LEARNING PROBLEMS

A COGNITIVE APPROACH

D1537826

John R. Kirby
Queen's University

Noel H. Williams
University of Windsor

Kagan & Woo Limited • Toronto

Canadian Cataloguing in Publication Data

Kirby, John R.
  Learning problems

Includes bibliographical references and index.
ISBN 0–921099–04–5

1. Learning disabilities.   2. Cognition in children.
3. Remedial teaching.   I. Williams, Noel Henry.
II. Title.

LC4704.K57 1991   371.9   C90–095621–6

Design: Joe Chin

Typeset, printed and bound in Canada

1 2 3 4 AP 94 93 92 91

Permissions

Every effort has been made to contact copyright holders of extracts reproduced in
this text. The publishers would be pleased to have any errors or omissions brought
to their attention.

The Kaiser-Permanente Diet (p. 45) is reproduced by permission of Pro-ed, 8700
Shoal Creek Blvd., Austin, Texas 78758-6897. Diagnostic Criteria for Attention
Deficit Hyperactive Disorder (p. 137) is reproduced by permission of the
American Psychiatric Association. The Matching Familiar Figures Test (p. 141)
is reproduced by permission of the Society for Research in Child Development
Inc. The Conners Rating Scales (pp. 142-144) are reproduced by permission of
Multi-Health Systems Inc., 908 Niagara Falls Blvd., North Tonawanda, NY
14120-2060 and 65 Overlea Blvd., Suite 210, Toronto, Ont. M4H 1P1: draft ques-
tionnaires printed in this text are not to be reproduced; forms are available from
Multi-Health Systems Inc. Sarason's Test Anxiety Scale (p. 146) is reproduced
by permission of Hemisphere Publishing Corporation, 79 Madison Ave., New
York, NY 10016-7892.

To J.P. Das,
   teacher, colleague, and friend

CONTENTS

PREFACE

Content and Approach

This book is about children who perform poorly in school, much worse than would be expected from their general level of mental ability. In the past, these children have been called underachievers, undermotivated, unlucky, brain damaged, poorly taught, and learning disabled. Many previous approaches have assumed that there is something wrong with these children, in particular with their brains; because of this, labels such as "learning disability" have associations of brain damage. Until there is more conclusive evidence one way or the other, we prefer to keep an open mind on the issue of brain damage, and accordingly use the less ominous description "learning problem".

Our approach differs from other approaches in several important ways. In the first place, for the reasons outlined above, we do not begin with a particular theory of what learning problems are, or how they are caused. The only clear facts concern the child's poor performance in school. It is important to discover the causes of that poor performance, but too often in the past we've let our initial theories distort and restrict our understanding of learning problems.

A second feature that distinguishes this book from other introductory books is that it is based upon a particular theory of cognition (thinking, learning, what the brain does). Other books try to keep everyone happy by mentioning all theories and approaches; in our experience, they succeed in keeping no one happy. Furthermore, that is a bad way to teach. Trying to learn seven theories at once is about as easy as trying to learn seven languages at once. We feel that it is preferable to learn one first, and well, particularly if that theory is a reasonably good one.

Obviously we think that the theory we use is a good one, otherwise we wouldn't use it! We call it PASS (for Planning, Attention, Simultaneous, Successive), though it has also been termed simultaneous-successive processing theory (Das, Kirby & Jarman, 1979). We think that it strikes a balance between being sufficiently comprehensive of current research and comprehensible by students. Needless to say, some individuals will disagree with us regarding one or the other of these factors.

The third feature of our approach is that we allow learning problems to exist in many academic areas, and at all levels of expertise, and we accept that learning problems may have different causes. Instead of concentrating upon one achievement area, usually reading, we deal with learning problems in the areas of reading, spelling, arithmetic and mathematics. Instead of focussing only upon *early* learning problems, such as in learning the basic skills in reading or arithmetic, we also include learning problems at the higher levels of comprehension and problem solving. We feel strongly that learning problems in areas other than early reading have been sadly neglected.

The fourth characteristic that helps distinguish our approach from many others is that we think the understanding of learning problems has as many implications for "normal" education as for "special" education. Learning problem children are far more like than unlike normal children and, in fact, it is quite "normal" for children to experience learning problems. Because we do not start out believing that learning problem children are fundamentally different from normal children, we have no need to restrict our thinking to them.

An important principle underlying our approach is that theory must be tied to practice whenever possible. At the very least, theory should point in the direction of practice, even if it cannot yet be applied. But this book is not a complete curriculum syllabus or a book on teaching methods. We provide guidelines for the design of remedial instruction, rather than attempting the impossible task of writing the Infallible Cookbook for Immediately Solving All Learning Problems. We hope you can take our guidelines and apply them, together with your own professional skills, to improve remedial instruction.

Audience

We aim this book at the teacher or teacher-to-be who wants to understand learning problems. No specific background in psychology or education is required; while some of the concepts we discuss are complex and not yet completely understood (at least not by us), we have tried to write about them as simply as possible. We've avoided undefined jargon, and useless jargon, to the best of our abilities.

On the other hand, there's no doubt that some previous knowledge of educational psychology, or some previous experience of teaching, will make this book easier to understand. (This is true of every educational textbook that we've ever seen.) While it has been designed to be read by undergraduates in psychology, educational psychology, or special education with no particular background, graduate students in those same disciplines should also benefit from this book.

Acknowledgements

We'd like to thank our colleagues and graduate students for their comments and encouragement, especially J.P. Das, John Biggs, Lorna Chan, Phil Moore, Louise Becker, Chris Gordon, Greg Robinson, and Moreen Sabourin. The dedication of Pam Kristensen, Denise Finnegan, Cindy Kissau, and Pat Roberts in producing the typescript is deeply appreciated. Elynor Kagan and Terry Woo have earned our appreciation and respect for their diligence in making that typescript into a book. (This may be the only page that Elynor doesn't get to improve!)

CHAPTER 1

What This Book Is About

THIS BOOK IS ABOUT children who perform poorly in their school work, much worse than we would expect given their general level of ability. These children are often labelled "learning disabled", but that term has come to mean too many things to different people; too often it includes assumptions about the *causes* of the learning problem. Instead, we will describe these children as having a *learning problem,* to indicate that there is something unusual about their school performance, without specifying *what* is wrong. Our purpose is to present a coherent theoretical account of the difficulties faced by these children and to indicate how theory suggests that diagnosis and remediation should take place. We hope to convince you that this is not just another dry academic theory, but an eminently practical one which can be applied by teachers and professional psychologists.

There has been concern for learning problem children throughout this century. Perhaps the initial indication of concern was the task given to the psychologist Binet in the 1890s by the school authorities in Paris, France. Binet's task was to find a means of determining which of the children who were performing poorly in the classroom could in fact benefit from school, and to distinguish between these children and those who perform poorly in the classroom but who cannot benefit from school. Today the former group of children would be called learning problem or learning disabled children, and the second group mentally retarded children. (The mentally retarded have a low level of general ability; therefore, it is not surprising that they perform poorly in school. When we refer to learning problem children, we do not include the mentally retarded.) After almost 100 years of research, we know a lot more about learning, and about the difficulties children have in learning, but the concern still exists. If anything, there is more concern today about maximizing the achievement of all children than there ever has been.

In the remainder of this chapter, we provide a background for what follows. We define what we mean by learning problems, differentiating such problems from learning disabilities. We describe our theoretical orientation, and examine three areas of theoretical controversy: intelligence, the brain, and affective problems. We conclude by presenting an overview of this book, and suggesting how you might want to study it. (No, don't groan, it's not going to be that terrible. Also, don't skip it, as some of these ideas are important. However, you may find that this chapter makes more sense after you've finished the book; why not re-read it then?)

Learning Problems and Learning Disabilities

We have decided to use the term "learning problem" because of the great confusion that exists over the term "learning disabled". As we will see later in this book, primarily in Chapters 2 and 3, the term "learning disabled" has been applied to describe both a broad category of children (similar to the category in which we are interested), and a relatively small group with very severe learning difficulties. Although there is still great debate among researchers about the concept and the term, many parents and practitioners regard a learning disability as a quasi-medical poblem, almost like a disease. We are sure that you have heard some children referred to as dyslexic or hyperactive. We have even met some teachers who describe themselves as dyslexic or hyperactive, perhaps only because they have difficulty reading their psychology textbook! There is confusion also about the role of the brain and of brain damage. Some theories describe learning disabilities as due to brain damage or at least to "brain dysfunction." Some teachers understand that learning disabilities are problems which can be overcome, while others think that, by definition, they cannot be remediated. There is always great danger, particularly in education, when some professionals use a term to refer to a very severe and specific disability while others (perhaps those more in touch with the children themselves) use it to refer to a milder and broader range of problems. In some cases children with relatively minor problems may be described with a label which makes teachers believe they have a more severe problem that cannot be fixed.

In our view, many of these confusions arise because the *phenomena* (what we observe) have become muddled with the explanations or the *causes* of the phenomena. What we observe are the children's failures in school, their otherwise normal ability, and their lack of major emotional trauma. At the observation level, the question is whether to define the problem narrowly (for instance, to be considered as having a learning problem, a child must be three years behind his or her classmates in achievement) or more broadly (one year behind). We have opted for the broader definition. At the causal level, we have opted to begin with an open mind, without a specific theory of how learning problems originate. Furthermore, we do not assume that all learning problems are of the same type, or at the same level. While we begin without a specific theory, please keep in mind that we are very much interested in discovering how learning problems are caused. Theoretical discoveries will be very important in helping children with learning problems, but much has yet to be attained. Such discoveries will depend, in our opinion, upon a solid understanding of how learning and thinking normally take place, and how they can go wrong. We simply do not know enough yet to begin with a theory of learning problems, and to try to do so might blind us in our *observations* of learning problems.

Another difficulty with the learning disability definition in our minds is that it emphasizes that the problems are the child's, eliminating by definition causes related to inadequate teaching, "social deprivation," and so on. It is more common to find children's problems in conjunction with teaching problems: children with learning problems may not have been exposed to the best teaching, or at least not to the best teaching for children with such problems. Nevertheless, the teacher is seldom entirely to blame. We seek to emphasize more the teacher-student interaction, and discuss instead the possibilities for remediation. Successful achievement usually requires the combination of a large number of factors, including ability, inclination, opportunity for learning, provision of teaching and so forth. Difficulty with any one or more of these can produce a learning problem.

The learning problem definition is a vague one. We accept that such a definition is not ideal in many people's minds, but we feel that it is the most appropriate form to apply to a vague concept. Learning problem children are not a distinct group of children, other than in the discrepancy between their ability and achievement. A child may have a learning problem in one area, but not in any others.

Furthermore, learning problems can exist to different degrees in different children; in any such situation there will always be more children with a minor problem than with a major problem. Any attempt to draw a firm dividing line between those with and those without problems will produce errors in classification. It is not the definition which is at fault in our view, but rather the perceived need to classify. Clearly some children have severe problems and do require special assistance. Our approach emphasizes that many other children can also have learning problems, and that the competent teacher should be aware of the variety of such learning problems, how to assess them, and what to do about them. Thus, our approach includes in the category of learning problems a number of children who have what might be termed "garden variety" problems, children who are excluded from any (though not all) definitions of learning disability.

In other words, what we have to say in this book has relevance to the education of "normal" children as much as it does to the education of children with major problems. The learning disabilities approach tended to encourage the belief that learning disabled children are a distinct group with particular problems associated with the early levels of achievement – for example, in basic reading skills. We believe that many children suffer from those problems to a mild degree, and furthermore, that there are yet more children who suffer from other problems associated with the later rather than early levels of achievement. We would like to consider the possibility that many children in high school have learning problems in the area of reading that are not necessarily associated with the basic reading skills of phonics or word recognition. Their problem instead may be more in the area of comprehension. More on this later (see Chapter 7, for example).

Cognitive Psychology and Education

In addition to being interested in cognitive problems, we intend to adopt a *cognitive approach* to such problems. In psychology, "cognitive" is used in this sense to mean that we are interested in how behaviour is produced, how internal psychological events might result in observed problems. To put it more simply, we are not interested in merely observing what children do, and the effects of whatever teachers do to help them. Our view is that you're more likely to know how to fix something if you know what is wrong, and you're more likely to know what's wrong if you know how it works normally. This is true for fixing an automobile engine, and we think it's true for fixing children's learning problems.

Unfortunately, we don't really understand very well how normal children's minds work. Current research in cognitive psychology describes a vast array of cognitive processes which must be considered. Speaking in very broad terms, these include such processes as perception, memory, comprehension, reasoning and strategies. Each of these processes can be further divided into sub-processes and those sub-processes divided again. Furthermore, many different theories exist to describe how these processes function. A question, then, is whether we should wait for cognitive psychology to understand the mind completely before we attempt to apply a cognitive theory in education. In our opinion it would be unrealistic to do so, in that complete understanding of the mind, if it is possible at all, is years away. Moreover, you do not need to understand something completely before you can apply your partial understanding. In our view, the field of learning problems can benefit from the current knowledge of cognitive psychology, and theories in cognitive psychology can benefit from a consideration of the difficulties faced by learning problem children.

What current cognitive psychology does emphasize, however, is that there are many mental components or processes responsible for producing even the simplest learning. Thus, there is need to consider a variety of explanations, a variety of factors which may be at fault, when attempting to understand a child's learning problem. Many theories can be faulted for concluding that all or many learning problems are due to a single cause.

(Curiously, many such theories began by considering previous theories and criticizing them for acknowledging only one type of learning problem of one type of cause.) We argue in this book that there are many different kinds of learning problems, many different potential causal factors, many different kinds of learning problem children and, therefore, many different correct approaches to remediating learning problems.

Our interest in this book is upon remediation. Too often children with problems are studied with the purpose of labelling or classifying them, with the naive expectation that this will somehow be of assistance to them. Many teachers have had the experience of referring a child to a psychologist or counsellor because the teacher has noticed the child is having problems – in reading, for instance. The result after several weeks of testing may be a report which describes the child as having a "reading problem" and recommends that the child needs further work with reading. This is little more than giving a name to the very problems that the teacher had noticed, and provides no further information about the cause of that problem or about how to overcome it. If diagnosis is to be useful, it must be tied directly to remediation.

This is not to imply that diagnosis or remediation are simple tasks, or that certainty can be attained with any ease. In many cases we will propose a variety of approaches to solving the problems, but leave the teacher to explore these possibilities, test them out, and choose among them. If children and their problems were easily classifiable and easily linked to remedial procedures, we would not have so many children today with learning problems. The very existence of so many learning problems implies that the problems are not easily classifiable, nor easily remediable. We suggest, however, that one reason for the lack of success in remediation is the lack of understanding about the problems themselves. A cognitive approach to these problems is intended to provide a deeper understanding of the problems and, therefore, to increase the chances of success in designing remediation.

Remediation itself may take many forms. In some cases, perhaps, the term "remediation" itself is not appropriate, in that children's problems are not so much fixed as circumvented by an alternative form of teaching.

Remediation may concentrate upon different levels of processes or skills. In some cases the child's problem may be in a quite specific achievement skill area, such as the addition of whole numbers. If this skill is the major source of the child's problem, then it is the appropriate focus of remediation. Other children may have difficulties with a broad array of cognitive tasks, all of which share a common underlying cognitive component; in this case it is more appropriate to concentrate upon the general cognitive processes than upon specific achievement skills. However, cognitive processes are merely means to an end. We should not forget that it is achievement which we are attempting to improve, not the cognitive processes. If our goal is to improve reading skills and we succeed only in improving a child's memory skills, we have not achieved our goal.

Remediation can also be either ability-oriented or strategy-oriented. As we shall see, some remediation is largely aimed at training abilities or capacities, including the teaching of new facts or of new skills. Other forms of remediation emphasize strategies, arguing that the child has enough of the required skills or abilities but does not know how to employ them appropriately in a given task. In this case remediation concentrates upon the child's approach to the task.

The Theoretical Approach

An important aspect of this book is that it is based upon a coherent theoretical description of how achievement and cognition normally take place. In our view it is necessary to understand a theory of achievement task performance before we can begin to understand how some children go wrong in these areas. (In common sense terms, you can't fix something if you don't know how it's supposed to work.) This view has many implications.

The first implication is the importance we attach to theory. Many textbooks on learning disabilities or problems attempt to describe all the existing theories in the area. In our experience this is an approach more relevant to experts in the area than to students beginning to learn about learning problems. In our experience a surplus of theories, instead of encouraging an appreciation of theory, tends to encourage the opinion that theory is unimportant: everybody seems to say something different and that doesn't seem to make much difference. (An analogy: learning a theory is like learning a language; it's easier to learn one first and then a second one, than to learn two or more at the same time.) Of course there are theoretical disagreements among researchers, but there are also many areas of agreement. More importantly, we believe that it is theory itself that is important; we hope to develop in you an interest in understanding how cognitive processes produce achievement – that is, in understanding a theory of achievement.

A second implication of our approach is that much of what we have to say reflects on understanding achievement in general, not just the poor achievement of learning problem children. While we will be mainly talking about children who are described as learning disabled, much of what we have to say also has relevance for children who are just performing relatively poorly in school, children who would normally not receive any special attention. In fact, fundamental to our approach to education and psychology are the ideas that children should be considered as individuals and that the teacher's task is to maximize the achievement (among other things) of every child. We also feel that few children are currently achieving anything like their potential. In this sense, one might even say that all children have some sort of learning problem, and would benefit from their teachers' having a deeper understanding of the cognitive processes underlying successful achievement.

How does one go about choosing a theory to present? If one is honest, one admits that one's own biases must come into the decision. We have chosen a theoretical approach which we like and with which we are familiar. Other authors would undoubtedly choose other theories. Our point is not that our theory is right and theirs are wrong, for at the moment it must be admitted that none of the theories is precise enough to be adequately tested

against another. However, the choice of a theory is not arbitrary. For our purposes, an adequate theory must describe cognitive processes and how they are involved in achievement performance. The theory must also suggest how those cognitive processes are to be assessed or diagnosed, and how remediation should take place. We feel that the theory presented in Chapters 4 and 5, and elaborated upon in the remaining chapters, fulfills these criteria. This is not to say that the theory task is completed. All theories are intended to describe what we know so far, but also to produce hypotheses about what we don't know. These hypotheses then need to be tested and the theory revised according to the results. In principle, then, all theories are intended to make suggestions about how they can be tested and ultimately altered. We believe that the theory we present in this book explains enough of what we know already for it to be of interest and *use* to teachers and other educational professionals. We also hope, of course, that our views stimulate research and application work which tests our hypotheses and, in the end, produces a better or more complete theory.

Intelligence

One theoretical issue which has plagued the field of learning disabilities concerns the role of intelligence. Traditionally, learning disabled children have been defined as those who perform poorly in school, relative to their level of intelligence. As long as one accepts the idea of intelligence as an entity, and one that is measurable, this definition provides few problems and is a great aid in identifying children to be so labelled. However, recent research and theorizing has cast doubt upon the usefulness of this definition for two reasons. In the first place, it is no longer all that clear what intelligence is and whether it can be usefully thought of as an entity. You may have heard that many years ago it was acceptable to define intelligence as "whatever IQ tests measure". Today this definition is seen as inadequate or even unacceptable; some would argue that it represents mysticism. The point is not that we need to be able to define something precisely before we can employ it, for we break this rule all the time, both in everyday life and in scientific life. (For example, scientists investigated and used the concept of electricity long before they had completely understood it. Perhaps it is not completely understood yet today.) Instead, the point is that we should attempt to understand what intelligence is rather than merely accepting that IQ tests measure it. (Which IQ tests? What kinds of IQ tests? Where do IQ tests come from?)

Secondly, intelligence is now seen less as a general mental ability – as implied in the learning disabilities definition – and more and more as the end result of a vast array of cognitive processes. In other words, intelligent behaviour is the result of cognitive processes, and a complete theory of intelligent behaviour would require a complete theory of cognition. In this sense, every cognitive process or component which contributes to intelligent behaviour has a role to play in a theory of intelligence. This is an important point because it suggests that no firm dividing line can be drawn between intelligence processes and achievement processes. In fact, achievement tasks represent some of the more valuable contexts in which we observe intelligent behaviour. Many of the components of achievement tasks, such as the processes underlying comprehension, are clearly related to the processes underlying intelligence test performance. To require that children be normal in intelligence processes is, in this sense, to eliminate the possibility of having a learning disability in those areas, contrary to the observations of many teachers.

This is a difficult theoretical point and we do not wish to belabour it here. Our point is that intelligence is now seen as the end result of a set of cognitive components, and that many of these same cognitive components have been implicated in the study of children's learning problems. If one adopts the learning disability definition, one runs into several problems. The first of these is how to say exactly in which aspects of intelligence, which cognitive components, the child has to be "normal"; the second is the difficulty in understanding learning problems or disabilities which are clearly linked to intelligence components.

A related problem has been the assumption underlying traditional conceptions of intelligence that it is unchangeable or untrainable. This is an assumption which, in our view, has plagued psychology for a hundred years or more. Only in the last ten years or so has it become respectable to discuss the training of intelligence (e.g., Sternberg, 1983), a change which has been facilitated by the reconceptualization of intelligence as the result of a set of cognitive processes. To train intelligence conceptualized as a general entity is an imposing task, though not necessarily an impossible one. (For example, most children become much more intellectually able between the ages of birth and sixteen. Perhaps educators should be more encouraged by this fact than the fact that children, on average, maintain their position relative to their age mates.) However, once intelligence is reconceptualized as a set of components, it seems much more feasible to consider training one or more of these separate components.

This is a very fundamental aspect of our approach to learning problems. We see behaviour, whether it be on an achievement test or on an intelligence test, as the result of a large number of cognitive processes and components. One or more of these components can be faulty (for various reasons) and can, therefore, disrupt behaviour. Disrupted behaviour in this sense represents a learning problem in our terms. That learning problem can be due in theory to any one or more of the cognitive components. Thus, many different types of learning problems may exist, some of which may be too related to factors which resemble intelligence for traditional learning disabilities theorists. Rather than shying away from these learning problems, we suggest instead that they are a major omission in current work in this area. (We will argue in later chapters that this omission has resulted in a lack of research on reading comprehension and mathematical problem-solving difficulties.) We are not saying that all of these components can be trained, at least not easily trained. All educators must eventually accept that some problems are insurmountable. We suggest, however, that attempts should be made to train as many components as possible; only after we have failed in a properly constructed attempt should defeat be accepted. In other words, we are suggesting that an open mind be maintained about the trainability of the various cognitive components and processes, and that a strict concern for intelligence test scores is not crucial in studying learning problems.

Our definition of learning problems does refer to "general mental ability", however. This is not an attempt to re-introduce IQ scores through the back door, but rather an admission that we see learning problem children as those with difficulties in a relatively small number of cognitive components or processes. The smaller the number of problem components, the greater the chances of successful remediation. We would suggest that children with difficulties in a large number of cognitive components are usually referred to as mentally retarded. This is what we mean by low general mental ability – a low level of performance in a large number of cognitive components. While much of what we say in this book will have some relevance to such children, they are not the children with whom we are primarily concerned.

We should mention here a result of our position regarding intelligence. In many school districts, particularly in the United States, an official label (e.g., "learning disabled") is applied to children who fit a legal definition based on a lag of achievement scores behind intelligence test scores. In such districts a particular discrepancy score must be obtained by a child in order to receive the special help which comes from being so labelled. Such definitions may be necessary for legal purposes, if only to ensure that the children needing help obtain it. However, such definitions encourage a variety of myths and misconceptions, not the least of which is that learning disabled children form a distinct, identifiable group in the same way that children with measles form a distinct group. Our experience, to the contrary, is that learning problems are distributed among children much like any other characteristic, with some children having many, others fewer, some none. The children form a continuous distribution, with no firm division between those with problems and those without. If we are right,

then any strict definition must be wrong. Our position, which will become clearer in the next few hundred pages, is that any such legal definitions need to be applied flexibly, and that in particular they must be sensitive to the professional judgements of teachers and psychologists working with individual children. To deny special help to a child because his or her IQ is 84 and our official cut-off for normality is 85 is, in our opinion, absurd. (More on this in Chapters 2 and 3.)

The Brain

A second problem which has plagued the learning disability field involves the role of the brain, both in children's problems and in our theories. Some early theorists described learning disabled children as resembling brain-damaged children, from which some people concluded that they too were brain-damaged (the learning disabled children, that is!). In the absence of any firm evidence of brain damage, other researchers invented the term "minimal brain damage" to suggest a type of damage which was, in principle, undetectable. Undetectable entities are crucial components in any form of mysticism, making any scientific person suspicious. With time, "damage" became "dysfunction", so that by the early 1970s it was not uncommon to hear learning disabled children described as having a "minimal brain dysfunction". Even now it is difficult to discuss learning disabilities without much of your audience inferring that you think those children have brain damage or dysfunction of some sort. This problem is accentuated when one's theories explicitly relate to the functioning of different areas of the brain (as does the theory developed in this book).

A basic feature of modern psychology is the hypothesis that all cognitive or mental activity is the result of, and is controlled by, the brain. As are all good hypotheses, this one is waiting to be disconfirmed by fact. There may, in fact, be spirits and demons out there affecting our cognitive processes which are yet to be discovered. If and when they are discovered, clearly the hypothesis will be disproved. In the meantime, it provides a sensible working basis for psychology and education. Learning and achievement are two obvious cognitive activities which according to this hypothesis are a function of the brain's activity. Thus, if a child has a learning or achievement problem, this problem is due to the activity of the brain. If the learning or achievement is at a lower level than desired, it is logical to say that the brain is not working properly, that there is dysfunction. However, it is a mistake to think that this statement says anything new at all. It is a circular statement, saying nothing more than that the child has a learning problem. Therefore, we see little value in talking about learning problem children or learning disabled children as having a brain dysfunction, whether it be minimal or otherwise.

At the same time, we feel strongly that psychology and education can learn much from the study of the brain. The theory which we will present in Chapters 4 and 5 of this book is strongly related to work concerning the brain, both in normal and in brain-damaged persons. The study of brain-damaged persons is necessary only to observe the functioning of different areas of the brain. It would be unethical to experiment upon normal human beings by removing bits of their brains. Because we talk about the brain you should *not* conclude that we think learning problem children have damaged brains. We talk about the brain in order to show what it does. Knowing what the brain does gives us a better theory of how cognitive or achievement tasks are performed, and thus of how they can be performed poorly – of what can go wrong. In studying the brain it is important to realize that things can go wrong for many different reasons. Brain damage – that is, physical insult to the brain – can disrupt cognition and behaviour. However, cognition and behaviour can also be disrupted by what could be termed *functional* problems. For example, we could teach you from an early age to say "arr" whenever we show you the letter B. In the long run this would disrupt your reading and spelling behaviour. The problem, though, is not structural or physical: your brain is not damaged by what we have taught you. The disturbance, instead, is of a functional nature: your brain is doing the wrong

thing. Many learning problems in children could be due to such functional disturbances, though of course not to such simple ones as that described.

Our conclusion in this area, again, is to maintain an open mind. There are undoubtedly children with damaged brains, and many of these children will exhibit learning problems. This does not mean that all children with learning problems have damaged brains. Even if learning problem children act like brain-damaged children, they are not necessarily brain-damaged themselves. Furthermore, even if they are brain-damaged, this does not mean that remedial instruction is useless. For this reason, the question of brain damage (particularly of the undetectable sort) is a red herring. At the moment we know virtually nothing about how to fix a damaged brain, so that diagnosis is unlikely to lead us to a quick solution to learning problems. On the other hand, we do know that brain-damaged individuals can learn to recover cognitive functions and lead normal lives. Brain damage does not mean that a child cannot learn, yet at the same time it does not provide a clear guideline for remediation. Our approach is, instead, to adopt an educational point of view, to concentrate upon what children can and cannot do, and upon the processes which underlie their successful and unsuccessful performances. The important question is whether children with learning problems can be trained to overcome those problems.

Emotional and Motivational Problems

The third problem that has plagued the field of learning disabilities concerns the role in learning problems of emotion and motivation – that is, of affective variables. Long before the concept of learning disabilities became common, many teachers referred to some children as underachievers or as unmotivated. It is still common today to hear teachers suggest that children who perform poorly do so because they aren't trying hard enough.

A related characteristic concerns what could loosely be lumped together as emotional factors. It has been widely observed that many children who perform poorly in school have poor self concepts, do not feel confident in their academic skills, may be depressed or anxious, and are unpopular with their peers and even with adults (see Chapter 10).

The important question is whether the affective problems are primary or secondary, whether they are the *source* of the child's problem in school or rather a byproduct of that problem. The traditional definition of learning disabilities (see Chapters 2 and 3) specifically excludes primary affective problems, without denying that such children exist. We adopt a similar approach; though many of our conclusions about how to teach children the cognitive processes underlying academic tasks will have relevance for such children, they are not the primary concern of this book.

We emphasize, however, that children do not fall cleanly into the two groups of primary cognitive problems and primary affective problems. Problems in either domain will tend to produce problems in the other, and in many cases it is difficult to determine which came first. Affective problems are often a result of difficulties outside the school, particularly in the home. Therefore, school personnel may find it difficult to change them, though they may be able to influence them. Teachers should be sensitive to affective problems and ensure that they are not worsened by what happens in school. Because school learning may be irrelevant to a child with severe affective problems, the first step may have to be to neutralize those problems.

If the affective problems are secondary, then the cognitive domain is the appropriate starting point. Teachers have more control over the development of cognitive skills and, therefore, should find it easier to operate in this domain first. Even in cases where the primary problem is affective, it may still be appropriate to work in the cognitive domain simply because of the difficulty or impossibility of working upon the child's affective problems. Furthermore, it may well be that some initial success in the cognitive domain begins to overcome the affective problems. Even if the child comes from a disastrous home environment, it is possible for the school to be a bright light in his or her life.

About This Book

In the remainder of this chapter we briefly outline the content of the book and the approach which we intend to take. We conclude with some suggestions about how to study this book, though of course these will probably be ignored by all students who would benefit from them.

Outline

This book is divided into four parts. Part I includes Chapters 2 and 3. In Chapter 2 we overview the history of the learning problems concept. Mostly this involves examining research concerned with "learning disabled" children. History is valuable, for as someone once said, "Those who ignore history are doomed to repeat it." The history of the learning disabilities field has been so confused and convoluted that we would like to help spare all of you the pain of repeating it. On the other hand, this is not a history book. Our treatment of history will be brief and aimed at emphasizing the major themes. The suggested readings given at the end of Chapter 2 should provide you with some starting points should you wish to pursue historical questions further.

Chapter 3 identifies several issues which recur throughout the book with regard to current approaches and legal definitions. Key questions concern how we are to define the type of problem in which we are interested and how we are to interpret theoretically the nature and causes of those problems.

The second part of this book consists of seven chapters which present our approach to learning problems, our frame of reference. In our view, this frame of reference succeeds in integrating much of the previous and current thinking about cognition and about learning problems, and also provides a basis for linking diagnosis and remediation. Chapter 4 describes the broad background of information processing theory, while Chapter 5 presents in more detail the PASS theory developed from the work of Luria and of Das. This theory describes three interdependent systems that produce and control cognition: arousal, processing and planning.

The remainder of Part 2 shows how different classroom phenomena are related to the three cognitive systems. Chapter 6 examines classroom behaviour, in particular the connections with arousal and attention problems. Chapter 7 examines current theories of reading and describes the reading process in terms of our theory. Chapters 8 and 9 do the same for spelling and mathematics. The purpose of Chapters 7, 8 and 9 is to describe how skilled achievement normally functions in information processing terms. This description then provides a checklist of potential problems which could produce low levels of achievement. The final chapter of Part II concerns the secondary affective consequences of learning problems. The secondary nature of these problems does not mean they are not important. In fact, affective problems may be the first ones to be noticed by the classroom teacher or the first ones of concern to parents.

The third part of this book applies the theory described in Part II to the diagnosis and remediation of learning problems. The theory emphasizes that cognition is the result of the coordinated activity of the arousal, processing and planning systems. It is not really possible to divide cognition into separate systems; however, it is helpful to consider the systems separately in order to elaborate on their nature, on how to measure them, and on what to do about problems. So while we present the systems separately in Chapters 11, 12, 13 and 14, we emphasize throughout their connections and dependence upon each other. Chapter 11 considers the arousal system and the attention disorders which can result from problems in arousal. Observational techniques and suggestions for remediation are included. Chapters 12 and 13 consider, respectively, successive and simultaneous processing, the two types of activity of the processing system. These chapters show that both forms of processing are involved in most achievement tasks, though to different degrees. These chapters provide examples of the poor achievement performance that can arise from successive or simultaneous processing problems. As do all the chapters of Part III, they describe how classroom teachers can observe these types of processing in the classroom, and how to

plan remediation of problems in these areas. The final chapter of Part III concerns the planning system, which integrates and controls the activity of the other systems. Again examples, observational techniques and remedial activities are suggested.

Part IV consists only of Chapter 15, which presents a retrospective overview of the book and the prospects for both learning problem children and the learning problem field. This chapter reviews the learning problem concept, and returns to the recurrent issues raised in Chapter 3. We describe what normally happens to learning problem children, and what could happen in the future. Lastly, we make some suggestions about needed research in the learning problems field, especially the need for implementation of existing research. Research has little purpose unless it is applied.

Boxes and Examples

In most chapters you will find boxed sections of text. The purpose of these sections is to highlight a case study example, a research finding, or some other aspect of the chapter content. These boxes do not provide a summary of the text's important points; however, they are not unimportant. In other words, don't read them instead of the text, but don't skip them either!

In the boxes and throughout the text we have tried to provide examples of children's learning problems. Sometimes these examples take the form of a case report, presenting a child's background and a teacher's description of classroom behaviour, while others are merely examples of children's poor achievement work. Please keep in mind that these examples are meant to illustrate more general points. They do not describe the only problems which are found, nor do they describe pure "types" of problems.

A Note on References

All references cited in this text are provided at the back of this book. Some references are also highlighted at the end of most chapters as suggestions for further reading. We have not attempted to provide an exhaustive list of references on any of the topics considered in this book, for in our experience such long lists are seldom useful to students. In fact, in our own work we tend to consult only the most recent of a long list of references, in the expectation that the most recent work would also refer to older work. Therefore, we have attempted to keep the reference list within manageable limits, though as you will see, the result is still quite long. Of course reference is made to older papers which cite key points; however, in general we cite only the most recent work where it encompasses the older work.

A Note on Solemnity and Seriousness

Throughout this book we have attempted to maintain a relatively light tone. We do this for several reasons, not the least of which are that we enjoy it and that we hope you will enjoy it too. We also feel that humour used appropriately can be very helpful for instructional purposes. Difficult concepts can be more easily understood through everyday examples, and a humorous anecdote may be remembered better than a more formal example. If each is equally informative, then the humorous one is preferable if it is the one more likely to be remembered.

Books about learning problems are usually very solemn in tone, perhaps because of the seriousness of the problems encountered by the children concerned. We, too, consider these problems to be of a serious nature, but do not see that this requires that they be treated in an overly solemn manner. Our humour (such as it is) should not be taken either as disrespect for you or as disrespect for learning problem children.

How to Study this Book

In our experience university students are not immune to learning problems themselves, though these problems are rarely as severe as those faced by younger children. One of the more persistent learning problems faced by university students is

not knowing how to absorb and comprehend information from the printed page. We have found many students who study textbooks either in a passive way, with no clear strategy, or with a variety of inappropriate learning strategies. Therefore, we offer some suggestions for how to read this book. If you feel you have your own system and that it works for you, stick with it. The most important point to remember is that the key to this book is the theory presented in Part II. This book contains many examples and many practical suggestions for diagnosing and treating learning problems, but none of these will correspond exactly to the problems which you face with an individual child. To understand this book, then, it is necessary that you internalize the theory and understand our approach. If you can do that, you should be able to see the general points which our examples illustrate, and be able to produce your own remedial plans for individual children. Your purpose in reading this book, therefore, should not be to learn just what we have said or what we have suggested, but rather to be able to elaborate upon what we say, to go beyond it to generate your own examples, implications, and conclusions. Everyone's ideas should be treated with a healthy scepticism, ours included.

A good way to test whether you have comprehended a chapter is to see if you can reconstruct it for yourself once you have finished reading it. At the end of the chapter, close the book and see if you can remember what we have said, and why we have said it. Don't be surprised if this is extremely difficult to do after your first reading of a chapter. If you're a normal human being, you'll probably have to go back and re-read entire chapters or particular sections of them in order to be confident that you have comprehended. If you still find you can't reconstruct an entire chapter, lower your sights and attempt to reconstruct a section. If that too fails, lower your sights again to a sub-section or even to a paragraph. Continue dropping down until something clicks, then try to climb back up, level by level. You should also find that the whole book makes a lot more sense the second time through.

One practical suggestion we would make is for you to become an active learner. In other words, underline what you think are the most important bits in the book. Take notes on those important bits. Summarize paragraphs, sections and entire chapters. In constructing your summaries, try as much as possible not to quote directly from the book but rather rephrase in your own words. Better still, construct your summaries with the book closed. When you can produce a good summary of a chapter with the book closed, then you can be certain you understand it.

Finally, be willing to seek help when you're confused. We have attempted to write this book as clearly as possible, with as much explanation as we feel is necessary to communicate the material. We don't feel that any of the concepts discussed in this book should be beyond a normal university student. However, some of the material is difficult and may cause problems, particularly on first reading. If you have re-read the material and carefully attempted to reconstruct our argument, and still cannot understand a section, it makes sense to seek assistance before proceeding too far. By all means attempt to complete the chapter and see if it becomes clearer with further reading. You might even wish to go back and read previous chapters to see if you've missed something. But if all that fails, consult your instructor. It is highly unlikely that the latter parts of this book will make much sense to you if you've missed any of the key concepts in the first part. In fact we suspect that missing the foundations is what happens to many children with learning problems in school. If you're seeking to help those children, there is little sense in trying to emulate them in your own work.

Summary

In this chapter we have introduced many of the ideas that will guide the rest of this book. If some of them are a bit hazy at the moment, especially the theoretical points, don't worry; they'll become clearer as you read on. You should also find them clearer when you re-read this chapter after reading the rest of the book.

Our approach to learning problems can be summarized in five points:

1. We begin by observing learning problems, and not with a specific theory of how they are caused.

2. We think that it is very important to understand how cognition normally works, in order to understand how it sometimes fails to work. Because of this, we devote a lot of time to presenting a general theory of cognition (Chapters 4 and 5) and specific theories of classroom behaviour and academic skills (Chapters 6 to 10).

3. Unlike many other approaches, we emphasize that learning problems can be of many types, due to many causes, in different academic areas, and at different levels of expertise.

4. This approach is not restricted to a small group of children who fit a narrow definition. In addition to thinking that many more children have learning problems than is often realized, we also think that learning problem children are far more like normal children than they are unlike them. For this reason, our approach has as much relevance to "normal" education as to "special" education.

5. It is very important to link diagnosis to remediation, never to lose sight of our goal – the improvement of children's academic achievement. This is an educational point of view which need not be inconsistent with a psychological point of view. Fundamental to this is the belief that most cognitive processes or skills are improveable – we start with that belief until we are proven wrong.

In this chapter we also raised three problems that have pestered the field:

1. the role of intelligence, both as a factor in the definition of learning problems, and as a factor which may need to be trained;

2. the role of the brain and brain damage, especially to make the point that our theory discusses the brain but does not assume that learning problem children have damaged brains; and

3. the role of affective factors – while many learning problem children may have affective problems, we specifically exclude those whose problems are mainly due to affective problems.

The remainder of the chapter has presented an overview of the rest of the book, and has made some suggestions about how you should study it.

PART ONE

An Introduction to Learning Problems

CHAPTER 2

Historical Overview

IN ORDER TO UNDERSTAND current opinions regarding children with learning problems, one should consider the past. In this chapter we provide a brief historical overview of the people, ideas and events that have had most influence in the development of the field of learning problems. As you read, keep in mind that the term "learning problems" is our own. Most of the authors to whom we refer would have used other terms, mostly "learning disabilities." For the sake of consistency and communication, we will use the former term, except when referring to the definitional issue.

There have been great changes in the field since the emergence of the term "learning disabilities" in 1962 (Kirk, 1962). Furthermore, even though the term is a recent one, the roots of the field can be traced back to the early 1800s. From these early beginnings we see three main influences that have contributed to our present-day understanding of learning problems. These influences are:

1. the type of disorder considered dominant to the learning problem, formulated from research, theoretical interpretation and remediation techniques;
2. changes in classification procedures; and
3. legislation.

In this chapter we will confine our discussion to the first of these influences, since it has had the most significant impact in the development of the field of learning problems. The second and third influences will be incorporated in Chapter 3 when discussing the problems of definition and the characteristics of learning problem children.

The characteristics with learning problems are multi-faceted, ranging from difficulties in reading and writing to general behavioural problems. To account for such characteristics, researchers have over the years undertaken countless investigations, attempting to discover the causes of the problems, and to develop remedial programs to overcome the problems and their causes. Traditionally, these researchers belonged to one of several schools of thought. One school considered learning problems to stem from disorders in perception and perceptual-motor development, and the other considered disorders of language to be the main culprit. Despite these differences, we can see several similarities in the two schools of thought:

1. Psychologists and members of the medical profession were the main investigators.
2. The cause of the disorders was seen as damage to the brain.

3. The subjects under investigation at first were brain-injured adults, then brain-injured children, and finally children with average intelligence with no physical evidence of brain impairment.

More recently, researchers have looked at learning problems from behavioural and cognitive points of view. What follows is a discussion of the work of some of the more prominent researchers from the areas mentioned above.

Disorders of Perception and Perceptual-Motor Development

Kurt Goldstein

The initial influence in this area came from the work of Kurt Goldstein (1936, 1939). Goldstein, a German physician, was responsible for the care of brain-injured soldiers during and after World War I. In his pursuit of the rehabilitation of his patients, Goldstein observed them in a variety of situations and presented them with numerous tasks. From this clinical framework, he observed six behavioural characteristics that were present to some degree in his patients. These were:

1. Forced responsiveness to stimuli. They would respond indiscriminately to all stimuli around them. They were easily distracted and would attend to any noise, object or movement.
2. Figure-ground confusion. The soldiers were unable to isolate the essential feature from the non-essential features of the various stimuli (for example, to isolate a word from the mass of words surrounding it on a page).
3. Hyperactivity. The patients displayed excessive gross motor activity that lacked any purpose. They appeared to be in constant motion.
4. Perseveration. Patients showed a tendency to repeat the same behaviour, over and over again. They appeared unable to stop their activities at will.

5. Meticulosity. The soldiers displayed a very rigid life-style. They would spend an inordinate amount of time structuring their daily routine.
6. Catastrophic reaction. This took the form of an emotional breakdown in the soldiers. According to Goldstein, it happened because of their inability to cope with their bizarre perceptions and chaotic behaviour.

Alfred Strauss and Heinz Werner

Goldstein's methods of research and findings influenced two other notable researchers in Germany, Alfred Strauss and Heinz Werner. Strauss, a neuropsychiatrist, and Werner, a developmental psychologist, both emigrated from Germany to the United States during the rise of Hitler to power. Within a short time after arriving in the U.S., they both joined the research staff of the Wayne County Training School in Northville, Michigan. Strauss and Werner were interested in children, and wondered whether the effects of brain injury in children paralleled the findings of Goldstein in brain-injured adults. Thus, they conducted similar experiments with brain-injured, mentally retarded children whom they called *exogenous* retardates. Exogenous meant that the mental retardation was due to brain injury (an external factor) and not a result of a familiar or genetic cause (an internal factor). Mental retardation due to internal factors was termed *endogenous,* Down's Syndrome being an example of this kind. Strauss and Werner did replicate in part the findings of Goldstein. Like the brain-injured adults, the exogenous mentally retarded children displayed:

1. a variety of perceptual disorders, e.g., figure-ground confusion;
2. perseveration; and
3. behavioural disorders including hyperactivity and impulsivity.

These results were extremely important for they demonstrated the similar effects of brain injury in both adults and children. Also, from these studies was coined the term "the brain-injured child", a term which will be discussed in Chapter 3. Werner and Strauss were interested in the education of these children, and because the brain injury could not be treated medically, they felt that the best method of teaching them was to place them in a structured environment, void of unnecessary stimulation.

Strauss and Werner's research and their ideas on educational intervention greatly influenced many scientists, among them Laura Lehtinen, William Cruickshank and Newell Kephart. These researchers expanded upon Strauss and Werner's theoretical and educational concepts.

Laura Lehtinen

Lehtinen was interested in the educational programs that would assist brain-injured children. The collaborative efforts of Lehtinen and Strauss were incorporated in the now-classic work *Psychopathology and Education of the Brain-Injured Child* (Strauss and Lehtinen, 1947). Given the fact that the children displayed such behaviours as hyperactivity, distractibility and various perceptual deficits, Lehtinen and Strauss suggested that the children should be taught voluntary control, and that the overstimulating external environment should be manipulated and controlled. Specific recommendations included the following:

1. The children should be taught in small groups.
2. Extraneous stimuli should be removed from the classroom; e.g., wall hangings and pictures should be removed and the windows should be covered to reduce outside stimuli.
3. The teachers should also avoid being a distracting influence. It was recommended that they wear plain clothes and not wear any form of jewellery.
4. The educational program should be highly structured, with daily routines established. Lessons should be short in duration, proceeding from simple to complex, and any instructional materials used should be simple.

This approach became the standard technique, particularly for mentally retarded and brain-injured children, for many years to come.

William Cruickshank

Most researchers would agree that William Cruickshank was and still is one of the most influential people in the field of learning problems. Working at the Wayne County Training School, he came under the influence of Strauss and Werner. In 1957, Cruickshank published the results of a study that replicated the work of Strauss and Werner except that it was conducted with cerebral palsied children of near average, average and above average intelligence (Cruickshank, Bice & Wallen, 1957). As a result of this study, Cruickshank concluded that perceptual problems were due to brain damage and not mental retardation. This study was significant because it was one of the first to extend Strauss and Werner's research to children of average intelligence.

A further extension occurred when Cruickshank included in his research a group of children who were hyperactive and behaviourally disordered, had perceptual difficulties, but were not known to have suffered any obvious brain damage (Cruickshank, Bentzen, Ratzenberg & Tannhauser, 1961). This study, commonly known as the Montgomery County Project, was aimed at teaching these children based on Strauss and Werner's structured environment approach. Essentially, the plan for teaching these children called for:

1. reducing extraneous stimuli;
2. reducing workspace of the child to a minimum;
3. providing a highly structured time-table; and
4. enhancing the intensity of the teaching materials.

In essence, this structured program was directed totally by the teacher: the teacher determined what activity the child should undertake, when the activity should be done and for how long. The rationale for this approach was that brain-injured and hyperactive children are unable to control their behaviour or make their own decisions until taught to do so. The structured environment approach has not been without its critics. For example, Gardner, Cromwell and Foshee (1959) claimed that increased visual stimulation reduced hyperactivity, a finding that is completely at odds with Cruickshank's approach. Burnett (1962) compared a regular classroom setting with the highly structured classroom, and found no significant difference in the speed at which a list of words was learned. Rost (1967) investigated the effectiveness of reducing the child's work space (e.g., by placing the child in a separate booth or cubicle), and found no evidence that it was beneficial for the brain-injured child or hyperactive child. In an extensive review of the structured environment approach, Hallahan and Kaufman (1975) concluded that there appears to be no relationship between the structured environment and academic achievement.

Newell Kephart

Kephart's association with Strauss resulted in the second volume of *Psychopathology and Education of the Brain-Injured Child* (Strauss & Kephart, 1955). This was an updating of the first volume by Strauss and Lehtinen. Kephart rose to prominence following the publication of his book *The Slow Learner in the Classroom* (1960), which detailed his approach to teaching children with learning problems. Kephart was more concerned with the perceptual-motor problems found in children and his philosophy was one of perceptual-motor training. Kephart's basic assumption was that good perceptual-motor development was a prerequisite for behaviour, language and learning. According to Kephart's theory, the child's first encounter with the environment is through motor activities, and this is essential for later learning. He postulated that combinations of motor skills and patterns lead to four motor generalizations, namely:

1. maintenance of balance and posture;
2. contact (reaching, grasping – the manipulation of objects);
3. locomotion; and

4. receipt and propulsion (the movement of objects toward and away from the child).

Furthermore, these generalizations become combined, which allows the child to progress systematically from movement control to systematic exploration, perception, intersensory integration and concept formation. Thus, children with learning problems were seen by Kephart to have had some disruption or breakdown of the sequence of motor generalizations, or a general slowing down of them.

The rationale of Kephart's training activities was based upon the perceptual-motor match. How does this occur? How does a child coordinate movement and perception of the environment? Kephart suggests that when a child observes an object it becomes three-dimensional only after the child has manipulated it. For example, when a child observes a toy across the room, it is observed as two-dimensional. When given the opportunity to touch it and squeeze it, the toy is perceived as a three-dimensional object. Thus, according to Kephart, the child has made a perceptual-motor match. To remediate learning problems, Kephart recommended training in the motor generalizations mentioned above. Children are first assessed using the Purdue Perceptual Motor Survey (Roach & Kephart, 1966). This instrument evaluates children from preschool through seventh grade in five areas. They are:

1. **Balance and Posture.** Here the child is rated on walking (forward, backward and sideways), jumping and hopping.
2. **Body Image and Differentiation.** Five specific movement patterns that reflect the child's body awareness are observed and scored. Some of these movement patterns are "Imitations of Body Movements" and "Identification of Body Parts" which involve the child following a series of instructions and imitating a series of positions of the arms.
3. **Perceptual-Motor Matching.** The child is rated on chalkboard activities, such as drawing circles and writing.

4. Ocular Control. The child watches the movement of a light first with both eyes, then with the left eye only, and then with the right eye.

5. Form Perception. Several visual forms (figures) are provided with the survey manual and are given to the children to copy. The children copy these forms with pencil on plain paper and are scored for organization and form.

The level of perceptual development of the child is obtained after the survey's administration, and if warranted, a training program is developed. According to what the evaluation revealed, training could occur in some or all of the recommended activities, which are:

1. Perceptual-Motor Training – training the child to walk forward, backward and sideways in a more efficient manner.

2. Perceptual-Motor Matching – the use of any activities that require the child to integrate movement and perception, e.g., eye-hand coordination activities.

3. Training Ocular Control – any activity that requires the child to follow a moving object with his or her eyes.

4. Chalkboard Training – any activity at the chalkboard that helps establish directionality, e.g., drawing circles.

5. Form Perception – activities based on the matching principle would suffice, e.g., matching objects and geometric figures; the use of puzzles.

Marianne Frostig

Frostig maintained that adequate development in visual perception is fundamental to academic achievement. She was concerned with the development of visual perceptual skills in children who are experiencing learning problems, and argued that the early remediation of such problems would prevent future difficulties. Frostig is best known for her test, the Marianne Frostig Developmental Test of Visual Perception – DTVP (Frostig, 1964; Frostig, Maslow, Laferer & Whittlesey, 1964) and the

remedial program (Frostig & Horne, 1964) that is based on the results of the test.

The test is composed of five subtests, each of which measures, according to Frostig, a distinct aspect of visual perception:

1. Eye-hand coordination – the ability to integrate body movements and visual skill.

2. Figure-ground discrimination – the ability to distinguish the essential figure from the non-essential background.

3. Form-constancy – the ability to recognize that a figure may vary in size, texture or position without altering its basic form.

4. Position in space – the ability to recognize a particular form in any position.

5. Spatial relations – the ability to recognize the position of two or more objects in relation to one another and to the observer.

The DTVP was developed to provide the teacher with an overall estimation of the child's visual perceptual development, and to identify the deficient perceptual areas that require remediation. The remedial program consists of hundreds of worksheets and various exercises that are quite similar to the tasks found in the subtests of the DTVP.

Several other perceptual-motor theorists have not been as influential as the ones discussed above, but still deserve mention. They are Gerald Getman, Ray Barsch, and the team of Glen Doman and Carl Delacato. Getman (1965) was an optometrist who worked closely with Kephart; he suggested that visual perception is learned, developmental, and necessary for learning. According to Getman, the child passes through six developmental stages that overlap in sequence. These are:

1. general motor development;

2. special movement patterns;

3. eye movement patterns;

4. visual language patterns;

5. visualization patterns; and

6. visual-perceptual organization.

Failure to pass adequately through these stages results in learning problems, which can, according to Getman, be remediated with training activities aimed at improving each of the six stages. Barsch (1965, 1967) believed that the development of spatial movement patterns is necessary for learning. The theory behind Barsch's beliefs is called Movigenics – the study of the child's movement in space and the consequences of this movement. According to Barsch there are twelve dimensions of movement that pertain to learning, and these are divided into three groups: Group 1 consists of muscular strength, dynamic balance, body awareness and spatial awareness that aid body control and movement. Group 2 includes tactual dynamics, kinesthesia, auditory dynamics and visual dynamics, the function of which is to process information. Group 3 involves bilaterality, rhythm, flexibility and motor planning, which affect the efficiency of the other dimensions. The child who is experiencing problems is trained in the above activities, the details of which are found in Barsch's Movigenic Curriculum (1965).

Glen Doman, a physical therapist, and Carl Delacato, an educational psychologist, developed in the 1950s a theory of *neurological organization* which formed the basis for the treatment and education of children with learning problems. Their approach has been the most controversial of all motor approaches to learning problems.

The Neurological Organization Approach of Doman and Delacato

The approach of Doman and Delacato is based on three principles: (1) full neurological organization; (2) ontogeny repeats phylogeny; and (3) if there is a problem in the central nervous system (CNS), treat the CNS.

Doman and Delacato maintain that, in order for a child to be an efficient learner in school, he or she must reach full neurological organization. This is accomplished by about the eighth year of life and is considered fully developed if the child has no problems in learning. Neurological organization is based upon the second principle: ontogeny repeats phylogeny. This refers to the belief that individual human development repeats the stages of evolutionary human development. Thus, the nervous system develops in stages, with each stage representing the highest degree of neurological development of certain animal species lower down on the evolutionary scale. There are five stages, hierarchical in nature, which are as follows: medulla, pons, midbrain, early cortex, and cortical hemisphere development (full neurological organization). Table 2-1 highlights the stages, giving the level of human development along with the corresponding highest level of species development and an example of mobility development.

When a learning problem appears, Doman and Delacato contend, the neurological development has not proceeded through the stages in a smooth manner, or some of the stages have not been reached.

Assessment and Treatment

The assessment procedure usually requires a visit to the Institutes for the Achievement of Human Potential in Chestnut Hill, Pennsylvania. Here a complete medical and developmental history is undertaken, along with a diagnostic evaluation which

TABLE 2-1
Stages of neurological development (after Doman and Delcato)

Highest Neurological Development	Level of Human Development	Species	Mobility
Medulla	Newborn infant	Fish	Trunkal movement
Pons	Four-month-old infant	Amphibian	Homolateral crawling
Midbrain	Ten-month-old infant	Reptile	Cross-pattern creeping
Early cortex	One-year-old infant	Primate	Crude walking
Cortical hemisphere	Eight-year-old child		Cross-pattern walking

usually takes three days. During this period, each level of neurological development is evaluated, the purpose of which is to identify at which level the weakness occurs. At the conclusion of the evaluation, a developmental profile of the individual is drawn up, emphasizing the individual's performance in three areas of expressive behaviour (mobility, language and manual competence) and three areas of receptive behaviour (visual competence, auditory competence and tactile competence).

If a weakness at a particular level is identified, a treatment program is developed, to improve neurological development and thus prevent or eliminate learning problems. The program usually consists of numerous activities, including breathing exercises; diet changes such as restrictions of fluids, sugar and salt; sensory stimulation; and the training of eye-hand use. Furthermore, the program calls for an imposed series of motor activities. If the individual is unable to perform the prescribed motor activities, the activities are imposed by another person or persons who move the limbs and sometimes the head through prescribed motions. The individual must relearn and perform correctly each stage of motor learning – creeping, crawling and walking.

Evaluation

While some reports have presented evidence supporting the approach (Delacato, 1966) most researchers (e.g., Robbins, 1966; Freeman, 1967; and Robbins & Glass, 1968) conclude quite strongly that the theory, treatment techniques and research evidence are inadequate. Freeman (1967), for example, provides a detailed critical analysis of the approach, listing nine objections ranging from the promotional methods aimed at parents and the rigid demands made during treatment to the legitimacy of the test instrument (Doman Dalacato Neurological Development Profile) and methodological flaws of supporting research studies. Such objections contributed to an official statement made by several medical, psychological and educational associations in both the U.S.A. and Canada decrying the approach and its use. A more recent critical statement has been made by the American Academy of Pediatrics (1982).

In spite of these strong criticisms, Doman and Delacato still treat children, and many parents become strong advocates of the approach. For those of you interested in learning more about the approach and its criticisms, we recommend that you read the primary sources mentioned above.

Was Perceptual-Motor Training Effective?

Research into the effectiveness of perceptual-motor training has yielded little empirical support for such methods. Several investigators (Bibacc & Hancock, 1970; Mann, 1971; Hammill & Weiderholt, 1973; Hallahan & Kaufman, 1976) have, to all intents and purposes, arrived at the same conclusions that:

1. the remedial programs lack a sound theoretical base;
2. the studies for the most part are poorly designed; and
3. when properly designed perceptual-motor studies are carried out, they show no significant improvement in academic areas.

Despite these criticisms, the training procedures are still in common use. According to Lahey, Hobbs, Kupfer and Delamater (1979) this is because, first, the poorly designed studies give the appearance of supporting such methods; second, other methods have not been forthcoming, particularly from commercial sources; and third, the choice of training procedures has not been based on reliable scientific evidence. As you will see in the final section of this chapter, some researchers are pursuing perceptual explanations of learning problems, but these researchers are using far more sophisticated theories of perception (within a broader theory of cognition), and their work has not yet led to the production of remedial materials.

Language Disorders

A puzzling feature in the history of learning disabilities is the scant attention given to language development. This is surprising since a defect in either the reception or production of speech would affect academic achievement. Hallahan and Cruickshank (1973) attribute the lack of interest in language development to the fact that Strauss and Werner, perhaps the most influential of all the early researchers in the field of learning disabilities, "paid relatively little attention to language problems in children" (p. 101). Despite this situation, there has been some notable research into the relationship between language disorders and problems in learning.

Early research involved the investigation of brain damage and its effects on language development (Broca, 1861; Wernicke, 1906; Head, 1926; Jackson, 1931), but most authorities would agree that the first solid link between language disorders and learning problems stemmed from the work of Orton. Along with Orton's work, the work of Myklebust and Kirk will be considered, since the influence of these researchers still permeates many classrooms today.

Samuel Orton

In the 1930s Samuel Orton, a neuropathologist, developed a theory of brain function which stated that one side of the brain dominated language processes (Orton, 1937). In his research he studied children who had no apparent brain damage but did have severe and distinct language problems. These problems included the following symptoms:

1. confusion of lower-case letters;
2. the tendency to reverse parts of words and whole syllables; and
3. mixed or confused dominance of eye, hand and foot.

Orton's explanation for such problems was the child's failure to develop hemispheric dominance. The brain has two hemispheres, each relating to opposite sides of the body (the left hemisphere to the right half of the body, and vice versa). Thus, when the cortex (the surface of each hemisphere) receives stimuli from sensory organs, it does so from the opposite side of the body. Figure 2-1 shows the nature of this cross-over. The hemispheres are connected by a large tract of fibres called the corpus callosum which transfers information from one hemisphere to the other. It has been demonstrated that for most people the left

F I G U R E   2 - 1
Schematic representation of the cross-over of visual stimuli, the words "cat" and "dog"

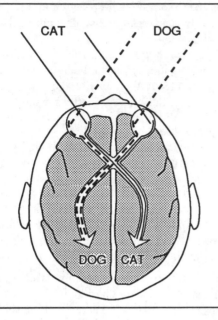

hemisphere dominates speech and language and the right hemisphere controls nonverbal spatial abilities.

Orton hypothesized that the non-verbal hemisphere stores mirror-images of words that are correctly stored in the dominant (verbal) hemisphere. When dominance fails to occur – that is, if the hemispheres do not develop their specialization – the reversed images are allowed to appear because they have not been suppressed by the dominant hemisphere. This then leads to the reversal of letters and words, a condition that Orton called Strephosymbolia (twisted symbols), and that was often accompanied by a variety of speech and comprehension problems. The aim of remediation was to develop cerebral dominance by using one-sided motor training. Further suggestions included:

1. removing students from regular classrooms;
2. using auditory channels as much as possible;
3. employing the phonetic approach to reading; and

4. establishing associations between sound and letter, so that when given the sound the child can produce the letter.

Little empirical evidence exists, as yet, for either Orton's theory or remediation techniques, but his influence continues today with many educators, among them Gillingham and Stillman (1970) and Slingerland (1974).

Helmer Myklebust

Myklebust's interest in learning problems and language disorders arose from his early work on deafness and aphasia. During this time he observed many children who were able to hear but failed to develop receptive language. Because of this observation he turned his attention to the diagnosis and remediation of auditory disorders.

Drawing from his early work on aphasia, Myklebust (1954) developed a theory of normal language development. He defined language as symbolic behaviour that includes the ability to abstract, to attach meanings to words and to use these words as a medium for thought and expression. Myklebust hypothesized five levels of abstraction: sensation, perception, imagery, symbolization and conceptualization. He also suggested that each stage was related directly to experience and that the stages were not mutually exclusive. The theory also includes five developmentally related levels of verbal behaviour:

1. inner language – auditory symbolic experiences;
2. auditory receptive language – comprehending the spoken word;
3. auditory expressive language – speaking;
4. visual receptive language – reading; and
5. visual expressive language – writing.

According to Myklebust, failure at any level within the developmental sequence will disrupt the stages that follow. For example, a child cannot learn to read until he or she understands speech. Central to Myklebust's theory is the assumption that the brain is made up of semi-autonomous systems. These are, he believes, neurological systems that function together or independently and include input-output systems, sensory modalities and the integration of these systems. When a system operates independently it is referred to as intraneurosensory learning, in which the integration of visual inputs and motor outputs or auditory inputs and vocal outputs occurs. An example of this would be the act of copying which integrates looking (visual) and drawing (motor). Combined functioning is referred to as interneurosensory learning that involves the integration of two systems that transfer information from one to another (visual-vocal or auditory-motor). An example of interneurosensory integration is reading. The child must look at a word (visual stimuli), which is then matched to its auditory equivalent (sound), and then expressed vocally (read).

While problems can exist in all three types of language (inner, receptive and expressive), Myklebust's remedial techniques concentrate on receptive and expressive problems, details of which can be found in the book *Learning Disabilities: Educational Principles and Practices* (Johnson & Myklebust, 1967). The work of Johnson and Myklebust has not been researched as extensively as other investigators, but two recent studies by Newcomer and Magee (1977) and Hessler and Kitchen (1980) provide some support of their principles.

Samuel Kirk

One of the most influential of all figures in the field of learning problems is Samuel Kirk. His influence stemmed from several important contributions. First, Kirk expressed the view that we should consider individual differences in children, particularly intraindividual differences (i.e., the child's individual strengths and weaknesses). Second, he helped to develop the Illinois Test of Psycholinguistic Abilities, ITPA (Kirk, McCarthy & Kirk, 1961, 1968) and the remedial program based on the test. Finally, he coined the term "specific learning disabilities" (Kirk, 1962).

The ITPA is based upon the communication model of Osgood (1957), and was intended to be a diagnostic instrument that could identify strengths and weaknesses in the way children process information. The test is made up of twelve subtests that measure abilities in three dimensions:

1. channels of communication – auditory-vocal, visual-motor;
2. the psycholinguistic processes – reception, organization and expression; and
3. levels of organization – representational and automatic.

The identification of the child's strengths and weaknesses allowed the teacher to cater to the individual needs of the child. The test, since its development, has become popular with teachers and school psychologists alike. However, researchers have questioned the test and remedial program on several grounds. Extensive reviews by Hammill and Larsen (1974) and Sedlack and Weiner (1973) point out that the ITPA has not shown constant effectiveness as a basis for differential diagnosis and remediation. Other authors have expressed doubts about the validity of the theoretical framework underlying the ITPA (Mann & Phillips, 1967; Mann, 1971).

Was Psycholinguistic Training Effective?

Not only has the theory behind the ITPA been questioned, but many doubts have also been expressed concerning the outcomes of training based upon the ITPA. Hammill and Larsen (1974) considered 39 studies that had been conducted, and concluded that no firm evidence for training effects had been established. Similar conclusions were reached by Sowell, Parker, Poplin and Larsen (1979) and Logan (1978). These conclusions have been disputed by supporters of psycholinguistic training (e.g., Lund, Foster, & McCall-Perez, 1978; Kavale, 1981). At the moment, it is still unclear how effective training based upon the ITPA has been. For our purposes, the doubts expressed about the theory itself are more damaging, for even if positive training results were shown, it would not be clear *why* they had occurred.

Because reading is a language-based skill, it seems clear that some reading problems are language-related. If language is seen to include skills such as sound-sequencing and sound-blending, then perhaps most reading problems are language-related. However, the mechanism is not clear from this type of description. Researchers have not abandoned the language domain in the same way that they have the perceptual-motor explanations. Instead they have concentrated upon developing more comprehensive theories of language, theories which now come within the broad class of cognitive theories. We will mention these developments in the final section of this chapter, and deal with them more fully in Chapter 7.

Behavioural Approaches

In the late 60s and early 70s a major shift in emphasis in the diagnosis and treatment of learning problems took place. Researchers began investigating learning problems as a form of maladaptive behaviour and not as the result of some underlying neurological impairment. Academic achievement, hyperactivity and impulsivity were seen as learned patterns of behaviour that could be modified just like other forms of abnormal behaviour. There are several reasons why this shift happened.

1. There was general dissatisfaction with perceptual-motor and psycholinguistic theories and training programs.

2. Hyperactivity, impulsivity and attention deficits became the focal points of study, and these behaviours were seen as obvious targets for behavioural intervention (Lahey *et al.*, 1979).

3. Behaviour modification became a sophisticated and well researched tool. It offered systematic ways of helping the teacher observe and change behaviour in the classroom.

4. Behaviour modification techniques had proved successful with other handicapped children, particularly the mentally retarded and emotionally disturbed.

While behaviourists agree that certain behaviours are governed by the central nervous system and that some behaviours are genetic in origin, their basic premise is that behaviour is governed by the principles of learning. Thus, behavioural and learning problems result from and are maintained by certain consequences in the environment. The technique of behaviour modification employs a structured environment and the reinforcement (rewarding) of behaviour that is considered desirable, along with the discouragement of undesirable behaviour. Traditionally, then, the technique has been used in the classroom to control and increase behaviours that are easily observed and measured, such as aggressive behaviour and out-of-seat behaviour. More recently, behaviour analysis techniques have been applied to the teaching of basic academic skills, such as reading and arithmetic (e.g., DISTAR: Engelmann & Bruner, 1974).

How effective is behaviour modification with learning problem children? In a concise analysis, Lahey *et al.* (1979) indicate that the results of studies aimed at improving attention, hyperactivity, impulsivity, perceptual and cognitive deficits were equivocal at best. A further finding from such studies is that the target behaviour – e.g., hyperactivity – might well improve, but specific academic problems remain. Another problem of existing behavioural programs appears to be that of generalization and durability. Maintenance of treatment gains following the termination of reinforcement has been poor (Keeley, Shemberg & Carbonell, 1976; Wahler, Berland & Coe, 1979). The regular failure of treatment gains to be maintained in non-treatment situations is also a problem with behavioural management interventions (Johnson, Bolstad & Lobitz, 1976).

Behaviour modification has also seen developments in recent years. In the last section of this chapter, you will see that researchers and practitioners have developed what is termed "cognitive behaviour modification", or more simply "cognitive control". Once again, these developments have taken place within a cognitive framework. Some of the methods of behavioural analysis, whereby complex tasks such as reading are broken down into component skills, have also been incorporated into cognitive approaches.

Recent Developments

As we have hinted throughout this chapter, each of the perceptual, language, and behavioural approaches has seen recent developments. What is significant, however, is that each of these developments has taken place within a frame of reference very different from those in which these approaches had their beginnings. The new frame of reference or theory, which is currently dominating psychology, is the cognitive one.

Cognitive theory attempts to describe and explain how the mind works, from the simplest of perceptions, through memory and strategies, to the most complex of decision processes. In this, it is quite different from many of the early theories which provided the underpinnings of traditional learning problem theories (perceptual, perceptual-motor and language theories); those theories tended only to address particular aspects of mind or behaviour. More importantly, modern cognitive theories are able to account for more of what we know of human behaviour. In particular, they have recently been applied to understanding academic tasks such as reading, spelling, arithmetic and mathematics.

Cognitive theory will be described in general terms in Chapter 4, and a more specific cognitive theory described in Chapter 5. This frame of reference will then be employed to understand both normal and learning problem behaviour in the areas of classroom behaviour (Chapter 6), reading (Chapter 7), spelling (Chapter 8), and arithmetic and mathematics (Chapter 9).

In Chapter 7, you will see the recent developments in the areas of perception (see reference to the work of Stanley and Hall, pp. 85-86) and language (see reference to the work of Stanovich, pp. 89-90). The behavioural approach has recently seen the proposal of cognitive behaviour modification, or more simply cognitive control. This approach, which aims to change children's cognitions so that they can control their own behaviour, is described in Chapters 11 and 14 (see reference to the work of Meichenbaum and Douglas, especially p. 152).

Our treatment of history in this chapter has been deliberately brief, more detail being available in other sources (see recommended readings at the end of the chapter). Following a discussion of important issues in Chapter 3, the remainder of this book is devoted to a cognitive approach to learning and learning problems. We hope to convince you that, in addition to being a worthwhile theory of human behaviour, this approach provides a useful framework for overcoming learning problems.

RECOMMENDED READING

For those of you who would like a more comprehensive history of the field, the following readings are recommended.

Hallahan, D.P. and Cruickshank, W.M.
1973. *Psychoeducational foundations of learning disabilities.* Englewood Cliffs, New Jersey: Prentice-Hall.

Weiderholt, J.L.
1974. Historical perspectives on the education of the learning disabled. In L. Mann and D.A. Sabatino (eds.). *The second review of special education.* Philadelphia: J.S.E. Press.

CHAPTER 3

Recurring Issues

FROM OUR BRIEF VISIT into the past, we can conclude that researchers have not agreed among themselves as to the nature of learning problems in children. This is understandable partly because different professionals are involved with children with such problems and each profession discusses learning problems from its own professional point of view. For example, the physician will diagnose and recommend treatment from within the confines of the medical model, while the educator often wonders about the usefulness of a neurological explanation. Because of these differences, several unresolved issues plague the field of learning problems. There is disagreement about an acceptable definition, and if we have trouble defining learning problems, then how can we be clear on:

1. the characteristic features of learning problems;
2. the identification of children with learning problems;
3. the cause of learning problems; and
4. the number of children having learning problems?

We will devote the remainder of this chapter to a discussion of these issues, which are clearly linked to each other. However, you should be warned that simple answers are elusive (and probably wrong!), and that these same issues will re-emerge throughout this book.

Definition

No other area in special education has had more trouble and confusion in defining its population than the field of learning problems. Such is the confusion that Clements (1966) noted thirty-eight terms and Cruickshank (1972) noted over forty terms, all used to refer to essentially the same child. There are several reasons for this variation: first, the differences in bias of the researchers, and second, the lack of a sound research base, in spite of the increased interest in the field of learning problems. Rourke (1983) discusses this problem, arguing that good definitions result only after extensive clinical observation and testing. Once this preliminary work is accomplished, research on disorders can proceed quickly. The field of learning problems overlooked this rigorous clinical investigation in its early stages: as a result, definitions have been developed prematurely and have been forced upon the scientific community. A third reason for confusion is that many investigators allow their theories about the *causes* of learning problems to intrude upon their definition of what a learning problem is.

Nevertheless, numerous attempts have been made at defining learning problems. These attempts have occurred in definite phases, each phase having its own focus. The first term to gain recognition was the "brain-injured child" (Strauss & Lehtinen,

1947), which implied that learning problems resulted from physical damage to the brain. With the passage of time it was criticized on numerous grounds and was replaced by "minimal brain dysfunction". This term was criticized in similar fashion, resulting in the emergence of the term "learning disability", which brought with it an educational focus.

The Brain-Injured Phase

As indicated in Chapter 2, the pioneering work in learning problems can be traced to the research of Alfred Strauss and Heinz Werner during the late 1930s and early 1940s. In their research, they witnessed a common behavioural pattern in children that were classified as mentally retarded, emotionally disturbed, autistic, behaviourally maladjusted and aphasic. Seeking a biological cause of the behavioural characteristics, Strauss suggested that the deviant learning and behavioural characteristics were manifestations of brain injury, and he created a new category – the brain-injured child. The basic Strauss definition (Strauss & Lehtinen, 1947) is as follows:

> The brain-injured child is the child who before, during or after birth has received an injury to or suffered an infection of the brain. As a result of such organic impairment, defects of the neuro-motor system may be present or absent; however, such a child may show disturbances in perception, thinking, and emotional behaviour, either separately or in combination. This disturbance can be demonstrated by specific tests. These disturbances prevent or impede a normal learning process. Special educational methods have been devised to remedy these specific handicaps. (p. 4)

Strauss theorized that the brain injury was exogenous, rather than endogenous (see Chapter 2, p. 17). Thus, the impairment was due not to a genetic cause, but to an injury that occurred outside of the genetic structure; for example, from anoxia (a lack of sufficient oxygen in the brain) or a fall on the head.

Strauss described the brain-injured child as having seven characteristics, four behavioural and three biological in nature. The behavioural characteristics were:

1. **Perceptual disorders.** When viewing pictures, these children see parts instead of wholes, and make figure-ground confusions.
2. **Perseveration.** They continue with an activity once started and have great difficulty in changing sets.
3. **Thinking or conceptual disorders.** The child is unable to organize materials and thoughts in a normal way.
4. **Behavioural disorders.** Children display such characteristics as hyperactivity, explosiveness, erratic or uninhibited behaviour.

The biological characteristics were:

1. **Slight neurological signs.** This refers to subtle problems in the absence of concrete evidence of neurological abnormalities. Awkwardness in gait, general clumsiness and fine motor problems are such examples.
2. **A history of neurological impairment.** This refers to evidence in the medical history that suggests damage to the central nervous system.
3. **No history of mental retardation in the family.**

The biological signs could be absent as far as Strauss was concerned and the child could still be diagnosed as brain-injured on the basis of behavioural characteristics.

Even though Strauss's work provided a meaningful and logical view of problem children, it was not without its critics. Stevens and Birch (1957) summed up the criticisms and arrived at four main objections to the term "brain injury":

1. The term indicates the supposed cause (etiology) of the problem and does not appropriately describe the behavioural characteristics of the condition. This is important because the condition is viewed in terms of behavioural characteristics, or symptoms, rather than etiology.
2. The term is associated with a variety of conditions such as cerebral palsy and epilepsy, which leads to confusion.

3. The term does not help in the development of a sound therapeutic approach; teachers and clinicians tend to approach the problem in terms of symptom reduction.

4. The term is too broad and leads to oversimplification.

On the basis of the above criticisms, Stevens and Birch (1957) recommended that the term "Strauss Syndrome" be used instead of "brain-injured" in describing the child who had difficulty in learning and did not fit into other classifications. Thus, the term was introduced to describe the child who exhibited several of the following characteristics (Stevens & Birch, 1957, p. 348):

1. Erratic and inappropriate behaviour on mild provocation;

2. Increased motor activity disproportionate to the stimulus;

3. Poor organization of behaviour;

4. Distractibility of more than ordinary degree under ordinary conditions;

5. Persistent faulty perceptions;

6. Persistent hyperactivity;

7. Awkwardness and consistently poor motor performance.

The Minimal Brain Dysfunction Phase

Research workers in the late 1950s and early 1960s observed that some children experienced learning difficulties that did not have the Strauss behavioural characteristics. Some children, for example, did not exhibit hyperactive behaviour, but were quiet and withdrawn. Thus, during the 1960s the term "minimal brain dysfunction" (MBD) became the label to include the Strauss-type child and other children with perceptual and learning problems. The shift in terminology resulted mainly from the work of Clements (1966) who defined MBD as follows:

... children of near average, average or above average general intelligence with certain learn-ing or behavioural disabilities ranging from mild to severe, which are associated with deviations of function of the central nervous system. These deviations may manifest themselves by various combinations of impairment in perception, conceptualization, language, memory, and control of attention, impulse, or motor function ... these aberrations may arise from other illnesses or injuries sustained during the years which are critical for the development and maturation of the central nervous system, or from unknown causes. (pp. 9-10)

This definition had much in common with the one of Strauss and Lehtinen (1947), but was more restrictive in that only children with near average, average or above average IQ were included. Strauss and Lehtinen did not impose such limitations. Furthermore, behavioural manifestations were expanded to include language and motor disorders. The term "MBD" differentiated the minimally involved child from the one with severe brain disorders.

Consider brain damage or dysfunction on a continuum from severe to mild, as found in Figure 3-1. At the severe end, extreme disturbances in behaviour are found, while at the mild end, subtle disruptions. For example, we see cerebral palsy on the severe end, characterized by major impairments of limb function and body movement. On the other end of the continuum we have minor impairments in fine motor coordination, e.g., poor eye-hand coordination, poor finger dexterity.

By the late 1960s the term suffered a fate similar to that of the "brain-injured child." Kauffman and Hallahan (1979), after considerable research by themselves and others (e.g., Freeman, 1976; Ross & Ross, 1976) argued that (1) the research evidence linking brain damage to specific behavioural characteristic is speculative and circumstantial in the majority of cases; (2) demonstrated damage of the brain does not positively result in the behaviours associated with the term; (3) the diagnosis of MBD does not bring with it specific implications for treatment; and (4) the 1972 term does not provide the clinician with any clear factors that can be identified and altered. As a result, the use of the term

FIGURE 3-1

The continuum from severe brain damage, or dysfunction, to mild or minimal brain damage/dysfunction

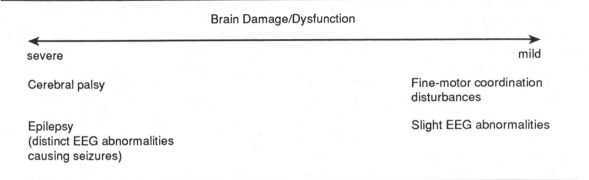

"MBD" might lead to a misinterpretation of the causes of inappropriate behaviour. For these reasons Kauffman and Hallahan have called for the abandonment of the term.

We can also see that the MBD definition contained within it a theoretical interpretation of the *causes* of learning problems. We would argue that such theoretical statements should *follow* extensive research into a problem rather than form part of the definition of the problem to be investigated.

The Learning Disabilities Phase

Even prior to the work of Clements (1966), a considerable number of professionals in the field of special education had begun to react negatively to labels that carried connotations of brain injury. The criticism here was that some children with major brain injuries do not have difficulty in learning. For example, some children with cerebral palsy have no learning difficulty, whereas others exhibit mental retardation. Furthermore, some authorities have asked the question in regard to the term "MBD": How much is minimal?

MBD can also be seen to be an empty, or at least circular, term. By definition, the child is not learning adequately, and we know that the brain is where the learning takes place. Thus, by definition we know that there is some sort of dysfunction in learning, and thus in the brain. MBD simply tells us that the child is not learning correctly, which is what we knew in the first place!

It became increasingly clear that terms and definitions that had greater educational implications were required. Hence, Kirk (1962) coined the term "learning disability" and defined it as follows:

A learning disability refers to retardation, disorder or delayed development in one or more of the processes of speech, language, reading, spelling, writing or arithmetic resulting from a possible cerebral dysfunction and/or emotional or behavioural disturbance and not from mental retardation, sensory deprivation, or cultural or instructional factors. (p. 263)

This definition was broader than Strauss's definition of the brain-injured child, since it specified that the disabilities may exist as a disturbance in one or more processes. For the first time we see the notion of specific learning disabilities, and a weakening of the theoretical link with brain dysfunction. However, the definitions of both Clements (1966) and Kirk (1962) do not include reference to the degree of severity of the learning disorder required to qualify for inclusion. Thus, the learning disabled definition became a "catch-all" term, whereby all children who had not been eligible under traditional handicapping conditions could be included.

Bateman (1965), a former student of Kirk, produced a definition that added a new dimension – the necessity to distinguish between capacity and achievement. Specifically, she argued that to have a learning disability with respect to a certain process, a child must perform significantly worse in that process than would be expected from the child's intellectual potential.

Because of the concern shown by special educators, the U.S. Office of Education became involved by providing financial funding for research. In order for the Office to act, a definition was required. One was developed in 1968 and was included in a U.S. Congressional Bill entitled *The Learning Disability Act of 1969*. The definition states:

> Children with special (specific) disabilities exhibit a disorder in one or more of the basic psychological processes involved in understanding or in using spoken or written language. These may be manifested in disorders of listening, thinking, talking, reading, writing, spelling or arithmetic. They include conditions which have been referred to as perceptual handicaps, brain injury, minimal brain dysfunction, dyslexia, developmental aphasia, etc. They do not include learning problems which are due primarily to visual, hearing or motor handicaps, to mental retardation, to emotional disturbance, or to environmental disadvantage. (USOE, 1968, p. 34)

This definition, really a development of the Kirk-Bateman definition, is an improvement in many ways, but still lacks educationally useful information on the diagnosis and treatment of learning problems. This definition was subsequently altered and expanded in 1977, and is now referred to as the (U.S.) Federal Register definition. Because of its importance within and beyond the United States, it is highlighted below.

A key phrase in the Federal Register definition – "a disorder in one or more of the basic psychological processes" – clearly reflects the shift in psychology in recent years toward theories which describe cognitive processes as opposed to mere behaviour or outcomes (more on this in Chapter 4). As yet, no precise and complete list of such psychological processes has been agreed upon, but it would include ones such as attention, perception, memory, transforming operations, strategies, and decision making. (Many researchers would feel that each of these terms is too broad and vague to be very helpful.) In our opinion the available research does not conclusively point to any one of these

processes as the sole cause of learning problems. Accordingly, we believe that the American legislators were wise (or at least wisely advised) to leave the issue open.

Not all investigators would agree with us, however. For example, Wepman, Cruickshank, Deutch, Morency and Strother (1975) argued that "specific learning disabilities" are the result of perceptual or perceptual-motor handicaps; Ross (1976) stated that they must be "associated with difficulties in sustaining attention" (p. 11); and Vellutino (1979) argued for the importance of verbal coding.

In our opinion, many authors are, once again, confusing *definitions* with theoretical statements about *causes* and with descriptions of *characteristics* commonly observed in the population in question. In our opinion, until we know a lot more about learning problems, it is preferable to employ a relatively open-minded definition while continuing to investigate potential causes. A definition, then, should emphasize observable features upon which most observers would agree (e.g., poor performance in school subjects, relative to estimated mental ability). Of course, it is also valid for a definition to exclude those cases which do not fall within the area of interest (for instance, the emotionally disturbed, or visually or auditorially impaired). It is then the task of theory, based upon research evidence and reasoning, to describe possible causes. Theories, you should keep in mind, are designed to be tested and improved; therefore, many of them are wrong. It is for this reason that theoretical statements should be avoided as much as possible in definitions; unlike definitions, they should change frequently.

Characteristics are yet a third category of statement: they are simply a list of features commonly observed in the population. As you will see in the following section, many characteristics are shared by many learning problem children. These characteristics (for example, poor self concept or poor memory skills) are not necessarily the *cause* of the learning problem, rather many of them may be by-products or side-effects of the original learning problem. This doesn't mean they are unimportant, because they should provide clues to the nature (causes) of the problem. However, they too should

The Federal Register Definition

The Federal Register Definition consists of two parts. The first part includes the following:

"Specific learning disability" means a disorder in one or more of the basic psychological processes involved in understanding or in using language, spoken or written, which may manifest itself in an imperfect ability to listen, think, speak, read, write, spell, or to do mathematical calculations. The term includes such conditions as perceptual handicaps, brain injury, minimal brain dysfunction, dyslexia, and developmental aphasia. The term does not include children who have learning problems which are primarily the result of visual, hearing, or motor handicaps, of mental retardation, of emotional disturbance, or of environmental, cultural, or economic disadvantage. (Federal Register, 1977, p. 65083)

The second part of the definition refers to specific criteria considered necessary to identify a learning disabled child:

(a) A team may determine that a child has a specific learning disability if:

(1) The child does not achieve commensurate with his or her age and ability levels in one or more of the areas listed in paragraph (a)(2) of this section, when provided with learning experiences appropriate for the child's age and ability levels; and

(2) The team finds that a child has a severe discrepancy between achievement and intellectual ability in one or more of the following areas:

(i) Oral expression;

(ii) Listening comprehension;

(iii) Written expression;

(iv) Basic reading skill;

(v) Reading comprehension;

(vi) Mathematics calculation; or

(vii) Mathematics reasoning.

(b) The team may not identify a child as having a specific learning disability if the severe discrepancy between ability and achievement is primarily the result of:

(1) A visual, hearing, or motor handicap;

(2) Mental retardation;

(3) Emotional disturbance; or

(4) Environmental, cultural or economic disadvantage. (Federal Register, 1977, p. 65083)

Essentially, this definition consists of four features:

1. The child has a disorder in one or more of the basic psychological processes.

2. The child has problems in learning, particularly in speaking, reading, writing, spelling and mathematical skills.

3. The problems do not stem *primarily* from other causes, such as visual, hearing or motor handicaps, mental retardation, emotional disturbance or environmental, cultural or economic disadvantage.

4. A severe discrepancy between actual achievement and assessed potential must be in evidence.

It is worth noting that this definition does not state a theoretical cause of learning problems, nor does it indicate how large a "severe" achievement-potential discrepancy must be.

be avoided in definitions, because it is not necessary for any one of them to be present for a problem to exist. In other words, many children with reading problems may have difficulty in paying attention, but this does not mean that *every* one will. This, in turn, raises an important point: there may exist more than one type of learning problem child; for example, the problems of some children may be due to perceptual problems, others to attention or verbal coding problems. We are not arguing that several types definitely exist, but rather that they *could* exist. This is another area in which we think it is helpful to keep an open mind.

Characteristics of Learning Problem Children

There are numerous characteristics that have been attributed to the child with learning problems. Perhaps the first concerted effort to delineate these characteristics appeared with Clements' (1966) investigation as part of a Task Force on Learning Disabilities. The report identified as many as ninety-nine characteristics. The ten most commonly reported characteristics in order of frequency were:

1. Hyperactivity;
2. Perceptual Motor Impairments;
3. Emotional lability (sudden emotional outbursts without obvious cause);
4. General coordination deficits (clumsiness and poor motor coordination);
5. Attention disorders (short attention span, distractibility, perseveration);
6. Impulsivity;
7. Disorders of memory and thinking;
8. Specific "learning disabilities" (reading, writing, spelling and arithmetic);
9. Speech and hearing disorders;
10. Equivocal neurological signs, such as electroencephalographic irregularities.

This list no longer reflects the present-day thinking on characteristic features. The 1977 Federal Register, for example, lists several discrepancies between ability and achievement as the dominant characteristic, thus placing academic problems on top of the list and not hyperactivity! Combining the features of the 1977 Federal Register and current research (Douglas, 1980; Torgesen & Dice, 1980), the characteristics of children with learning problems may be listed as follows:

1. **Discrepancy factor.** This refers to a child's achieving well below what would be expected from his or her intellectual potential. (As we have seen, this is a crucial component of the definition of a learning problem.)

2. **Language problems.** As a result of the discrepancy factor, difficulties can occur in oral language, listening comprehension, reading skills and/or arithmetic reasoning. (Again, because these comprise the major academic skills, they are also virtually a part of the definition of an academic learning problem.)

3. **Attention problems.** These are most often (i) the inability to maintain attention over a required period of time (short attention span), (ii) the inability to respond to relevant characteristics of stimuli (focus of attention) and (iii) the inability to make accurate stimulus discriminations (selective attention).

4. **Impulsivity.** There is a tendency for the children to be unduly impulsive, characterized by their quick response during problem-solving tasks and their apparent lack of problem-solving strategies that are necessary to give a correct response.

5. **Activity problems.** Four types of motor disorders can be seen: hyperactivity, hypoactivity, gross and fine-motor problems.

6. **Memory problems.** Here the child experiences difficulty in the encoding, storage and retrieval of information.

7. **Perceptual problems.** These appear to result from the child's inability to recognize, discriminate and interpret sensation.

8. **Affective problems.** These are the social-emotional problems that usually emerge, apparently as consequences of the cognitive problems and of repeated failure in school.

As we have indicated, characteristics 1 and 2 really form part of the definition of a learning problem. These issues will be elaborated in the following section, in the context of identifying learning problem children. Characteristics 3, 4, 5, 6 and 7 are more ambiguous in nature; they can be seen either as hypothetical *causes* of learning problems or as by-products (consequences) of those problems. Characteristic 8 is now generally regarded as a consequence of learning problems, though some educators continue to see affective problems as primary causes of learning problems.

A word of caution! Children with learning problems are a heterogeneous group, in which individual differences dominate. These characteristics can be found in many combinations and it is these combinations that contribute to the child's academic problem. Furthermore, some characteristics are often found together, revealing identifiable symptom clusters. For example, the hyperactive child displays excess gross motor activity, impulsiveness, short attention span and emotional lability.

Identification

The identification of exceptional children is an arduous task at best, and is usually governed by examining the parameters of the definition of the exceptionality in question. The identification of the child with learning problems is made more difficult by differences of opinion among authorities regarding an acceptable definition. As was discussed earlier in this chapter, these differences are large, but because the acceptable working definition is that of the 1977 Federal Register, the procedure for identification should demonstrate that:

1. a discrepancy between achievement and intellectual ability exists in one or more of the following areas: (i) oral expression, (ii) listening comprehension, (iii) written expression, (iv) basic reading skill, (v) reading comprehension, (vi) mathematics calculation or (vii) mathematics reasoning;

2. the discrepancy is not *primarily* the result of (i) a visual, hearing, or motor handicap, (ii) mental retardation, (iii) emotional disturbance or (iv) environmental, cultural or economic disadvantage;

3. the child has been provided with good educational opportunities.

The key factor in this procedure is the determination of the discrepancy between achievement and ability, to which we now turn.

Discrepancy

In order to determine that a difference exists between the child's potential and level of achievement we have to:

1. identify the child's present level of achievement;

2. assess the child's potential for learning; and

3. determine the amount of discrepancy between achievement and potential that is considered significant.

In doing this, we are presented with several problems. First, the problem of measurement error – we can never be sure that achievement test scores truly reflect the child's present ability. Second, there is the difficulty of measuring potential. This is usually done with some type of intelligence test, but you should be warned that different tests can give different results, and that there are serious questions about what intelligence is, how it can be measured, and even whether it can be meaningfully measured at all. It is also not clear that there should be a perfect relationship between measured intelligence and academic performance.

Third, there is the question of what is considered a significant discrepancy. The problem here lies in the fact that this amount would differ from age to age and grade to grade. For example, a nine-month discrepancy in reading in grade two is a more severe problem than a nine-month discrepancy in grade ten.

Despite these difficulties, the practitioner needs to make decisions using the available quantitative data. Thus, several techniques have been developed to calculate discrepancies, the most common being: (1) the mental grade method, (2) the years-in-school method, and (3) the learning quotient method. These techniques are summarized below.

Calculation of Discrepancies

The Mental Grade Method

This method was developed by Harris (1961) and is probably the best known and simplest method. It uses the following formula:

$$RE = MA - 5$$

or

$$RE = \frac{CA \times IQ}{100} - 5$$

where

RE = reading expectancy grade

MA = mental age $(MA = \frac{chronological\ age \times IQ}{100})$

5 = 5 years of age at school entry

Let's look at an example. Jean is 10 years old and has an IQ of 110. Using the formula, Jean's reading expectancy grade is 6.0. If Jean reads at 4.0 grade level, she would be two years below her expected reading level.

Years-in-School Method

This method was first developed by Bond and Tinker (1967) who criticized the mental grade method because it does not take into consideration the years of teaching to which the students have been exposed. To incorporate this factor, they suggested the following formula:

$$RE = \frac{YIS \times IQ}{100} + 1$$

where

RE = reading expectancy grade

YIS = years in school

Using this formula, the RE of Jean, who has been in school for 5 years, would be

$$RE = \frac{5 \times 110}{100} + 1 = 6.5$$

Using this method, if Jean reads at a 4.0 grade level, she would be 2.5 years below her expected reading level.

Learning Quotient Method

This method, first developed by Myklebust (1968), takes into account three factors: mental age (MA), chronological age (CA), and grade age (GA). Three factors are averaged in order to reduce the errors that accompany the factors, and the average is called the expectancy age (EA). Furthermore, in this method either a verbal MA or a performance MA, based on the verbal and performance IQs as measured by the revised Wechsler Intelligence Scale for Children (WISC-R), may be used. The EA is obtained using the following formula:

$$EA = \frac{MA + CA + GA}{3}$$

The learning quotient (LQ) is then considered to be the ratio of achievement age (AA) to expectancy age (EA), multiplied by 100:

$$LQ = \frac{AA \text{ (achievement age)}}{EA \text{ (expectancy age)}} \times \frac{100}{1}$$

An LQ of 89 or below is considered by Myklebust to indicate the presence of a learning problem.

To obtain an estimate of the verbal MA, the verbal IQ is multiplied by the CA and then divided by 100:

$$\text{verbal MA} = \frac{\text{verbal IQ} \times CA}{100}$$

Performance MA is obtained in similar fashion:

$$\text{performance MA} = \frac{\text{performance IQ} \times CA}{100}$$

Grade (GA) is obtained by adding 5.2 to the present grade placement (Grade + 5.2).

Let's consider Jean, using this method. Jean is 10.0 years old, in grade 5.0 and her full WISC-R IQ is 110. Her verbal IQ is 108 and her performance IQ is 111. Her reading achievement score is 4.0, which transforms into a reading achievement age of 9.0.

Using Verbal Information

$$\text{verbal MA} = \frac{\text{verbal IQ} \times CA}{100}$$

$$= \frac{108 \times 10}{100} = 10.8$$

$$EA = \frac{10.8 \text{ [MA]} + 10 \text{ [CA]} + 10.2 \text{ [GA]}}{3} = 10.3$$

$$LQ = \frac{9 \text{ [AA]}}{10.3 \text{ [EA]}} \times \frac{100}{1} = 87$$

Using Performance Information

$$\text{performance MA} = \frac{\text{performance IQ} \times CA}{100}$$

$$= \frac{111 \times 10}{100} = 11.1$$

$$EA = \frac{11.1 \text{ [MA]} + 10 \text{ [CA]} + 10.2 \text{ [GA]}}{3} = 10.4$$

$$LQ = \frac{9 \text{ [AA]}}{10.4 \text{ [EA]}} \times \frac{100}{1} = 86$$

Since both of Jean's scores are below 89, this method indicates that she has a learning problem: she learns only 87 percent and 86 percent respectively, of what she is capable of learning in both areas.

A word of caution! While discrepancy formulas do have certain advantages (and some sort of measure of discrepancy is required by the definition of learning problems), there are difficulties associated with them. In particular, the results may vary across grade levels and they definitely depend upon which formula is used (Macy, Baker & Kosinki, 1976; Bruininks, Glaman, & Clark, 1973).

The identification of a disability is a most difficult task and the discrepancy formula assists in this procedure. However, the scores produced act merely as a starting point, for they do not address other factors that contribute to learning problems, such as motivation, health, family background, attendance at school, teacher expectations and teacher style, to name but a few. All these factors need to be considered, and the 1977 Federal Register recommends that this is done via a multidisciplinary team approach. It has been said that nothing can replace good clinical judgement and experience in the identification of learning problems (McLeod, 1979). If several professionals are involved in the identification process, this approach might be the best at this point in time.

The Causes of Learning Problems

The search for an explanation of the factors underlying children's learning problems dominates the field today. This search has probably produced much of the controversy that surrounds learning problems, but we hasten to add that controversy surrounds almost all aspects of learning problems! There are basically three categories of causal factors which have been discussed: biological, environmental and psychological.

Biological Factors

The brain is the control centre of behaviour, and any injury or insult to the brain results in physical, mental and emotional changes. Scientists have not yet fathomed the finer workings of the brain, but present-day knowledge does provide support for the belief that brain damage disrupts basic brain processes, which in turn results in disordered behaviour and learning. Brain damage may result from three influences: physical damage (brain injury), heredity and biochemical disturbances.

Brain Injury

Physical damage to brain tissue can occur before birth (prenatal), during birth (perinatal), and after birth (postnatal).

Prenatal Factors   Pasamanick and Knoblock (1973) provide an extensive review of prenatal factors and list the following among the most common to cause physical damage to the brain:

- rh factor incompatibility;
- X-rays;
- maternal diabetes and hypothyroidism;
- infectious diseases, e.g., rubella, syphilis;
- excessive intake of alcohol, nicotine and drugs resulting in oxygen deprivation;
- maternal kidney infection and bleeding.

Perinatal Factors   During labour, complications can arise resulting in brain damage. This damage can occur as a result of anoxia or physical insult. Anoxia is the lack of sufficient oxygen in the fetus resulting in respiratory difficulties. It is commonly the result of difficult and prolonged labour, strangulation of the fetus by the umbilical cord, or improper use of anaesthetics. Physical insult to the brain results from difficult birth (breech birth and poor presentation), use of forceps, narrow pelvis and birth canal, and enlarged fetal head. It should be pointed out that usually a combination of the above factors, rather than a single factor, results in brain damage.

Postnatal Factors   During the early years of life, the child is perhaps at his or her most vulnerable time. Colletti (1979) points out that by the age of 6, approximately twenty percent of all children may have suffered from some brain insult, caused by infections and trauma. The most common infections are meningitis and encephalitis. The brain and spinal cord are covered by a thin protective layer called the meninges; an infection of this layer is known as meningitis. An infection of the brain is known as encephalitis. Encephalitis may occur as a complication following some common childhood diseases, such as mumps, chicken pox and measles.

Physical damage results from such things as accidents in and around the home. Such accidents damage brain tissue or can cause bruises to the surface of the brain, swelling of brain tissue, and blood clots which can lead to tissue damage. Parke and Collmer (1975) indicate that one of the leading causes of brain damage in children is child abuse, an aspect of the home situation that warrants immediate attention.

DIAGNOSIS OF BRAIN INJURY   Apart from the hard signs of brain injury, e.g., observed brain tissue damage or hydrocephalic conditions, how can the diagnosis of brain injury and its relationship to learning problems be undertaken with any sense of confidence? Unfortunately, it cannot! Admittedly, indicators of brain injury appear to be more prevalent among children with learning problems, but these indicators also appear in children who do not experience learning problems, e.g., some children with cerebral palsy. Researchers have been trying to develop methods that identify brain injury in learning problem children with some degree of reliability, some of which will now be discussed.

EEG Studies A technique for recording the electrical activity of the brain was developed by Hans Berger in the early 1930s. He showed that it was possible to monitor brain waves from the scalp. These brain waves he called electroencephalograms or EEGs, and they have been used since their discovery to relate brain activity to behaviour, both normal and abnormal. To record an EEG, small metal electrodes are attached to the scalp. The electrical signals that are picked up are then amplified and recorded on paper. Figure 3-2 shows examples of such recordings. How have these recordings been used to investigate the relationship of brain function and learning problems? According to Lubar and Deering (1981) three EEG techniques have been utilized: traditional EEGs, split-screen EEGs and evoked potentials.

Traditional EEGs are usually requested by the pediatrician, performed by the electroencephalographer and interpreted by the neurologist. What the neurologist looks for are differences in the wave patterns, such as frequency (in cps – cycles per second – or Hz – Hertz) and amplitude (voltage). Notable differences have been found between learning problem children (particularly children with reading problems) and normal controls (Hughes, 1978). The main finding is that children with problems tend to exhibit excessively slow wave activity, characterized by the small amplitude of the EEGs. Satterfield and Dawson (1971) suggest that this is evidence for a state of low arousal, particularly in hyperactive children. (More on this in Chapter 11.)

In the split-screen technique, a television is used. Half the television displays the EEG and the other half displays the child's behaviour. The importance of this technique is that the connection between EEG irregularities and environment events can be noted and marked on the EEG record, thus avoiding possible mistakes in interpretation.

FIGURE 3-2

Some typical EEG patterns, their names, frequency and the physiological state they represent. The vertical markers on the right of the patterns indicate a voltage of fifty microvolts.

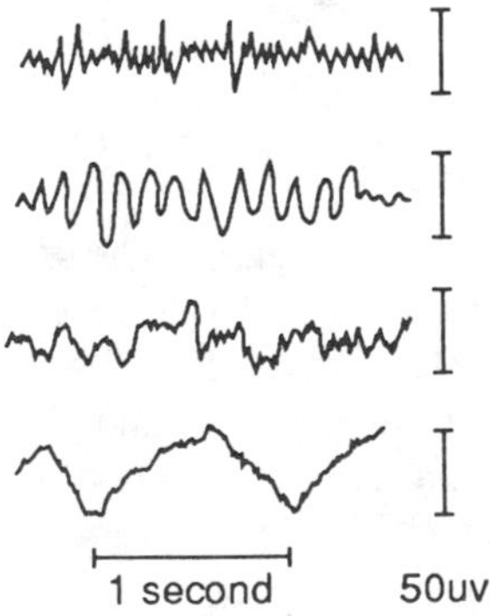

EEG Pattern	Name	Frequency (cps or Hz)	Physiological State
	Beta	14 - 30	Alert-Excited
	Alpha	8 - 13	Relaxed
	Theta	4 - 7	Drowsy
	Delta	1 - 3	Deep Sleep

1 second   50uv

Many people believe that traditional EEGs are crude indicators of electrical activity (Evans, 1977) and that they should be measured when the brain is being challenged by outside stimuli. The evoked potential technique is concerned with the brain's response to distinct events over time. Over the last ten years the technique has become more widely employed in the study of learning problems. The evoked potential technique is discussed in the box opposite.

Brain Electrical Activity Monitoring   A further application of the EEG and the evoked potential is seen in a new technology called Brain Electrical Activity Mapping (BEAM). This technique was pioneered by Duffy and his colleagues (Duffy, 1981; Duffy, Denkla, Bartels & Sandini, 1980), and provides "new insights into the regional differences in the brain electrical activity in dyslexic children" (Hynd & Cohen, 1983). A significant feature of this technique is that it condenses and summarizes brain electrical activity across the cerebral cortex into a type of topographical map, which can be displayed on a computer colour graphics monitor. Early research using BEAM has found differences between children with learning problems and control children (Duffy *et al.*, 1980); further research and refinement of BEAM may help our understanding of learning problems.

Other techniques have been developed recently to study the brain, notably Computer Axial Tomography, Positron Emission Tomography, and Magnetic Resonance Imaging; we describe each of these in turn.

Computer Axial Tomography (CAT)   is a radiological tool that scans the skull and allows visualization of the brain. An X-ray is passed from an emitter through the brain and the radiation that emerges is absorbed by a detector on the opposite side of the brain. This process is repeated at different angles, approximately three degrees apart, until full rotation occurs. The result is a collection of images of thin slices of the brain, which are then assembled by computer to produce a unified picture of the brain.

Positron Emission Tomography (PET)   is an extension of CAT, and can detect brain function while the subject is performing cognitive tasks. A radioactive isotope of glucose is injected into the carotid artery which carries blood to the brain. Because of differences in metabolic activity, more blood, and thus more of the isotope, are absorbed by the parts of the brain which are more active at any point in time. The PET scan is able to distinguish the different rates of uptake of the isotope, and thus can determine which parts of the brain are most active. By doing a PET scan while a subject is performing a task, the researcher can see which parts of the brain are most involved in that task. Such techniques may eventually tell us a lot about the sources of some children's learning problems.

Magnetic Resonance Imaging (MRI)   was known previously as "nuclear magnetic resonance imaging", but the name was shortened in the mid-1980s because of public concern over the connotations of the word "nuclear". When a strong magnetic field is applied to the brain, MRI measures the electrical responses of hydrogen protons in brain cells. With the help of a computer, these signals are converted and enhanced, creating a coloured picture of the part of the brain being investigated. One of the advantages of this technique is that it does not use radiation, in spite of the concern about the word "nuclear".

Neuropsychology

Neuropsychology, the study of brain-behaviour relationships, has recently provided further insight into the nature of learning problems. The usual procedure of the neuropsychologist is to give a series of psychological tests, the results of which are interpreted based on present-day knowledge of brain function. The tests used cover a wide range of abilities which often include the assessment of sen-

The Evoked Potential

The evoked potential (EP) is the response of the brain to a distinct event (e.g., a flash of light, or a specific sound). If an individual is subjected to a flash of light, the stimulus will *evoke* a change in the brain's electrical activity that can be detected in the EEG. To obtain the EP, a stimulus is presented, usually between fifty and one hundred times, at intervals of about one second. The electrical changes in the brain are then averaged by a computer and the EP is displayed as a single response. Because the EP is averaged, it is also called an averaged evoked potential (AEP). Typically, the AEP lasts for about .75 of a second and consists of many peaks, some positive, designated P, and some negative, designated N. These peaks are numbered sequentially as P_1, N_1, P_2, N_2 and so on. Figure 3-3 represents a typical AEP. It should be pointed out that AEPs will differ somewhat, depending on where the electrodes are placed on the skull.

You might now be asking how this measurement can help in the understanding of learning problems. The AEP is considered to provide information about the subject's cognitive processing ability and state of arousal. For example, peaks P_1, N_1, P_2 reflect the attentional state of the individual, and N_2 reflects arousal. P_3 is affected by more specific cognitive tasks, such as stimulus selection processes and decision making. In studying children with learning problems, then, researchers look for differences in the shape of the AEP, paying specific attention to the amplitude of peaks and latency (time) between specific points on the AEP.

FIGURE 3-3
Sample average evoked potential (AEP)

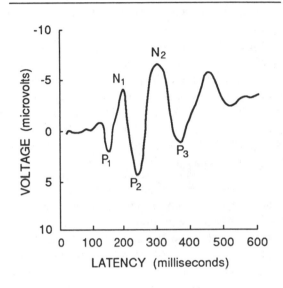

Since the early 1970s research activity has increased dramatically. For example, early researchrs such as Conners (1971) and Shields (1973) demonstrated differences in the AEP of learning problem children and normal children, suggesting that basic information processing deficits underlie the learning problems. Since this early research, the measurement of AEPs has become more sophisticated, as seen for example in the work of E. Roy John and his colleagues (John, 1977; Prichep, John, Ahn & Kaye, 1983). John has developed a powerful tool for assessing brain dysfunction called Neurometrics, which investigates aspects of the

EEG and AEP simultaneously from different areas of the brain. This technique has, according to John, demonstrated significant differences between learning problem and normal children, lending further support to the theory of an information processing deficit. As time passes, techniques for examining the electrical activity of the brain will no doubt improve with continued research. For those of you who would like to know more about AEPs, see the list of recommended readings at the end of this chapter.

sory acuity, lateral dominance, sensory stimulation, perception, speech and language, and intelligence.

With the use of such tests, neuropsychologists have, according to Gaddes (1983), made significant contributions to the field of learning problems, including:

1. the provision of additional diagnostic information in the analysis of learning problems;

2. the development of better methods of subtyping;

3. the improvement of assessment techniques for the early identification of children at risk;

4. the emergence of better remedial techniques.

Since the application of neuropsychology to the educational scene is a recent one, the above contributions are most encouraging, and the future looks very promising for the role of neuropsychology in education.

Heredity

Does heredity play a role in the development of learning problems? Researchers for the past eighty years or so have suggested a genetic link to learning problems. For example, Thomas (1905), in discussing "congenital word blindness", stressed its familial nature by pointing out that it is often present in more than one member of the family. Furthermore, the presence of genetic factors in other conditions that negatively affect learning – e.g., Phenylketonuria (PKU) and Down's syndrome – suggest that the idea of a genetic link in learning problems cannot be ruled out.

Hermann (1959) found that reading problems were more likely to be experienced by both members of a set of genetically identical twins than by both members of a set of fraternal (genetically different) twins. It is also common for learning problems to "run in families" (Denckla, 1973: Hallgren, 1950; Owen, Adams, Forrest, Stolz & Fisher, 1971; Silver, 1971). However, in most of these studies it is impossible to tell whether the similarities are due to similar genes or to similar learning environments. (Remember: you can inherit money, but that doesn't mean it's genetic!)

Biochemical Imbalance

A biochemical imbalance has been thought by some researchers to result in learning and behaviour problems (Wender, 1973; Lubar & Deering, 1981). It has been suggested that certain glandular disorders and vitamin deficiencies contribute to such imbalances, but the main line of evidence comes from the notion of an abnormal neurochemical imbalance. A detailed discussion of this aspect will be undertaken in Chapter 11, when we consider problems of arousal.

Environmental Factors

Researchers today are of the opinion that some learning problems are associated with certain environmental factors. The basic belief here is that the development and behaviour of children result from an interaction of the child's own individual characteristics and the environment in which the child lives. If this interaction is not a harmonious one, problems in learning and behaviour result. In recent times, research has centred on the environment, investigating not only the home, but also the school and the effect of environmental toxins on health and learning.

The Home

It has been found that learning problems are more prevalent among culturally disadvantaged children (Hallahan & Cruickshank, 1973). However, it is still not clear if these problems are the result of inadequate learning experiences or poor nutrition and inferior medical care (Cravioto & DeLicardie, 1975).

The School

Poor teaching has been suggested as a contributor to learning problems (Bruner, 1971; Cohen, 1971). According to Adelman (1971), poor teaching refers not only to inadequate instruction, but to such things as the teacher's lack of knowledge of individual differences in children, teacher bias, classroom environment, and poor curriculum. Larson (1976) and Lieberman (1980) concur with this view, and Bateman (1974) suggests that in many cases the term "learning disabilities" may be replaced by "teacher disabilities", so that attention may be brought to bear on teacher inadequacies. Proponents of this view suggest that the training of teachers be thoroughly overhauled, with a view to preparing teachers better to handle the individual differences that permeate our classrooms. It is also possible that the curriculum is inadequate, either in requiring students to learn in ways that are not appropriate for them, or in forcing them to begin learning academic skills at too early an age (e.g., Elkind, 1983).

Environmental Toxins

A recent concern has been the possible link between environmental toxins and learning and behaviour problems in children. Certain chemical elements, such as lead, have been shown to be poisonous and many others are being investigated. It is believed that these toxins either result in damage to the central nervous system or produce a chemical imbalance affecting learning and behaviour.

Typical of the research in this area is that of Pihl and Parkes (1977). They investigated the level of mineral elements in learning problem children. In part of the study, a group of third and fourth grade learning problem children were compared with normal children and were matched for age, grade, sex and socioeconomic level. Pihl and Parkes found significantly higher levels of toxic elements lead and cadmium in the learning problem group. They point out that this does not prove that these minerals caused the learning problems, but such a possibility cannot be ignored.

Toxins ingested with food have been in the headlines for some time. Feingold (1973, 1975) argued that learning problems and hyperactivity are directly related to food additives, and that a diet void of such additives results in a decrease in hyperactivity and improvement in learning. Feingold's diet and the reaction of the research community are explored in the box overleaf.

Psychological Factors

In order to have an overall understanding of the learning process, researchers over the years have developed models to explain learning, and these models have been applied to help explain the nature of learning problems. For example, Osgood's (1953, 1957) model of language was elaborated upon by Kirk (Kirk *et al.,* 1968) who developed the ITPA, a test based on the premise that learning problems are language-based. Other models have sought perceptual (Frostig & Horne, 1964) and perceptual-motor (Kephart, 1960) explanations, criticisms of which were discussed in Chapter 2. While these early models have been an important feature in the field of learning problems, today's consideration of psychological factors essentially revolves around (1) the concept of a maturational lag, and (2) a cognitive deficit, resulting from inefficient cognitive processes or strategies.

Maturational Lag

The basic premise of this approach is that each child has a predetermined developmental timetable

The Feingold Diet

In 1975, Ben Feingold published a book titled *Why Your Child is Hyperactive*. Since then his diet has received much attention from the media in TV talkshows and newspaper and magazine articles. In the years following the publication of the book, so many parents of learning and behaviour problem children have become firm believers in the diet, that Feingold Associations with thousands of members have been established. By 1980, an estimated 200 000 children had tried the diet (Feingold, 1980).

An unfortunate but common feature in the field of learning problems is the emergence of treatment "fads" that claim to have remarkable effects but are without scientific proof. Is the Feingold diet one such fad? To answer this question, let us examine Feingold's hypothesis, diet and research evidence and the reaction of the research community.

Basic Premise

In an unequivocal manner, Feingold has stated that artificial food colourings and flavours and naturally occurring chemicals (salicylates) have the ability to produce negative reactions in the body that affect all biological systems. Disruption of the central nervous system then results in the development of a variety of learning and behaviour problems, in particular hyperactivity. Feingold states that (1) those problems are allergic reactions, against which the body has no natural defences, and (2) children who react negatively to the additives do so because they have a constitutional predisposition to develop learning and behaviour problems.

Treatment

Feingold's answer to these problems is to place the children on a restrictive diet which eliminates (1) all foods containing artificial colourings and flavours, (2) all foods containing naturally occurring salicylates, and (3) certain miscellaneous items such as any compounds containing aspirin, toothpaste and toothpowder. The diet, known as the Kaiser-Permanente Diet, is outlined below.

Research Support

Early support for the diet came from Feingold's own clinical judgements and anecdotal reports and from several research studies (Feingold, 1974). Spring and Sandoval (1976) examined these studies and pointed out the various inadequacies in their experimental design. A more recent reappraisal of the diet was conducted by Mattes (1983), who examined both supportive and non-supportive studies. Among the supportive studies examined were those of Rapp (1978) and Swanson and Kinsbourne (1980), and both were criticized as having numerous methodological flaws. Rapp (1978), for example, did not analyze her results statistically and Swanson and Kinsbourne (1980) were questioned on several accounts, one being the way in which the hyperactive children were identified.

Studies that question the efficacy of the diet far outnumber supportive studies. One of the earlier doubting studies was by Harley and his colleagues (Harley, Ray, Tomasi, Eichman, Matthews, Chun, Cleeland & Traisman, 1978). In their investigation, Harley *et al.* (1978) identified forty-six hyperactive children who were randomly assigned to experimental and control groups. Inclusion in the study also depended upon parental consent, since all family members were placed on the respective diets. Subjects assigned to the experimental group were placed on the

Feingold diet. The control diet consisted of the usual levels of additives, colourings and salicylates. The families did not know which diet they were being given. Both diets were comparable in appearance, nutritional value, variety and palatability.

At the end of one month the diets were changed between the groups, and again lasted for one month. The effects of the diets were evaluated using parent and teacher questionnaires, neuropsychological tests and direct observation in both classroom and laboratory. Overall results showed no marked diet effect, and the conclusion of Harley *et al.* was that their study provided little support for the Feingold diet.

Other well designed studies such as those by Weiss, Williams, Margen, Abrams, Caan, Citron, Cox, McKibbern, Ogar and Schultz (1980) and Mattes and Gittleman-Klein (1981) came to the same conclusion: the Feingold diet had no marked effect. As a result of these studies, several organizations have conducted further independent investigations, and have reached similar conclusions. For example, the Nutritional Advisory Committee on Hyperkinesis and Food Additives (1980), reporting to the Nutrition Foundation, stated emphatically that the diet appears to be of no value and future research is not warranted. In less strong a statement, the National Institutes of Health (1982) suggest that the relationship between diet and hyperactivity is limited and recommend continued research to clarify the issue once and for all.

The Kaiser-Permanente (K-P) Diet (after Feingold, 1976)

Omit the following as indicated:

I. Foods containing natural salicylates

   Almonds
   Apples (cider and cider vinegars)
   Apricots
   Blackberries
   Cherries
   Cloves
   Cucumbers and pickles
   Currants
   Gooseberries
   Grapes or raisins (wine and wine vinegar)
   Mint flavours
   Nectarines
   Oranges
   Peaches
   Plums or prunes
   Raspberries
   All tea
   Tomatoes
   Oil of wintergreen

The salicylate-containing foods may be restored following four to six weeks of favourable response, provided that no history of aspirin sensitivity exists in the family.

II. All foods that contain artificial colours and flavours

III. Miscellaneous items:

   All aspirin-containing compounds

   All medications with artificial colours and flavours

   Toothpaste and toothpowder (substitute salt and soda or unscented Neutrogena soap)

   All perfumes

Note: Check all labels of food items for artificial colouring and flavouring. Since permissible foods without artificial colours and flavours vary from region to region, it is not practical to compile a list of permissible foods. Each individual must learn to read the ingredients on the label. When added colours and flavours are specified, the item is prohibited. If in doubt, the food should not be used. Instead, it is advisable to prepare the substitute at home from scratch.

that consists of stages that are predictable and orderly. A child with learning problems is considered to pass through these stages at a slower rate than his or her normally achieving counterparts – it is a maturational lag not an ability deficit that contributes to the learning problem. While research studies are sparse, several deserve mention.

Silver and Hagen (1966) carried out a follow-up study of children with specific reading problems. Several years after the initial evaluation, when students were young adults between 16 and 24, they were re-evaluated. The improvement seen in such areas as auditory discrimination and spatial orientation, according to Silver and Hagen, was due to maturation. In another follow-up study Koppitz (1971) re-examined 177 learning disabled students after a five-year period, and described their problems as a result of slow maturation. She described them as immature and in need of more time in order to reach the level of their normally achieving peers.

More recent investigators such as Kinsbourne and Caplan (1979) argue that the uneven patterns of development often seen in children with learning problems are due to the fact that their mental maturation proceeds by "fits and starts". More specifically, Pelham and Ross (1977) and Tarver, Hallahan, Cohen and Kauffman (1977) offer the possibility that learning problem children exhibit a lag in selective attention and verbal mediation.

The link between learning problems and maturational lag theory is incomplete at this point in time. Before the application of such a link can be used with any form of assurance, further research is warranted, paying particular attention to the reliability and validity of the measures used.

Cognitive Deficit

A more dominant view today is that learning problem children have some sort of specific cognitive deficit (such as poor memory skills or poor cognitive strategies). This does not necessarily mean that the deficit is permanent, or that it was genetically determined, but it does mean that it is unlikely to disappear by itself with the passage of time. Some cognitive deficit theories argue that the problem

existed before school was encountered, others allow for the possibility that the problem was acquired in response to school experience. Many different cognitive deficits have been proposed; this suggests the possibility that various subtypes of learning problems exist. For example, some learning problems may be due to a low level of a particular skill (such as sequential memory), while others are due to particular strategies (ways of trying to remember things in order).

The remainder of this book considers learning problems from a cognitive point of view, a view more related to the deficit than maturational lag positions. As you will see, however, this does not constrain the number of potential explanations to any great extent.

The Causes of Learning Problems: A Summary

As you can see, many causes have been suggested for learning problems, and many different *kinds* of causes. The biological and environmental causes are clearly more basic, but even they must work through a psychological mechanism; for example, lead poisoning does not cause a learning problem directly, but it may cause subtle brain damage, which in turn disrupts some psychological mechanisms (such as attention), which in turn prevents learning from taking place normally. We'd like to leave you with three thoughts:

1. The evidence for biological and environmental causes is not conclusive, and in any case would not guarantee that *all* learning problems are so caused.

2. Even if the biological and environmental explanations are valid, they still operate upon psychological and educational factors to produce learning problems.

3. The biological and environmental explanations point to ways to *prevent* future learning problems, whereas the psychological explanations suggest ways of *solving* current learning problems.

Prevalence

What proportion of children suffer from learning problems? There have been many attempts to determine the percentage with learning *disabilities,* but the estimates have ranged from a low of one percent to a high of forty percent (Meier, 1971)! The great discrepancy in these figures is due to many factors, primarily disagreements over definition and causation, and the changing social acceptability of having children labelled "learning disabled". We have seen in the preceding sections that definitions vary greatly and that many different causes have been implicated. If, for example, a maturational-lag explanation were accepted, and a relatively slight discrepancy between ability and achievement taken as the criterion – say, achieving one year behind potential – then it would not be difficult to imagine large numbers of children with learning problems/disabilities. On the other hand, if a more precise brain-damage hypothesis were accepted, or if a more strict criterion for including adopted – say 2.5 years behind potential – it would be very difficult to imagine many more than one or two percent of children being included.

Social factors have also played a role. From time to time it has been seen as preferable to have one's child labelled "learning disabled" rather than alternatives such as "slow" or "retarded". In those times (and they vary from country to country, state to state, and even year to year) it seems easy to find children "qualified" to be included. Some school authorities, trying to be helpful, have even gone so far as to provide extra funds when more than a certain number of such children have been located: while the intentions of these authorities were laudable, such funding programs obviously encouraged abuses. At other times and in other places, the term "learning disabled" has been seen as a stigma, to be applied to children with supposedly little academic future, who are, therefore, about to receive a second-class education. In such cases it is not surprising that parents resist having their children so identified.

There is great disagreement among learning disability theorists over whether the learning disabled

FIGURE 3-4

Two different conceptions of learning problems. Shaded areas represent learning problem/disabled children.

I. *Discontinuous distribution* (Learning problem children form a distinct subgroup.)

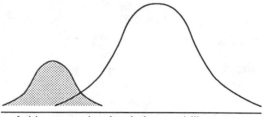

Achievement level, relative to ability

II. *Continuous distribution* (Learning problem children form a tail-end of the distribution.)

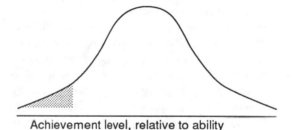

Achievement level, relative to ability

represent a distinct group of children (distinct probably because of different brain structures, functions or damage), or whether they simply represent the tail-end of the distribution of all children, when both achievement and ability are taken into account. If they are indeed a separate group, as are, for instance, the brain-damaged mentally retarded, then researchers should aim to devise diagnostic tests to separate these children from other children. On the other hand, if the children in question are merely behind other children in the development of academic skills relative to their intelligence, then there is likely to be a *continuity* in the distribution of test scores, rather than a firm dividing line (see Figure 3-4).

The question of how many learning problem children there are only makes sense in the former case (Part I of Figure 3-4). In the other case (Part II of Figure 3-4), the answer would depend largely upon where one draws the dividing line. Draw it far enough to the left, and you have very few children who qualify; draw it further to the right, and vast numbers of children qualify. Today the line is drawn in different places in different school jurisdictions, but it is often drawn by administrators acting as much on the basis of what funds are available as on the advice received by teachers.

The distinct group description is usually, although not always, associated with causal explanations of brain damage, or at least severe brain dysfunction. Researchers functioning within this framework are often said to work in the "medical model". The continuous distribution description is more associated with educationally oriented researchers, who are more likely to ascribe learning problems to inadequate teaching or to suboptimal cognitive processes and strategies.

We believe that there is some validity to both points of view. On the one hand, there are children who clearly do suffer from brain damage, and others whose difficulties are so severe that brain damage becomes a very plausible hypothesis. On the other hand, for the vast majority of children who fit the Federal Register definition, there is at best only the thinnest of evidence for brain damage.

In our view, the correct way to approach questions of prevalence is to accept a theoretically uncommitted definition of the larger group of children – those who fit the Federal Register definition. From the teacher's point of view, these children are performing much worse in school than they should; for them the term "learning problem" seems more appropriate. The "how many" question does not arise; teaching resources have to be shared among all students, and the number of children who can be given special help will depend upon the resources available. However, as research proceeds, it is likely that subgroups of these children may be identified, whose problem is more severe and can be plausibly linked to brain damage. At the moment there are at least two such subgroups within the "learning problem" population, those with "attention deficit hyperactive disorders" (who will be examined in more detail in Chapters 6 and 11), and the "deep dyslexic" (mentioned in Chapters 7 and 11). The "phonological dyslexic" (mentioned in Chapters 7 and 12) may be a third group. For these children the general label "learning disabled" seems more appropriate, although that term is not as valid or as useful as the specific diagnostic category terms.

Summary

In this chapter we have examined several recurrent issues that have plagued the study of learning problem children. We have seen that these issues are linked, and that one cannot be resolved without having implications for other issues. The definitional problem is perhaps the easiest to resolve first, if only because the legislators have taken the problem of out of the hands of researchers and answered it from a legal point of view. (This has happened not only in the United States but also, to a lesser degree, in other parts of the world.) As it happens, the Federal Register definition provides quite a useful basis for studying learning problem children.

One of the difficulties with many of the earlier definitions was that they included statements as to the *causes* of the problem, without any unequivocal evidence in support. A second difficulty was the implication that all learning problem children were basically of one type and that their problems stemmed from one basic cause (perceptual-motor disturbance, selective attention, etc.).

In the remainder of this book we develop an approach to learning problems based upon the following principles:

1. Learning problem children are those performing worse in academic areas than their intellectual ability suggests they should, and whose problems are *not primarily* due to sensory, motor, emotional, or environmental deprivation factors.

2. While some subgroups can be argued to have some form of brain damage, there is no evidence that the majority of learning problem children do.

3. Many of the characteristics of learning problem children can be helpful in determining the nature of their difficulties, but many can be side effects or byproducts of the primary problem(s).

4. Because learning problems occur in the performance of cognitive tasks such as reading and arithmetic, it is useful to examine the cognitive (psychological) processes normally involved in such tasks, and to examine the performance of learning problem children to determine which cognitive processes are functioning abnormally.

5. The complex nature of cognitive tasks such as reading and arithmetic suggests that different learning problem children could have quite different learning problems, even within the same academic area (e.g., reading).

6. From the educator's point of view, it is important to translate any suggested cognitive process problems into suggestions for remedial activities designed to overcome them.

RECOMMENDED READING

Most of the topics covered in this chapter are found in journals and books with which most teachers would be familiar. A few general references are:

Winzer, M., Rogow, S., & David, C.
1987. *Exceptional Children in Canada.* Scarborough, Canada: Prentice-Hall.

Journal of Learning Disabilities.

Journal of Special Education.

Learning Disability Quarterly.

Remedial and Special Education.

Canadian Journal of Special Education.

Neuropsychology

The following books are recommended for those who wish to pursue the relationship between brain function and learning problems:

Rourke, B.P., Bakker, D.J., Fisk, J.L., & Strong, J.D.
1983. *Child neuropsychology: An introduction to theory, research and clinical practice.* New York: Guildford Press.

This book provides an introduction to the neuropsychology of children with learning problems. Case studies are used extensively.

Tarnapol, L. & Tarnapol, M. (eds.)
1977. *Brain function and reading disabilities.* Baltimore: University Park Press.

This book includes many useful chapters, for instance, the one by Evans on evoked potentials.

Prichep, L., John, R.E., Ahn, H., & Kay, H.
1983. Neurometrics: Quantitative evaluation of brain dysfunction in children. In M. Rutter (ed.). *Developmental neuropsychiatry.* New York: Guildford Press.

This chapter is a challenging one, examining the analysis of both EEG recordings and evoked potentials.

Torello, M.W. & Duffy, F.H.
1985. Using brain electrical mapping to diagnose learning disabilities. *Theory into Practice, 24*(2), 95-99. This article avoids technical jargon and introduces BEAM and its use in diagnosing learning problems.

Heredity

Smith, S. (ed.)
1986. *Genetics and learning disabilities.* San Diego: College Hill Press.

This book provides an up-to-date discussion of the relationship between learning problems and heredity.

Diet

Silver, L.B.
1987. The "Magic Cure": A Review of the current controversial approaches for treating learning disabilities. *Journal of Learning Disabilities, 20,* 498-504. In addition to reviewing the effect of diet on learning problems, this article describes other questionable techniques, such as "patterning" and optometric visual training.

Lewis, M. (ed.)
1986. *Learning disabilities and prenatal risk.* Urbana: University of Illinois Press. A broad array of factors is discussed, including nutrition, drugs, genetics, and low birth weight.

PART TWO

An Integrated Frame of Reference

CHAPTER 4

What the Brain Does: Information Processing

BEFORE YOU CAN UNDERSTAND why something is not working properly, you first have to know something about how it works when it *is* working properly. For example, you're not going to be able to repair a car's engine if you don't know something about how engines work. So when we look at children with learning problems, and we want to "repair" those problems, we first have to find out how children normally function. This means that we first have to understand the psychology of children's learning, specifically how the brain *processes information.*

What does psychology know about how the brain works? The easy answer is "Not much"! Psychology is a much younger science than, say, physics, and brains are a lot more complicated than engines. So we have to admit that there are few definite answers where the brain is concerned, and even fewer simple answers. However, tremendous advances have been made in the last twenty years, and are still being made.

Behaviourist Psychology

Perhaps the greatest change that has taken place in the last twenty years is the way that psychologists think about the brain. Until the 1960s, the dominant theory in psychology, particularly in North Amer-

ica, was *behaviourism;* behaviourists observed people's behaviour, but they didn't theorize about what was happening inside the people's heads. The brain was accepted as a mystery, a mystery that didn't have to be solved.

Today, most psychologists see themselves as *cognitivists,* or at least they accept that some sort of cognitive theory about the brain is the most accurate. A cognitive theory is one which explicitly tries to describe what is going on in the brain, in addition to observing what behaviour that brain produces.

What happened to change psychology from a behaviourist to a cognitivist point of view? Until recently, the only description of learning that could be imagined by psychologists was one that saw the brain as an old-fashioned switchboard, the kind at which the operator sits, frantically trying to connect blinking lights with wires. By this view, learning was thought to be the connecting of a *stimulus* (a thing that is observed by the person to happen in the environment) with a *response* (an action by the person). For example, the stimulus of a red traffic light is connected with the response of putting on the brakes. This *stimulus-response learning theory* works pretty well to describe how very simple animals learn, or even how more complex animals learn relatively simple things.

Behaviourist psychologists assumed that the same sort of theory could be applied to *all* forms of learning, including all human learning. At this point, the behaviourists divided into two groups: one group decided to try to describe human learning in stimulus-response terms, a truly monumental task. Because they had to start somewhere, they picked very simple kinds of learning, hoping to go on to complex learning once they had completely described simple learning. Unfortunately, even simple learning proved to be too complex. As a result, this first group of psychologists continued to study very simple learning, often in animals (who seem to be more tolerant of simple learning and of behaviourist psychologists!).

The second group of behaviourists realized that a stimulus-response theory would be very complicated, and difficult to produce quickly. Because they wanted to help people quickly, they decided to give up the theory altogether: they are the ones who accepted the brain as a mystery not to be investigated. Instead, they investigated people's behaviour, without worrying too much about why they produced that behaviour. These psychologists have become the proponents of behaviour modification, the altering of people's behaviour by means of manipulating its consequences (by rewards and punishments).

The Cognitive Revolution

The big change happened in the 1950s, and didn't begin in psychology. It began with the development of computers, complex information processing machines. Computers managed to liberate psychology from its stimulus-response theory prison. If machines could be built that operated in more complex ways than an old-fashioned telephone switchboard, why should we deny that human beings' brains could work in a similarly complicated way? Of course the computer consists of wires that are connected to each other, but you don't need to follow each of the wires through all of its connections to be able to use, understand, and even repair the computer. Psychologists began to see parallels between computers and human beings: computers take in lots of information (*input*), they possess prodigious memories (*storage*), they transform information in complex ways (*operations*), and they do complex things (*responses*), all according to some on-going plan of action (*program*). The difference, of course, is that humans choose their own plans (to some extent), while computers still need humans to supply their programs.

Thus the computer became psychology's new metaphor for talking about the brain. Unlike the telephone switchboard metaphor, the computer metaphor was capable of a level of complexity that meant that complex learning could be described. (Psychologists are not the only ones to recognize the benefits of computers; even telephone companies have replaced their old switchboards with computers now. Nothing like disposing of the old metaphor entirely!)

Relevance for Learning Problems

The shift to a cognitive approach to psychology has been important for the learning problems field. Some children's problems can be well described in a behavioural way – for instance, the child whose major problem is that he or she cannot sit still in class. This behaviour may very well be due to a lack of a particular response (sitting still) in a particular stimulus situation (the classroom, while the teacher is talking). It may also be true that a behavioural type of treatment (rewarding sitting-still behaviour, ignoring or punishing fidgety behaviour) would alleviate this problem. Great successes with behavioural treatments (often called *behaviour modification*) encouraged many psychologists to adopt this approach with learning problem children. (See the list of readings at the end of this chapter for some examples of psychologists dedicated to the behavioural approach.)

There are two problems with the behavioural approach to learning problems. The first is that while the *problem* can be described in behavioural terms, the *cause* hasn't been! Consider a poor child with an ants' nest below her seat: this would surely produce fidgety behaviour, but we'd hope that she didn't have to wait for some earnest behavioural psychologist to come along for her problem to be solved. Also, we might agree that teaching that poor girl to sit still in such a situation would be an exercise in torture! That is basically a silly example, but intended to make the point that understanding the problem's cause may give you some helpful ideas about how to eliminate it. There's nothing fundamentally wrong with the behavioural approach; it's just that there are other approaches that may be more helpful in many situations. The psychologist who tackles every learning problem as though it were a behavioural problem is like the carpenter who only carries one tool: very effective in some cases, disastrous in others.

The second problem with the behavioural approach to learning problems is that the problems with which we are concerned usually involve very complex learning, rather than very simple learning. Behavioural psychology took for its classic example of learning a rat in a box learning to press a bar to obtain food. *Some* learning problem children may have problems that resemble that situation, but most have problems that are more related to reading, writing, spelling and arithmetic. So the problem is that the behavioural approach *tends* to treat all children as though they suffer from the same sort of simple problem, when in fact many of them suffer from problems in much more complicated areas.

We have seen so far that there are two problems with the behavioural approach: it ignores the causes of problems, and it tends to treat all children as though they have simple problems. The cognitive approach certainly tries to overcome these difficulties. In this chapter and the next, we describe a cognitive explanation of what the brain does. Then, in the remainder of Part II, we will use this cognitive theory to explain what is happening when children are in classrooms. In Chapters 6, 7, 8 and 9 we deal with problems with attention, reading, spelling and doing arithmetic; in Chapter 10 we describe some of the emotional or affective consequences of these cognitive problems. In Part III we will make use of this frame of reference to explain how the information processing approach can help in the diagnosis and remediation of learning problems.

Basic Ideas in Information Processing

In the remainder of this chapter we are going to describe the fundamental concepts of information processing, the ones that almost all cognitive psychologists would accept. In Chapter 5 we present a more detailed description of a particular cognitive theory that we think is very helpful in understanding learning problems.

The most basic statement of information processing psychology is this:

(1) Information is entered into the system; (2) it is held briefly while it is examined for importance; (3) some of it is selected for processing, and (4) the results of that processing are stored in a relatively permanent form. (5) Responding, or acting, usually involves the coordination of information previously learned and of information currently entering into the system. (6) All of this takes place under the direction of a program or plan of action.

This description of information processing is illustrated in Figure 4-1. As you can see, each of the numbered parts of the description also appears in the diagram. This is a general model: in the next few chapters we will see some more specific models, for instance, of how reading works.

Each part of the general model deserves some further description.

Incoming Information (1)

We are constantly bombarded with information: sights, sounds, tastes, smells, internal physiological sensations (like hunger, a stiff leg, a sore muscle) and our own thoughts. It would not be possible for us to pay attention to all of these stimuli; there is simply too much happening around (and within) us. One of the most important functions of the informa-

FIGURE 4-1
The information processing system

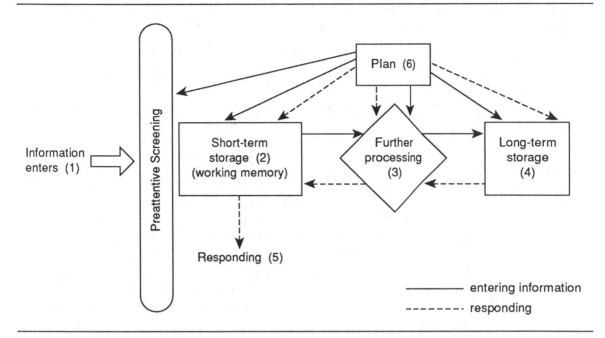

tion processing system is to screen out this surplus of incoming information, to protect us from an overload. This screening-out takes place in two stages, *preattentively* and *attentively*. Preattentive screening happens before we become aware of it: an example of this is when you literally do not hear your mother calling you to dinner because you are totally absorbed in a TV program. Your "plan" has determined what is important, and for the moment that doesn't include your mother. Of course your mother can overcome this preattentive screening by shouting more loudly, cuffing you about the ears, or tickling your feet. Attention-getting devices like telephones, fire alarms, and TV commercials are designed to overcome preattentive screening. In terms of Figure 4-1, preattentive screening occurs before stage 2 of the model.

Information Storage (2)

In some ways this is the most important stage of the model. Information that has not been screened out

preattentively is held briefly in what is called *working memory*. Working memory is really the core of the information processing system. It contains what we are currently aware or conscious of. Incoming information has to be held there while we (or our plans) decide what to do with it. Unless you do something with it, or to it, this information will fade away in twenty seconds or so. What we decide to do to this new information *also* takes place in working memory. Just to make the situation even more complicated, it is also true that our plan (see [6] below) resides in working memory. To illustrate this, let's re-draw our model, as Figure 4-2.

Working memory has been described as the cognitive scratchpad or workbench. By this we mean that what we are actively thinking about takes place in working memory. Working memory is often referred to as a "space", or as a "place" where processing occurs. Space is used metaphorically; it does not mean that working memory is a physical location with a physical size. Working memory has one overwhelming feature: it's very limited. There

FIGURE 4-2
*The re-drawn information processing system,
emphasizing working memory*

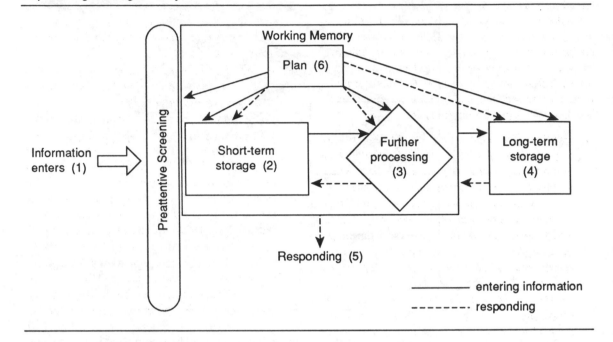

is a very strict limit to the number of "things" that we can place in it. The most obvious example of this is remembering numbers: if someone reads you a list of random numbers once, you'll be lucky to remember more than six or seven of them.

Fortunately there is a way around this limitation. While we can only hold a certain number of "things", there is no real limit to how much each of those "things" can contain. So if our "things" consist of individual numbers, we'll be able to hold only six or seven. However, if each "thing" is itself a meaningful pattern of numbers, such as

2 4 6 8   1 3 5 7   2 4 6 8   1 3 5 7   2 4 6 8,

then we should be able to remember far more individual numbers, even though it is the same number of "things". Psychologists refer to these "things" as *chunks;* that is, chunks of information. In the pre-

ceding example, each group of four numbers could be a chunk.

Now you may not be too concerned about remembering numbers, whether they are in patterns or not. But think instead of the implications for reading, or even for listening to someone. If all you could remember of a book, even this book, was the first seven words (or the last seven words), you wouldn't be very far ahead. Instead, what you should be doing is packing (or *encoding,* to use the technical term) lots and lots of extra information into each of your available working memory spaces. Like the screening-out process, this encoding can occur preattentively (or automatically) or attentively. Automatic encoding should happen when you see "2 4 6 8"; you really shouldn't have to do too much thinking to see this as a pattern. Attentive encoding, like attentive screening-out, is described in the next section, on further processing.

Further Processing (3)

It is accurate to say that *processing* starts as soon as light hits your eye or sounds hit your ear, etc. So even the initial stage of holding the information briefly involves *some* processing. However, once the information has been received – that is, initially encoded – you only have a brief amount of time before it fades away. In that brief amount of time, about twenty seconds, one of three decisions has to be taken. The three possibilities are:

(a) Delete it. The information doesn't appear to be important, so you decide to delete it. This is attentive screening. A good example is when you hear your mother calling you to dinner, but you consciously decide to ignore her. Similarly, in reading you often encounter details which are not important for the text's meaning; in order for the text's meaning to be understood, these details have to be discarded. (How details are recognized as unimportant is not a simple matter; see Chapter 7.) This deletion procedure is very important, because it's our most efficient way of cleaning up our workbench to make way for new information.

(b) Rehearse it. The second possible decision is to go over the same information again, in the same form. Psychologists call this rehearsal. If someone read the numbers "2 7 3 9 6 4 2" to you, you'd probably repeat them to yourself if you wanted to remember them. This is rehearsal. Rehearsal is a good way of increasing the life expectancy of information in our working memory, but not for long. One or two rehearsals of something doesn't prolong its life a great deal. If, however, you rehearse something many times, as an actor would in preparing for a play, you can acquire an almost permanent copy of it. (One of the authors of this book was required in high school to memorize a soliloquy from Macbeth, as punishment for some misdemeanour. Try as he might, he still cannot forget it!) It should be emphasized that pure rehearsal, simple repetition without any interpretation or thinking, is incredibly boring and open to errors: if perchance you make a mistake on your forty-ninth repetition, you really have no way of detecting it. *Rote learning* has its place, in the learning of things that don't yet make much sense; skilled teachers mix rote learning with *meaningful learning* (see next paragraph) to maximize learning and student interest.

(c) Recode it. To "re-code" something means to change its representation, and it's what we do when we see meaning in the raw information that we have received. So when we receive "9 7 5 3 1", we could recode it as "the first five odd numbers, in reverse order". By doing this we have replaced five chunks of information with two ("the first five odd numbers", and "in reverse order"). The recoding process is cyclical: we can recode what we have already recoded, etc. This is important in language processing, as we will see more extensively in Chapter 7. Just to give you some idea of what will be said there, when we read, we actually see little lines and curves on the page. These marks are recoded (preattentively) into letters. Letters are also preattentively recoded, into syllables or perhaps words. Beyond that stage, attentive recoding usually takes over: words are chunked into phrases, phrases chunked into meaningful phrases, and then ideas chunked into main ideas. By recoding intelligently, we can pack an astounding amount of information into relatively few chunks.

How does recoding happen? How do we know how to recode our current working memory contents? Recoding is controlled by two factors: our current plan (see [6] below) and what we already know (see [4] below). For example, if you are driving along a remote highway and you see a service station, you will interpret or recode that perception according to your current goals; if you are low on gas, you'll see it as a gas station; if you are hungry, you'll see it as a potential place to purchase food; and so on. If you are of dishonest persuasion, you may even see it as a place to acquire sudden wealth.

We can recode current input *only* on the basis of what we know. Our long-term memory (see [4] below) contains a lot of information about how the world normally works, about words and their meanings, and about how to do things. So when new information comes in, it is compared with what we already know. This comparison process can occur automatically or consciously. An example of automatic comparison would be when you walk down a familiar street – you're not aware of it, but your long-term memory is checking the street for familiarity. If something is unfamiliar, such as a new building, you're alerted to it. Comparison can also occur consciously, for instance when you see a photograph of someone, and you try hard to remember who that person is.

When long-term memory information is used to recode incoming information, we are engaged in *meaningful learning*. In fact, a good definition of something's *meaning* consists of what it is related to in long-term memory; this is literally all that we know about it, all the meaning that we have for it.

As recoding proceeds, our interpretation of the incoming information becomes increasingly abstract, that is, more remote from the input and more related to what we had inside our heads beforehand. Some abstractions retain the ability to regenerate the input accurately, such as "the first five odd numbers, in reverse order". This *accurate* regeneration ability is lost in more remote abstractions: "Macbeth is about ambition and its frustration".

Long-Term Memory (4)

Our long-term memories contain at least three different types of knowledge: facts, schemes, and procedures. Facts are the easiest to describe. We simply know a lot of things, many of which are relatively arbitrary and unconnected with anything else that we know. Examples of factual knowledge are that the capital of Mongolia is Ulan Bator, that your first English professor's first name was Peter, that "kitchern" means giggle in German, and what your brother looks like. While we possess a vast number of such facts, the difficulty with them is that, once they've been lost, there's no easy way to find them again. Facts have been essentially rote learned, and are not often very abstract in nature.

Long-term memory contains also some very abstract information which, unlike facts, is usually connected in very complex ways to other things that we know. Psychologists describe this kind of knowledge as *schemes*. Take for example the word "friendly"; you may have a precise definition of it in your memory (thus it may be like a fact), but you also "know" a lot more about friendliness. When you hear the word, you may think of particular people or incidents in your life. Friendly also means something quite different, depending upon whether you're describing a person, a country or a computer! In other words, you have an implicit, complicated, vague and schematic definition of "friendly" which is most unfactual!

Another example of a scheme: if you're reading a story in which the hero goes into a restaurant and is served a can of tomatoes, you know that something is wrong. Your scheme of what a restaurant is doesn't accept the serving of cans very easily. We'll see many more examples of this in Chapter 7.

Our long-term memories also contain *procedural* knowledge – that is, knowledge about how to do things. How to ride a bicycle, how to draw a house, how to write a computer program, how to study a book are all procedures that we may have stored in our long-term memories.

Responding (5)

Responding is clearly related to knowledge, and can happen in various ways. Some responding is very simple; for example, "What is your name?" should provoke a very simple, automatic factual response. In this case the answer was immediately known, and the production of the response was not complicated. In other cases you could know the answer, but its production would be more complicated: for example, the response to "Tell me what happened during your summer vacation." There are also examples in which you don't know the answer right away, even though it is uncomplicated (such as, "What is 97236 divided by 3?"), and ones in which you don't know the answer right away and it is complicated to produce, such as "Divide 97236 by 3, add your age in months, multiply by the number of Canadian provinces, and find the square root."

The most important aspect of responding is how automatic it is. An automatic response, such as walking, or adding "2+ 2", or making toast, does not require much conscious planning and therefore does not absorb much working memory. Less automatic responses, such as mountain climbing, multiplying "7 × 21", or preparing a full dinner, take up more space. Very un-automatic responses, such as making the next move in a chess game (if you're not a great chess master) can take up all the available space: "If I move here, then he'll move there, so I'd better move there, but then he'll move there and attack my queen, so I'd better try to protect her by moving...."

Response automaticity can change. When you were seven years old, "2 + 2" may have absorbed all of your processing resources; it shouldn't absorb much any more! Drill and practice, whether they are in the classroom (reading, writing, doing arithmetic), sport (practising plays in football), or art (practising a piece of music), are intended to increase response automaticity to free working memory space. Paradoxically, by practising something so that you can do it without thinking, you become able to use that information to think about more important things in your now available working memory space! (We'll discuss this again in Chapters 7, 8 and 9, when discussing the relative merits of "drill" and "understanding".)

The Plan (6)

All of this complicated processing has to be controlled, so that the right thing happens at the right time. Plans can be *automatic,* in which case they don't take up much working memory space, or *conscious,* in which case they do. Furthermore, conscious planning can make use of plans that we already have, or we may have to create a new plan. Creation of new plans is the most consuming type of planning.

Plans can exist at many levels, and any level of plan normally calls upon lower-level plans. For example, when you carry out a plan to multiply 27 ×

32, you'll need to use sub-plans that are concerned with adding and "carrying". Moreover, each of these sub-plans will have to call upon an even lower-level plan to write down the actual numerals.

(If you know anything about computer programming, you'll recognize that plans are like programs, and that sub-plans are like subroutines. If you don't know anything about computer programming, maybe you'd better start learning!)

Putting It All Together

That concludes our "brief" overview of what information processing is and how it works. A naive person would be excused for thinking that it is not difficult to understand why information processing sometimes doesn't work, and wondering instead how it can ever happen properly!

In the next chapter, we will describe information processing in a more detailed manner, and begin to discuss some of the difficulties that learning problem children *could* have.

Summary

Our purpose in this chapter has been to introduce you to the basic ideas of information processing. These basic ideas, at least in their broad outline, would be accepted by most cognitive psychologists today. While we see cognitivism as the dominant force today, you should be aware that there are still many active behaviourists. These psychologists would disagree with the approach taken in this chapter (and in most of this book).

The basic description of information processing is as follows: Information is taken in; it is held briefly in working memory and examined for relevance. Some is selected for further processing (deletion, rehearsal, or recoding) and is stored in long-term memory. Responses are made. All of this takes place under the control of a plan. We'll make this description more detailed and precise in Chapter 5, and even more so in Chapters 6 through 10, with regard to school performance.

RECOMMENDED READING

Behaviourism/Behaviour Modification
Bandura, A.
  1969. *Principles of behaviour modification.*
  New York: Holt, Rinehart and Winston.
    This is the classic presentation of
  behavioural principles.

Information Processing
Lindsay, P. & Norman, D.A.
  1977. *Human information processing.* New
  York: Academic Press.

There are many information processing
theories, applied to many different areas of
human activity. This book is an excellent
general text that will lead you into many of the
different manifestations of information
processing.

Gardner, H.
  1985. *The mind's new science: A history of the
  cognitive revolution.* New York: Basic Books.
    This view of the history of the cognitive
revolution addresses the roles of philosophy,
anthropology and computer science in
cognitive science.

CHAPTER 5

PASS: A Theory of Information Processing

IN THIS CHAPTER we will present a more specific theory of information processing, which we will call PASS, for Planning, Attention, Simultaneous, Successive. This theory accepts the general description of information processing that was given in Chapter 4, but it goes on to give much more detail about several features. The main differences are that this theory (1) gives more detail about what types of processing take place; (2) emphasizes the role of arousal in attention; and (3) deals with individual differences. The theory is helpful in describing how children normally perform tasks like reading, spelling and arithmetic. By knowing how these school tasks are normally performed, we can begin to appreciate some of the ways in which children can *fail* to perform them well. The consideration of arousal processes is helpful in understanding many classroom behaviour problems.

The Brain

The PASS theory comes partly from the study of human behaviour, for instance in classrooms or laboratories, but it also comes from the study of the brain. Because the brain is where the information processing system is, you'd think that it would be a very sensible place to start looking if you wanted to understand information processing. Unfortunately, the brain is incredibly complex. To give you some idea of just how complex it is, consider some facts:

– The brain is composed of cells called neurons, about 10^{11} of them. That is 100 000 000 000 cells!
– Each of these cells can be connected to as many as 60 000 other neurons.
– Cells can connect with each other one-to-one, as in a chain, or bundles of cells can generate electrical fields called *slow waves* that can travel through the brain.
– Connections between cells can change in response to learning.

So the brain has many more connections than does the largest computer, and the actual connections between bits are more complex and changeable than in a computer. Just to make it worse, there's no easy way to open up the brain and watch what is happening; in any case, most brain owners would object strenuously to any attempts at opening up!

Ready to give up on the brain? Well you wouldn't be the first. Many psychologists, and even more educators have decided that the brain is too complex for them to understand, and that even if they did understand it, they don't see how that understanding would make them more effective in helping children with learning problems. We think that the decision to give up on the brain is wrong, for several reasons. First of all, we don't have to wait until we *completely* understand the brain before we start doing something with that knowledge. Second, we are beginning to learn about some very important aspects of the brain. Third and most important, the brain is where information processing takes place: if children are having information processing problems, we should be able to understand their problems better if we can understand even a little about the mechanism that is doing the processing.

One of the ways of studying the brain is to examine brain-damaged people, to see what sorts of damage produce what sorts of problems. People can continue to live, and lead reasonably normal lives, even though major parts of their brains have been removed or damaged. Careful psychological research can reveal some very subtle difficulties that these people have, as well as the more obvious ones. By combining the evidence obtained from studies of brain-damaged people with that from studies of normal people, we should be able to construct a theory of information processing that describes how the brain works, and also how it fails to work.

Are Learning Problem Children Brain-Damaged?

As soon as anyone mentions brain-damaged people in a book on learning problem children, someone leaps to the conclusion that learning problem children are brain damaged, or at least that the authors think so. So we'd like to state something very clearly: WE DON'T KNOW! Some learning problem children may have some damage in their brains, but then so may many children whom we call normal. What we can be sure of is that if they do have damaged brains, the damage is nothing like the damage in the brains of people who have had bullets shot through their heads, and so on. It is also very unlikely that *all* learning problem children have brain damage, since there are so many of them, they are mostly otherwise normal, and they are of so many different types.

Why is the brain damage issue such an emotive one? Because most people think that if the brain is damaged, then there's nothing we can do about it. This kind of argument has been used in the past to rationalize not trying to help learning problem children: if their brains are damaged, then by definition we can't make them normal. That line of argument is simply false: many people with severe brain damage, much more extensive than the damage a learning problem child could have, can lead lives that are close to normal. What they require is careful teaching to train other parts of the brain to do what the damaged part used to do, or to teach them to accomplish old tasks in new ways. So even if some learning problem children are brain-damaged, that is no reason for thinking that there is nothing we can do for them. And don't forget, there is *still no good reason* for believing that they are brain-damaged.

How is the brain damage research relevant, then? As we see it, the brain damage research helps to describe the structures of the brain and what they do. After examining many cases of brain damage in many parts of the brain, we have a better idea of what is there, and what it does. So when we encounter a learning problem child who is not performing "normally" in school, we try to find out what parts of his or her information processing are not working normally. The brain damage research gives us ideas about parts of the brain that may not be working properly, as do other types of psychological research.

Notice that we have said "not working properly" rather than "damaged". Brain damage is an extreme form of "not working properly", and learning problem children are likely to have much more subtle forms. If you like analogies, it's like a plumber looking for a drainage problem: the cause could be a broken pipe (equivalent to brain damage), or a blocked pipe (equivalent to the learning problem child's "not working properly"). The result could be the same – no water getting through – but the recommended remediation would be quite different. Brain damage research can tell us about the structures and functions of the brain, but only educational research will tell us what to do about it.

PASS

Where the Theory Came From

The theory had its origins in the clinical work of Alexander Luria with brain-damaged patients (1966a, 1966b, 1973). Briefly, Luria observed the deficiencies that his patients exhibited after damage to various parts of the brain. He compiled observations from many patients, concluding that the brain was organized in three *functionally interdependent systems.* Damage in particular areas consistently affected the same behaviours in different patients, though very slight changes in location could produce differences in severity and in the level of behaviour disrupted. The term "functionally interdependent" means that even though the systems can be described separately, in the normal brain they interact with and *depend upon* each other.

Of course, Luria's work was with the brain-damaged. J.P. Das and his colleagues have taken Luria's basic theory and developed it in ways more relevant to normal and learning problem children (see Das, Kirby & Jarman, 1975, 1979; Das, Leong & Williams, 1980; Kirby, 1984; Kirby & Das, 1990; Das, Naglieri & Kirby, in press; Naglieri, 1989; Naglieri & Das, 1988). The work of Das and his colleagues has been oriented in four directions: studies of different cultures (not relevant here), studies of the mentally retarded (also not relevant here), studies of normal and learning problem children (very relevant), and development of a battery of tests that can be used with these children (also relevant). This work has led to the production of two individualized test batteries (Das & Naglieri, 1990; Kaufman & Kaufman, 1983).

What the Theory Says

PASS theory states that cognition is the result of three distinct, but functionally interdependent neurological systems (see Figure 5-1). The systems are (1) the *attention and arousal system,* located in the brain stem and lower cortex, responsible for maintaining alertness and cortical tone; (2) the *process-*

FIGURE 5-1
Three neurological systems. Each system is identified by a shaded area (after Luria, 1970).

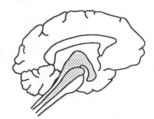

Attention/Arousal System

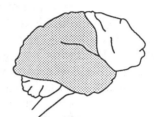

Processing System

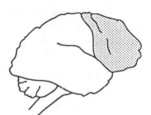

Planning System

ing system, located in the posterior (occipital, parietal, temporal) cortex and responsible for the input, storage and transformation of information (the two types of processing in which the system engages are called *simultaneous* and *successive* processing), and (3) the *planning system,* located in the frontal cortex and responsible for the organization and monitoring of processing (see Figure 5-1 for the location of these systems in the brain). It is important to note that these systems are interdependent – just as weaknesses in one system can be compensated for in other systems, those same weaknesses could disrupt the other systems. Thus, an observed deficiency in memory, for example, is not necessarily due to processing system problems: arousal or planning could just as well be involved.

The three systems of the model are illustrated more schematically in Figure 5-2. It can be seen that input is analyzed by the processing and attention systems, though probably quite primitively in the latter. Input is encoded on the basis of information stored in the long-term memory (processing system), and that encoding is stored in the working memory (processing system). It can be maintained there, or manipulated (recoded, either on the basis of other new input or other long-term memory codes), or transferred to long-term storage. While all of that occurs within the processing system, the processing is guided or controlled by the planning system. In the case of familiar input or a familiar task, an habitual plan may be executed in an automatic fashion, taking up little additional processing space. In a less familiar situation, a new processing plan may have to be constructed, and execution of this plan will take up additional processing space. When an habitual plan is implemented, no new "planning" is required, so in a sense the planning system is involved largely in an historical fashion; it is also possible that the execution of any plan necessarily involves the planning system to some degree. When a nonautomatized plan is executed, processing space is necessarily occupied, decreasing the space available for the other information and operations (cf. Case, 1980). Both the processing and planning systems rely upon appropriate levels of arousal. Although the mechanism is not clear, arousal that is too high or too low interferes with attention and appears to decrease the amount of short-term processing space available, decreasing the amount of information and the complexity of plans that can be handled.

In the remainder of this chapter, we will describe each of the PASS systems (planning, attention, simultaneous and successive processing) more fully. In each section we'll give examples of potential learning problems, though each of these systems will be dealt with more completely in Chapters 11, 12, 13 and 14. Finally, we shall raise two

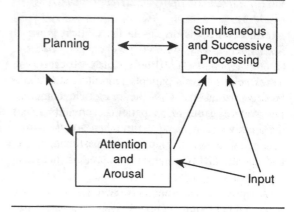

FIGURE 5-2
Three information processing systems

important issues: how this theory relates to the concept of intelligence, and how the theory accounts for school achievement. School behaviour and achievement will then be described more fully in Chapters 6, 7, 8, 9 and 10.

Attention and Arousal System

The attention and arousal system is responsible for maintaining an appropriate level of activity in the brain, and for ensuring that important stimuli are given the required processing. Early descriptions of PASS presented only the arousal aspects of this system (e.g., Das, Kirby & Jarman, 1979), but more recent versions (e.g., Das, Naglieri & Kirby, in press) focus on both arousal, as the mechanism of this system, and on attention, as the behaviour which we can observe more easily. We refer to this system as either the attention and arousal, or just the attention system, but you should remember that both arousal and attention are involved.

The most obvious learning problem attributed to inappropriate attention or arousal is hyperactivity. In theory, low cortical arousal results in poor behavioural control, and thus in behavioural overactivity. Ross (1976) has argued that many learning disabled children show the characteristics of hyperactive children, even if they are not themselves behaviourally over- active. He claimed that the central feature of hyperactivity and of learning disability is poor selective attention, which in the model would appear as reduced short-term processing capacity, or inefficient planning. If arousal is the fundamental problem – i.e., it causes the poor selective attention – then the arousal system could be said to be at fault. However, poor selective attention (which is really an emergent property of all three systems) could be due to inefficiencies in any one or more of the three systems. Hyperactivity, and the role of attention in causing it, are discussed in Chapters 6 and 11.

Attention system interventions are of several sorts. Probably the most common response is to wait in the expectation that these children will "grow out of" their problems. This would be true if they have, as Ross suggests, a developmental lag in attentional skills. However, several years of school failure while selective attention is developing are likely to produce a severe academic skill deficit, as well as negative attitudes toward school. The initial attention problem would leave a residue of academic problems that would be difficult to alter in adolescence.

A second approach involves the use of stimulant drugs. The argument is that these increase cortical arousal, thus improving behavioural control, calming the child so that instruction may take place, and perhaps allowing the child to learn. While the drugs do decrease the behavioural activity level, there is still much argument about whether they facilitate learning in the long term. One difficulty may be with the dosages given the children, the "standard dose" being too much for one child and too little for another. If the drugs happen to sedate the child into a sluggish stupor, it is unfortunately true that most teachers would be less concerned about the hypoactive child than the former hyperactive tone (Das, 1973). Stimulant drugs are discussed further in Chapter 11.

If it is the attention system *per se* that is at fault, and the inappropriate arousal level can be detected (perhaps electrophysiologically from the reticular activating system in the brain stem), some sort of biofeedback technique might be applicable. In biofeedback, people are trained to control their own physiological responses. (Would the average hyperactive child be likely to sit through the usually long biofeedback session obediently? Probably not.)

By far the most promising techniques hardly involve the attention system at all: most are better characterized as teaching the planning system to control attention, or to bypass its worst effects. These techniques will be discussed in the Planning System section below and in Chapters 11 and 14. At the moment, attention system problems have direct solutions only in a medical sense; indirect solutions are more psychological in nature, and are more promising. Chapter 11 will provide further examples of attention problems, as well as suggestions regarding diagnosis and remediation.

Simultaneous and Successive Processing

The functions of the processing system can be characterized through a series of dichotomies. For example, one can discuss processing in terms of the *amount* of processing required (little *vs.* a great deal), the *content* processed (verbal *vs.* spatial), the *memory* involved (working *vs.* long-term), and the *type* of processing involved (simultaneous *vs.* successive). None of these dichotomies should be taken too seriously – the first is clearly a continuous dimension, and the other "dichotomies" probably represent separate abilities (i.e., it's not a question of verbal *or* spatial content being processed, but rather of different skills and knowledge structures being required for each). We emphasize the "type of processing" dichotomy in this book, because we feel it has most application to learning problem children.

Because the processing system is basically responsible for the storage and transformation of information, disabilities attributed to this system are described in terms of insufficient processing, inappropriate processing, lack of requisite knowledge schemes, or lack of sufficient processing

FIGURE 5-3
*Schematic illustration of simultaneous
and successive processing*

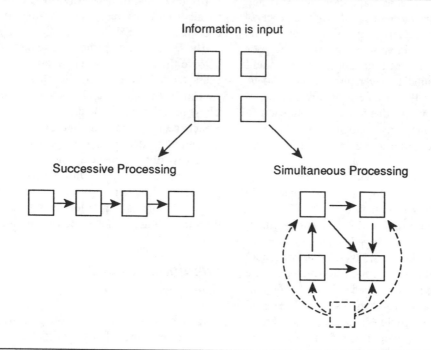

space. These alternative descriptions can be difficult to distinguish and, in fact, all could be functioning to produce the observed disability. Again, it
can be seen that some of these processing system
problems, especially those related to *choice* among
alternative types of processing, may have their
source in the planning system.

Luria (1966a, 1966b, 1973) and Das *et al.* (1979)
distinguish between two types of processing, called
simultaneous processing and successive processing. The difference between them concerns what
happens to information when it enters the processing system. In *successive processing* the pieces of
incoming information are coded into a *temporal
sequence,* so that the only connections among them
are the ordinal links of one piece to the next. Thus,
the code that is formed is one-dimensional in nature

(see Figure 5-3). This type of processing is important when it is necessary to keep every piece of
information, and in its correct order. For example,
in remembering a telephone number you need to
know both the actual digits and their order to have
any success. Luria's data demonstrate that successive processing is performed in the fronto-temporal
areas of the brain (see Figure 5-4). Successive processing is involved in rote memory, in the breaking
down or analyzing of information into an ordered
sequence (as in analyzing a word into its constituent sounds; see Chapter 7), and in the operation of
complex plans (to keep track of what steps have
been carried out, and which remain). As we will see
in Chapter 7, many children with learning problems
in reading have difficulties with successive processing, and this type of processing is also involved

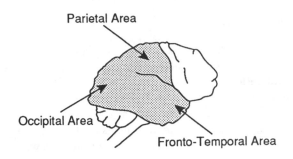

in spelling, arithmetic and mathematics problems.

In *simultaneous processing,* the incoming information is coded into a form that is more "holistic" or multi-dimensional (see Figure 5-3). In this case, the pieces of information are linked to each other in more complex ways, and order is usually lost. The easiest way to describe simultaneous processing is to say that it allows the *relationships* among the pieces of input information to be seen (as opposed to successive processing, in which the only "relationship" seen is the temporal one). According to Luria, simultaneous processing takes place in the parietal-occipital areas of the brain (see Figure 5-4). Simultaneous processing is involved whenever patterns are detected, whether they are spatial or verbal. To describe a set of lines as forming a cube is to use simultaneous processing, just as it is to say that the words "dog", "cat" and "canary" share the characteristic, "pet". Just as successive is required to keep information ordered, simultaneous is required to keep information related. Difficulties with simultaneous processing can result in learning problems in each of the achievement areas, problems which will be different from those due to successive processing difficulties.

Simultaneous and successive processing are related to the functioning of working memory. Successive processing refers to the *holding* of chunks

of information, greater successive processing being required to hold more independent chunks of information. Simultaneous processing refers to the *formation* of chunks, more simultaneous processing being required to form more complex chunks.

Two points need to be stressed with respect to simultaneous and successive processing: (1) they normally work in conjunction with each other, and (2) a difficulty in using either type of processing can be due to a *lack of ability* or to the *inappropriate use of abilities.* Normal cognitive activity (including that involved in academic achievement) requires both simultaneous and successive processing. For example, in reading it is necessary to be able to analyze a word into its component sounds (successive) but also to relate it conceptually to other words (simultaneous). In "The dog bit John", word order (successive) is crucial so that a meaningful and accurate image can be constructed (simultaneous). Educationally our goal should not be to have children use one or the other form of processing, but rather to be able to use both appropriately.

What does it mean to have a "difficulty" in using one or the other form of processing? Luria has presented case studies of people who have undoubtedly suffered brain damage in either the parietal-occipital or front-temporal regions and have lost some of their ability to use simultaneous or successive processing. These persons clearly have a *defect* which prevents their normal functioning. Depending upon the severity of the damage they may or may not be able to regain the affected functions. Learning problem children are not likely to have a defect to the same extent, though they may be less likely than other children to be able to use one or the other form of processing (in the same way that some children cannot run as fast as others, and so on). If the problem is that they are less *able* to use a form of processing, then that *ability* may have to be trained within the processing system, or an alternative method found for performing the task in question. On the other hand, a learning problem child's "difficulty" may be that he or she is *inclined not to use* a particular type of processing.

This disinclination may be due to poor teaching (as when the successive aspects of reading are overemphasized), to a history of failure with a type of processing (for example, producing a dislike of spatial problems that normally require simultaneous processing), or even to a lower level of skill with one of the types of processing. In the last case, an initial lower level of skill could produce a disinclination to use it, which in turn, through lack of practice, would result in an even lower level of skill. To the extent that the problem is one of disinclination, remediation will concentrate upon the children's strategies (planning system). In most cases it is likely that both the processing and planning systems will have to be involved in remediation (see Chapters 12, 13 and 14).

Planning System

The preceding discussion of the attention and processing systems emphasized that many of their problems are actually problems of planning, or that they are best solved through the planning system. Yet the planning system is the one which we know least about; accordingly, a list of planning functions and disabilities is necessarily incomplete and vague. The discussion which follows is largely based upon work by Kirby and Ashman (1982, 1984), with Luria's theory as a conceptual framework.

The planning system is responsible for the construction, execution, and monitoring of plans for processing. A plan that is well established is probably stored in long-term memory and functions automatically; as such, little "planning" is required for execution of such a plan. On the other hand, that same plan at an earlier stage in the development of automaticity would require a great deal of "planning". As plans become more automatic, they require less of the limited capacity processing space. Although this space is "in" the processing system, the determination of what is placed in it is a function of the planning system.

Kirby and Ashman (1982, 1984) have divided planning system functions into three levels: stra-

tegy, attention, and metacognition. Each of these will be described and related to learning problems in turn.

Strategy Level

Planning at this level is related to being able to use a relatively specific plan to solve a type of problem. Straightforward examples would include using rehearsal to memorize random numbers, or imagery to remember concrete nouns.

Psychological research contains many examples of strategy teaching, many of which have been with the mentally retarded. A difficulty that has been encountered is generalization (e.g., Butterfield, Wambold & Belmont, 1973): although a particular strategy can be taught in a particular task context, the retarded are unlikely to apply a similar strategy in a related task, and may even fail to use that strategy in the same task on the next day. A possible reason for these failures is that generalization itself must be taught if the retarded are to generalize. More important, however, is that the tasks which have been addressed, usually rote memory tasks, are quite trivial as far as the students are concerned (in the words of Brown and DeLoache, 1978, they lack "ecological validity"). It is possible that strategies and tasks which form integral parts of a retarded person's life (e.g., relevant to their home or workplace) and which result in clear and meaningful rewards, would be more likely to be retained and generalized.

Strategy teaching has been more successful with learning problem children (Worden, 1983). Studies by Krywaniuk and D. Kaufman (see Das et al., 1979, Chapter 9) have shown that successive processing can be taught, largely in a strategic sense, resulting in achievement gains. In studies such as these, it is always difficult to know whether a particular *process* is being improved (processing system) or whether the strategy for *using* that process is being improved (planning system). It is likely that both are occurring, perhaps differentially across subjects. Similarly, it can be seen that some strategy training relates more to use of particular knowledge schemes, while other training concerns the use of appropriate processes or operations.

Current research has detailed the sorts of strategies that are used in memory tasks (e.g., Flavell, 1970), and that the learning disabled do not use them very well in such tasks (e.g., Torgeson, 1977; Worden, 1983). What is needed now, in addition to attempts to train those memory strategies, is an effort to discover the strategies that are normally used in important, classroom-relevant, ecologically valid tasks such as reading and mathematics. These are the strategies that would be most usefully taught to the learning disabled.

Selective Attention Level

Selective attention is the result of the interaction of all three cognitive systems, especially the attention and planning systems. There are examples of selective attention which are largely controlled by the attention system; in these examples, selective attention is said to operate "automatically" or "effortlessly". This is a very important characteristic, because it allows limited processing and planning resources to be devoted to more pressing tasks. However, there are also examples of selective attention which are more controlled by the planning system; in these examples, selective attention is nonautomatic and effortful. In this section we are discussing planning-controlled selective attention; don't forget that the other type also exists.

The planning system determines what is to be placed in the short-term limited capacity processor. This function can be elaborated to encompass the fundamental role of selective attention: information is sampled from the environment, meaningful codes to interpret that information are sampled from the long-term memory, operations to apply to that information are selected, etc. At the level of selective attention many quick decisions must be made to reduce the complexity of the task situation confronting the individual. These decisions involve resource allocation.

Difficulties in selective attention have been argued to be the basis of many learning problems,

including hyperactivity (e.g., Ross, 1976). Thus, learning problem children have been described as impulsive, lacking in self-control, inattentive, distractible, and so on. It is important to note that some or all of these could stem from attention or planning system problems. Since selective attention improves with developmental level, it could be that the original problem disappears with age; in this case, learning problem children would have been suffering a developmental lag. However, the years of school failure would produce a residue of academic problems: low academic skills, low academic self-concept, and poor attitudes towards school.

If planning system problems in selective attention are evident, the teaching of general attention-controlling strategies would be indicated. The area that has been most studied concerns the visual searching of a display to select a stimulus item that meets certain conditions, and the most studied task has been Kagan's Matching Familiar Figures (Messer, 1976). (This task is examined more closely in Chapters 11 and 14.) A remedial technique that is increasing in use is Meichenbaum's (1977) cognitive behaviour modification, in which strategies rather than responses are taught. Meichenbaum's approach is also important because it incorporates Luria's theory of the internalization of verbal self-control. Briefly, external verbal instructions from another person control action at an early stage of development; at later stages, overt verbal *self*-control, and then *covert* self-control direct behaviour (see also Chapters 11 and 14). By teaching verbal self-control, it may be possible to accelerate the developmental process of selective attention in particular task domains.

One weakness of this approach has been generalization: for example, visual scanning instruction may improve visual scanning performance, but not classroom performance. Again, it can only be said that some skills may not be of great relevance or of recognized relevance, and that generalization must be specifically catered for in instructional programs. (If you want to teach visual scanning, why not use letter and word materials?)

Metacognition Level

Metacognition is a term which began to be used widely in the 1980s. It can refer to cognition that is beyond the normal processing level of cognition, or to cognition that is more highly developed than normal (Garner, 1989; Lawson, 1980, 1984; Wong, 1986). It is cognition *about cognition,* the conscious awareness of ways of approaching tasks, of processing information, and of monitoring success. As such, it is the highest level of planning, and is related to many other planning and processing activities. Metacognition is usually assessed in an interview situation in which the subject is asked how he or she would handle a particular task and why. Alternatively, the subject can be asked to indicate task parameters which might be relevant to possible solutions. Although there has been concern that metacognition, as it is currently measured, may be a function of verbosity rather than task performance (e.g., Cavanaugh & Perlmutter, 1982), other studies (Kirby & Ashman, 1982) indicate that metacognition is a central intellectual ability.

Can metacognition be taught, to improve academic performance? At the moment, this question cannot be answered with any confidence. A number of studies have attempted to answer this question, particularly with reference to the area of reading (e.g., Paris, Lipson & Wixson, 1983). While metacognition was not taught in the Kirby and Ashman study, its results did indicate that selective attention might act as a prerequisite for the effectiveness of metacognition. In other words, a suitable level of selective attention may have to be attained before instruction in metacognition can have any benefit. This is most likely to be true of learning problem children; in fact, it may be that after that level of selective attention was attained, the learning problem could be said to exist no longer. In this case, metacognition training may serve more of an enrichment than a remedial function.

The planning system will be dealt with more completely in Chapter 14.

Relation to Intelligence and Achievement

We've come this far without indicating exactly how attention, processing and planning are related to intelligence and achievement. We've done this because the answer depends upon what you mean by intelligence or achievement. This is not the place to discuss theories of intelligence, but it can be said that there are many theories and even more separate aspects of intelligence that can be measured. The same is true for achievement tasks, as we will see in Chapters 7, 8 and 9.

The important point to keep in mind here is that PASS theory describes how the brain or cognitive system works. The brain is responsible for intelligent (or nonintelligent) actions, for achievement (or failure) in school. Because the three information processing systems are *interdependent,* we cannot say that intelligence is here, and that achievement is there. Instead, we have to admit that the situation is complicated; the entire cognitive system is involved in the production of intelligent actions and school achievement. Nevertheless, we can use our knowledge of the entire system to study children who are having learning problems. As we will show in the next five chapters, it is possible to analyze children's learning problems in terms of the theory just presented. Armed with a better understanding of the mechanics of children's problems, we are in a much better position to design remedial procedures, which will be discussed in Chapters 11, 12, 13 and 14.

Before proceeding to describe the achievement areas and learning problems, we will conclude this chapter by outlining how the information processing skills we have described are related to achievement and how learning problems can arise (see Figure 5-5). The achievement areas of reading, spelling, arithmetic and mathematics require a large number of cognitive skills, and difficulties in using these skills can produce learning problems in one or more areas. More broadly, normal classroom behaviour requires attention skills and controlled levels of arousal. As is indicated at the top of Figure

FIGURE 5-5

How learning problems are caused. Problems at any level cause problems at levels below. The higher the original source of the problem, the broader the problem. However, higher areas can be affected by secondary learning problems.

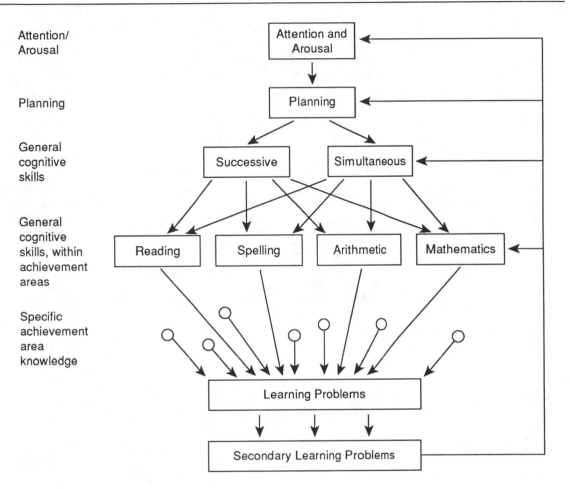

5-5, attention or arousal problems can disrupt classroom behaviour generally, usually leading to broad academic problems (see Chapter 6). Inappropriate attention or arousal would act to disrupt planning (the second level in Figure 5-5), which would in turn disrupt simultaneous and successive processing (level three), and achievement areas. Even if attention or arousal are within tolerable limits, planning problems could disrupt all lower levels, or only specific subsets of them. Similarly, one or both of the general cognitive skills (simultaneous or successive processing) may be weak, producing a particular type of learning problem across achievement areas. For example, poor successive processing could affect word analysis in reading, resulting in overemphasis upon visual cues in spelling and an inability to follow a plan in problem solving. (These examples are described more fully in Chapters 7, 8 and 9.)

It is also possible for one or more of the general cognitive skills to be weak, but only within one or more of the achievement areas. For example, the student may have difficulties using successive processing in spelling when segmenting a word, but may function adequately in the successive processing aspects of reading. In this case, it is clear that the weakness is not in "successive processing", but rather "successive processing in spelling", a subset of successive processing (and of spelling) skills.

We will also see that many learning problems can stem from causes which have little to do with the general information processing skills. Instead, they are due to lack of knowledge relevant to the particular content area. The knowledge lacking may be about the world in general (such as when a child has problems reading a story dealing with something he or she knows nothing about), or about specific skills (as when a child has problems in arithmetic because he or she never learned how to do long division).

Furthermore, learning problems themselves can give rise to secondary affective problems, which can feed back upon the higher levels of Figure 5-5. In this way, a reasonably specific problem on a low level can produce quite a broad problem. Secondary learning problems are discussed further in Chapter 10.

Summary

In this chapter we have described a more detailed theory of how the brain works, a theory that has been called Planning, Attention, Simultaneous and Successive processing theory. We have described three brain systems that are responsible for producing and controlling behaviour: the attention, processing, and planning systems. The most important aspect of the processing system for our present purposes is that it engages in two types of processing, successive and simultaneous. These two types of processing operate in working memory to hold

information in order and to integrate that information.

A number of important issues have appeared in this chapter, issues that reappear throughout the book. One concerns the role of brain damage in explanations of learning problems: while brain damage may be at the root of learning problems in some children, this is not necessarily the case for all or even most learning problem children. A second issue concerns the causes of learning problems: some may be due to ability problems, whereas others may be caused by the child's use of inappropriate strategies. Finally, we looked at how this theory is related to intelligence and achievement. No one cognitive system or type of process can be identified with either intelligence or achievement: instead, intelligence and achievement are seen as the results of the harmonious functioning of all of the cognitive systems and processes.

RECOMMENDED READING

The best sources on simultaneous and successive processing are:

Das, J.P., Kirby, J. & Jarman, R.F.
   1979. *Simultaneous and successive cognitive processing.* New York: Academic Press.

Das, J.P., Naglieri, J.A., & Kirby, J.R.
   In press. *The assessment of cognitive processes.* New York: Allyn & Bacon.

Kirby, J.R. & Das, J.P.
   1990. A cognitive approach to intelligence: Attention, coding, and planning. *Canadian Psychology, 31,* 320-333.

With regard to the planning system, you could consult many of the chapters in:

Kirby, J.R. (ed.)
   1984. *Cognitive strategies and educational performance.* Orlando, Florida: Academic Press.

While Luria's work is not easy to read, the following is the most approachable of his books:

Luria, A.R.
   1973. *The working brain.* Harmondsworth: Penguin.

CHAPTER 6

Classroom Symptoms of Attention Problems

IT IS A MONDAY MORNING in November, and John Doe, a University Education major, is on his way to Roseland Elementary School. He is going to his first teaching practice session. He is fairly confident about the weeks ahead. He has some basic ideas about primary teaching methods, classroom management and a good idea of what qualities are considered essential for developing into an excellent teacher. After the first few days his confidence and enthusiasm appear to have disappeared. What has happened to shatter one prospective teacher's expectations?

John has run into two related problems: classroom management and individual differences in attention skills. In order for learning to take place, the students have to be paying attention: while they seem to do so some of the time, John doesn't think they do it often enough for much learning to take place. Fortunately, with time, John's classroom management skills will improve (or he may consider a more relaxed career as a police officer or paratrooper). However, the second problem will remain: no matter how good his management skills, he will still see some children willing to sit and work all day long, while others get fidgety after five minutes. In other words, some children are able and willing to pay attention long enough for learning to have a chance, and others aren't. What's worse, the children who stop paying attention to John easily transfer their skills, it seems, to annoying the other children, and to annoying John. In no time at all, children are arguing or even fighting with each other. As poor John says to himself as he trudges home in the afternoon, "What chance does learning have?" Is it any wonder that many children have learning problems?

Fortunately, and perhaps amazingly, learning does occur. You may be forgiven for thinking that children learn in spite of school rather than because of it, but the vast majority of children do benefit from schooling. Our point is that *more* children should so benefit, and that many children currently achieving *adequately* could be doing *better*.

The key to understanding John's problems is the concept of *attention*. For learning to take place, children need to be paying attention, and this seems to be particularly difficult from some children much of the time (and for all children some of the time). When attention is lacking, either the class as a whole or the individual child stops learning and starts doing something else, often something disruptive. Lack of attention thus leads to inappropriate classroom behaviour which is both a symptom and cause of poor learning. Classroom behaviour may be the first sign of learning problems to be noticed.

In this chapter, we briefly discuss the importance of attention and its relationship to the behaviours mentioned. We also discuss the importance of identifying classroom behaviour problems as primary, secondary or tertiary in nature. In doing this we rely heavily upon the work of Virginia Douglas (1980). We conclude the chapter with a brief discussion of how these behaviours fit into our theoretical framework (Chapter 5); diagnosis and remediation of attentional problems will be considered in detail in Chapter 11.

What Is Attention?

Attention has been considered a central construct in psychology since the time of William James (1890), and in recent years has been an important area of investigation in children with learning problems. Research on attention has usually been divided into two areas of study, psychological and psychophysiological, a consequence of which has been the emergence of many models or descriptions of attention. For example, Posner and Boies (1971), as a result of reviewing the physiological research on attention, suggest that attention consists of three major components:

1. **Alertness,** which refers to the ability to maintain attention for a required period of time;
2. **Selectivity,** the ability to focus on and select specific aspects of a stimulus while excluding other features of the stimulus; and
3. **Processing capacity,** the ability to focus simultaneously on more than one stimulus (related to the idea of working memory presented in Chapter 4).

Attention is complex because it is really two different types of process. The first type is automatic, or effortless attention, and is governed by the attention/arousal system; it is effortless only because it is not normally controlled consciously. The second type is conscious or effortful attention, which is more governed by the planning system; this is the system which allows us to control what we attend to, and even override the attention/arousal system.

We will argue that appropriate attention requires the involvement of the complete information processing system described in Chapters 4 and 5. Just to give you an idea of how it works, consider what is necessary for selective attention to occur: the stimuli have to be quickly encoded and checked for relevance; relevance is determined by long-term memory information, working memory information (what has happened recently), and the current plan; the information selected for attention must be further processed, again in terms of what we know and what we are trying to do; finally, throughout all this, arousal must be kept at an appropriate level. Too low and we lose interest, too high and we lose track of what we're doing.

Attention in Learning Problem Children

Much of the work investigating the development of attention and its concomitant problems in children has focused on selective and sustained aspects of attention.

Selective Attention

At any time in the classroom the child is bombarded with numerous stimuli. It is impossible to attend to all of these stimuli because of the limited nature of the information processing system, particularly of working memory. In order to focus on the relevant aspects of the stimuli, the irrelevant ones must be screened out. This is usually referred to as selective attention.

Sustained Attention

Sustained attention refers to one's ability to maintain attention over an extended period of time. This is crucial for many school-related activities – children must concentrate for several minutes or more while reading or doing mathematics if learning is to occur. This type of attention has also been referred to as vigilance or alertness.

Children who have poor attention skills may be described as inattentive and easily distracted. They appear to respond to most stimuli, relevant or irrelevant, in the environment. They cannot stay on-task for any appreciable length of time, which usually results in the failure to complete tasks undertaken. A further problem that might be seen to occur is an increase in the children's activity level. (Increased activity level is called *hyperkinesis* or *hyperactivity*.) They become fidgety, restless and take to wandering around the classroom for no apparent reason. This wandering may have a disruptive influence on the classroom, and as a result peers might reject such students. Yet another feature is that the children appear disorganized, displaying impulsive behaviour that results in poorly developed problem solving skills. And the list goes on. The point to be stressed here is that children with poorly developed attention skills will display several kinds of behaviour that not only disrupt their learning but also have adverse effects on their acceptance in the class by both peers and teacher.

Many teachers and researchers have observed that children with learning problems also have attention problems, as well as activity level problems (hyperactivity, hyperkinesis). (See Ross, 1976, for a review.) Would it be fair, then, to conclude that the attention problems have *caused* the learning problems? If so, remediation should concentrate upon the attention problem first. Or is it the activity level problem that has caused the attention problems? It may even be the case that the learning problem, say in reading, has caused the attention and activity level problems. As we will see in the remainder of this chapter, psychologists distinguish among three kinds of attention problems: primary, secondary, and tertiary, and the recommended intervention or remediation approach may depend upon which type the child has.

Three Types of Problems

The complexity of the connections among learning problems, attention problems and activity levels has been shown in many studies. Silver (1979)

reporting on his own research and that of others, points out that if we consider learning disabled children as a whole, approximately 40% of them will display hyperactive behaviour. Furthermore, when these children are seen in a clinical setting, they invariably show evidence of social-emotional problems. Lahey, Stempriak, Robinson and Tyroler (1978), on the other hand, found that four separate factors could be distinguished in characteristics of behaviour problem children: conduct problems, learning "disabilities", personality problems, and hyperactivity. In other words, children could be hyperactive without displaying a learning problem, and vice versa. They concluded that many children labelled as hyperactive are, in fact, experiencing primarily behaviour problems. Lambert and Sandoval (1980) found that 42% of their 280 hyperactive subjects could qualify as being labelled "learning disabled".

The solution to this confusing situation is to try to understand what has caused different children's problems, to divide them accordingly and treat them differently. Three types of children are described in Table 6-1, according to the causal nature of their problems. The first type, whose primary problem is emotional, does not of course fit the definition of learning problem children used in this book. The second type, whose other problems all stem from an academic problem, does fit. The third type, whose primary problem is an attention deficit, is a special case, forming a distinct subgroup of learning problem children; as such, they may require a distinct approach to remediation. Let us consider each of the three types in turn.

Type I: Emotional Problem

In the classroom, such children are constantly out of their seats, disturbing others, being argumentative and just plain nuisances. These children experience difficulty with "on task" behaviours, are easily distracted, and appear to be unduly impulsive. Their academic performance is uneven, and they may be unable to hold a conversation on a topic for any considerable length of time. Based on these behaviours, some teachers would say that such a

TABLE 6-1
Primary, secondary and tertiary problems in the classroom

Problem	Type of Child		
	Type I	Type II	Type III
Primary	Emotional problem	Specific learning problem	Attention deficit – Hyperactivity
Secondary	Hyperactivity	Emotional problem	Specific learning problem
Tertiary	Specific learning problem	Hyperactivity	Emotional problem

child is emotionally disturbed, while others may suggest that such a child is hyperactive. The point to be stressed here is that the same behaviours may be considered primary, secondary or even tertiary in nature. If we investigate such a child further and find that the family situation is not good, we may surmise an emotional problem as being primary in this case. It may be that the father is an alcoholic and there is constant discord between mother and father. The child is mistreated at home and, as a reaction to the home situation, comes to school emotionally distraught, exhibiting the behaviours described above. Thus, the secondary problem may be hyperactivity, which in turn could lead to (tertiary) academic problems. As we have said in Chapter 1, these children are not the subject of this book.

Type II: Learning Problem

Here we see the specific learning problem as primary – for example, a severe reading deficit. As time passes, such children become frustrated by their inability to read at the level required and become emotionally upset at the situation this produces. They may become aggressive in the classroom and refuse to cooperate. As a result they may develop avoidance behaviours and display hyperactive behaviour. In these children, then, we see academic learning problems as being primary, emotional upset as secondary, and hyperactive behaviour as tertiary.

Type III: Attention Deficit Problem

In this case, hyperactivity is the consequence of an attention deficit, which is the primary problem. Children with this problem have a tendency to be easily distracted, are impulsive and constantly move around the classroom for no apparent reason. This behaviour directly affects their academic performance, resulting in problems with learning (secondary), only to culminate in the development of emotional problems (tertiary), as a result of school failure and possible peer rejection. We describe attention deficit problems more in Chapter 11.

It is important to know what type of children you are treating, because you should probably do different things with the different types. For the learning problem child (Type II), the most sensible approach is to teach the academic skills which are lacking. That approach may have disastrous effects upon the Type I child, and no effect upon the Type III child. On the other hand, a behaviour-oriented program that may be appropriate for the attention deficit child could be ineffective or worse for the child whose problem is really in reading.

Children with emotional problems are really quite different from those whom we describe as having learning problems; accordingly, as we have said several times already, we do not consider them further in this book. Note, however, that many Type II and Type III children will show emotional problems: because these problems are not primary, they do fall within the scope of this book.

A crucial problem in learning problem research is to distinguish between Type II and Type III children – that is, between learning problems (of the general variety) and attention deficits (a more narrow category of learning problem). Of the researchers who have undertaken this task, one of the foremost has been Virginia Douglas of McGill University. Douglas has, over the last few decades, devoted much of her time to identifying the exact nature of attention deficit (which she has called hyperactivity) and to eradicating much of the confusion surrounding attention deficit and learning problems. To this end, Douglas and her colleagues have sought (1) to develop clearer definitions of the two groups and (2) to elaborate on the cognitive deficits found in attention deficit and learning problem children. Douglas (1980) maintains that the underlying problem in attention deficit children is a predisposition towards poor control of impulsivity, an inability to sustain attention and effort, and poorly modulated arousal levels. In contrast, learning problem children face more cognitive and academic problems.

In Figure 6-1 you will see a schematic representation of the distinction between these two types of children. This diagram is based upon one used by Douglas (1980), but we have adapted it to suit our purposes and conform to our terminology. Consider first the attention deficit child. Douglas believes this child is born with a constitutional predisposition towards an impaired ability to sustain attention and effort, towards poor inhibitory control and towards poorly modulated arousal level, which results in the child's tendency to seek stimulation. Thus, we see a child who is poor at on-task behaviour, is impulsive in nature and displays excess gross motor activity. As a consequence of such original deficits, both the child's cognitive development and motivation will be impaired. This results in less effective learning and, thus, in the ineffective development of cognitive skills (planning, simultaneous and successive processing and achievement-area skills).

Especially affected by attention problems are what Douglas calls "search strategies", part of what we call planning. She argues that attention in young children is exploratory, which means that it is controlled by the most salient features of the stimulus. With repeated experiences of the environment, the exploratory nature of attention is replaced by the child's concentration on more critical aspects of the stimuli, making the environment more meaningful. Thus, we see a change in the child's search strategies from being exploratory to being specific and relevant, resulting in organized and purposeful behaviour. (Attention deficit children, as a result of impaired attention and impulsivity, have difficulty making the transition from exploratory search strategies to ones that are specific.)

In terms of motivation, Douglas suggests that children who succeed in mastering most problems required of them in the classroom will develop effective intrinsic motivation. Attention deficit children repeatedly experience difficulty with academic tasks, and that often results in their giving up. This kind of experience does not provide a good base for the development of intrinsic motivation. Repeated failure would result in the development of an avoidance pattern of behaviour when confronted with problem-solving tasks. In turn, the child's original problems would be enhanced, resulting in increased concentration problems, impulsiveness and arousal levels. The cycle would continue with a snowballing effect (Douglas 1980).

On the other hand, the learning problem child has a problem which is primarily cognitive in nature, *stemming from* the knowledge, processing strategy, metacognitive or planning area problems which in the hyperactive child are the *consequence* of that child's problem. Repeated failure in the classroom can possibly result in the child's developing avoidance patterns of behaviour. Thus, the child becomes easily distracted, is restless, impulsive, and has difficulty concentrating on academic tasks. With the appearance of such behaviours, other cognitive abilities of the child might, in turn, be disrupted; thus the problem may well spread to areas that were not originally affected (refer back to Figure 5-5 to see how this could happen). The final outcome is that the child loses interest, motivation is lowered, further failure results and, as with the attention deficit child, the cycle continues.

A schematic representation of the distinction between a learning problem and attention deficit child (after Douglas, 1980)

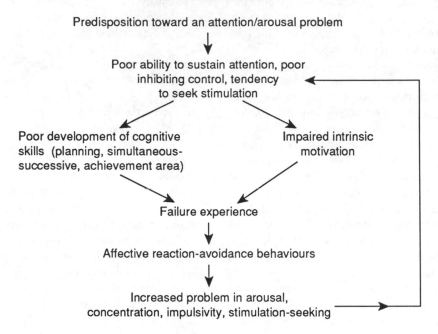

Attention Deficit Child

Predisposition toward an attention/arousal problem

Poor ability to sustain attention, poor inhibiting control, tendency to seek stimulation

Poor development of cognitive skills (planning, simultaneous-successive, achievement area)

Impaired intrinsic motivation

Failure experience

Affective reaction-avoidance behaviours

Increased problem in arousal, concentration, impulsivity, stimulation-seeking

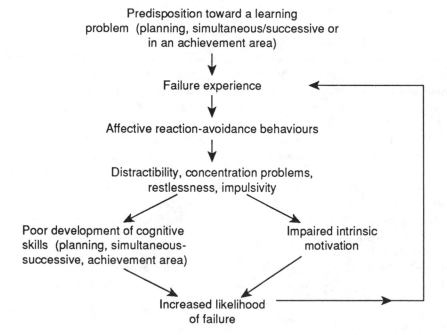

Learning Problem Child

Predisposition toward a learning problem (planning, simultaneous/successive or in an achievement area)

Failure experience

Affective reaction-avoidance behaviours

Distractibility, concentration problems, restlessness, impulsivity

Poor development of cognitive skills (planning, simultaneous-successive, achievement area)

Impaired intrinsic motivation

Increased likelihood of failure

Attention Problems and PASS

As you saw in the previous chapter, PASS theory considers the brain to consist of three interrelated systems: attention, processing and planning. While all systems have an influence on behaviour, the arousal and planning systems appear to have the main influence on the behaviours discussed above.

It is the arousal system that is the source of the problems of attention deficit (Type III) children. It is this system that creates difficulty in sustaining attention, inhibiting impulsivity and so on. A deficient attention system can result in a child being over- or under-active. An over-active state has an effect on the planning system in such a way that the child is unable to deal effectively with information that comes from the processing system. This over-stimulation results in the child's being unable to make decisions; in behaviour that is erratic, unfocused and inappropriate, as seen in the attention deficit child; and in the distractibility of the child. An under-active state may make the child unresponsive, leading to withdrawn behaviour. (The complex connection between activity level, arousal and attention will be further dealt with in Chapter 11.)

It is important to remember, however, that many of these same behaviours can arise in Type II children, from problems in the planning system, or perhaps even in the processing system (refer back to Figures 5-5 and 6-1). Poor planning may result in poor regulatory control of behaviour – that is impulsiveness and distractibility. Only when the learning problem arises from an attention system problem should we say that the child is Type III, that is, that he or she has an attention deficit. As you will see in Chapter 11, many suggestions have been made for the treatment of such children, including the use of drugs which supposedly affect the attention/arousal system.

A Type II child, whose problems stem from the cognitive domain (processing and planning systems), is unlikely to be helped by attention system treatments, because that system is merely showing symptoms of the real problems. Chapters 12, 13 and 14 will consider the nature of these problems and suggestions for designing remediation.

As we said earlier in this chapter, inappropriate classroom behaviour may be the first sign of a learning problem. The next three chapters provide greater detail on the consequences for academic skills; it is important to remember that these academic problems may or may not be accompanied by behaviour problems as considered in this chapter.

Summary

This chapter focused on the classroom behavioural symptoms of learning problems, with particular emphasis on the relationship between attentional problems and the consequences of those problems. We stressed the need for a better understanding of the underlying factors contributing to the attention problems, since different types of exceptional children may appear to display the same behavioural patterns. Thus, we emphasized the importance of identifying attention problems as primary, secondary, and tertiary. We identified three types of children: those with emotional problems (Type I), those with learning problems (Type II), and those with attention deficit problems (Type III), and demonstrated how each could be considered a primary, secondary or tertiary problem. Since our book does not deal with primary emotional problems, we concentrated on the importance of distinguishing between attention deficit and learning problem children. To this end, we adopted the work of Virginia Douglas who maintains that attention deficit children (Type III) essentially have a predisposition toward impulsivity, hyperactivity, and poorly modulated arousal levels in contrast to the more cognitive and academic problems of learning problem children (Type II). While all systems of PASS theory (attention, processing and planning) have an influence on behaviour, the attention and planning systems appear to have the main influence on the behaviours discussed.

RECOMMENDED READING

Hale, G.A. & Lewis, M. (eds.)
1979. *Attention and cognitive development.*
New York: Plenum Press.

   This book is comprehensive in its coverage of the relationship between attention and learning, and also in its coverage of attentional problems in children, particularly hyperactive children. An excellent book.

Kaufman, J.M. (ed.)
1981. Attentional disorders: Implications for the classroom. *Exceptional Education Quarterly, 2,* 1-93.

   This issue of the journal is entirely devoted to a discussion of attention deficits in children with learning problems.

Krupski, A.
1986. Attention problems in youngsters with learning handicaps. In J.K. Torgesen & B.Y.L. Wong (eds.). *Psychological and educational perspectives on learning disabilities.* Orlando, Florida: Academic Press.

   This chapter provides a good analysis of the relationship of selective and sustained attention to learning problems.

CHAPTER 7

Reading

THE HUMAN SPECIES spent many million years evolving the ability to walk comfortably on two feet. It has spent perhaps one million years evolving to use and understand oral language. Both of those developments have taken eons, and it can be truly said that our physical and neurological structures have changed in order to be able to do them. In contrast, consider how long we have been reading and writing – that is, using written language. Even 1000 years ago it was rare for a member of a given culture to be able to read, and there were many cultures in which written language was unknown. In fact, until roughly 100 years ago, with the advent of compulsory schooling, reading was not a widely expected skill in our Western societies. Adult literacy, and illiteracy, remain serious issues for much of today's world, even for our supposedly well-educated societies.

The recency of reading and writing may begin to account for some of the extraordinary difficulties that some of our children have with these skills, and the considerable effort that most children (and teachers) have to devote to acquiring them. This effort is in great contrast to the seemingly effortless acquisition of oral language between birth and age 5. Biggs and Telfer (1981) have argued that we as a species are *biologically prepared* to learn oral language – that is, we have evolved genetically to facilitate oral language learning – while we are bio-

logically *unprepared* to learn written language. Instead of falling back upon existing neurological structures in our written language learning, we have to learn them painstakingly from scratch. The computer analogy would be that we have the *hardware* available to support oral language learning, but must learn written language only through the *software* or programs that we can develop ourselves. Biggs and Telfer's argument is a fascinating one, though proof of it would be hard to discover; in any case, there isn't much we can do about it! What their hypothesis does do, however, is help us understand why learning to read can be so difficult.

In this chapter our main purposes are to show how reading normally works, and to show how it can fail to work in learning problem children. To set the scene for these topics, we will begin by briefly reviewing the history of reading, and of how it has been taught and conceptualized.

Approaches to Reading

Forms of Written Language

The first evidence of written language dates from approximately 4000 B.C. in Sumeria. The early written languages that have been identified can be described as *logographic* languages, in which objects were represented by pictures that originally resembled them. Over time, it seems that the pictures gradually changed, to a point at which they resembled the original object in only a very abstract way.

The advantage to logographic languages is that they are easy to begin to learn – there is no difficulty in getting a child to appreciate that a picture of a cat can stand for a real cat. The disadvantages are that vast numbers of separate pictures are required, and that some abstract concepts are very difficult to represent pictorially. For instance, how would you picture "honesty"? Some sort of convention would have to be adopted, accepting that a picture such as an open hand meant honesty; nevertheless, such a picture is hardly as representative a picture of "honesty" as would be a cat's picture for "cat".

Chinese is the best modern example of a logographic language, and serves as testimony to both the feasibility of such a language (after all, one billion Chinese people seem to manage with it quite nicely, thank you!), and to some of its difficulties. Modern Chinese is said to consist of some 50 000 characters, of which perhaps 4000 are known automatically by a given reader (see Rozin & Gleitman, 1977). This is not the place to discuss logographic languages more fully, though some further readings are suggested at the end of this chapter. Let us leave you with a problem: How would you construct a Chinese typewriter?

The second type of written language is called a *syllabary.* In these languages (Korean and parts of Japanese are examples), every different syllable is represented by a different character. Even though syllabaries usually require several characters per object, depending upon the number of syllables in a word, their effect is to decrease dramatically the number of characters required to represent speech. This is achieved only through losing the correspondence between the written symbol and the object that is being represented. Instead of representing the visual object, syllabaries take the first step toward representing the sound of the oral language.

The final (at least the latest, so far) major development in written language was taken by the Phoe-

nicians around the year 1000 B.C. They developed an *alphabetic language,* that was based upon the *phonemes* rather than the syllables of oral language. For example, "kangaroo" has three syllables, but seven phonemes (the "oo" is only one). Again the overall effect is that the total number of characters (letters) required to write the language decreases, the final number depending upon the number of different sounds used in a particular oral language. It is worth noting that many languages, notably English, cheat by using the same letter to represent different sounds and by using combinations of letters to increase artificially the number of sounds that can be represented.

Alphabets and Phonetic Regularity

In a "perfect" alphabet, there would be exactly the same number of letters as sounds in the oral language. In English, such an alphabet would require many more letters than we currently have. An alternative would be to have strict rules about representing some sounds by certain letter combinations; for instance, the rule could be that the "oo" sound in "pool" would be represented as "oo", whereas "book" would require a different spelling.

The degree to which an alphabetic language has a strict correspondence between letters and sounds is called *phonetic regularity.* Some languages, such as Spanish, are very close to being phonetically regular, while others, such as English, are more irregular.

One of the reasons English is irregular is that it has evolved in a haphazard way. As we will see in Chapter 8, it is only within the last few hundred years that words were thought to have a "correct" spelling; previously many authors spelled words differently, sometimes to represent different pronunciation in different areas of the country (England, that is).

Another more sensible reason for English's phonetic irregularity is that it attempts to maintain some sort of *morphological regularity.* A morpheme is a word part that has some meaning – for instance, the "sign" in "signature". By keeping the "sign" unit in words like "signature", "significance" and "signify", the written language shows that the words are meaningfully related to the word "sign", even though the morpheme "sign" is pronounced differently. It might be easier for a child to learn to pronounce "sine" rather than "sign", but then it would be more difficult to relate the meanings of "sine" and "signify".

If you are interested in the history of written language, the suggested readings at the end of this chapter offer a starting point. For the purposes of this chapter and book, we will confine ourselves to English, accepting it the way it is. As we will see below, English's phonetic irregularity may be a contributor to some of the difficulties in learning to read.

How to Teach Reading

In the hundred years or so that reading has been systematically taught to large groups of children, there have been several substantial changes in approach and emphasis (see Crowder, 1982, Chapter 10, for a very readable summary). The most traditional method, termed the ABC method, can even be traced back to the ancient Greeks. The essence of this method is that children must learn the letter *names,* and use them when learning new words. For instance, the child is supposed to learn "See-Aye-Tee, cat". This method clearly involves phonic skills, but seems peculiar in that it emphasizes the letter *names* rather than their sounds.

Objections were raised to the ABC method, arguing that it was low-level, boring, and ineffective. The opposition favoured the "whole-word" method, in which new words were associated with their meanings, without reference to individual letters or sounds (those analytic skills were to be acquired later).

Not surprisingly, the whole word method was opposed in turn, by those supporting the phonics approach. This approach was an updated version of the ABC method, in that it stressed analytic skills, but it emphasized letter sounds rather than names.

The simplest description of the history of teaching reading is that it has been a tension between two competing orientations, the analytic phonics approach and the meaningful whole-word approach. As time has gone by, the debate has become more interesting because the successive versions of each approach have been improved, just as the phonics method itself was an improvement on the ABC method. As you will see in the remainder of this chapter, each approach has its virtues, but not in isolation. Either approach alone can produce reading problems. (For further information about the history of teaching reading, see the recommended readings at the end of this chapter.)

How Skilled Reading Works, and Fails to Work

In this section we describe how skilled reading works, in competent readers. We emphasize the hierarchical nature of reading, and detail eight levels within the reading hierarchy. These different levels can be used to describe *potential* sources of reading problems.

We begin by listing the eight levels and giving a brief example of each. With that as a framework, we will then delve into each of the levels, describing how it works and can fail to work.

Overview of the Eight Levels

Reading can be thought of, analyzed, or studied at various levels. These levels form a smooth progression from the visual detection of lines all the way up to the interpretation of complex themes and messages. We have divided this progression into eight levels, following Kirby (1988), levels which make intuitive sense and correspond to the ways in which researchers and teachers have approached reading. These are not the only levels possible: for instance, someone else could combine several of ours, or draw the line dividing two at a different place. It is also possible to discuss other levels: for example, we start with the visual perception of lines, but a neurophysiologist might be more interested in how particular points are detected within the eye. We think the eight levels we've picked out are the most useful for describing reading but, as always, you should be aware that other approaches are possible.

The eight levels are:

1. **Features.** Features are the lines or curves of which letters are composed, for example, ⊂, ⊃, |, and so on. Each letter is composed of a different set of features, which the brain must learn to recognize.

2. **Letters.** Letters should be familiar to all of you, as they are the basis of our alphabet. Early in the reading process, we learn to recognize letters, using automated feature detection. (If we shift to a different alphabet, such as the Cyrillic alphabet, we have to go back to learning feature recognition.)

3. **Sounds.** This is the level at which sounds become attached to letters or letter combinations. Early in reading, it seems helpful to "sound words out", as this process allows our oral language skills to recognize visually unknown words. Later on we seem to bypass the sound stage, only returning to it for difficult materials. The sound or syllabic level remains important for spelling (see Chapter 8).

4. **Words.** Again you should know these. What you may not know is that words are stored in long-term memory, and that recognizing a word involves searching that memory. Skilled readers are seldom aware of working at levels below the word level (i.e., levels 1, 2 or 3).

5. **Chunks.** A chunk is a group of words making a meaningful phrase, for example "the tall children", "we went fishing", "it goes", or "the little brown puppies". A sentence could consist of only one chunk, but usually consists of several in material intended for high school audiences or above.

6. **Ideas.** An idea is a basic statement, usually having at least a subject and a verb. Unlike the previous levels, ideas are no longer exact replicas of what is on the page; instead they are abstractions of meaning, though admittedly low-level abstractions. The set of ideas in a text is the set of all things that are said in the text. Fancier terms for ideas are "propositions" or even "micropropositions".

7. **Main ideas.** The main ideas of a text provide a summary of what it says. Main ideas are constructed from the elements at the idea level; some ideas may not be used, some may be combined with each other or with what we already know, or a main idea may even be stated in the text as an idea. The main ideas of a novel would be a summary of the plot. A fancier term for "main ideas" is "macropropositions". (The distinction between micropropositions and macropropositions comes from the work of Kintsch and van Dijk, 1978.)

8. **Themes.** Just as main ideas represent an abstraction from ideas, themes are an abstraction from main ideas (Kirby & Cantwell, 1985). Themes usually provide an underlying message which is not stated explicitly in the text; they usually have to be constructed by the reader. Some texts have very clear themes or morals (such as Aesop's fables), while others are more obscure (try reading an abstract modern play; if you were a below-average reader in high school, most Shakespearian plays would fit the bill).

Coordination across Levels

Information processing can be occurring at all of these levels, though the reader is usually only consciously thinking or working at one or two of them. In order to work at a particular level smoothly, it is necessary for the lower levels to function automatically. For this reason, if the reader is having difficulty identifying words (level 4), chunking (level 5) or simple comprehension (level 6) become very difficult. In order for any level to work well, lower levels must function automatically. In other words, effort expended at any level prevents effective functioning at higher levels.

The factor which acts to limit the reading system is working memory. As we saw in Chapters 4 and 5, working memory is severely limited in the number of "things" which it can hold, though there is no limit to the amount that each "thing" or chunk can hold. If working memory is devoted to holding four or five features, as it might be in learning a new alphabet, it may be possible to identify some syllables, but not easily. Certainly word identification and comprehension processes beyond will be very difficult.

When reading is working smoothly, features are being automatically chunked as letters, and letters as syllables or words. Words are identified, usually automatically, and formed into syntactic chunks: unless the syntax is unusually complex, this too happens automatically. At the working memory level, several syntactic chunks are held until their meaning (a microproposition) is computed. At this point, the separate syntactic chunks are dropped, leaving only the one microproposition taking up one place. Other syntactic chunks are similarly processed into micropropositions, until several micropropositions can be processed into a macroproposition. Individual macropropositions can depend upon large numbers of micropropositions, so it is unlikely that the working memory could hold all the micros before producing the macro. Instead, it is probable that a macro is produced after several micros, and then updated as new micros are produced. Macropropositions are transferred to long-term memory when "complete", though they can be recalled for updating. If several macros are recalled at the same time, it becomes possible for the reader to use them to compute a more abstract thematic proposition.

The preceding paragraph describes reading working in a *bottom-up* fashion, proceeding from the printed page to thematic comprehension. Reading also works in a *top-down* fashion, using an existing element at one level to predict or facilitate the identification of elements at a lower level. Thus, a macroproposition could "predict" or "expect" the existence of a certain microproposition, either setting the reader to search for it, or leading the reader to presume that it had been seen. For example, if the macro "They robbed the bank" has been produced, it expects the micro "A weapon was used". The reader may either regress to check that a weapon was used, or simply proceed on the assumption that one was.

Top-down processing can occur between any pair of levels: for example, if the word "bank" is expected (on the basis of current macros, micros and chunks), the "m" in a misspelling, "bamk", may not be attended to. The important point to remember is that bottom-up and top-down processing occur interactively, with control passing from one level to another and back again. (See Rumelhart, 1981, for a more extended description of the interactive model of reading.)

It is not necessary for our purposes to expand on the nature of skilled reading. Please consult the recommended readings at the end of this chapter for more information about the nature of reading. We now turn to the ways in which the reading system can fail, producing reading problems.

How Reading Fails

By now it should be clear that the skill of reading is a very complex one, and that there is more than one thing that can go wrong. Therefore, right from the beginning we should expect that there is more than one kind of learning problem in the area of reading. As we will see below, *potential* problems exist at each of the levels of reading. However, we will also see that recent research has tended to emphasize two areas of reading problems, one being the letters-to-sounds-to-words area, and the other the words-to-chunks-to-propositions area.

Features and Letters

As you should remember from Chapter 2, an early and very dominant interpretation of learning problems (which were mainly reading problems) was that they were due to "visual perceptual" problems. Even though some of the early theories were quite vague about what a visual perception problem was, in modern cognitive terms it would have to be described as a problem at the feature and letter level, perhaps progressing up to the (visual) word level. More recent research in this area (see Chapter 2) has been quite negative about the validity of this visual perception explanation.

In the 1970s, however, several studies were performed which brought the visual perception interpretation back, but in a far more detailed and sophisticated form. The most important of these studies were by Stanley and Hall (1973). They were interested in the very early stages of information processing, when the stimulus material is held very briefly in the sensory register. For adults, information is held in the sensory register in a very accurate form (like a picture) for about a quarter of a second. If any of this information is to be retained, it must be selected for processing during this period, and transferred toward working memory. Any information not so selected is wiped out by the next stimulus input. This characteristic is crucial because in reading the eyes typically fixate upon the page for about a quarter of a second, before moving very quickly to their next fixation. (For more on eye movements, see the recommended readings at the end of this chapter.) Any features not begun to be processed into words are immediately lost, preventing word identification and comprehension, and interfering with the next fixation's input.

Stanley and Hall (1973) investigated the hypothesis that reading problem children may not perform this initial processing very efficiently. Their hypothesis was that such children may have sensory register images that persist longer than those for normal children, thus interfering with subsequent incoming stimuli. They presented their subjects with stimuli in two parts: first one part, then a brief pause, then the second part. Normal children were unable to tell that they had seen two separate pictures if they had been separated by less than 100 msec (that is, one-tenth of a second). Their reading problem subjects were between 8 and 12 years old, and were 2.5 years behind in reading. These children needed a gap of 140 msec before they could detect that they had seen two separate displays. Stanley and Hall concluded that reading problems may be caused by sensory register images that persist too long in these children, overlapping with subsequent inputs. If this were the case, then eye movements and sensory register processes would be "out of sync", rather than cooperating smoothly.

In a second study, Stanley and Hall (1973) claimed that reading problem children take longer to transfer information from the sensory register to short-term (working) memory. In this study they presented a letter for a standard amount of time, then left a brief gap, then presented a "mask". A

mask is a stimulus that should obliterate the previous display, if it occurs after a short enough gap. For normal children, the letter could be recognized if the mask was delayed for 50 msec; reading problem children needed a further delay of 15 msec before they were as successful.

Stanley and Hall's conclusions have not been without their critics. The basic criticism has been that their technique relied upon the children's report of when they saw two pictures or a letter, etc. If for some reason the reading problem children are more hesitant to judge, their performance could be as Stanley and Hall observed, but for very different reasons. Several years of failure in reading could produce such a hesitancy, without any need to implicate weaknesses in the feature level of visual processing in reading. In fact, when further studies were performed with different techniques, the predicted differences between good and poor readers did not emerge (e.g., Fisher & Frankfurter, 1977). For further information about this dispute, you should consult Vellutino's excellent review (1979, pp. 94-106); until further research clarifies this issue, we find no reason to disagree with Vellutino's conclusion that "there is no convincing evidence that reading disability is attributable to deficient form perception resulting from dysfunction in initial-stage processing" (Vellutino, 1979, p. 115). It is also worth noting that if poor readers were deficient at the featural level they should demonstrate difficulties in many more areas than reading alone, as the same featural analysis is required in all visual perception. The lack of clear evidence and the logical difficulties with the hypotheses are heartening for teachers, as it is by no means easy to see what we could do in a regular classroom to assist children with feature-processing problems.

Sounds

To attach sounds to letters is to engage in phonetic, or phonological coding. This coding requires reference to oral language, unlike the preceeding visual coding. There is now extensive research showing that children with reading problems tend to have problems with phonetic coding, and that children with poor phonetic coding skills (in oral language) tend to develop reading problems.

The difficulty that poor readers have with phonetic coding is shown in a longitudinal study by Mann, Liberman and Shankweiler (1981, cited by Liberman & Mann, 1981). They measured the phonetic coding ability of a group of children in kindergarten, and then examined the same children for reading ability in first grade. Phonetic coding was measured in two ways, by a syllable-segmentation test, and by a memory for words test. Before describing the experimental results, it is necessary to describe these tests to ensure that the connection with phonetic coding is clear. Both tests also represent measures that could be used by classroom teachers.

The syllable-segmentation test was presented to the children as a game in which the experimenter would say a word and the child had to tap on the table to indicate how many *syllables* were in the word. For example, "cat" should produce one tap, "kangaroo" three, and so on. This is a skill that 50% of children can pass successfully at age 5, 90% at age 6. (As we will see below, it is also possible to give a *phoneme*-segmentation test, which children find more difficult.)

In the memory for words test, children were read sequences of words which they then had to repeat. Two types of word sequences were used, rhyming and nonrhyming. If a child codes a word phonetically – that is, represents the *sounds* heard in memory – he or she finds rhyming strings of words much more difficult to remember than nonrhyming. This has been shown in many studies with children and with adults (e.g., Conrad, 1964). On the other hand, if children represent the words they've heard in their memories in a non-phonetic way (for example, only visually or semantically), then rhyming words should not be any more difficult than nonrhyming words. Therefore, if you want to see the extent to which children are using phonetic coding, check the difference between their memory for rhyming and nonrhyming words. Children who make far more errors on rhyming words are likely to be using phonetic coding extensively, while children whose number of errors is consistent across rhyming and nonrhyming sequences are not likely to be using phonetic coding (or at least aren't using it very effectively).

Now back to Mann *et al.*'s (1981) results. They measured reading ability in first grade, and divided their subjects into three groups – good, average, and poor readers. These three groups did not differ in IQ or in nonverbal memory; however, they did differ greatly in phonetic coding (see Table 7-1). As you can see in the table, children with large differences between rhyming and nonrhyming word memory who were also successful on the syllable-segmentation test were far more likely to become good readers in first grade.

TABLE 7-1
Performance of readers (as identified in first grade)
on phonetic coding tasks (in kindergarten)
(Adapted from Liberman and Mann, 1981)

| | % | Memory for Words | | |
Reading Ability Group	Passing Syllable Segmentation Test	Rhyming Errors	Nonrhyming Errors	Difference
Good	85	13.4	8.1	5.3
Average	56	15.4	12.8	2.6
Poor	24	15.0	13.2	1.8

These results support the hypothesis that some degree of sound analytical skill is necessary in order to become a good reader, and that poor readers are less able (or less willing) to use phonetic coding. However, we have to be careful of such results, because they are only correlational in nature; for example, it is possible that phonetic coding and good reading are both characteristics of some children, but that the former does not *cause* the latter. In fact, some research has suggested that being taught to read actually improves your phonetic coding ability (Morais, Carey, Alegria & Bertelson, 1979). Thus it may be more accurate to say that phonetic coding and sound analysis skills develop along with reading, each helping the other. The point is not that phonetic coding is *absolutely necessary* for learning to read (after all, congenitically deaf children can learn to read to some degree, although not very well; Furth, 1966), but rather that it is a great help.

As it turns out, the syllable-segmentation task described above is easier than, and is not as good a predictor of reading as, a phoneme-segmentation task. In the phoneme-segmentation task, the child is asked to tap once for each sound in the word. At age 5, no children are able to segment phonemes (Liberman, Shankweiler, Fischer & Carter, 1974), even though 46% could do so with syllables. At age 6, 17% could segment phonemes, 48% syllables. By age 7, when over 90% were able to segment syllables, only 70% could do so with phonemes. To illustrate the relation to later reading ability, when the 7 year olds were tested one year later, none of the children who had failed the phoneme test was in the top third of the class in reading (Liberman *et al.,* 1980). On the other hand, one half of the bottom third had failed the phoneme test the year before.

Sound analysis skills appear to be a crucial (or at least very helpful) component of early reading skills. Barron and Baron (1977) have shown, however, that children can also access word meaning visually. Most skilled adult readers are able to read silently without subvocalization, at least until they encounter difficult material. The results of Liberman and associates may indicate that sound analysis is a step which should not be skipped by beginning readers, even if they are to bypass it later.

Can children's reading skills be improved through phonetic-oriented instruction? This is a far more complicated question than it appears, for several reasons:

1. Much reading instruction has always been phonetically oriented, and even when other approaches are attempted, some phonics surely creeps in (even if only at home!).

2. Most children seem to learn to read reasonably well, regardless of how they are taught.

3. "Phonics instruction" as it would be found in most reading programs would not conform to the principles laid down by researchers in the field (e.g., Liberman, Shankweiler, Camp, Blackman & Werfelman, 1980).

4. Some children may have reading problems because they don't know how to (or don't want to) use the phonetic coding *ability* they have (that is, they could use it if they had been properly taught). On the other hand, there *may* be another group of children who don't have the ability to phonetically code efficiently. The first group should improve through phonetically oriented instruction but the second, by definition, shouldn't.

We will return to remedial issues in Chapters 11 to 15.

Words

Both the visual and phonic skills of the previous levels are required for competent word recognition, i.e., lexical access, at least in early reading. As we have seen in the preceding section, skilled readers appear to bypass the phonic level, at least when they are reading material within their ability level.

For reading to proceed smoothly, words must be identified quickly so that syntactic chunks can be formed and meaning computed. For meaning to be computed or comprehended, the subsidiary units must be held *at the same time* in working memory. It is for this reason that word recognition is so crucial. If words are recognized slowly, the first word of a group may have faded before the rest have been recognized; chunk boundaries may therefore be incorrectly located and important elements of meaning lost. In other words, there is only a limited amount of "attention" available to the reader: if he or she devotes it to figuring out what a word is, much less will be available for determining sentence meaning. Convincing evidence now exists that poor readers do take appreciably longer to recognize words, and that this slowness has damaging consequences for comprehension.

First let us look at the evidence that poor readers take longer to recognize words, as opposed to other visual stimuli. Stanovich (1981) has presented the clearest demonstration: he had his subjects (first-grade children divided into skilled and less-skilled readers) sit in front of a screen, and verbally name the pictures they were shown. Pictures were of five types: colours, line drawings of common objects, numerals (1 to 10), letters, or words. The children were asked to name the pictures as quickly as they could, and an electronic clock measured the length of time that elapsed between the presentation of the picture and the subject's oral response.

Stanovich was investigating whether poor readers would be slower to name the displays, indicating that they were slower to access their long-term memory representation of the displays and make a response. More specifically, he was trying to see if this slowness was general, or if it was confined to letters and words, or just words. For example, if both letters and words were named more slowly, the difficulty could well be at the featural level. Word-naming slowness alone would implicate, instead, word recognition processes or the organization of word knowledge in long-term memory.

Stanovich's results are shown in Table 7-2. Just in case you're worried that some of the less-skilled readers may not have known the words they were supposed to name, you can be assured that Stanovich did not count those trials; the results shown are only for those in which the subjects answered correctly. Stanovich's statistics confirmed what you can see from the table: poor readers were significantly slower than good readers only when they

TABLE 7-2

Length of time taken by skilled and less skilled readers to name pictures in Stanovich's experiment (Adapted from Stanovich, 1981). Times are milliseconds (i.e., thousandths of a second).

Type of Picture	Less Skilled	Skilled
Colour	766	821
Line Drawing	835	869
Numeral	653	660
Letter	774	775
Word	1351	1008

had to name words. The difference in naming time is massive, over a third of a second *per word!* This means that over a ten-word sentence, the less-skilled reader would be three seconds (i.e., about three words) behind a more skilled peer. If that sentence had three syntactic chunks, the poor reader would be very likely to have "lost" the first one before the end of the sentence, interfering greatly with comprehension. Re-reading would allow sentence-level comprehension, but would slow down reading even further. This, in turn, would hinder comprehension of meaning across sentences.

Inefficient (i.e., slow) word identification could be the result of problems at lower levels (visual or phonetic analysis), or of a difficulty in the way in which words and their attributes are stored in long-term memory. Word identification results from the simultaneous contribution of several kinds of information from the visual, phonetic, and meaning realms. We have already considered the visual and phonetic, and have hinted at meaning. Meaning arises in reading as a text is processed. Our sense of the meaning of what *has* been read guides and restricts our expectations of what words and meanings we are *about* to see. We do *not* think that this results in what some authors have termed the "psycholinguistic guessing game" (Goodman, 1967), in which meaning takes over the dominant role in word identification. There is no doubt that meaning plays an important role, but not to the exclusion of visual and phonetic factors.

Difficulty in the phonological analysis of words is the most commonly noted characteristic of children with reading problems (Stanovich, 1982a, 1982b). Individuals have been identified who, in spite of good educational experience, have extraordinary difficulty in learning to "sound out" words (e.g., Crowder, 1982, Chapter 11). It seems very plausible that these individuals have a *disability,* one that could be termed "phonological dyslexia", which is the result of abnormal functioning in the part of the brain responsible for associating sounds to visual symbols. On the other hand, it is not at all clear that the majority of children with phonological problems have such a disability. In many cases it may be more true to say that they have not been well taught or, at least, that they have not successfully learned phonological coding. You should demonstrate that competent teaching of phonological coding fails before you reach for the "phonological dyslexic" label. However, you should also be aware that such a distinct disability may exist, and that it may be an appropriate diagnosis for some children.

The traditional approach to word identification training has been the flash-card technique, in which children are drilled to recognize (i.e., name) new words. A more "progressive" approach relies upon "word experience", in the belief that children will come to know words through encountering them in their reading. An information processing analysis would doubt either of these techniques in isolation. In the first place, there is far more to word identification than the mere naming of the word, though this is an important component (as Stanovich showed). In fact there is also far more to word identification than being able to give a definition to the word, a technique favoured in vocabulary instruction. Skilled word identification allows the naming or defining of a word, but also opens up a network of associations containing sounds, images, and alternative senses of the word. This *semantic network* provides a rich context for the guiding of further processing. Put more simply, word identifica-

tion should result in the activation of a scheme, not merely a name or a synonym-like definition. Scheme activation is the necessary ingredient for improved comprehension beyond the word level.

Beck, Perfetti and McKeown (1982) examined previous vocabulary-training research and found that definition-oriented instruction did not benefit comprehension. Comprehension was facilitated, as predicted, when vocabulary instruction included techniques specifically designed to develop a rich semantic network. The instructional techniques Beck *et al.* employed included requiring the subjects (fourth graders) to generate sentences with the vocabulary words and to contrast the meaning of new words with those of old ones. Their techniques can be seen as examples of fostering simultaneous processing (see Chapter 13).

The word level is the appropriate place to discuss a rare phenomenon, termed "deep dyslexia" or even "word-blindness". This is a severe disturbance of reading, first identified by Hinshelwood in 1895 (see Hinshelwood, 1917), in which the person is unable to recognize words. This disability is most common in persons who have suffered unequivocal brain damage, but there have been case studies reported of "developmental deep dyslexia" (e.g., Crowder, 1982, Chapter 11; Coltheart, Patterson & Marshall, 1987), in which the disorder is congenital. Children suffering from deep dyslexia may initially resemble other learning problem children with word identification problems, but will show very little progress in learning even the simplest reading tasks, despite considerable efforts to teach them (cf. Crowder, 1982, Chapter 11). Deep dyslexic children are a distinct subgroup of learning problem children, one deserving the label "learning disabled". There is plausible evidence (e.g., Ingram, 1970) that their brains are different, perhaps due to genetics, and that their problem is very difficult or impossible to resolve. Please note that such children are very rarely discovered, and that they are not typical of other learning problem children. It is also instructive to remember that even experts in this field are unconvinced that the neurological explanation is necessary (Benton, 1975).

Syntactic Chunks

English is a language which relies upon word order to tell the reader or listener what function a particular word has. For instance, "John loves Mary" is very different from "Mary loves John", and much confusion will result if John does not realize this difference! When we talk of a word's function, we mean its grammatical class; e.g., as subject, adjective, verb, object, etc. We need to employ a grammatical analysis of a sentence in order to break it up into syntactic (grammatical) chunks. These chunks allow the recoding of words into a smaller number of units, releasing pressure upon working memory and facilitating further comprehension. For this process to work smoothly, grammatical analysis must happen automatically. This can present great difficulties for the reader who is not familiar with a particular sentence's syntax, or is not familiar with the syntactic role of a particular word. An example of an unfamiliar syntax would be:

Jack built the house that the mouse that the cat that the dog scared chased played in.

The following should be more familiar:

The dog scared the cat that chased the mouse that played in the house that Jack built.

An example of a word taking on an unfamiliar role, and one which presents beginning readers with problems, is:

Jack walked into the circus tent.

Most beginners think of "circus" as a noun and, therefore, as the place that Jack walked into, and as the end of a reasonable sentence. This of course leaves with them with the extra word "tent", which they don't know how to handle.

Syntactic analysis is also very difficult if an unknown word is in a crucial role. For example, there is no *syntactic* problem in:

The tall plants on the shelf were all mimsy.

because we know by the time that "mimsy" is encountered that "it" must be an adjective (as is "yellow") or a noun (as is "weeds"). However, in

The tall plants mimsy the shelf were all yellow.

too many possibilities exist: "mimsy" could be a preposition (as is "under"), a conjunction ("and"), a verb ("The tall plants died ..."), or several other types of word ("The tall plants that ..."). Of course, the remainder of the sentence limits these possibilities, but only after we have paid conscious attention to the problem, absorbing working memory space and interfering with comprehension.

Many studies attest to the difficulties imposed upon the reader by complex syntax. For example, Tatham (1969-1970) found that second and fourth grade children had higher reading comprehension scores on material that was written in familiar as opposed to unfamiliar syntax. When this conclusion is combined with the finding that reading problem children are less competent with even standard syntax (Semel & Wiig, 1975), the likelihood of syntax being involved in reading problems increases.

If syntactic chunking does slow information processing in reading, then *pre-chunking* of text (i.e., dividing it into chunks typographically so that the reader doesn't have to do it) should facilitate deeper processes such as comprehension. This is precisely what Cromer (1970) found, for adults. To test the applicability of this work for reading problem children, Kirby and Gordon (1988) repeated this study with children in grades three to six. They had children read either an "appropriate chunks" or an "inappropriate chunks" text. An example of an appropriate chunks text is the following:

Michael was born
  in an industrial city
    in Northern England
      where he spent the early years
      of his life.

As you can see, each line corresponds to a good syntactic chunk. Compare this to the following:

Michael was born in an industrial
  city in Northern
    England where he spent the
      early years of
      his life.

These inappropriate chunks are, in fact, more like normal text, in that a line ends where it ends, without much concern for the reader.

Kirby and Gordon (1988) found that poor readers (defined as the bottom third of each grade in reading comprehension) performed far better on a reading comprehension task when they had read the appropriate chunks text.

Of course the solution is not to reprint all reading material into appropriate chunks form, though experience with some material in that form may help poor readers acquire the skill of syntactic chunking. Familiarity with different syntactic forms also needs to be explicitly taught. However, as syntactic chunking is dependent upon successive processing (because of its reliance upon word order), there may well be children who have particular difficulty in this area. The degree to which such skills can be directly taught will be considered in Chapter 12.

Micros, Macros and Themes

While reading *requires* the processing of features, letters, sounds, words and syntactic chunks, these are not what reading *is*. If reading is mainly anything, it is mainly the extraction of meaning from sentences, paragraphs and larger texts.

Surprisingly, there is not much evidence that reading problems emanate from these levels. Of course problems at the lower levels can produce a lack of comprehension, but that is not fundamentally a *comprehension* problem. To demonstrate a problem in comprehension, one would have to have eliminated any problems at preceding levels. Because that has never been done, it is difficult to prove that reading problems can be due to comprehension problems. Furthermore, it is likely that students showing reading comprehension problems would also show other types of comprehension problems, such as in listening. (As we argued in Chapter 1, many children with comprehension problems may also have problems with some of the reasoning tasks found on IQ tests and, therefore, would have been eliminated from the traditional "learning disabilities" category.) For these reasons,

it is worth indicating what kinds of reading comprehension problems could arise at each of the levels of ideas, main ideas, and themes. These problems would be accentuated by problems at lower levels.

At the higher levels, the major potential problems stem from (a) the number of components or chunks to be integrated into the proposition, (b) the availability of prior schematic knowledge in long-term memory, (c) the difficulty in recognizing relationships between chunks so that an integrated representation can be formed, and (d) the reader's intention to process information to the given level. Problem (d) is a strategic one, and will be considered further in Chapter 14. Problem (b) can be solved either by teaching the student the appropriate content, or by designing instructional aids (such as advance organizers; see Kirby and Cantwell, 1985) that activate the desired scheme. Problem (a) concerns successive processing and how much can be held in working memory; accordingly it will be dealt with in Chapter 12. Problem (c) concerns simultaneous processing, the topic of Chapter 13.

How Reading Skill Develops

In the previous section we saw how reading functions in a skilled reader and which processes can go wrong. It is also important to study how reading skills develop in the individual child. Not surprisingly, the steps identified in the preceding section are related to those observed developmentally. When we examine how reading skills develop in the normal child, it is possible to see three distinct periods (Kirby, 1988). These periods can be seen as *stages,* but this does not mean that a child is *in* one stage at a certain time, nor does it mean that there is a sudden transition from one stage to another. Instead, these periods or stages are more like *phases,* each one dominating the child's reading for a while, but still existing beneath the surface during the other phases. Another point to remember is that the phases depend more upon reading skill than they do on chronological age. For example, an eight-year-old is likely to be in Phase 2, but could be in either of the others instead. It is also possible for a child to shift phases in response to task difficulty: a difficult text may cause a child to revert to a former phase, whereas easy material may allow progression to the next phase.

The three phases are:

1. **Global Phase.** This phase is a pre-reading one, in which the reader treats the text as a whole, and does not have any means of identifying an unknown word. The reader responds on the basis of what he or she thinks the story is about, regardless of what it actually says. This phase provides a good, meaningful orientation for reading, but must be left before reading skill can improve significantly. If the global phase persists, reading problems can result. A mild form of this problem occurs when the child guesses what a word is on the basis of its first letter or two.

2. **Analytic Phase.** In this phase the child "cracks the code" – that is, begins to analyze words into their constituent parts, attaching sounds to the visual symbols. This stage is less meaning-oriented than the previous one, but it is an important one on the way to skilled reading. However, if a child becomes "fixated" at this stage, perhaps because a teacher stresses correct pronunciation of words, a different kind of reading problem can develop.

3. **Synthetic Phase.** The third phase represents skilled reading, in which the reader puts together an orientation towards meaning with the analytic ability to identify words quickly and precisely.

The following sections will elaborate what happens in these three phases, stressing the information processing skills that are required.

Global Phase

This phase can be said to begin the first time children encounter a book in a meaningful way – for instance, when their parents first read them a story.

Children are aware very early in this process that "reading" means getting a story from a book, though they are unaware of how this happens. For example, Johns (1980) has shown that when pre-readers are asked questions such as, "Can you read?", they often respond, "Yes". Furthermore, if they are shown a particular book, they will say they can read it if they know the story. These children may indicate that they can read a picture, or that an upside-down page of text can be read. Children in this phase have little conception of what a word is, that it is composed of discrete sounds, or that printed words are composed of letters which represent different sounds.

The important characteristic of children's thinking about reading in this phase is that it is global, or holistic. Children in this phase do not break the act of reading down into its component parts, but rather deal with it as a single, complete entity. A number of researchrs have shown that this is the normal beginning phase of reading (Biemiller, 1970; Barr, 1972). In the information processing terms used in Chapter 5, we would describe this type of "reading" as relying heavily upon simultaneous processing.

A cynic might say that this phase is not a reading phase at all, as the child clearly has no conception of what reading is about. We would disagree, because reading *is* about the extraction of meaning from text, which global phase children recognize in their peculiar way. They know what reading is supposed to do, but they don't know how to do it. Another reason for recognizing the global phase as a stage of reading development is that its influence can persist into later stages, even if only in a mild way.

Virtually all children are able to become aware, soon after instruction begins in reading (if not before) that reading involves words, and words involve letters. The global phase, in its pure form, fades into the background as soon as this awareness is realized. At this point the reader should begin to learn to *analyze,* to break words down into their component letters and sounds (analytic phase). This requires a switch from simultaneous to successive processing, to allow the breaking down of a holistic entity into a sequence of parts.

Children can persist with simultaneous processing even though they realize that reading involves words which involve letters and sounds. If they do so persist, they attempt to deal with words and letters holistically – for example, by guessing what a word is, based upon its first letter or so. In a sense, these children are trying to approach reading *too intelligently!* Rather than develop the low-level letter-sound rules (word-attack skills), they adopt the global approach of going directly to meaning without dealing with the details. While this may be a good approach for the skilled reader (in the synthetic phase), it is disastrous for the beginner. Beginning readers who fail to switch to the analytic approach are very likely to develop reading problems.

Why do some readers fail to become analytic? There are three possible reasons:

1. **They are not taught to.** As we have seen above, it has been fashionable from time to time to teach reading in a non-analytic or whole-word manner. Even if this approach is taken exclusively, most children succeed in "cracking the code", in figuring out what reading is really all about. Some unfortunate children are not so successful in solving the puzzle, and persist with their earlier strategy, which is reinforced by the teacher.

2. **They are not able to** (or perhaps are *less* able to). These children may have low successive processing ability, making it difficult to carry out the necessary visual and auditory analysis.

3. **They may not choose to.** The alternative possibility is that even though they possess the required successive processing ability, they choose to approach reading in a way that does not make use of that ability. For these children the problem is strategic, and may stem from a lack of appreciation of what is required in reading.

We'll see in Chapter 12 how successive processing problems can be diagnosed and remediation designed. Chapter 14 will concentrate similarly upon strategic problems.

Analytic Phase

For some people, the analytic phase is "what reading is all about". This is the phase in which the child learns the sounds associated with the letters, learns how to analyze spoken words into their component sounds and thus letters, and learns how to blend letter sounds into properly pronounced words. As mentioned in the previous section, all of these skills require successive processing: the holding of information in correct sequential order, the forming of associations between parts, and part-by-part analysis of visually or auditorially perceived words.

It is worth emphasizing that these skills *require* successive processing; they are *not exactly the same as* successive processing. In other words, they are members of the group of skills which require successive processing; a particular child may use them ineffectively in some cases, without necessarily being poor at all other forms of successive processing. There is a tendency for children weak in one area of successive processing to also be weak in others, especially within the same content area (e.g., reading), but this is not necessarily always the case.

Readers can become "stuck" at the analytic phase, again resulting in reading problems. Reading may be slow and word-by-word, if not letter-by-letter, especially if the child fails to master the successive processing skills of this stage. On the other hand, it is possible for the child to master these analytic skills, but not progress beyond them to the synthetic phase; in this case, the reader is very effective at pronouncing text ("barking at print" as Wardhaugh, 1969, says), but fails to extract much meaning from it.

Reading problems at this phase can be attributed to several causes:

1. **Teacher emphasis of correct pronunciation alone.** Just as problems can result from *not* stressing word attack skills, they can also stem from *over-stressing*.

2. **Lack of successive processing ability.** If the reader lacks the information processing ability to master the analytic skills, he or she can

become fixated upon them. In this case, the teacher must work to improve these abilities, or must devise ways to allow the reader to use other abilities.

3. **Lack of simultaneous processing ability.** The reader may well master the analytic skills, but fail to progress beyond. Again, teachers should either improve the abilities lacking or find a way around them.

4. **Reader strategy.** It is also possible that readers themselves may choose to approach reading in a mainly analytic manner. This may be because they are good at it, and see no need to go further, or it may be because they are not good at it. In the latter case, readers may feel that this is what reading "really is", and they'd "better keep working at it".

Successive and simultaneous processing problems will be discussed in Chapters 12 and 13 respectively, and strategic problems in Chapter 14.

Synthetic Phase

This phase represents the combination of the best parts of the previous two, an orientation toward meaning in the presence of competent word attack skills. These two aspects contribute to each other's effectiveness: a rough idea of likely meaning guides word identification, speeding it up so that more words are likely to co-exist in working memory, thus increasing the likelihood that they will be recoded meaningfully.

The most important aspect of this stage is the flexible use of several sources of information. At times, reading is very "data-driven" or "bottom-up", relying upon the analysis of printed words. At other times reading is "conceptually-driven" or "top-down", guided by the reader's goals and by previously processed meanings. In information processing terms, both simultaneous and successive processing are orchestrated by a smoothly operating strategy or plan.

Are there reading phases beyond the synthetic phase? It depends upon what you mean by reading.

A number of recent researchers have argued for a phase of "meta-comprehension", in which readers not only comprehend, but comprehend *how* they comprehend (e.g., Brown, Campione & Day, 1981; Kirby & Moore, 1988; Lupart & Mulcahy, 1984). Readers in such a phase should be far more aware of how to use texts for their own purposes, and of how to select particular reading strategies to meet those purposes. In this phase, the reader tries to understand the author's purpose in writing a text.

It is debatable whether it is necessary to speak of this fourth phase of reading. It is arguable that it is not a *reading* phase at all, but rather a phase of cognitive development, specifically that of formal operations (see, for instance, Flavell, 1976). If we choose not to include it as a separate stage, we can see these characteristics as the later part of the synthetic phase. Whether we identify it as a separate stage or not, should we associate the lack of this skill with a type of learning problem in reading?

We suggest that the answer is "Yes", even though this goes against the tradition of the "learning disabilities" field. A reading disability is usually thought of as a difficulty in attaining the synthetic phase of reading, roughly equivalent to a reading age of 10 to 12. Once children attain that level of reading skill, they are said to be "functionally independent". Supposedly such readers have mastered reading and now have to get on with their learning via that medium. However, our position is that learning problems can occur after functionally independent skills have been attained. These problems are associated with difficulty in perceiving the deeper meanings of texts, or in organizing one's use of a text for some complicated purpose (such as studying for an exam). The higher levels of reading skill (i.e., the theme levels) involve a "meta-comprehensive" awareness of the implicit structure and meanings of text. These skills are demanded by the later years of secondary school and university, though it seems that many students pass through without mastering them. These skills separate the student who can tell you the *plot* of Shakespeare's *Macbeth* from the student who can explain what themes underlie it.

You might object that these "meta-comprehension" skills are too close to what are normally considered to be intellectual skills, or "intelligence". We agree that they are so related, but this does not mean that they are unrelated to reading. Nor does it mean that these skills cannot be learned or improved. As will be discussed in Chapter 14, careful instruction in strategic reading can begin to overcome these problems.

Summary

This has been a long chapter, mainly because more is known about reading than about other achievement areas, and because reading is so important. We have seen that reading problems can occur at any level, not only at the basic level of word analysis or recognition. Once reading problems at the comprehension level are accepted, it can be seen that they have terrible consequences for areas far beyond what is normally called "reading" in schools.

Our purpose in this chapter has been to give you a good grasp of how skilled reading functions, and of how reading skills develop, so that you will have a better understanding of how reading problems can occur and what their many causes could be. Only by understanding how reading works can we understand why it's not working, and understanding why it's not working is an important step toward making it work better.

We have described reading at eight levels of analysis (features, letters, sounds, words, chunks, ideas, main ideas, and themes), and the development of reading skills in three phases (global, analytic, and synthetic). Each of these levels and phases can be associated with different kinds of reading problems, which call for different kinds of remediation.

Reading is a complex activity; it is unlikely that there are simple reading problems, and less likely that reading problems have simple solutions. Don't despair if you can't see immediately how to cure all reading problems. We hope that some solutions will become clearer as you progress through this book, but don't expect miracles. The general framework presented in Chapters 4 and 5, the description of reading provided in this chapter, and the suggestions in Chapters 11 to 14 should help you to understand and attack reading problems, but they will not tell you where the magic wand is hidden.

RECOMMENDED READING

Written Language
Gelb, I.J.
1963. *A study of writing.* Second edition. Chicago: University of Chicago Press.

This is the classic work in the area, to which most subsequent sources refer.

Taylor, I.
1981. Writing systems and reading. In G.E. Mackinnon & T.G. Waller (eds.). *Reading research: Advances in theory and practice*, Vol. 2. New York: Academic Press.

How Reading Has Been Taught
Crowder, R.G.
1982. *The psychology of reading.* New York: Oxford.

Chapter 10 of this excellent book presents a brief and very readable overview.

Eye Movements and Reading
Rayner, K. (ed.)
1983. *Eye movements in reading: Perceptual and language processes.* New York: Academic Press.

This is a recent, but surely not the last, treatment of the matter. A briefer treatment can be found in Crowder's (1982) Chapter 2.

Theories of Reading
Pearson, P.D. (ed.)
1984. *Handbook of reading research.* New York: Longman.

This is a comprehensive treatment of the various aspects of reading, and of modern theoretical approaches.

Smith, F.

1978. *Understanding reading.* Second edition. New York: Holt, Rinehart & Winston.

Smith is one of the leading proponents of the "psycholinguistic" approach to reading, which emphasizes the meaningful nature of the task. Many critics feel that Smith and others overstate the case, and therefore *underestimate* the importance of phonological processes. A powerful force in educational circles, however.

Comprehension

Kintsch, W. & van Dijk, T.A.

1978. Toward a model of text comprehension and production. *Psychological Review. 85,* 363-394.

Be warned: this is not a paper for novices, but it is a landmark paper in the history of understanding comprehension.

Pearson, P.D. & Johnson, D.D.

1978. *Teaching reading comprehension.* New York: Holt, Rinehart & Winston.

This one you'll be able to understand! One of the most valuable sources on improving comprehension skills.

CHAPTER 8

Spelling

WE HAVE SEPARATED the study of spelling from that of reading (see Chapter 7) for the sake of convenience (to break up an otherwise overly long chapter) and because researchers have considered the two separately (see Frith, 1980). By doing so, we are not denying that the two sets of skills are inextricably linked, that problems in one are likely to be accompanied by problems in the other, and that the two should be taught in an integrated fashion.

We begin by briefly describing the history of spelling and approaches to teaching it. The second section presents an information processing analysis of skilled spelling, and the third section concentrates upon a particular area of research that points towards two qualitatively different spelling strategies. Finally, in the fourth section, we discuss the two major ways in which spelling fails to work, tying these in to our information processing model presented in Chapters 4 and 5.

Approaches to Spelling

Spelling as we know it today consists of a complicated set of rules and conventions for writing down words. If English were a phonetically regular written language (see Chapter 7, pp. 82-83), a set of rules would be sufficient, each sound having its corresponding letter. Because English is not entirely regular, conventions are needed; for instance, "ph" often (though not always) is pronounced as "f". Many conventions apply only to a few words: the way to pronounce "enough" is one example. The result is a tangled web of simple and complex rules, and a large collection of exceptions to them.

Yet spelling has not always been an issue in English. Until the fifteenth century, the written language was controlled by scribes, who were responsible for *trans-scribing* books, one at a time, by hand. According to Vallins (1965), these scribes freely used different spellings of the same word to represent different dialectical pronunciations. (If this were done today, imagine the difficulty a Bostonian would have in reading a book written by an Alabaman, and the total bewilderment each would have with a book written by an Australian!) It was not even unusual for the same author to spell the same word in different ways on the same page.

Since the fifteenth century, with the advent of the printing press, spelling has been gradually standardized. The few disputes that remain are between "British English" and "American English", the former being accepted to varying degrees by the British, the Australians, the Canadians and other (non-U.S.) parts of the now defunct British Empire. Thus we have variations such as colour or color, defence or defense, and standardise or standardize.

Since the standardization of spelling and the beginnings of compulsory schooling in the nineteenth century, educators have swung back and forth in deciding on the importance of spelling. From many accounts it seems that in the early days reading was taught *by* spelling, for example, "See-Aye-Tee says *cat*." Modern educators are astounded that anyone learned to read that way, but they did. When it came to spelling, one had either to remember the visual appearance of "cat" or to recall the sequence "See-Aye-Tee" and then record the written letter associated with each of those sounds. If you have a sadistic streak, consider the difficulties such spellers would have had with the letter "w" (pronounced "double-you", i.e., UU) or with spelling the word "queue" (in which the whole word is pronounced in the same way as the first letter!).

Many educators reacted against such nonsense by arguing that spelling itself was not important; if children could read well, then eventually they would learn to spell as they became more familiar with the written language. Furthermore, they argued, who cares if they *don't* learn to spell in the standard manner? These opinions became associated with a "progressive" attitude towards education, which also included a bias towards teaching reading by the "whole word" approach (see Chapter 7). As we will argue in the remainder of this chapter, the "anti-spelling" approach (especially when combined with the "anti-phonics" approach to reading) leaves the learner unprepared to attack unfamiliar words. While the inability to spell *may be* unimportant, it contributes to difficulties with a phonic approach to word attack skills, and thus to reading problems. Furthermore, it is arguable that spelling *is* important, because it allows us to communicate more effectively with others and because others will judge our written work (and us) by our spelling. To deliberately not teach spelling would be to disadvantage the very children who are most in need of its support.

How Spelling Works

There seem to be two types of words that we spell: those that we can spell immediately, without thinking about them (e.g., c-a-t); and those that require more thought (e.g., c-a-t-a-s-t-r-o-p-h-e). The former are clearly spellings that we have rote learned, and they are usually correct. While we don't know of any research on this particular topic, we suspect that there are great individual differences in the number of words that can be spelled immediately.

In this chapter we are more concerned with the second class of words, those that even skilled spellers spell slowly and after some thought. These are not necessarily hard words, because most spellers spell most of them correctly. They are words whose spelling has not been rote learned and so must be "re-invented" on each occasion. These are also the words that poor spellers have great difficulty in spelling.

How do we go about spelling these words? What we suggest below is a "task analysis" of this kind of spelling, based upon our observations of good and poor spellers' spelling, and based upon our understanding of how human information processing takes place (see Chapters 4 and 5). Farnham-Diggory (1978) has suggested a very similar model to describe how spelling takes place. We emphasize that the model describes how spelling *should* take place, not how it *does* take place in poor spellers. As such, it should provide ideas about what poor spellers are doing wrong, and about the design of remedial activities.

The model is illustrated as a flow diagram in Figure 8-1. It consists of four rectangular boxes, indicating actions to perform, and three diamond-shaped boxes, indicating decisions to be made. Believe it or not, we have kept the model simple to emphasize its overall structure. In fact, each of the individual actions or decisions is itself complex.

The sequence begins with the auditory input of a word to be spelled. This can come either from the "outside" – that is, from a teacher – or from the "inside", as in, "The next word I want to write is 'elephant'".

FIGURE 8-1

Information processing model of spelling (Start at the top and proceed downwards.)

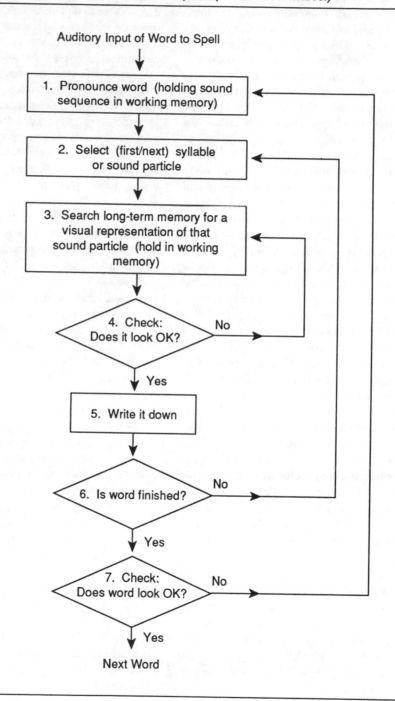

The first thing that the speller must do, according to the model, is repeat the word, either silently or aloud, to establish a working memory representation of it. This is not as easy as it sounds (excuse the pun): particularly when the input word comes from the outside, the acoustic stimuli must access their sound representations in long-term memory, in order to allow the speller to say the word. To acquire some idea of how difficult this can be, have one of your friends, who speaks a language that you don't, read you a list of words in that language for you to repeat. If the words are long or the sound-combinations unfamiliar, you should have some difficulty. For the speller, if the wrong sounds are pronounced, trouble is sure to result.

The pronunciation of the word should produce a sequence of sounds held in working memory (step 1). Skilled spellers then select the first syllable for spelling (step 2). Less skilled spellers may have to work with a smaller particle, such as a phoneme. As we saw in Chapter 7 (see pp. 86-88), the breaking up of a word into syllables or phonemes is not performed well by children before age 6, and much later by poor readers or spellers.

Long-term memory is then searched for a visual representation of the first sound segment (step 3). This representation, one or more letters, is held temporarily in working memory, for visual checking (step 4). This step is purely visual and very dependent upon the speller's experience of words: does the selected version of the sound particle look correct? Because many syllables have two or more written representations, this checking is necessary. For example, spell "kangaroo". The first syllable could be represented by "can", but competent spellers who are at all familiar with the word will quickly reject that, probably even before it is written down. It is possible, especially for poor spellers, that the writing down of the particle (step 5) occurs before step 4. If the syllable doesn't look correct, the speller goes back to step 3, to find another representation. When this first check is passed, the speller goes on to another: Is the word finished? If the answer is yes, as it would be in a one-syllable word, the speller goes on to the next word, etc. In a multiple-syllable word, the speller should go back to his or her working memory representation of the

word's sound sequence, to select the next syllable or particle for spelling. Presuming that the speller has kept track of where in the word he or she has reached, or that the written version produced so far can provide this information, the cycle repeats until the check at step 6 decides that the word is finished.

The final step is again a visual step, to ensure that the word "looks right". If English were perfectly regular, so that each sound sequence had only one written representation, this check would not be necessary. Because English has complicated sound-spelling relationships, however, it is necessary. A speller could get to this stage with "catastrofee" for "catastrophe"; only if the speller has encountered the written word before is it likely that he or she will reject the incorrect version. Again, this is a visual check. If the version is rejected, then the whole cycle may have to repeat to locate the error.

It should be clear that this model relies upon two sorts of skills, phonetic and visual. As we have explained previously, the former rely upon successing processing and the latter upon simultaneous processing. Phonetic skills are involved in the initial pronunciation of the word (step 1) and in the segmenting of it into a sound sequence (step 2). Visual skill is required for the two checking operations at steps 4 and 7. Step 3 requires the integration of phonetic and visual information, as the former must access the latter. Step 6 requires phonetic skill, to check that all the sound segments have been finished; alternatively, step 6 requires the integration of visual and phonetic skills to allow the speller to pronounce what has been written so far, to see if the word is finished. Skilled spelling thus relies upon the efficient integration of simultaneous and successive processing.

Sound Words and Sight Words

The model in Figure 8-1 provides a reasonable description of how many words are spelled. As we said at the beginning of the last section, words whose spelling we know by rote do not have to be processed in that manner. But how does the model work with what are called "sight words", those that are spelled in peculiar ways with little reference to

TABLE 8-1
Common sight words

are	for	light	right
buy	goes	me	said
could	he	new	their
done	I	of	who
eat	no	put	you

TABLE 8-2
*Typical "Phoenician" spelling errors
(from Payne, 1984)*

Correct Word	Misspelling
congratulate	congrachulate
promotion	promoshion
gratitude	gratachooed
employer	emploire
freeze	freese
grief	greaf
kerosene	carosiene
necessary	nesasary

spelling "rules"? (See Table 8-1 for a list of common sight words.) Take for example the word "yacht"; the skilled speller pronounces it, selects the one syllable to be spelled, and long before "yot" reaches consciousness, it is rejected. Good spellers seem to "know" that certain words are exceptions, and that more exotic long-term memory representations need to be searched for. The phonetic representations of these words need to be "tagged" in some way, to avoid a lot of tedious misspelling-checking-searching cycles. Often this tagging is incomplete, in the sense that we know there is something peculiar about how a given word is spelled, though we aren't quite sure what. A good example of this is the word "rhythm"; many skilled spellers start to spell it knowing that it is a peculiar word and that there is a strange series of y's and h's in it. Accordingly, few skilled spellers start to write "rithm". However, many write "rhythym", and then (visually) realize that that is not correct.

Two Spelling Strategies

If skilled spelling requires the integration of phonetic and visual skills, then individual differences in these skills should produce different approaches to the task of spelling. For instance, we would expect persons who lack phonetic skill to rely upon their visual skills more heavily than do most people, and vice versa. This is precisely what Jonathan Baron and his colleagues have found in a series of research studies (e.g., Baron, 1979; Baron & Strawson, 1976; Baron, Treiman, Wilf & Kellman, 1980). Baron's research has led to the identification of two groups of spellers, one which relies

upon phonetic sound-symbol rules, and the other which relies instead upon specific visual associations. The former group is referred to as "Phoenicians" (recalling the invention by that culture of the original alphabet), and the latter as "Chinese" (because of their logographic written language; see page 82). We will use those same terms here and, like Baron, we intend no ethnic slur! Let us emphasize, however, that these two groups are merely the ends of a continuum (or perhaps of two continua), and do not really stand apart from more average spellers.

Phoenicians and Chinese can be distinguished in both their reading and spelling. In spelling, Phoenicians are more likely to rely upon phonetic rules, even if the word they are spelling is an "exception"; this suggests that such children have failed to "tag" exception words as such in their long-term memories. Table 8-2 shows some typical Phoenician spelling errors. In reading, the Phoenicians are more likely to pronounce a word as though it were regular (e.g., pronouncing the "w" in "sword", or the "s" in "island"). In other words, the reader tends to overgeneralize a rule, a common finding in developmental research (see for example Flavell, 1976). The reader often proceeds from (1) obtaining the wrong answer, to (2) obtaining the right answer some of the time by using a simple rule, to (3) obtaining the wrong answer by generalizing too far from that simple rule, to (4) obtaining the right answer by using a more comprehensive rule.

TABLE 8-3
*Typical "Chinese" spelling errors
(from Payne, 1984)*

Correct Word	Misspelling
congratulate	congrtachalet
promotion	protion
situated	sitchuwached
membership	mebership
splendid	spleded
employer	inployue
unusual	unushale
excitement	exitment

On the other hand, in spelling the Chinese rely more upon a visual association for the spoken word. This can be successful for irregular words (e.g., "know"), but disastrous for regular words. Table 8-3 contains some typical Chinese misspellings. As you can see, they usually involve either an idiosyncratic arrangement of letters (congrtachalet), or the omission of a syllable unit (protion). The former appears due to a visual association ("congratulate" has a "t" in a peculiar place), the latter to a failure to phonologically check the written product. In reading, the Chinese are more likely to make *meaning-preserving* errors (e.g., reading "done" as "did"; see Baron, 1979).

One question that emerges when you inspect spelling errors is whether the Chinese are doing something different (referring to visual associations), or doing what the Phoenicians are doing (attempting to apply sound-symbol rules), but not as well. If they are doing something different, then it seems legitimate to talk of two spelling strategies; on the other hand, if they are not, then it would make more sense to talk of one skill – for instance, phonological or phonetic ability – and see the Chinese as having a low level of this skill. The distinction between strategies and abilities is a complex one, which we can't resolve here. For our purposes it is worth keeping the question in mind (it has remedial implications; see Chapters 11 to 14), and it is also worth remembering that a difference

in ability (weaker phonetic coding) could produce a difference in strategy (reliance upon visual information). Similarly, a difference in strategy (reliance upon visual information) could produce a difference in ability (less phonetic ability, due to lack of practice).

In theory, an over-reliance upon either phonetic or visual information should result in spelling errors. Payne (1984) found that second grade poor spellers were equally likely to be classed as Phoenician or Chinese, but that fifth grade poor spellers were almost exclusively Chinese. This suggests that the initial difference is strategic in nature (perhaps partly dependent upon ability), but that gradually good spelling comes to depend more and more upon phonetic ability. These findings also suggest that children who continue to rely upon visual associations to the exclusion of phonetic analysis are likely to become poor spellers.

Sources of Spelling Problems

As we have argued in the previous chapter, phonetic analysis skills rely upon successive processing. In spelling, successive processing is required for the initial break-down of the stimulus, and for the holding of the resultant sound sequence in working memory. Inadequate successive processing would result in three problems:

1. Failure to repeat correctly the word to be spelled;
2. Failure to break it correctly into sound segments; and
3. Inability to retain one's place in the word being spelled (resulting in an omission or repetition of a sound unit).

These problems will all result in Chinese-like spelling, in that a normal pronunciation of the result will not produce sounds recognizable as the word being spelled.

Simultaneous processing is similarly involved in the visual skills of finding a written pattern for the sounds and of checking the written result. Inadequate simultaneous processing will result in two types of problem:

1. Incorrect sound-symbol matches (perhaps at the letter level, but more likely at the syllable level), and

2. Spellings based upon sound-symbol matches that are usually correct, or correct for other words, but not for the word in question. A specific instance of this second problem is the failure to realize that a given word is a "sight" word, and not to be analyzed phonetically.

These problems will result in spelling of a Chinese kind, if the poor visual codes are used anyway. However, spelling will be Phoenician if the speller decides, instead, to use regular sound-symbol rules.

Simultaneous and successive processing problems are related to specific types of misspelling. Attention and planning problems produce more generally poor performance, usually extending beyond any specific achievement area and beyond any specific subskill (see Figure 5-5). A possible result of a planning problem that could be specific to spelling would be the failure to employ alternative spelling strategies – that is, a failure to switch strategies when one has clearly failed. Yet another planning problem, in this case related to simultaneous processing, would be the failure to monitor performance, to fail to perform the visual checks found at steps 4 and 7 of the model. These steps, for example, may be omitted by a child described as impulsive. Attention and planning problems are linked, and are described further in Chapters 11 to 14.

The task analysis of spelling presented in this chapter is a good example of how modern cognitive psychology operates. Spelling (or reading, or arithmetic, or anything else) is not dealt with as a unitary skill; instead, it is broken down (theoretically) into parts or steps: sometimes this is easy, sometimes difficult, and sometimes impossible. The approach draws on careful research studies to validate the accuracy of such models, and to locate the steps which are causing most problems. Once those steps have been found, more research can be done to test the hypothesis that improving them will help overall performance. We'll see more examples of task analysis in the next chapter.

Chapters 12 and 13 will deal with successive and simultaneous processing, how to measure them and how to improve poor skill in using them. As we will see there, successive or simultaneous processing may be weak across a variety of achievement areas, or the problem may be confined to particular skills such as spelling. In either case, remediation will be better designed if it is based upon an understanding of the cognitive skills which underlie the observed achievement problems.

Summary

In this chapter we presented a cognitive model which describes how spelling should take place ideally. This model contains both phonetic and visual steps, emphasizing that both are important and that either could be the source of spelling problems. Phonetic skills are dependent upon successive processing, visual skills upon simultaneous processing.

Spelling errors can be classified according to whether they are produced by relying too much on phonetic or on visual information. Children who produce phonetically based errors have been labelled "Phoenicians"; those who produce visually based errors, "Chinese".

RECOMMENDED READING

Frith, U. (ed.)
    1980. *Cognitive processes in spelling.* New York:
        Academic Press. A collection of papers on the cognitive psychology of spelling. Almost all of the 22 papers can be highly recommended.

Farnham-Diggory, S.
    1978. *Learning disabilities.* London: Open Books.

This little book is a good introduction to the cognitive psychology of learning problems, even though many of the author's conclusions are at variance with ours. The spelling task analysis in Figure 8-1 is similar to one presented by Farnham-Diggory in her Chapter 12. An interesting aspect of her treatment (which does not happen to coincide with our view) is that she ascribes the visual checks to the right hemisphere of the brain, while the remainder is performed by the left.

CHAPTER 9

Arithmetic and Mathematics

THE VAST MAJORITY of research concerning learning problems has been done in the area of reading and associated areas such as spelling. It is possible to see several reasons for this concentration. The most notable are, first, that reading is seen as a more important skill than arithmetic and mathematics, and second, that poor performance in arithmetic and especially mathematics is attributed simply to lack of ability. It is certainly not valid to claim that there are fewer problems in arithmetic/mathematics than in reading. However, some teachers do feel that arithmetic/mathematics problems, where they are not due to "low ability", are secondary to a reading or general learning problem; that is, that the problems in arithmetic/mathematics are *caused by* the other (presumably more important) problems.

In this chapter we present a rationale for considering arithmetic and mathematics as important areas of learning problems. Without denying the importance of reading, we emphasize the importance of arithmetic and mathematics. In particular, we challenge the "low ability" explanation of poor performance in these areas; this argument is often circular in nature, and has long been an excuse for poor teaching, especially of female students. As we have done in the two preceding chapters, we approach the topic by first developing models of how arithmetic and mathematics problems are

normally performed, and then using this framework to identify potential sources of learning problems. But first some definitions.

Arithmetic and Mathematics

It is worth distinguishing between two parts of the general area of mathematics – arithmetic and mathematics. By *arithmetic* we mean the computational aspects of employing the basic operations (+, –, ×, ÷) with numerals. Arithmetic problems can range from the simple (2 + 2 = ?) to the complex (685+ (712 + 2) = ? + 397). In skilled arithmeticians, simple problems usually involve the *recall* of *number facts,* whereas more complex problems require the use of one or more *algorithms*. Algorithms are simply procedures for calculating the answers for problems to which we do not have an "automatic" answer.

By *mathematics,* we mean the rest! That includes algebra, geometry, calculus and many other more complicated areas of mathematics. What all of these areas have in common is *problem solving:* that is, there is not usually an immediate path seen to solution, as there should be in arithmetic. Many mathematics problems require the student to perform considerable amounts of thinking and effort to transform the task at hand *into* an arithmetic problem. "Word problems" are a good example of this:

> If three men each work seven hours a day for five days, earning $10 per hour and having to pay $5 each day for lunch, how much will they have earned as a group?

To solve this the student must first see that the problem has to be transformed or translated into arithmetic. Mathematical problem solving is required to perform this translation:

> How much do they receive? Well take 3 times 7 times 5, all times $10. That is, $3 \times 7 \times 5 \times 10 = ?$

The student then performs this *arithmetic* problem, and obtains, if correct, the answer of $1050. Then more mathematical problem solving is required to realize that something has to be subtracted, and to figure out how to do that.

> Well, they each eat one lunch per day, so that's three men times five days, times $5 per day, or $3 \times 5 \times 5 = ?$

Again, the arithmetic is performed, obtaining $75. If the problem solving continues well, the need to subtract that answer from the previous number is realized, the arithmetic is set up, and performed.

Of course not all mathematics reduces to arithmetic. The best counter-example is geometry, in which problems can simply require the proof of the equality of two angles, without quantifying their actual size.

How important are arithmetic and mathematics? They are more important today than they have ever been before. From comparing prices in grocery shopping, to balancing a chequebook, to completing an income tax form, arithmetic skills are an important part of everyday life. Hand-held calculators may be more and more common, but we still need to know which algorithms to use, how to understand the results, and how to identify possible errors. To be non-mathematical today is like being illiterate in the recent past: you become a passive spectator rather than an active participant in the modern world. Advanced mathematics is also more and more involved in many careers, in business,

government, science and education. Not all children may be proceeding to such careers but they do, at least, deserve the opportunity.

An important point in this chapter concerns automaticity. You should recall our argument in Chapter 7 concerning automaticity in reading: you need to be able to recognize words automatically, effortlessly, and without absorbing any working memory space, in order for there to be space left over for deeper levels of comprehension. The same argument holds true in mathematics: if the lower-level arithmetic computations ($2 + 2 = 4$) absorb conscious effort, less space will remain to retain the larger problem, the solution strategy, or the point in the solving of the problem that has been reached.

Approaches to teaching arithmetic and mathematics have varied in the same ways that approaches to teaching reading have. Traditionally, mathematics education emphasized drill and the performance of arithmetic computation. The 1960s saw a swing in the opposite direction, emphasizing a conceptual understanding of mathematical processes, the "new math". In many cases, that emphasis upon mathematical "meaning" failed, partly because many children did not acquire sufficient automaticity in the basic operations, and partly because many of the teachers themselves did not understand what they were supposed to be teaching! By now you should understand how a cognitive psychologist views such disputes: the choice between "basic skill" and "meaning" is a false one. Adequate automaticity is required in basic skills, in order to make more advanced meaningful learning possible, the latter being the ultimate goal of instruction.

Information processing task analyses, such as those that were shown in Chapters 7 and 8 for reading and spelling, can also be produced in mathematics. In fact, the task-analytic approach had its beginnings in the understanding of mathematics skill (e.g., Gagné, Mayor, Garstens & Paradise, 1962). This is because the cognitive processes involved in mathematics are more obvious than they are, say, in reading. In both reading and mathematics the input data (words and numbers) are equally clear, but that is not true with respect to what the learner does with them. As we will see below, when the problem "2 + 7 = ?" is presented, it is quite easy to suggest a model of what cognitive processes are occurring when the student solves it, and even possible to investigate how the *operation* (adding) is performed. As should have been clear in Chapter 7, this is far more difficult to do in reading: for instance, what is the operation performed when the student reads "The cat is up the tree"? We can describe how the words are pronounced, but we are only beginning to be able to speculate about how they are comprehended. The study of mathematics and mathematical learning problems should allow a deeper appreciation of how *operational* factors influence performance.

Arithmetic

What cognitive processes are involved in performing simple arithmetic calculations? Let us begin with a simple example, 3 + 7 = ?. The first actions that the subject must perform are to *encode* the numbers 3 and 7, by which we mean that those visual stimuli on the page must access their representations in long-term memory, and result in representations of them being activated in working memory. This is comparable to the process of *lexical access* described in Chapter 7. Next (or perhaps at the same time) the + sign must be encoded, activating an *operation* or action which is then directed toward the contents of working memory. Then this operation must be executed, and a result obtained. As we will see below, there are several plausible ways in which this execution can take place. Finally, the result obtained in working memory must access its visual-motor representation in long-term memory, resulting in the writing down of the answer. In terms of simultaneous and successive processing, the information *holding* relies upon successive processing, as does the maintenance of one's place in solving the problem. Number encoding, in the recognition of particular patterns (e.g., 2+ 2 = 4), requires simultaneous processing, in that a unitary code is involved. Operation *execution* also requires simultaneous

processing, because a relationship must be constructed between items.

All of these processes should be familiar to you from Chapters 7 and 8, with the exception of the operation activation, and the operation execution. In reading, the comparable processes would include generalizing or making an inference; the nature of reading is such that operations are seldom blatantly indicated on the page, and it is much less easy to see which have been executed and how successfully.

In general, there are two explanations or models of how the operation in simple tasks like 3 + 7 = ? is carried out:

1. The encoded numbers fit a familiar pattern (like a well-known word in reading) to which there is a connected response, "10". In this case rote memory is used, and no real computation. This model is plausible for skilled arithmeticians or for children dealing with single-digit or very familiar problems.

2. The sum is computed by counting on until the desired numbers have been added. This general model is the more appropriate one for beginning arithmeticians, and even for skilled arithmeticians in many cases (Resnick & Ford, 1981). Suppes and Groen (1967) identified three more specific variants of this second model, which are illustrated in Figure 9-1.

(a) A mental "counter" is automatically set to 0, and then incremented by 1s until the first number (3) is reached. Then the counter is again incremented by 1s, until the number of increments indicated by the second number (7) has been reached. By this model the subject would first count to 3, then count on 7 more times, reaching 10. Assuming that counting is a relatively automatic procedure, and that it occurs at a constant rate, the time taken to solve a problem of the form a + b = ? should be a function of the number to which the subject must count – that is, a+ b or in our example, 10. If this model is correct, then the difference between the time taken to add 4 + 2 and the time taken to add 4 + 4 should be the same as the difference between the times for 4 + 4 and 4 + 6 (i.e., each pair is different by two "counts"). Also, there should be no difference between the times taken for 7 + 2 and 2 + 7.

(b) In the second model, instead of starting at 0, the counter is set to the first number, in our example 3. The counter is then incremented by 1s according to the second number, reaching 10. In this case, the time taken is a function only of the second number, so that 1 + 7, 2 + 7,

or 9 + 7 should all take the same amount of time.

(c) The third model is similar, except that the initial counter is set to the larger of the two numbers to be added, after which the smaller number of increments is counted on. This would save a great deal of time, and mean that adding time is a function of only the lesser of the two numbers to be added. Therefore 1 + 7 would be faster than 9 + 7, though 1 + 7 would take the same amount of time as 3 + 1.

FIGURE 9-1
Three models of adding by counting (based upon Suppes and Groen, 1967)

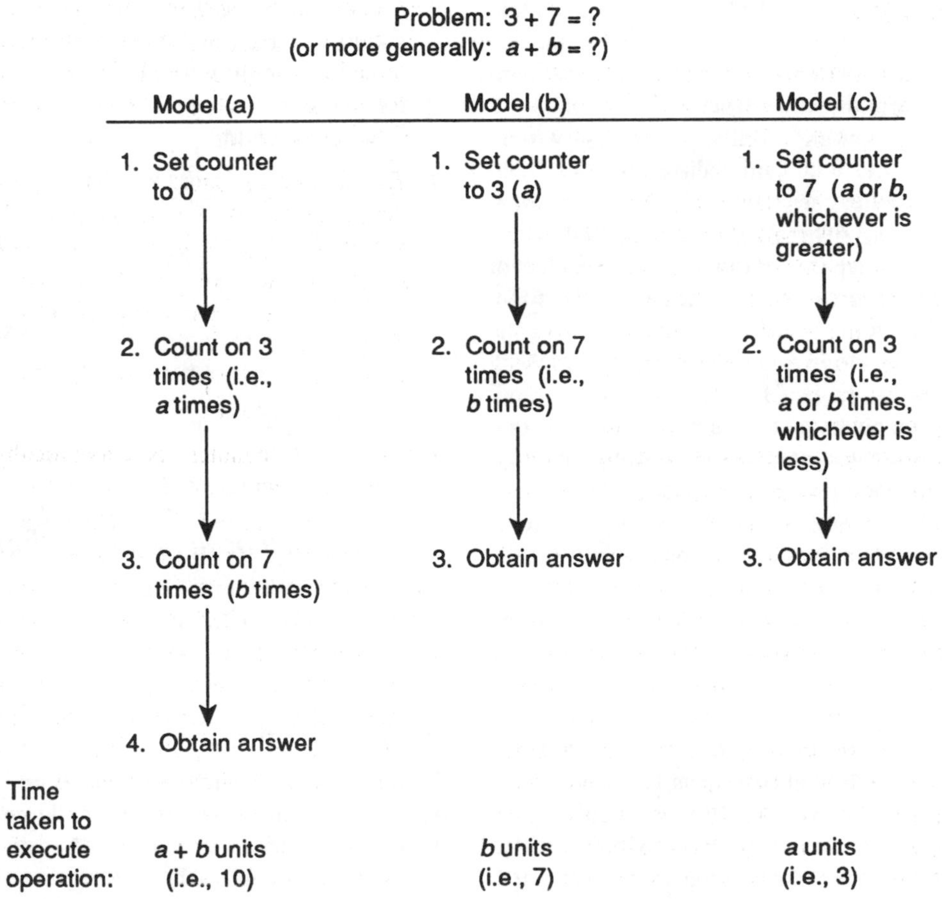

Problem: 3 + 7 = ?
(or more generally: a + b = ?)

Model (a)	Model (b)	Model (c)
1. Set counter to 0	1. Set counter to 3 (*a*)	1. Set counter to 7 (*a* or *b*, whichever is greater)
2. Count on 3 times (i.e., *a* times)	2. Count on 7 times (i.e., *b* times)	2. Count on 3 times (i.e., *a* or *b* times, whichever is less)
3. Count on 7 times (*b* times)	3. Obtain answer	3. Obtain answer
4. Obtain answer		

Time taken to execute operation:	*a* + *b* units (i.e., 10)	*b* units (i.e., 7)	*a* units (i.e., 3)

A series of studies has shown that this third model is the most accurate for describing first graders' addition (e.g., Groen & Parkman, 1972) and stays valid at least until grade 3 (Ashcraft & Fierman, 1982). Groen and Resnick (1977) even showed that many pre-schoolers, taught how to add by the first model, spontaneously shift to the third model within several weeks.

Comparable models have been devised for subtraction. In $a - b = ?$, model *(a)* says the student sets the counter to a, then counts down b times, whereas in model *(b)*, the counter is set to b and the student counts up to a. If b is smaller than the difference $a - b$, then the first approach will be faster. Model *(c)*, of course, says to select whichever approach is faster. Woods, Resnick and Groen (1975) demonstrated that while some second graders use *(a)*, most second graders and all fourth graders adopt approach *(c)*, suggesting that as the children become more experienced in arithmetic, they spontaneously adopt the more efficient approach.

These "computing" skills are necessary only when the answer is not immediately known. Ashcraft and his colleagues (Ashcraft, 1982; Ashcraft & Battaglia, 1978; Ashcraft & Fierman, 1982) have demonstrated that the arithmetic performance of even third graders shows evidence of the more automatic solution, in which the execution of the operation seems to involve something like looking up the result in a table. Clearly, as we become more skilled, we do not have to "count on" to find out that $2 + 2 = 4$. However many skilled adders will count on in a more complex problem, such as $2 + 7 + 3 + 9 + 3 = ?$; furthermore, counting on serves as a foolproof solution to any problem should you forget the "automatic" answer. Developmentally children may well progress through models *2(a), 2(b)* and *2(c),* to model *1* (the most advanced model); they may regress to an earlier model when faced with difficult tasks.

Another way of looking at these early computing strategies is to compare them to sounding-out strategies in early reading. Just as skilled readers may not have to sound out many words, skilled arithmeticians may not have to count on very often. However, just as the phonetic skills provide a fall-back, so do the counting skills. Furthermore, and perhaps most importantly, the early counting skills may provide a sound structural basis for the learning of higher level skills, just as phonetic analysis provides a sound basis for the integration of oral and written language and for the understanding of the structure of written words.

What are the implications of this task-analysis work for children with arithmetic learning problems? There are several, which are only beginning to be explored by researchers. The task analysis presented on pages 108-109 provides a checklist of possible sources of difficulty for such children: number encoding, operation encoding / activation / selection, and operation execution. The last of these can be analyzed in more detail. For example, learning problem children may have begun their arithmetic careers with the wrong strategy; instead of adding by counting on, they may have tried to recall answers only from memory (there is no evidence yet that this causes problems, but it may). Alternatively, children with arithmetic problems may have *begun* like other children with the simplest counting-on strategy, but may have failed to switch to the more flexible strategies that the other children develop relatively quickly. A final alternative is that such children may just be slow at executing arithmetic operations; perhaps this slowness is part of their nature, or perhaps they simply haven't practised executing the operations often enough. The possibilities will be explored in the following section.

Learning Problems in Arithmetic

Before we can begin to decide the *causes* of arithmetic learning problems, it is necessary to see what kind of problems there are.

Types of Errors

There have been a number of studies examining the types of arithmetic errors that children make. In fact, any teacher or parent could repeat these studies; all they require is the construction of a reasonably large number of arithmetic problems of various sorts, careful recording of what children do in each one, and attention to where they make their errors. Lankford (1972; cited by Resnick & Ford, 1981) found that a group of grade seven "good computers" could be distinguished from "poor computers" by the types of strategies they employed in solving problems. In other words, there was often a logic to the errors that the poor computers made: they were not so much making mistakes (e.g., 2 × 4 = 9) but rather following an incorrect procedure or strategy (e.g., 2 × 19: "two times nine equals eighteen, so write down 18; two times one equals two, so write down two; the answer's 218"). Lankford also found that the poor computers knew fewer number facts, such as the multiplication tables, so that they had to reinvent what they should have known (e.g., 4× 5: "well 4 × 4 = 16, so I have to add another 4", which could produce further errors). Overall, Lankford's results could be summarized as follows (based upon Resnick & Ford, 1981):

1. Poor computers more often get the wrong answer by "correctly" following the wrong procedure than by incorrectly following the right procedure.

2. Poor computers' knowledge of number facts is less extensive and less automatic than that of good computers.

3. Good computers are more likely to sense that an answer is incorrect, and go back to correct it.

Several studies agree that the first of these conclusions is true (e.g., Brown & Burton, 1978; De Corte & Verschaffel, 1981). De Corte and Verschaffel's study is noteworthy, because they based much of their argument upon European and Soviet research which is not widely known by researchers in English-speaking countries. They concluded that 78% of the 1633 arithmetic errors that they observed by first and second grade children were errors of "thinking", that is, errors due to selection of an inappropriate strategy or operation. By contrast, only 13% of the errors were due to incorrect execution of the correct operation. Like Lankford's older poor computers, De Corte and Verschaffel's subjects made little effort to verify the correctness of their answers.

Task Analysis Components

Earlier in this chapter (pp. 108-109) we described a task analysis of how a simple arithmetic task would be performed by a student. Kirby and Becker (1988) employed a similar task analysis to compare the performance of normal grade 5 children with those they termed "arithmetically disabled"; the latter children had performed more poorly than the normals on an arithmetic test, and much worse than they had themselves on tests of reading and intelligence. For comparison purposes, Kirby and Becker also had a third group of subjects who were "reading disabled", in that their reading scores were worse than those of the normals, and worse than their own arithmetic and intelligence scores. By the careful construction of a series of reaction time tasks, Kirby and Becker were able to measure how long each of the students took to perform each of the components of the task analysis.

In the most complex task (in which all of the components were involved), subjects were shown equations such as 7 − 2 = 4, and had to say as quickly as possible whether each equation was true or false. The task components that Kirby and Becker hypothesized were: encoding (of the three numerals), selection of operation (deciding to subtract, in this case), operation execution (carrying out the subtraction), and comparison (comparing the computed answer with the given answer, and responding).

Kirby and Becker's results (see Table 9-1) showed clearly that comparison processes did not differentiate the three groups. While encoding times were higher for the arithmetically-disabled, these differences were not statistically significant; it is possible that a larger study might show this difference to be significant, but it is worth noting that the difference (approximately 75 msec, compared with the average of the normal and reading disabled groups) is much lower than the difference in word encoding time between good and poor readers (about 340 msec; Stanovich, 1981).

Selection of operation produced more confusing results. This component was assessed by measuring the difference between the time children took when they knew what the next operation was to be, and

TABLE 9-1

Amount of time (in milliseconds) taken by three groups of children
to perform processes involved in arithmetic tasks
(Adapted from Kirby and Becker, 1988)

	Group		
Process	Arithmetically Disabled	Normal	Reading Disabled
Encoding	333	276	237
Comparison (True)	898	930	895
Comparison (False)	1029	992	1028
Operation Execution (addition)*	1355	924	823
Operation Execution (subtraction)*	2813	1857	1674
Selection of Operation (addition)	473	858	772
Selection of Operation (subtraction)	1160	608	625

* indicates groups are significantly different in this process.

the time taken when the next operation was unknown; presumably selection is involved in the latter, and not in the former. For addition, many of the arithmetically disabled appeared to take as long to answer both types of problems, giving them a selection time that was much *shorter* than that of the normals! For subtraction, their selection times were higher than those of the normals, though not significantly so. For our present purposes, it seems wisest to conclude that Kirby and Becker's results do not demonstrate a real difference in selection times. As this component relates to the strategic or thinking aspects of the task, it is worth remembering that other studies have shown selection of operation to be important (e.g., De Corte & Verschaffel, 1981).

Kirby and Becker's most important results concerned the operation execution component. As Table 9-1 shows, they found arithmetically disabled children much slower than normal or reading disabled children in this component, particularly for subtraction. Keep in mind that these were grade five children who had been doing single digit subtraction problems for four years, that none of the problems involved any number greater than 9, and that incorrect responses were not included in calcu-

lating the component times. These operation execution times are much higher for the arithmetically disabled, and the magnitude of the difference (over a full second for subtraction) is much greater than, say, the difference in word encoding times for good and poor readers.

These results are very interesting, for unlike those of the reading research, they have examined the importance of the operation efficiency factor, the facility with which operations are executed. Kirby and Becker's results are more ambiguous with respect to encoding and selecting; it is possible that other research, using other tasks, will emphasize those factors (as do, for instance, the studies of Lankford, 1972; and De Corte & Verschaffel, 1981).

How should we interpret Kirby and Becker's results? While we know that children with arithmetic learning problems take longer to solve very simple items, and that the component that is taking longer is that involved in the actual execution of the operation, we still do not know *why* the operation execution takes longer. Kirby and Becker's research was not designed to determine *how* the operations were executed (as were the studies of Groen & Parkman, 1972, and others). Therefore we can only presume, following Ashcraft and Fierman (1982), that the normal subjects were solving most of the problems by means of a relatively automatic retrieval process. In some cases, especially with the less automatic subtraction problems, some actual calculations might be necessary, probably by means of the more flexible models described previously (see pp. 108-110). If that is what the competent arithmeticians are doing, what could the arithmetically disabled be doing? It seems likely that the arithmetically disabled do not have automatic access to the basic number facts or that, if they do, they refuse to use them. It appears as if they must, instead, actually perform the calculations (by one of the models described on pp. 108-110). It is further possible that they are not even using the more flexible models, but are engaging in the most time-consuming computational procedures possible.

Only future research will resolve the details of the operation execution explanation. However, for the purposes of remediation, it is clear that substantial work is required with these children to teach them first the faster, more flexible approaches to computation, and second to automate their number fact retrieval skills. There is no reason to be pessimistic about this remedial approach, as there is yet no suggestion that there is anything fundamentally wrong with their information processing systems. However, as operation execution is related to simultaneous processing primarily (see pp. 197-200), it is possible that weaknesses in simultaneous processing could restrict progress in arithmetic (cf., Das, Kirby & Jarman, 1979, pp. 73-78). The possibility of improving simultaneous processing skills will be considered in Chapter 12.

We should not lose sight of the results obtained by Lankford (1972) and De Corte and Verschaffel (1981) regarding subjects' strategies. Those authors and others have argued that one of the characteristics of children with arithmetic learning problems, perhaps the most important, is that they go about solving problems with the wrong procedures. At the most general level, this could be a problem of strategy selection, strategy construction, and performance monitoring. At the level of simple arithmetic tasks, however, it can be seen that these are problems of operation execution, in which the simplest procedures may be carried out correctly, but in which the more complex procedures (e.g., carrying) are not followed correctly. It is very possible that the simple procedures are carried out slowly, inefficiently, and at great working memory cost, interfering with the more complex procedures and, in particular, preventing any performance monitoring (i.e., obvious error checking) from being carried out.

Mathematics

Mathematics and Problem Solving

While it is usual to think of a child as having a learning problem in the area of arithmetic, it is more unusual to think the same thing in the area of mathematics. This should remind you of our discussion in Chapter 7, in which we stated that reading problems are usually thought of at the earlier stages of reading (at letter, sound or word identification levels). Problems at the higher levels of meaning extraction (ideas, main ideas and themes) are not usually considered within the ambit of reading *disabilities* because they may not be specific to reading, and because they may be related to intelligence. Similar arguments are employed with respect to mathematics: a child who can not solve mathematical problems may have a general *thinking* problem not specific to mathematics. Mathematics, in fact, provides more grist for the mill because many so-called tests of intelligence contain problems with either mathematical or spatial content. Yet how can you have a child who is of normal intelligence but performs poorly on questions often included in tests of intelligence?

As we have argued throughout this book, the higher-level thinking and problem solving skills are at least to some degree learned and are, therefore, just as subject to "learning problems". Furthermore, the inclusion of mathematical problems in intelligence tests is merely an artifact of the test construction, and probably based to some degree on the unstated belief that mathematical ability is largely innate. Our point of view is that there is considerable learning involved as well, and that it is a more sensible strategy to assume that these problems too can be overcome, at least until the attempt has been made.

We begin by describing in information processing terms how mathematical problem solving is normally performed, by competent mathematicians such as students who are achieving normally for their age. Then we examine the potential sources of learning problems in mathematics. Before beginning, however, it is necessary to emphasize that much less information processing research has been done in mathematics. As a result, our descriptions are somewhat vague and speculative. They should provide a framework for considering mathematical learning problems, and clarify some directions for future thinking and research in this area.

How Skilled Mathematics Works

The major difference between mathematics problem solving and arithmetic is that in the latter the path toward the solution is obvious. We may not know the answer to $647 + 1032 + 93 = ?$ immediately, but even elementary school children should know exactly how to go about finding it. In problem solving, however, the task is usually set out in such a way that we first have to decide *how* we're going to tackle it. What we have to do is apply rules to the problem as it is set out, in order to transform it into a problem that we do know how to solve immediately. Consider the following:

> John leaves home with $5.00. On the way to school, he buys two 25¢ candy bars. At lunch time, he pays a dollar for a sandwich, and 25¢ for an orange juice. How much money does he have left after that?

When competent high school mathematicians read this problem, they first decide that it requires subtraction, and transform the problem into

$$5.00 - 2 \times .25 - 1.00 - .25 = ?,$$

which they know how to go about solving. Although that seems easy, look back at the actual

wording of the problem and try to list all of the knowledge that one must have to reach that point. Clearly, a lot of knowledge about the world is required (the worth of a dollar or a cent) plus a good deal of reading ability. As problems become more complicated, more background knowledge is required to solve them, and many more intermediate steps are required in order to transform the problem into one (or more) that we know how to solve.

We have represented this problem roughly in Figure 9-2. Having read and comprehended the problem (step 1), the first question is whether the solution procedure is immediately known. If it is, as it should be for simple arithmetic problems (such as $647 + 1032 + 93 = ?$), the solution operations are performed, after which the answer should be checked, to ensure that it answers the question. In Figure 9-2, that process is described as path A. If the solution procedure is not immediately known (as would be the case for an average 10-year-old in the money example above), then the second question is asked: Can a solution *strategy* be seen? In this case, by strategy we mean a general approach to the problem. In the money example above, we would hope that most senior elementary children would realize at this stage that the problem is one requiring representation as an arithmetic statement and subtraction. If a strategy is seen (path B), the next step (box 4 in the model) is to transform the problem accordingly. Once this has been done, the solver goes back to step 2, checks whether the solution procedures are now clear; if they are, path A is followed. If the answer at step 2 is still "no", however, something has gone wrong, and step 3 must be taken again. If this happens, either the strategy adopted is incorrect, or the transformation is incomplete. If the strategy is incorrect, another must be selected (step 3); if the transformation is incomplete, it must be completed (step 4). These transformations result in different *representations* of the problem information (Mayer, 1985).

As long as a strategy can be seen, things proceed reasonably smoothly. If, however, the answer at step 3 is "no", the much more demanding path C must be taken. The skilled problem solver has sev-

FIGURE 9-2
Model for solving mathematics word problems

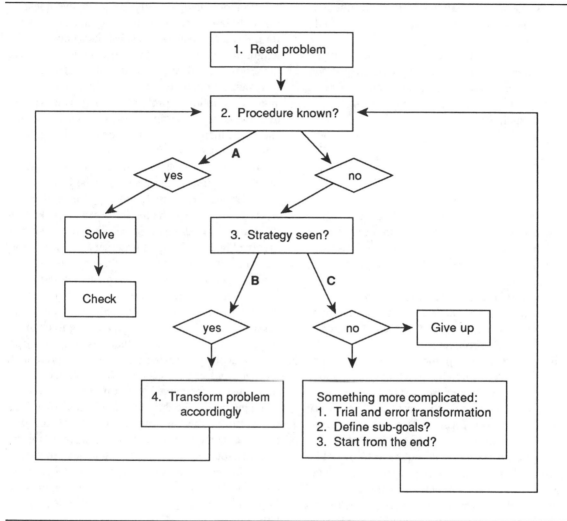

eral back-up path C methods available. One is to engage in some trial-and-error transformation of the problem (or of bits of the problem), in the hope that these will produce a version of the problem (or of part of it) that can be seen to have a clear solution strategy back at step 3. In many problems, this involves listing all the facts given, and all the possible results of combining them. Trial-and-error transformation is not very certain of a positive result, and is properly used only as a method of last resort.

A more hopeful technique is attempting to define sub-goals. One may not be able to see how to get from the given information to the desired result, but it may be possible to see that certain intermediary goals will have to be attained. A simple example of this would be in a geometry problem that asks for the area of a figure all of whose dimensions first had to be calculated. In this case, the individual dimensions are sub-goals, on the way to the final result.

The third technique listed in Figure 9-2 is "working backwards", which can be done only if you know what the answer is, the real question being how you get to it. This is commonly seen in "proof" problems, such as:

Prove that the area of the triangle ABC is one quarter the area of ADE, if AB is equal to BD and BC is parallel to DE.

In this case, rather than listing all the possible true statements derivable from the problem, it should be easier to start with the goal (ABC = ADE/4) and work backwards. (We'll leave you to solve this one!)

The three path C techniques have one thing in common, they reduce the load upon working memory. Normally (in paths A and B) one would have to hold the required problem information and the proposed solution strategy at the same time in working memory, in order to be able to tell that the solution will work. If this procedure exceeds the available working memory space, then path C is necessary. Trial-and-error transforming of problem information does not require the holding of a solution, and even the transformations do not have to be held if they are written down. Selecting a sub-goal reduces the size of the problem and thus the amount of information that has to be held. Working backwards has the advantage of starting with one piece of information, rather than with the massive amount presented in the problem.

A necessary element of path C is the box labelled "Give up". After a certain amount of effort, one has to admit defeat; this amount of effort will vary with the individual, and will depend upon the individual's knowledge and history of success in the area. A characteristic of good problem solvers is that they go through the possible solutions systematically, keeping track of what they've tried and what they haven't, and give up only when all options have been attempted.

Particularly in the case of path C, it is necessary for the problem solver to check at the end that the solution obtained actually answers the question asked. For instance, in using sub-goals it is possible for the student to answer a subsidiary question (the length of the rectangle) and forget to go on to solve the original problem (the area of the rectangle).

As we admitted at the outset, this is a relatively vague description of problem solving. This is partly due to the vague definition of what problems are, and to the many different methods of solving them. Yet even this speculative task analysis gives a reasonable idea of what is involved in mathematical problem solving, and of what could be going wrong in a learning problem. In information processing terms, it is clear that the flexible use and evaluation of strategies is crucial. Successive processing is involved in the holding of necessary problem information, but that can be side-stepped by, for instance, writing down the given and derived information. In more complicated problems (i.e., those with many steps to the solution), successive processing will also be involved in keeping track of the stage of problem solution that has been reached. Simultaneous processing will be very important, in that *relationships* between bits of problem information must be perceived for solutions to be seen. More generally, the decisions made at steps 2 and 3 of Figure 9-2 are based upon the information *pattern* recognized at that point, clearly requiring simultaneous processing. Simultaneous processing is also implicated because many such problems are either explicitly spatial (e.g., in geometry) or implicitly spatial (e.g., when drawing a diagram helps) in nature.

Potential Problems in Problem Solving

By the reasoning of the last section, skilled problem solving requires the following:

1. The necessary world knowledge about the problem content (e.g., dollars, cents).

2. The necessary reading skills to be able to decipher word problems (semantics and syntax).

3. A store of information patterns, and the corresponding operational procedures for obtaining answers (relevant to step 2 in the model), or for transforming information into meaningful representations (step 4).

4. A store of larger and more general information patterns, and the corresponding strategies for selecting operational procedures (relevant to step 3).

5. Sufficient successive processing skill (available working memory space) for keeping track of progress in problem solution.

6. Strategy monitoring and performance evaluation, in order to switch strategies when one has failed and to check that the answer obtained is acceptable.

These skills, in turn, provide a list of possible sources of learning problems in problem solving, in particular in mathematics.

As there is little research that has considered mathematical problem solving from a learning problems perspective, it is not yet possible to indicate which of these skills is the source of mathematical learning problems. Similarly, it is difficult to predict with certainty which skills can be readily improved through remedial instruction. We will consider each of the skill areas in turn.

1. World Knowledge

Given normal intellectual ability, the only impediment to possession of sufficient world knowledge is lack of familiarity through lack of experience. Learning problems caused by lack of world knowledge should be minor in nature – that is, not generalized beyond the area of the specific knowledge deficit (e.g., money). As such, they should be easily detected and corrected by the teacher.

2. Reading Skill

Mathematical word problems contain some of the most complicated syntax and semantics that children encounter in school. Peculiar syntactic constructions such as "If a man had ... and if someone were to ... then how many ... would he have?" are common, clearly presenting a source of potential confusion to many children. Furthermore, relatively odd expressions abound (e.g., "at least as much as", "the greater of the two"), and much specific knowledge must be possessed for problem solving to proceed smoothly. It is undoubtedly true that many children fail at the word problem level, in mathematics and science, because of reading problems, and because they are being asked to read material which far exceeds their reading ability (MacDonald, 1980). As we have seen in Chapter 7, reading problems can be of many kinds, and due to many causes. Refer to that chapter for more on reading problems.

3. Operations and Transformations

In order to solve a problem, the student has to be able to *represent* that problem in a form which contains the relevant information, and in a way which accesses the problem solution. Consider the following example (you may have been tormented with such problems when you were in school):

> The Salmon River flows at 5 km per hour. John has just bought a red motorboat for $5000. In still water, this boat can go 20 km per hour. John travels upriver at the boat's maximum speed; he takes two hours to get to the village. How long will it take him to get back to where he started?

There is too much information there to be able to see a solution immediately; you have to sort through the information that has been presented, decide what is important, and then *re-present* it to yourself. The difficulty is that you have to know something about the problem before you can make the correct decisions. If you are familiar with this type of problem, you may think to yourself, "This is one of those distance-rate-time problems ... usually they give you two of them, and you have to figure out the third ... or something like that." In these distance-rate-time problems, the price of the vehicle, its colour, and the location of the destination are *never* important. So if you reached this point, you might eliminate information, to be left with the following:

Current goes 5 km/hr; boat goes 20 km/hr with no current; trip takes 2 hrs against current; how long with current?

The next step is to represent the problem information so that it can be solved. This process has several parts, some of which have already begun by the time you have decided what kind of problem it is. Some of the problem representation processes are normal reading comprehension processes, which help to identify the problem type. (See skills 1 and 2 above: What does "upriver" mean? How do rivers flow? How do motorboats move?) Others allow you to go from this vague level of representation ("He's going to go slower against the current, and faster with it") to a mathematical representation that connects with a solution ("You need to find the distance he travels ... d= t × r ... We know his upstream rate is 20 minus 5, or 15, and we know his upstream time is 2 hours ..." and so on).

In many ways, this problem representation stage is more difficult than the problem solution stage which follows. Once you have the equations set up (the end of the representation process), all you have to do (usually) is follow simple rules. The art is in setting up the correct equations. Not surprisingly, children with learning problems have difficulty with problem representation, but careful teaching can begin to overcome these difficulties (Hutchinson, 1989).

The student must also be able to recognize information patterns and carry out appropriate transformations. Often this requires only the implementation of an arithmetic operation, such as adding or dividing. Other transformations can be more complicated, such as rotating a shape in a geometry problem, or listing the possible conclusions from given mathematical information. Clearly, these operations and transformations require considerable arithmetic and mathematical knowledge which should be functioning with some degree of automaticity. We have seen in the first half of this chapter that operation execution can be the locus of learning problems in arithmetic, and presumably could be in mathematics too. It would be hoped that a teacher would be able to detect such a pattern in a child's responses (i.e., having difficulties with the arithmetic aspects of mathematics problems) and act accordingly. We have discussed means of overcoming operational problems earlier in this chapter (see p. 113). Difficulties in the more complex types of operations or transformations, such as deriving conclusions from given facts, should be comparable in nature, if not in degree. Some difficulties will be due to the child's not knowing the facts at all (comparable to not knowing how to divide), and others to the child's not knowing the facts well enough (i.e., lack of automaticity). Practice at conclusion generation (e.g., "From the information given, list everything that we can conclude") should be an effective remedial procedure. Further remedial suggestions will be given in Chapter 13.

4. Strategy Recognition and Selection

Both skills 3 and 4 require pattern recognition – that is, the simultaneous processing of input information in order to detect a regularity that is associated in long-term memory with a procedure. As we argued in the first half of this chapter, the recognition of the correct situation for an arithmetic operation is an example of simultaneous processing. The recognition of a general situation as being appropriate for a particular strategy is another example of simultaneous processing, but of a more abstract and more difficult nature. Whereas the arithmetic operation requires recognition that "x+ y" implies that whatever x and y are should be combined or added, strategy recognition involves a pattern which has more than three simple elements. An example of a pattern recognition that is somewhat more complex would be the following:

$$687 + 432 + 117 = 432 + 117 + x$$

The overall pattern must be seen, so that lower-level operations of addition are *not* begun. The more efficient strategy requires recognition of the similarity between left and right sides of the equation, and consequently operations of cancellation.

More complex patterns would be involved, for example in the recognition that a word problem was an "area" problem. Yet more complex pattern recognition would be required in the choice of geometric representations for some elaborate word problems. As the patterns to be recognized become more complex, it is clear that the sub-units of the pattern must be recognized effortlessly (i.e., automatically) if the larger pattern is to be seen. Insufficient automaticity of lower level information will be a major impediment to simultaneous processing at this level. Techniques for improving simultaneous processing will be discussed in Chapter 13.

5. Working Memory Space

Once we go beyond basic arithmetic tasks, most problems require the execution of a series of operations, each of which may depend upon the outcomes of previous steps. We have seen examples of this in previous chapters, such as in spelling (Chapter 8). The plan of action must be held in memory long enough and in enough detail for the problem solver to be able to tell that it will accomplish the desired goal. Then the first operation must be selected and performed, perhaps requiring the execution of sub-operations. Next, the problem solver must return to the correct place in the original plan and proceed. Retention of the plan and one's place in it places a heavy load upon working memory, unless one is familiar with the particular plan. Methods for improving available working memory space (successive processing) will be dealt with in Chapter 12.

6. Strategy Monitoring

In situations in which a strategy is not immediately obvious (path C of Figure 9-2), or in which an incorrect strategy has been selected, some monitoring of success is required, both to know when to stop an ineffective strategy and to know when to stop a strategy that has succeeded (how can you know you've succeeded unless you monitor progress?). The minimum monitoring should occur at the very end, to ensure that the answer obtained appears to answer the question asked. However, more sophisticated monitoring can be very helpful

at earlier stages, particularly if one does not know that the strategy currently being followed is the correct one. This is most often true when trial-and-error processing is occurring.

While strategy monitoring has not been studied with respect to learning problems in complex problem solving tasks, it has been widely studied with respect to learning problems in other tasks, such as reading comprehension. Children who are inexperienced in the task they are performing often fail to monitor their success, sometimes because they do not understand the task well enough to realize what success comprises (as when a child reads without attempting to understand), and sometimes because lower-level information is not well enough automatized to allow higher-level monitoring to occur.

It is likely that comparable difficulties will produce corresponding learning problems in mathematical problem solving. Methods for overcoming strategy problems will be discussed in Chapter 14.

Summary

In this chapter we have presented an outline of how arithmetic and mathematics "work". In many ways this outline has been more vague than we would like, but we hope that it has succeeded in giving you a deeper understanding of these skills, and of how they can fail.

Arithmetic was described as requiring number encoding, operation selection, operation execution, and various comparison and response skills. Obviously, as the nature of the arithmetic problem becomes more elaborate, so would this list of skills. The skills required in mathematics problem solving are more numerous and vague. We listed the following: world knowledge relevant to the problem content; reading skills (because most problems are presented in writing); operating, transforming, and representing skills; strategy recognition and selection; working memory; and strategy monitoring.

We have indicated some sources of learning problems which are well validated by research studies, others which are more speculative. These ideas, together with the diagnostic and remedial suggestions contained in Chapters 11 to 14, should give you a good basis for tackling learning problems in these areas. Perhaps the most important assertion in this chapter is that learning problems in the arithmetic and mathematics areas, particularly those concerned with problem solving, shouldn't be ignored by educators.

RECOMMENDED READING

Resnick, L.B. & Ford, W.W.
1981. *The psychology of mathematics for instruction.* Hillsdale: Lawrence Erlbaum Associates.
    This book covers both arithmetic and problem solving. The task analysis approach to basic arithmetic skills is well described in the first half of the book; the second half concentrates more upon mathematical reasoning.

Carpenter, T.P., Moser, J.M., & Romberg, T.A. (eds.)
1982. *Addition and subtraction: A cognitive perspective.* Hillsdale: Lawrence Erlbaum Associates.

Ginsburg, H.P. (ed.)
1983. *The development of mathematical thinking.* New York: Academic Press.
    See especially the paper by Allardice and Ginsburg, Children's psychological difficulties in mathematics.

You will find many articles on the cognitive processes involved in arithmetic and mathematics in the following journals:

Cognition and Instruction
Educational Studies in Mathematics

CHAPTER 10

The Affective Consequences of Learning Problems

RESEARCHERS IN THE LEARNING disabilities field have traditionally focused their investigations upon the academic problems that children have, and upon the cognitive processes that may be responsible for these problems. Other factors, particularly in the affective domain (social or emotional problems), have been less studied, even though it is common for learning problem children to have such problems (T. Bryan, 1976; J. Bryan, 1981; Pearl, Donahue & Bryan, 1986). Previous researchers may have discounted affective factors because they do not appear in definitions or diagnostic criteria of learning disabilities. Furthermore, as discussed in Chapters 1 and 6, the affective problems may have been considered the primary problems in many cases and, thus, the children labelled "emotionally disturbed" rather than "learning disabled".

While the emphasis of this book is cognitive, we would be amiss if we did not address some of the affective consequences that appear to accompany many "long term" learning problem children. The school provides a setting not just for academic development, but for social and emotional development too. Such a provision is crucial for the psychological well-being of the child. Social experiences affect not only the child's own feelings of competence, but also the perceptions of teachers, fellow students, and parents. Self-perceptions and the perceptions of others can be affected by academic performance, and in turn can affect academic achievement. Children whose *primary* problem is affective are not the concern here. However, it is important to understand the affective consequences of academic or cognitive problems, because those affective consequences may limit the effectiveness of remediation. In our discussion we concentrate on the effects that learning difficulties have on the child, and then look at some of the more pertinent problems that occur both in the classroom and the home.

The Child

How do children with learning problems feel about themselves? Researchers have tried to answer this question, and the following characteristics are representative of current findings. Many learning problem children:

1. lack self-confidence;

2. are poorly motivated;

3. have a negative self-concept;

4. have poor self-perception;

5. often do not understand social cues; and

6. lack task persistence.

121

Such characteristics result from continued academic failure. Seligman (1975) has described this group of symptoms as "learned helplessness". In reviewing the effects of repeated academic failure in children with learning problems, Licht (1983) concurs with Seligman that such failure will lead most likely to the development of a feeling of helplessness. The affective problems of learning problem children can be well understood under the label of learned helplessness.

Learned Helplessness

Learned helplessness results when individuals learn from a repeated number of failure experiences that they have no control over the outcome of events, and come to believe that no amount of effort (internal or external) will bring about an appreciable change.

The theory of learned helplessness was originally developed in the laboratory of Seligman and his colleagues (Seligman & Maier, 1967; Overmeir & Seligman, 1967) as an outcome of their experiments (believe it or not) with dogs. Seligman (1975) extended his findings to include certain human experiences, one of which was academic failure. Like most psychological theories, Seligman's has been investigated by other researchers; and because of their often conflicting results, Seligman (Abramson, Seligman & Teasdale, 1978) reformulated his hypothesis, and now bases his theory on the attribution theory of Weiner (1974). Weiner's theory used the concepts of causality (internal-external) and stability (stable-unstable) to which Seligman added the concept of globality (specific-global). Causality refers to whether the outcome is caused from within (internal) or outside (external) an individual; stability refers to whether the causal factor is long-lived or short-lived; and globality to whether the outcomes do or do not lead to generalized expectations.

How does this model apply to learning problem children? Consider children with poor mathematical computational skills. When they fail to solve basic arithmetic problems they could attribute their failure to (1) lack of ability (an internal stable factor), or (2) lack of effort (an internal unstable factor). They could also attribute it to a variety of external causes. According to Seligman, however, if failure is attributed to internal, stable factors such as lack of ability, the concept of globality should be included. Thus, if children feel that they have failed because they are stupid (internal-stable-global cause), the situation will be generalized. That is, they will develop an expectancy of failure which in turn will, in all likelihood, be accompanied by feelings of hopelessness and eventual withdrawal from future academic problems. Seligman argues further that the feeling of inadequacy may generalize to all situations in the classroom (particularly if more than one failure has been experienced), building up a feeling of total inadequacy and helplessness.

Consider now Figure 10-1, a schematic representation of how learned helplessness may develop in children with learning problems. (This figure expands the box labelled "Secondary Affective Problems" in Figure 5-5.) The child first experiences failure at school in an academic area. As a consequence of this failure, the child receives negative feedback from both the school and home. The teacher complains about poor work, possibly being sarcastic, while at home parents exert pressure to improve. With these pressures and repeated failure, the child develops doubts about his or her capabilities to succeed in the classroom. At this point, the child becomes frustrated and develops a sense of shame. Negative feelings concerning self-worth are internalized, and efforts to achieve decline. With this reduced effort, failure increases and negative self-feelings become strengthened. Whereas the initial failure might have been in a specific subject area, e.g., reading, other school-related activities become interpreted in the same way. The child loses all initiative to succeed and has, to all intents and purposes, become helpless – a condition that has been learned.

What experimental support is there to show learned helplessness as being characteristic of learning problem children? Several researchers have recently reviewed the literature (Thomas, 1979; Canino, 1981, and Licht, 1983) and found considerable support. Typical of the research in this

FIGURE 10-1

Schematic representation of the development of learned helplessness in children with learning problems

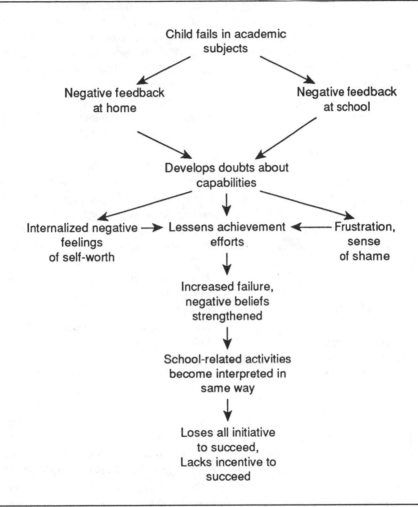

area is the study conducted by Palmer, Drummond, Tollison and Zingraff (1982). Attributions (i.e., explanations of outcomes), expectancies, affective reactions, and persistence were studied in normal and learning problem children. The subjects were randomly assigned to one of three groups: a completion condition (the subjects were given sufficient time to complete three coding tasks); a noncompletion condition (the subjects were given insufficient time to complete three coding tasks); or a control condition (the subjects were given no coding task). Results showed that attribution differences between the groups depended on whether they did or did not complete their tasks. While both the learning problem and normal subjects considered ability an important factor in determining success, the learning problem group considered their general lack of ability to perform tasks as more significant in determining failure than did the normal group. Learning problem children were also less persistent. Furthermore, the teachers considered the performance of the learning problem children to result from learned helplessness. The teachers rated the learning problem children as showing less persistence and "response initiative" on both non-academic and academic tasks than normal children. (For a more detailed analysis of the research in this area, see the above-mentioned review articles.)

We have discussed the way in which learning problems can affect the child. The next question is, how are learning problem children perceived by the people who are in daily contact with them, namely their teachers, peers, and family members? Let's consider the school situation first.

The School Situation

The social-emotional development that occurs in school is a result of the interaction among the children, their peers and teachers. At times, this interaction is disrupted because a child is considered "different." Unless the child is accepted socially, interaction is limited. This can be the case for children with learning problems.

Numerous studies have investigated the social consequences for learning problem children in the classroom. These studies have considered variables such as teacher attitude, teacher interaction, special classes vs. regular classes, age, sex and social class to name just a few. It is not our intention to discuss all of these variables: at the end of the chapter you will find a list of suggested readings for more information on them. In this chapter, we will consider the teacher-child and peer-child relationships.

Teacher-Child Relationships

Teaching children in a regular classroom is a challenging job at best, but the extra demands that are placed on teachers of children with learning problems can have negative effects on teacher-child interaction. Just what kind of relationships exist between teachers and learning problem children? One aspect of the relationship that has been explored is the effect of teacher attitude.

Myklebust, Boshes, Olsen and Cole (1969) studied teachers' ratings of academic achievement and behaviour in learning problem children. Learning problem children were judged less competent in motor ability (general coordination), auditory comprehension (vocabulary, sentence length) and orientation (time concepts). The finding that should be emphasized here, however, concerns the rating of behaviour. Teachers considered learning problem children to be less attentive, less able to organize themselves, less able to complete assignments, less cooperative, less able to cope with new situations, less accepting of responsibility, less accepting of others and less tactful than other children. Bryan and McGrady (1972) used the same rating scales and found much the same results: from the behavioural viewpoint, learning problem children were considered less desirable in the classroom by their teachers.

Following the same line of investigation, Keogh, Tchir and Windeguth-Behn (1974) obtained teachers' views of learning problem children. Some of the behaviours ascribed to learning problem children were aggressiveness (cruel, violent, destructive – 66% of the teachers), hyperactivity (63%), short attention span (44%), withdrawn (44%), no sense of responsibility (44%), and poor interpersonal relationships (41%). While many of these teacher attitudes may be based in fact (and many may not), what is important is that these attitudes must affect teachers in their dealings with learning problem children.

In terms of teacher-child interaction, research suggests that children with learning problems have more interaction with teachers, including both positive and negative interaction. For example, Bryan (1974a) found that over 50% of teacher interactions with learning problem children concerned academic issues, while for normal children only one-quarter of the relations were academic in nature.

Bryan also found that the interactions between teachers and learning problem children involved more punishments than those between teachers and normal children. It has also been shown that in regular classrooms the interactions with learning problem children are usually negative, though they are more positive in small groups and in the resource room (Forness & Estvellt, 1975).

These conclusions were supported in a recent study by Siperstein and Goding (1985). They observed teachers' interactions with learning problem children and non-learning problem children, and found that teachers initiated more interactions with learning problem children, corrected them more often, and used more negative verbal and nonverbal behaviour with them. Siperstein and Goding went one step further: they provided the teachers with feedback regarding their interaction patterns. Following feedback, teachers maintained their number of interactions, but the negative tone of these interactions was reduced. Both students and teachers may benefit from the monitoring of teachers' behaviour in the classroom if that monitoring is used to provide constructive feedback to teachers.

Teacher expectancies have also been investigated. Several researchers have found that learning problem children were expected to do poorly academically and, in some cases, these expectancies persisted despite dramatic improvement by the children (Foster, Schmidt & Sabatino, 1976).

One aspect of teacher-child relationships that has not been investigated to any great degree is the feelings that teachers develop regarding *their* self-worth while working with children whose improvement is limited. Because most teachers are achievement oriented, or at least committed to improving children's skills, they might well become frustrated when children have difficulty succeeding in their classes. How teachers cope with this situation has not really been investigated. One might speculate that some teachers become angry and frustrated and take their frustrations out on the children. Some teachers might feel guilty about their own inadequacies in teaching children with learning problems, and develop an attitude of learned helplessness about teaching them. This is an area that warrants further investigation!

Peer-Child Relationships

What relationship exists between learning problem children and their peers? Several studies have considered this question, and the general indication is that the relationship is a poor one. Many of these studies have used sociometric measures, in which children are asked to nominate which other children in the class they'd like to sit beside, work with, and so on.

Bryan (1974b, 1976) investigated peer relationships in third, fourth and fifth grade classes in which learning problem children had been mainstreamed. Results showed that learning problem children received significantly higher scores on the social rejection scale and significantly lower scores on the social attraction scale than their peers. An interesting feature of this investigation was that twenty-five of the learning problem children were included in both the 1974b and 1976 studies; they received rejection votes in each, suggesting that their popularity had not improved over time.

A study by Siperstein, Bopp and Bak (1977) also shows that learning problem children are likely to be rejected by their peers. Siperstein *et al.* studied fifth and sixth grade children on such ratings as physical appearance, athletic ability and academic achievement. Learning problem children were found to be less popular than their peers, particularly when students were asked to name peers who were the best looking, most athletic and liked best.

Some researchers have been more specific in defining their learning problem population. Wiener (1980), for example, wondered whether a specific type of learning problem would be more acceptable to the peer group than other types of learning problems. Wiener found that children with sequential problems (that is, problems in sequencing or visual / auditory memory – successive processing in our terms) had less difficulty acquiring positive peer relationships than children with spatial and conceptual problems (e.g., poor body image, poor verbal expression ability – simultaneous processing in our terms). A further finding was that the more extreme the learning problem, the more negative the peer relationship. Pelham and Milich (1984) reviewed the literature on peer relations in hyperactive children (defining hyperactivity in a loose way), and concluded that hyperactive children, particularly those who are also aggressive, have extremely poor peer relations.

The Family Situation

A good place to start this section is to draw your attention to the work of Wender (1971). Wender, a child psychiatrist, based his findings on clinical reports and not on well-documented research studies. His opinions were based on interviews with parents, many of whom probably needed help desperately; as a result, their views may have been extreme. According to Wender, parents of children with learning problems describe their children as stubborn, obstinate, bossy, fidgety, difficult to discipline and defiant of adults. Is there support for such descriptions? Let us examine some studies that have investigated attitudes of parents with learning problem children.

Owen, Adams, Forrest, Stolz and Fisher (1971) interviewed parents of children with and without learning problems, to elicit their feelings about their children. The parents were matched on age of child, age of siblings, social class and race. Parents of learning problem children described them as having poor verbal ability (i.e., they had difficulty expressing themselves, they did not listen and were difficult to talk to) and as having more difficulty in controlling their impulses. They also reported that these children showed more anxiety than their siblings. In another study, Strag (1972) interviewed parents of learning problem, mentally retarded and normal children, and asked them to rate their children on questions pertaining to behavioural and emotional problems and neurological impairment. The learning problem children were rated as showing less consideration for others, being less able to receive affection, and demonstrating more clingingness than normal children. They were different from the mentally retarded, being characterized as

less stubborn, more jealous and clinging, and less able to receive affection.

Other researchers have lately continued with this line of research. Chapman and Boersma (1979) compared the attitudes of mothers of children with and without learning problems. They found that the mothers of learning problem children in the third to sixth grade were more negative about the efforts of their children in school-related tasks. These mothers also considered the efforts of their children to be considerably poorer than those of other children in the family. Similarly, Pearl and Bryan (1982) found that the mothers of learning problem children viewed their children's success less positively and their failures more negatively. Furthermore, they attributed any success by their children to luck, and failure to lack of ability. (In other words, they had developed a source of learned helplessness for their children, just in case these children didn't have one themselves!)

Do parents' perceptions of their learning problem children change over time? McLaughlin, Clark, Mauck and Petrosko (1987) compared eighty learning problem adolescents and their parents, using a questionnaire that focused upon the extent of the learning problems, current levels of performance in the social and academic domains, social relationships, problem solving skills, and subsequent occupational status. While parents and children agreed that cognitive, academic and social problems persisted into adolescence, parents were more concerned about the consequences that would follow their children into adulthood. Parents did not expect their learning problem children to enter postsecondary institutions, and were subsequently dissatisfied with the type of jobs their children had. McLaughlin *et al.* concluded that more effort should be devoted to working with parents, to help them develop more positive attitudes towards their children.

Implications for the Classroom

We are not suggesting in this chapter that learning problems can be overcome by intervening in the affective domain: no matter how happy children feel about themselves, if they can't read they still have a learning problem. However, unless intervention takes account of their affective problems and tries to understand how they feel, much remedial effort will be wasted.

In some cases it may be useful to attack affective problems directly, in the context of addressing the child's cognitive problems (see the recommended readings for a list of affective intervention techniques). An awareness of affective problems should, at least, provide a basis for setting the emotional atmosphere surrounding intervention, thus assisting the child to overcome feelings of inadequacy and contributing to his or her well-being both within and outside the classroom.

Specific suggestions, to be used in conjunction with the cognitive techniques described in the following chapters, are to:

1. Reduce failure to a minimum. (Move in small steps to ensure that the child is "with you".)

2. Provide a supportive environment in the classroom. This may be accomplished by stressing the importance of effort, and by demonstrating the positive effects of increased effort by the child.

3. Provide encouragement for feelings of competence and control. Place emphasis on the strengths that the children possess, and utilize them to their maximum. Increase feelings of self-control by structuring lessons to allow the children, where possible, to make their own choices in choosing activities.

Summary

The purpose of this chapter has been to describe briefly the affective consequences for children with learning problems. We have seen that repeated failure in the classroom contributes to a negative feeling of self-worth in children that can lead, in turn, to feelings of helplessness. The child with learning problems also experiences poor interpersonal relationships both in the school and home. These children require not only intervention on the academic level but also consideration in regard to the problems in the social / affective domain.

RECOMMENDED READING

Learning Disability Quarterly, 1982, *5,* 334-446.
This issue of the journal is entirely devoted to affective development in children with learning problems. Topics range from affective influences and assessment of affective problems to the training and improvement of affective development in learning problem children.

Schumaker, J.B. & Hazel, S.J.
1984. Social skills assessment and training for the learning disabled: Who's on first and what's on second? Parts I & II. *Journal of Learning Disabilities, 17* (7) 422-431; (8), 492-499.
This two-part review article discusses the long-term effects of learning problems on social development. Both assessment and treatment of social problems are discussed.

Gresham, F.M.
1988. Social competence and motivational characteristics of learning disabled students. In M. Wang, M. Reynolds and H. Walberg (eds.). *The handbook of special education. Research and practice.* Elsmford, New York: Pergamon Press.

PART THREE

Diagnosis and Remediation of Learning Problems

CHAPTER 11

Attention and Arousal

IN THIS CHAPTER we discuss the nature of attention and arousal. We describe how the attention and arousal system (or, more simply, the attention system) normally works, how it can produce learning problems, and how these problems can be overcome.

Before we begin, however, it is important to review what aspects of attention are included in this system, and to describe the connections between attention and arousal. Attention can be a confusing term, because it can refer to relatively automatic processes (which are the topic of this chapter), and can also refer to much more conscious and effortful processes (which are a function of what we call planning, which is dealt with in Chapter 14). Remember: the attention system concerns lower-level or automatic attention.

The attention system includes both attention and arousal. Whereas attention is a cognitive process, arousal is not; yet arousal is the factor that drives the attention system. The ways in which arousal affects attention and other processing are an important focus of this chapter.

As you will see, one of the most common descriptions of children with arousal or attention problems is "hyperactive"; this is an old term, derived from the tendency of some children to engage in excessive motor activity. The modern term is "attention deficit hyperactive disorder"

(American Psychiatric Association, 1987), which emphasizes the central role of attention problems. We spend much of this chapter discussing this type of problem; we also deal with two other manifestations of attention / arousal problems, hypoactivity and test anxiety.

A word of warning, which we will give at the beginning of each of the chapters in this section: learning problems are complex, and seldom appear in a pure form. Even though a child's problem may *stem* from an attention or arousal problem, it may spread through the child's cognitive systems to produce what appears to be a general and widely based problem. Look back at Figure 5-5 in Chapter 5. The purpose of this figure is to emphasize that problems can begin in many places, but have effects upon virtually all others. We emphasized this in Chapter 6 too: children whose attention problems are secondary in nature – that is, are caused by problems in other components – may behave similarly to children with *primary* attention system problems. Clearly, these are different types of children and ideally remediation should (probably) differ according to the primary nature of the learning problems. However, there is still dispute among researchers about how attention problems are caused, whether different types can be identified, and how these problems may be overcome. Bear with us as we try to unravel some of the intricacies of attention in psychology, and some of the mysterious ways in which attention and arousal have appeared in studies of learning problem children.

The Nature of Attention and Arousal

It is rare for arousal to appear in theories of cognition, perhaps because it is hardly a *cognitive* process. Unlike cognitive or thinking processes like memory and strategies, arousal is a more primitive, almost emotional factor in human functioning. Yet arousal has profound effects upon attention, which is very much a cognitive process. Therefore, we concentrate here primarily upon arousal and its effects upon attention.

The concept of arousal has origins in psychology and in physiology that are consistent with each other; furthermore, you should find that arousal means roughly what you think it means. Arousal has been defined as "energy mobilization" (Cannon, 1915) and as the "degree of excitement" (Duffy, 1934); basically, it describes a dimension which ranges from near-death comatose inactivity, through drowsiness, to increasing alertness and attentiveness, to excitement, distractibility, emotional disturbance, and disorganized high anxiety! Two points can be emphasized about this dimension. The first is that in describing it we have brought in other concepts which are intimately related to arousal, for instance activity level, attention, and distractibility. The second point is that both ends of the dimension, drowsiness and emotional disturbance, can have equally fatal effects upon performance.

The Inverted U Curve

Hebb (1955) described this relationship between arousal level and performance as an inverted U relationship: at both ends performance is low, whereas in the middle it is quite high. The relationship is illustrated in Figure 11-1. As you can see, the middle area of the curve defines the *optimal* level of arousal; movement in either direction will tend to disrupt behaviour.

FIGURE 11-1

The inverted U curve, showing the relationship between behavioural efficiency and arousal level

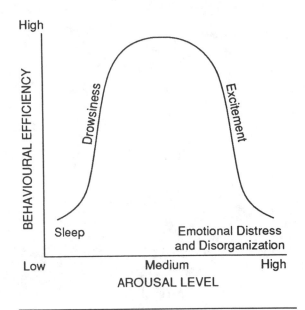

Task Differences

Unfortunately, our responses to the world are more complex than Figure 11-1 suggests; this complexity is partly due to different types of tasks, and partly to different types of people. Let's consider tasks first. Tasks that are very intricate or complicated have a *lower optimal arousal level* than tasks which are more simple (this rule, illustrated in Figure 11-2, is often called the Yerkes-Dodson Law, after the two people who first proposed it; Yerkes & Dodson, 1908). Take, for example, some of the different tasks performed by the members of a football team. The task of some of the defensive linemen is quite simple: use brute strength and basic skills to tackle the ball carrier. A high arousal level is quite appropriate for such tasks, and may even be necessary. The quarterback, on the other hand, has a much more complex task: he must read defences, plan plays, and respond to very subtle changes as a play begins. A high arousal level in a quarterback may

F I G U R E   1 1 - 2
The effect of arousal levels upon tasks of two different levels of complexity (the Yerkes-Dodson Law)

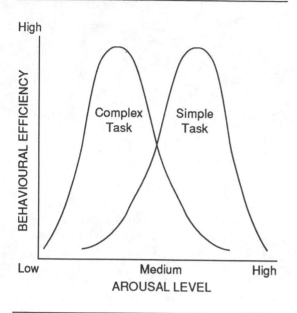

lower levels. High arousal seems to act upon working memory: as the optimal level is passed, less information can be held active at the same time. Since complex tasks require more information to be active, they suffer from too high a level of arousal. Arousal that is too low, however, can also cause problems: it appears that some degree of arousal is needed to "energize" behaviour; once arousal falls below that level, plans or responses cannot be executed efficiently.

One of the most frequently mentioned instances in which arousal affects performance is test anxiety. We're sure you know many students (you may even be one yourself) who have gone into an exam and just gone "blank": even though they knew the material well an hour before, they can now remember nothing! Unfortunately many examining practices encourage high anxiety, even though high arousal is certain to be contrary to the high level of thinking required by most exams.

Person Differences

The second factor which complicates the inverted U curve is that people differ in their *preferred* levels of arousal and also in their *optimal* levels of arousal. (What still isn't clear is whether people who prefer high arousal necessarily perform best under high arousal.) You must know some people who love pressure and claim they do well under it, and other people who hate stress or pressure and seem to fall apart when it hits them.

Eysenck (1967) has proposed that two important personality dimensions are (a) the normal level of arousal at which a person works, and (b) the quickness with which a person's arousal level can change. Dimension (a) is the resting level of arousal. Eysenck refers to persons with high resting levels of arousal as *introverts:* they are already highly aroused, and therefore do not require additional stimulation; in fact, additional pressure may "send them off the deep end" to the right in Figure 11-1. People with low resting levels of arousal are called *extroverts:* they crave additional stimulation to push them from the left-hand side of Figure 11-1 towards the middle.

produce tremendous enthusiasm and spirit, but is unlikely to produce well-organized planning. The quarterback's more complex task has a lower optimal arousal level. (Before you football players start complaining, let us admit that this is a simplification: modern professional linemen need to employ rather complicated skills and tactics, so the old high arousal levels may not be as appropriate today as they once were. Also, complex skills can be practised to the point that they no longer take up much working memory space, and are thus no longer disrupted by slightly higher levels of arousal. But you get the idea: simple tasks – high arousal; complex tasks – low arousal.)

The same holds true for academic tasks: simple tasks, such as copying words or adding single digit numbers, can stand a higher level of arousal, whereas more complex tasks, such as comprehending a difficult passage or problem-solving, require

To understand how a person will respond to increased stimulation, you also have to keep the rate of change dimension in mind. Eysenck terms this the "neuroticism – stability" dimension. Neurotics change arousal levels quickly whereas stable individuals do so more slowly and less drastically. (Beware: the definition of neurotic may be different from the one you normally use.) Thus, stable extroverts may be able to handle the extra stimulation they desire, whereas neurotic extroverts should have considerably more difficulty handling the extra arousal they seek.

Whether or not Eysenck's theory is correct or complete, the points to remember are that people will differ in the amount of arousal they seek, and in the level of arousal at which they perform best. Taken in conjunction with considerations of task differences, this point confirms that Figure 11-1 is a simplification. The figure makes an important point, but you should not forget that there will be individual and task differences.

The Mechanism of Arousal

So far we have been discussing arousal as a psychological construct; we hope this view hasn't been too different from the way in which you would have thought about arousal. As a relatively primitive process, however, arousal has been studied physiologically, and a great deal is now known about how the arousal system of the brain works. We present here an overview of the physiology of arousal to provide you with a general indication of what is known. This is particularly important with regard to learning problems in attention, because there is evidence that *some* of these problems are due to physiological weaknesses in arousal. At the same time, our goal is not to make you into a neurophysiologist or to suggest how you might overcome physiologically based learning problems.

The seat of arousal in the brain is the *reticular formation,* which is located at the base of the brain, in the brain stem (see Figure 11-3), and which is part of the attention system described in Chapter 5. This structure was first described by Moruzzi and Magoun in 1949. It is said to be reticular because a

FIGURE 11-3
The reticular formation in the brain (The brain is facing towards the right, and the right half of it has been removed to show the centre.)

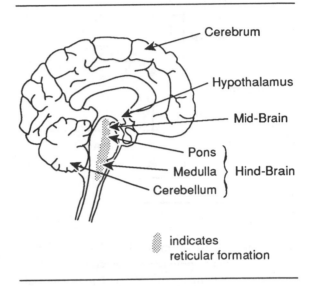

F I G U R E   1 1 - 3
The reticular formation in the brain (The brain is facing towards the right, and the right half of it has been removed to show the centre.)

Cerebrum
Hypothalamus
Mid-Brain
Pons ⎫
Medulla ⎬ Hind-Brain
Cerebellum ⎭

⦙ indicates reticular formation

microscopic examination of its tissue shows that it consists of a diffuse aggregation of cells forming a dense network (*reticulum* means network). It is also called the *reticular activating system* (RAS) because it is responsible for maintaining the activation level of the brain and consciousness. Electrical stimulation of a normal RAS can bring a human being or animal out of a state of sleep, but damage to the RAS can produce a state of coma. (The actual effect of damage or stimulation depends upon their exact location in the RAS, Lindsley, 1960.)

Three types of stimuli, each with a different source, can affect arousal levels (Golden & Anderson, 1979). The first source is within the body itself, from metabolic processes – for example, when a person is hungry or thirsty. The second source is the environment, for instance, when a loud noise makes you alert or when a lecturer with a monotonous voice sends you to sleep. In contrast to these two "input" factors, the third source is the higher centres of the brain (the processing and planning systems, especially the latter). Thus, for example,

Relations among input and the attention/arousal, processing and planning systems

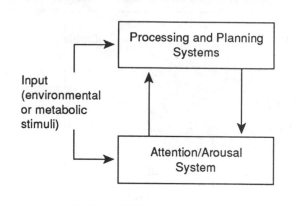

the planning system may alert the attention / arousal system to a potentially dangerous situation, or "reassure" it that some recent environmental event is not cause for alarm. The effects of activating the attention / arousal system are to ready the cortex (processing and planning systems) and the rest of the body for action. The relationships among this system and the higher centres are illustrated schematically in Figure 11-4. For more on the physiological nature of arousal, consult the recommended readings given at the end of this chapter.

Learning Problems in Attention

The attention system is basically nonspecific in nature, so problems in it tend to spread throughout most cognitive-achievement processes (refer back to Figure 5-5). Therefore, attention-based learning problems are likely to be seen in general classroom behaviour, without being restricted to any particular achievement area. This is most true of what could be termed *primary* attention problems, in which the attention system itself is at fault. Atten-

tion problems can also be generated as a *secondary* effect, the result of lack of knowledge or strategies either generally or in a specific achievement area. While such an attention problem could be confined to a single achievement area, it is still likely to generalize to others. It is also possible to see *tertiary* attention problems, which are caused by broadly based academic failures or even emotional disturbances (see Table 11-1).

Research concerning learning problems in attention / arousal has been dominated by two problems, attention deficit and test anxiety, both of which would normally be seen as instances of over-arousal (but read on: some theories argue that attention deficit is due to *under-arousal!*). Accordingly, these two problems dominate Table 11.1. We include also a more speculative problem, hypoactivity, which would normally be seen as an instance of under-arousal (same caution as above).

Hyperactivity

Let us begin by considering the case study on page 137. This study would remind most teachers of many children they've dealt with in the early elementary grades.

Peter's behaviours (inattentiveness, overactivity, distractibility, impulsiveness, aggressiveness, poor peer relationships, etc.) are characteristic of many children who have been rather loosely labelled hyperactive. All of these symptoms are not necessarily present in every hyperactive child, but many are, much of the time. In fact, the looseness of this collection of symptoms has contributed to the theoretical confusion on which we commented in Chapters 2 and 3. Some researchers think that hyperactivity causes attention and social problems, others that attention problems are the cause of the hyperactivity and social problems, while still others believe that hyperactivity and attention problems are separate disorders which happen to co-occur in some children. Some authors even suggest that hyperactivity and attention problems are characteristic of all or most learning disabled children (Ross, 1976).

TABLE 11-1
Learning problems ascribed to arousal

Problem	Learning Problem Symptoms	Causal Description
Attention Deficit	Excessive movement; impulsivity; distractibility; short attention span	Defect in or incomplete development of attention system (primary)
	Aggressiveness; social immaturity; poor peer relationships	Lack of task-appropriate knowledge or strategies (secondary)
		General failure or emotional disturbance (tertiary)
Test Anxiety	Fear and avoidance of tests and test-like situations	Personality bias towards anxiety (primary)
	"Going blank" in test situations	Lack of automatic (overlearned) knowledge and strategies (secondary)
		History of failure in tests (tertiary)
Hypoactivity	Failure to attend to novel stimuli; over-exclusive attention; self-stimulation	Defect in or incomplete development of arousal system (primary)
	Social isolation; withdrawn behaviour in inappropriate situations	Lack of task-appropriate knowledge and strategies (secondary)
		General failure or emotional disturbance (tertiary)

The American Psychiatric Association attempted to resolve this confusion by introducing the term "Attention Deficit Disorder" (ADD) in the third edition of their Diagnostic and Statistical Manual (DSM-III) in 1980, and more recently the term "Attention Deficit Hyperactive Disorder" (ADHD) in the revision of the third edition (DSM-III-R, 1987). The diagnostic criteria for ADHD are shown in Table 11-2. For the ADHD diagnosis to be made, eight of the fourteen behavioural symptoms must be present; thus, combinations of behaviours are allowed for. The behaviours must occur much more frequently than would be expected normally for children of the same mental age, must have been present before the age of seven, and should not be the result of a "Pervasive Development Disorder"

(such as mental retardation or childhood schizophrenia).

Like all definitions, ADHD is not without its critics (e.g., Lahey, Schaughency, Hynd, Carlson & Nieves, 1987). Its value in diagnosis and treatment has yet to be established, but it is a valuable attempt to add some precision to a confusing area. The vagueness that remains may not be an inadequacy, but may rather reflect the vague nature of the diagnostic category being observed. In the remainder of this book, we use the term "attention deficit" to refer to ADHD. We use this term when referring to older research too, even though the original authors used the term "hyperactivity".

Definitions like DSM-III-R are clearly attempting to address what we have termed primary

TABLE 11-2
Diagnostic criteria for Attention Deficit Hyperactive Disorder

Consider a criterion met only if the behaviour is considerably more frequent than that of most people of the same mental age.

A.   A disturbance of at least six months during which at least eight of the following are present:

1. Often fidgets with hands or feet, or squirms in seat (in adolescents, may be limited to subjective feelings of restlessness).
2. Has difficulty remaining seated when required to do so.
3. Is easily distracted by extraneous stimuli.
4. Has difficulty awaiting turn in games or group situations.
5. Often blurts out answers to questions before they have been completed.
6. Has difficulty following through on instructions from others (not due to oppositional behaviour or failure of comprehension), e.g., fails to finish chores.
7. Has difficulty sustaining attention in tasks or play activities.
8. Often shifts from one uncompleted activity to another.
9. Has difficulty playing quietly.
10. Often talks excessively.
11. Often interrupts or intrudes on others, e.g., butts into other children's games.
12. Often does not seem to listen to what is being said to him or her.
13. Often loses things necessary for tasks or activities at school or at home (e.g., toys, pencils, books, assignments).
14. Often engages in physically dangerous activities without considering possible consequences (not for the purpose of thrill-seeking), e.g., runs into street without looking.

Note: The above items are listed in descending order of discriminating power based on data from a national field trial of the DSM-111-R criteria for Disruptive Behaviour Disorders.

B.   Onset before the age of seven.
C.   Does not meet the criteria for a Pervasive Development Disorder.

Criteria for severity of Attention Deficit Hyperactive Disorder

Mild   Few, if any, symptoms in excess of those required to make the diagnosis *and* only minimal or no impairment in school and social functioning.
Moderate Symptoms or functional impairment intermediate between "mild" and "severe".
Severe   Many symptoms in excess of those required to make the diagnosis *and* significant and pervasive impairment in functioning at home and school and with peers.

Attention Deficit Hyperactive Disorder: A Case Study

Peter was the second of three children, having an older brother and a younger sister.

School Situation

Half-way through second grade, Peter was referred for a psycho-educational assessment by his teacher because of his poor academic performance and the constant display of disruptive behaviour in the classroom. Throughout grade 1 and part of grade 2, Peter was observed to be constantly "on the go" and easily distracted. Rarely was he seen to sit down and complete tasks that were required of him – he had difficulty concentrating. He was frequently out of his seat, which disturbed the other class members; his overactivity lacked purpose. When he was sitting down he was constantly fidgeting. His teacher noticed that when he was asked a question or required to solve a problem he responded very quickly and usually gave the wrong answer. He would often call out in class. His relationship with his peers was very poor and he often threw temper tantrums when he did not have his own way. He did not have any friends. In the gymnasium he did not do well either – he was slightly uncoordinated, as evidenced by his clumsiness in various physical activities.

Peter's reading level was way behind and he had great difficulty with the alphabet. His memory for numbers was poor. His teacher described him as poorly organized. His performance on the WISC-R (Weschler Intelligence Scale for Children, Revised) revealed a verbal IQ of 85 and a performance IQ of 102.

Home Situation

Peter's parents reported that he was constantly on the move at home. They claimed that they often felt worn out at the end of the day, particularly if it was a weekend. He had difficulty sharing with his siblings and had frequent arguments with them.

Developmental Milestones

These appeared to be normal, although his parents felt that he was just that little bit slower in developing speech than his brother or sister.

Medical History

There were no labour or delivery problems or any serious health problems. His parents reported that he had difficulty with sleep over the first two years and appeared to cry a lot during the first year.

attention problems – that is, problems which are in some sense inherent to the attention system itself and not a response to some type of experience. Even if the problem becomes apparent before the child starts school, of course, it is still not clear that it is not due to some other environmental factor, such as lead poisoning or an unpleasant home life. In any case, we can accept that many children may begin school with an attention problem, while others will develop theirs in response to school experiences. While this latter group of children may exhibit similar behaviours in the school years, the solutions to their problems may be quite different. To foreshadow the final section of this chapter, some authors have argued that primary attention problems may require a medical solution.

Primary attention problems that would fit the DSM-III-R criteria could be due to some defect in arousal – a defect that would continue to be present – or to a lag or delay in the development of the attention / arousal system. In the latter case, the original arousal problem may disappear after several yars, but leave behind it a residue of academic failure. This residue would encourage the child to hate school and to believe that he or she will never be a success at school. It insures that the child lacks the necessary basic skills for more advanced learning. Thus, a temporary problem becomes magnified and permanent through lack of treatment.

Some of the possible causes of primary attention problems which have received some empirical support are heredity, neurological damage, biochemical imbalances, food additives, toxic reactions, lead poisoning, radiation stress, fetal alcohol syndrome, and maternal smoking. Such a list suggests that even primary attention deficit children (if such a distinct group exists) are not homogeneous in nature, though all of these factors may act to damage the attention system.

Secondary and tertiary attention problems (Table 11-1) appear more as responses to experiences, particularly after school has begun. To take a specific example of a secondary problem, consider a boy who has not learned many word attack skills: when the teacher asks him to read, he may well look about himself in a distracted manner, impulsively guess at words, and act rudely and aggressively in order to escape this unpleasant experience. In this case, the lack of specific knowledge has led to behaviour which will soon be hard to distinguish from that of the primary or "true" attention deficit child. What we are calling tertiary attention problems come from more general experiences, such as several years of school failure or an emotional disturbance. Such experiences can produce general lack of interest, or even hate, for school, and consequently many of the distracted and aggressive behaviours mentioned above.

If the causes of attention deficit are many and varied, at least the explanations of how it operates are only two in number. Perhaps paradoxically, it is not yet clear whether the behavioural *over*-activity which we observe is due to *over-* or to *under*-arousal.

The over-arousal theory argues that attention deficit results because the child is unable to filter out irrelevant stimuli and deal effectively with relevant stimuli, and is overly sensitive to incoming stimuli. Thus, irrelevant information is present in working memory and, as a result, behaviour is disorganized and inappropriate. One of the first studies to support this position was that of Laufer, Denhoff and Solomon (1957), and it is still considered today by some researchers to provide the strongest support. Laufer *et al.* argued that a part of the attention system called the diencephalon (responsible for filtering out irrelevant information) fails to function in attention deficit children. Instead of messages in the brain converging upon relevant actions, impulses are more diffuse and connected to many different (and irrelevant) responses, and more of the brain is aroused. Thus, behaviour is disorganized and over-active (Ferguson & Pappas, 1979).

These days, there is, perhaps surprisingly, more support for the contrary theory, that attention deficit children have under-aroused brains. This theory suggests that these children seek extra stimulation to increase their (brain) arousal level. Support for this position comes mainly from psychophysiological studies in which attention deficit children have exhibited low levels of arousal in the *autonomic nervous system* (as measured by galvanic skin response or heart-beat), and in the brain in general (as measured by EEG). Other support comes from studies in which attention deficit children's behaviour has improved following the administration of *stimulant* (arousal-increasing) medication.

The autonomic nervous system is a part of the brain which is thought to reflect one's mood or internal state. For example, if one is over-anxious, perspiration increases, resulting in increases in the electrical conductance of the skin. This response is measured as skin conductance level (SCL), or, following the presentation of a stimulus, as a galvanic skin response (GSR). (You've seen such things as lie detector tests in movies.) Satterfield and Dawson (1971) found that attention deficit children had lower SCLs and smaller GSRs than control children, exactly contrary to what would be expected for over-anxious subjects. Furthermore, the administration of stimulant medication (see the final section of this chapter) increased the attention deficit children's SCLs and GSRs, and decreased their amount of inappropriate behaviour. Williams (1976) confirmed the findings of lower SCLs and smaller GSRs for children whose activity levels had been determined by classroom behaviour ratings. Satterfield (1973) found lesser cortical arousal in attention deficit children, as measured by EEG (electroencephalogram).

Wender (1973, 1976) has taken the under-arousal theory further, to attempt to understand the cause of the under-arousal. He considers it to result from a biochemical disorder, due to a deficiency in neurotransmitters. Neurotransmitters are chemical messengers that connect one nerve cell to another. A nerve cell releases the chemical, which is taken up by the next cell causing it to "fire". If there is an insufficient amount of the neurotransmitter from the first cell, the second cell will not fire. The result is a disruption of the complex interconnections between nerve cells, and a malfunction of the part of the brain in which the disruption occurs. Wender believes that, in the attention deficit child, this disruption occurs in the attention / arousal system. This results in under-arousal, the consequences of which are problems in attention, problems in activity level and probably some lack of control. Wender's support for his hypothesis comes from the positive effects of stimulant medication. Stimulants increase the efficiency of neurotransmitters, allowing more efficient connections between nerve cells, and having the effect of increasing attention skills and self-control.

The under-arousal hypothesis, we believe, is most appropriate for those attention deficit children who respond positively to stimulant medication. They appear to have a primary arousal problem. However, there are many other children who exhibit attention problems but who do not respond positively to such medication (see the treatment section below). These children may not necessarily fit the DSM-III-R definition of attention deficit, particularly the requirement that the problem begin early. However, even if they do show an early onset of over-activity, their problems may be more secondary or tertiary in nature. Perhaps these children do not have under-aroused brains, or even over-aroused brains, for that matter; instead, their symptoms may be caused by problems in the processing and planning systems. This remains a question for future research.

Test Anxiety

We have dealt with attention deficit at length because attention deficit problems have long been accepted as characteristic of the learning disabled child. Test anxiety is a very different type of problem, normally seen in older or even adult students, and therefore not traditionally considered relevant to learning *disabilities*. Because test anxiety seems to be a cognitive or arousal process which interferes with learning, we see it as very relevant to learning problems.

Test anxiety is merely a name for a particular type of anxiety about school, which is in turn an aspect of general anxiety (Phillips, 1978). Test anxiety may be manifested both cognitively (by statements or actions concerned with avoiding testing situations, etc.) and physiologically (by increased sweating, heart rate, etc.). Anxiety is thought to have two aspects: *trait* anxiety and *state* anxiety (Spielberger, 1972). Persons who have high trait anxiety are generally anxious; i.e., anxiety is a part of their personality. State anxiety on the other hand is more transitory, and is a natural reaction to various events or thoughts. The stable personality trait of anxiety may have some primary basis in arousal but probably also involves more cognitive factors. State anxiety would appear to function in a more secondary or tertiary manner, arousal being affected, perhaps, by the cognitive systems. Both aspects of anxiety can play a role in test anxiety, and can even compound each other's effect (Burch-field, Stein & Hamilton, 1985).

Test anxious persons have low self-esteem and low performance expectations (Wine, 1982). They are also more self-preoccupied in test situations, which means that they are more likely to have thoughts about themselves in working memory than information which is more task-relevant; accordingly, they are less likely to succeed. This characteristic has led several investigators to suggest that the major problem in test anxiety is attentional in nature (Geen, 1980; Wine, 1982). Test anxious persons are also less likely to have coping strategies to deal with stressful situations. Many of these characteristics should remind you of the affective consequences (e.g., learned helplessness) suffered by younger learning problem children (see Chapter 10). To some degree, test anxiety may function as an affective consequence of a more cognitive problem (if you don't know the material, you should be afraid of the test), but in another sense it operates upon cognition to reduce the amount of relevant information that is in working memory. Unlike attention deficit children, test anxious persons appear to be over-aroused mentally, the over-arousal and concentration upon personal factors acting to block out needed information. Thus, even though a student knows the correct information, he or she may not be able to access it in a test situation. In particular, he or she won't be able to employ it in a complex task.

Hypoactivity

In 1973 Das warned that, in concentrating upon hyperactivity as a learning problem, educators were failing to consider hypoactivity, a problem of potentially equal magnitude. Hypoactivity refers to the opposite of hyperactivity – extreme quietness, social isolation and inactivity. The reasons for ignoring this problem, if it is real, are not difficult to understand: hyperactive (i.e., attention deficit) children may be extremely disruptive in the classroom, whereas hypoactive children may even be seen as ideal, though unintelligent, pupils. While

we do not know of any empirical studies of hypoactive children, at least not in terms of arousal levels, we do wish to point out that hypoactivity may represent an important learning problem.

Hypoactive children would appear in school as isolated or withdrawn, perhaps even mildly autistic. This may be the result of their having been "captured" by some stimulus or thought that is probably not relevant to the academic task at hand, or of their preference for a very low amount of stimulation or arousal. A very speculative hypothesis would be that hypoactivity is caused, contrary to hyperactivity, by mental *over*-arousal. There has been some support for this interpretation, if hypoactivity is accepted as a mild form of autism. For example, Dunlap, Koegel and Burke (1981) have reviewed evidence that autistic children's attention is *overselective* in nature, in contrast with the underselectivity shown by attention deficit children. They suggest overselectivity can be seen as an attempt to reduce stimulation and thus arousal. Goldstein and Lancy (1985) have recently proposed that autistic children prefer and need extremely low levels of mental arousal; the normal world would produce a state of over-arousal in them.

We emphasize that this hypothesis is speculative, and is based upon the suggestion of a *mild* form of autism. Normal autism is a severe disability, much more debilitating than what we are considering as learning problems. A true autistic child would be very unlikely to reach a normal school. We are more confident in stating that many children do suffer from extreme withdrawal (e.g., Conger & Keane, 1981), a problem which can at least be seen as an affective consequence of a learning problem. Our suggestion is that such withdrawal may also be a direct cause of learning problems, operating through arousal to affect attention.

Observation and Assessment of Attention and Arousal

It is difficult to measure arousal by itself, as the most valid measures are physiological in nature (e.g., GSR) and are, therefore, not employable by most psychologists, much less by teachers. We do not describe physiological methods here; if you wish to pursue those, consult the references at the end of this chapter. Instead we describe measures that have been used in the assessment of attention deficit (these falling into the categories of performance measures and rating scales) and one questionnaire measure of test anxiety. No specific measure of hypoactivity exists, but it could be indexed by performance on the attention deficit measures that was opposite to that of attention deficit children.

Attention Deficit: Performance Measures

A variety of instruments may be employed in the analysis of the primary symptoms of inattention, distractibility and impulsivity. For example, a choice reaction time task, a serial reaction time task, or a vigilance task such as the Continuous Performance Test (Rosvold, Mirsky, Sarason, Bransome & Beck, 1956) may be used to measure inattention. Distractibility has been measured using the Colour Distraction Test (Santostefano & Paley, 1964) and the Stroop Colour Distraction Test (Stroop, 1935). Impulsivity is most often measured by the Matching Familiar Figures Test (MFFT) (Kagan, Rosman, Day, Albert & Phillips, 1964); because of its extensive use among researchers, this last test will be discussed in some detail.

The Matching Familiar Figures Test (MFFT)

The MFFT was developed by Kagan and his colleagues (Kagan, Rosman, Day, Albert & Phillips, 1964) to investigate the nature of impulsivity. In this test the child is asked to select from a set of six figures one which exactly matches a given standard figure (see Figure 11-5). Two cognitive styles are assessed, reflectivity and impulsivity. Children who evaluate and analyze their responses before answering often select the correct answers and are

FIGURE 11-5
An item from the Matching Familiar Figures Test. The child is asked to select one of the six lower figures which is exactly the same as the one above. (From Kagan et al., 1964)

considered reflective. Children who check the standard less often, use fewer systematic scanning strategies, respond more quickly, and usually give inaccurate responses are considered impulsive. Impulsivity, of course, is characteristic of attention deficit children.

It should come as no surprise to you that the MFFT has also been considered as a measure of planning, because the reflective children are using better strategies than the impulsives. Therefore, we will see this test again, in Chapter 14. (Messer, 1976, presents an extensive review of research involving the MFFT, as well as of criticisms of the concepts of the reflective and impulsive styles.)

Attention Deficit: Rating Scales

Numerous rating scales have been developed to measure hyperactivity and attention deficit, for use by teachers and parents (Achenbach, 1978; Bell, Waldrop & Weller, 1972; Davids, 1971; Kendall & Wilcox, 1979; Sandoval, Lambert & Sassone, 1980; Werry, 1968), but the most widely used have been those developed by Conners (1969, 1970, 1973).

Conners Parent Scale

Conners (1970) developed a ninety-three-item parent scale, grouped into twenty-five headings which included such problems as fears, perfectionism and bowel problems. However, the version most frequently used is the one revised by Goyette, Conners and Ulrich (1978) which consists of forty-eight items (see Figure 11-6).

Each item on the questionnaire is answered by one of the following: "not at all", "just a little", "pretty much", or "very much", with the points 0, 1, 2 and 3 being assigned respectively. Attention deficit children are identified usually by calculating the average score of the items on the scale checked in Figure 11-6, an average of 1.5 being accepted as the minimum lower limit.

FIGURE 11-6

The 48-item version of the Conners Parent Symptom Questionnaire

PARENT'S QUESTIONNAIRE

Name of Child   Date

Please answer all questions. Beside each item below, indicate the degree of the problem by a check mark (√)	Not at all	Just a Little	Pretty Much	Very Much
1. Picks at things (nails, fingers, hair, clothing).				
2. Sassy to grown-ups.				
3. Problems with making or keeping friends.				
4. Excitable, impulsive.			√	
5. Wants to run things.				
6. Sucks or chews (thumb; clothing; blankets).				
7. Cries easily or often.		√		
8. Carries a chip on his shoulder.				
9. Daydreams.				
10. Difficulty in learning.				
11. Restless in the "squirmy" sense.				√
12. Fearful (of new situations; new people or places; going to school).				
13. Restless, always up and on the go.				√
14. Destructive.		√		
15. Tells lies or stories that aren't true.				
16. Shy.				
17. Gets into more trouble than others same age.				

	Not at all	Just a Little	Pretty Much	Very Much
18. Speaks differently from others the same age (baby talk; stuttering; hard to understand).				
19. Denies mistakes or blames others.				
20. Quarrelsome.				
21. Pouts and sulks.				
22. Steals.				
23. Disobedient or obeys but resentfully.				
24. Worries more than others (about being alone; illness or death).				
25. Fails to finish things.			✓	
26. Feelings easily hurt.				
27. Bullies others.				
28. Unable to stop a repetitive activity.				
29. Cruel.				
30. Childish or immature (wants help he shouldn't need; clings; needs constant reassurance).				
31. Distractibility or attention span a problem.				✓
32. Headaches.				
33. Mood changes quickly and drastically.			✓	
34. Doesn't like or doesn't follow rules or restrictions.				
35. Fights constantly.				
36. Doesn't get along well with brothers or sisters.				
37. Easily frustrated in efforts.				✓
38. Disturbs other children.			✓	
39. Basically an unhappy child.				
40. Problems with eating (poor appetite; up between bites).				
41. Stomach aches.				
42. Problems with sleep (can't fall asleep; up too early; up in the night.)				
43. Other aches and pains.				
44. Vomiting or nausea.				
45. Feels cheated in family circle.				
46. Boasts and brags.				
47. Lets self be pushed around.				
48. Bowel problems (frequently loose; irregular habits; constipation).				

FIGURE 11-7
The Conners Teacher Rating Scale

TEACHER'S QUESTIONNAIRE

Name of Child				Grade	

Date of Evaluation

Please answer all questions. Beside each item below, indicate the degree of the problem by a check mark (√)	Not at all	Just a Little	Pretty Much	Very Much
1. Restless in the "squirmy" sense.				√
2. Makes inappropriate noises when he shouldn't.				
3. Demands must be met immediately.				
4. Acts "smart" (impudent or sassy).				
5. Temper outbursts and unpredictable behavior.			√	
6. Overly sensitive to criticism.				
7. Distractibility or attention span a problem.				√
8. Disturbs other children.			√	
9. Daydreams.				
10. Pouts and sulks.		√		
11. Mood changes quickly and drastically.			√	
12. Quarrelsome.				
13. Submissive attitude toward authority.				
14. Restless, always "up and on the go".				√
15. Excitable, impulsive.			√	
16. Excessive demands for teacher's attention.				
17. Appears to be unaccepted by group.				
18. Appears to be easily led by other children.				
19. No sense of fair play.				
20. Appears to lack leadership.				
21. Fails to finish things that he starts.				√
22. Childish and immature.				
23. Denies mistakes or blames others.				
24. Does not get along well with other children.				
25. Uncooperative with classmates.				
26. Easily frustrated in efforts.			√	
27. Uncooperative with teacher.				
28. Difficulty in learning.				

Conners Teacher Scale

Conners (1969, 1973) also developed a thirty-nine-item rating scale to be used by teachers. It has also been revised and shortened by Goyette *et al.* (1978), and now consists of twenty-eight items, being scored on the same 0 to 3 scale as the Parent Scale. The twenty-eight items are shown in Figure 11-7. Like the Parent Scale, the minimum average score for the identification of attention deficit children is said to be 1.5, on the items checked in Figure 11-7.

Evaluation

Rating scales are less than an ideal way to assess hyperactivity (or anything else, for that matter), but they are often all we have. They do distinguish hyperactive children from other children (Barkley, 1981). Their great advantage is that they allow the persons dealing most with the child to supply their opinions. Often, however, rating scales have not been investigated well enough for us to have great confidence in the results they provide; sometimes it is not even possible to see why certain items are included. Despite these criticisms, rating scales appear to be the preferred method of identification. They are easy to administer and inexpensive, and they can provide information from a wide rage of behaviours without time-consuming interviews. Furthermore, they provide information about the child's behaviour over an extended period of time in his or her "natural environment", namely the home and the school. See Poggio and Salking (1979) for a critical review of the instruments used to measure hyperactivity.

Test Anxiety: Rating Scales

Test anxiety is usually measured by asking the student to fill out a questionnaire. While it is also possible to monitor physiological responses during testing, there is not much evidence that the test anxiety necessarily manifests itself as arousal of the autonomic nervous system (Burchfield, Stein & Hamilton, 1985). Instead the arousal seems more cognitive in nature; for this reason, and because it is important to listen to the person with the problem, questionnaires may be the better way to go.

Sarason's Test Anxiety Scale

I. Sarason (1978) has presented a representative measure, the Test Anxiety Scale. This questionnaire is based upon previous work by Mandler and S. Sarason (1952, the Test Anxiety Questionnaire), and upon a previous version of the Test Anxiety Scale (I. Sarason, 1958). The 1978 version (see Figure 11-8) consists of thirty-seven true-false questions. While it is designed for college students, relatively minor changes in wording could make it suitable for high school students. (A separate Test Anxiety Scale for Children, appropriate for elementary students, also exists; S. Sarason, Davidson, Lighthall, Waite & Ruebush, 1960). The test is scored by counting the number of questions which are scored with a "test anxious" response, sometimes true, sometimes false (see Figure 11-8). While no formal norms exist, I. Sarason (1978) reported that the average scores for Washington undergraduates were 16.72 for males, 19.74 for females. It is not possible to determine from that information how high a score a student would need to have to be identified as having a test anxiety problem, but clearly, the higher the score, the more likely it is that there is a problem. (It is worth keeping in mind that students, even adult college students, may not realize they have a test anxiety problem. Therefore, such a questionnaire, even if it tells them only that they are so far above average, may be informative, and may lead them to consider some form of treatment.)

FIGURE 11-8
Test Anxiety Scale Items (Keyed answers are in parenthesis)
(Sarason, 1978).

(T) 1. While taking an important exam, I find myself thinking of how much brighter the other students are than I am.

(T) 2. If I were to take an intelligence test, I would worry a great deal before taking it.

(F) 3. If I knew I was going to take an intelligence test, I would feel confident and relaxed beforehand.

(T) 4. While taking an important examination, I perspire a great deal.

(T) 5. During course examinations, I find myself thinking of things unrelated to the actual course material.

(T) 6. I get to feel very panicky when I have to take a surprise exam.

(T) 7. During tests, I find myself thinking of the consequences of failing.

(T) 8. After important tests, I am frequently so tense that my stomach gets upset.

(T) 9. I freeze up on things like intelligence tests and final exams.

(T) 10. Getting a good grade on one test doesn't seem to increase my confidence on the second.

(T) 11. I sometimes feel my heart beating very fast during important exams.

(T) 12. After taking a test, I always feel I could have done better than I actually did.

(T) 13. I usually get depressed after taking a test.

(T) 14. I have an uneasy, upset feeling before taking a final examination.

(F) 15. When taking a test, my emotional feelings do not interfere with my performance.

(T) 16. During a course examination, I frequently get so nervous that I forget facts I really know.

(T) 17. I seem to defeat myself while working on important tests.

(T) 18. The harder I work at taking a test or studying for one, the more confused I get.

(T) 19. As soon as an exam is over, I try to stop worrying about it, but I just can't.

(T) 20. During exams, I sometimes wonder if I'll ever get through college.

(T) 21. I would rather write a paper than take an examination for my grade in a course.

(T) 22. I wish examinations did not bother me so much.

(T) 23. I think I could do much better on tests if I could take them alone and not feel pressured by a time limit.

(T) 24. Thinking about the grade I may get in a course interferes with my studying and my performance on tests.

(T) 25. If examinations could be done away with, I think I would actually learn more.

(F) 26. On exams I take the attitude, "If I don't know it now, there's no point worrying about it".

(F) 27. I really don't see why some people get so upset about tests.

(T) 28. Thoughts of doing poorly interfere with my performance on tests.

(F) 29. I don't study any harder for final exams than for the rest of my course work.

(F) 30. Even when I'm well prepared for a test, I feel very anxious about it.

(T) 31. I don't enjoy eating before an important exam.

(T) 32. Before an important examination, I find my hands or arms trembling.

(F) 33. I seldom feel the need for "cramming" before an exam.

(T) 34. The university should recognize that some students are more nervous than others about tests and that this affects their performance.

(T) 35. It seems to me that examination periods should not be made such tense situations.

(T) 36. I start feeling very uneasy just before getting test paper back.

(T) 37. I dread courses where the professor has the habit of giving "pop" quizzes.

Overcoming Attention Problems

By far the greatest amount of remedial work has concerned attention deficit; much less has been devoted to test anxiety and virtually none to hypoactivity. Accordingly we begin, and concentrate upon, the treatment of attention deficit.

Treatment of Attention Deficit

Over the last thirty years or so, the management of attention deficit has been dominated by three approaches: behaviour modification; the use of stimulant medication; and, more recently, cognitive behaviour therapy (cognitive control). Without question, the preferred choice, particularly in North America, has up to recently been the use of medication. The popularity of such treatment is a result of (a) the child's being viewed from the medical model, and (b) the apparent success of medication with a significant percentage of attention deficit children. Recently, however, concern has focused on:

1. the relationship between academic achievement and medication;

2. the side-effects of medication; and

3. the fact that many attention deficit children do not respond positively to medication.

As a result of such concerns, alternative methods of treatment have been sought, including behaviour management techniques and cognitive control.

Drug Therapy

Since the early studies of Bradley (1937) and Bradley and Bowen (1941), the use of drugs has been the primary tool in the management of attention deficit children. The drugs most commonly used are the amphetamines (the stimulant drugs), particularly methylphenidate (commonly known as Ritalin, and probably the most frequently used), d-ampheta-mine (Dexedrine), and pemoline (Cylert). The stimulants are so called because of their power to increase the arousal of the central nervous system (CNS). All of the stimulants can be taken by mouth, and are rapidly absorbed into the bloodstream, thus having a relatively quick effect on the child. They appear to have their strongest effect on behaviour between one and two hours after ingestion. The effects diminish four to five hours after ingestion.

POSITIVE ASPECTS   Over the last twenty years, studies have shown that attention deficit children show a positive response to stimulant medication (Whalen & Henker, 1976; Swanson, Kinsbourne, Roberts & Zucker, 1978). From such studies it has been estimated that anywhere from seventy to eighty percent of attention deficit children respond in a positive manner, while the remainder do not improve and some become worse. The positive responses, according to Weiss (1981), are as follows:

1. concentration is improved;

2. goal directed behaviour replaces purposeless activity;

3. general classroom behaviour is improved;

4. aggressive and impulsive behaviour is reduced;

5. motor activity, rote learning and figure-ground discrimination skills are facilitated.

One would expect a positive impact on school learning to accompany such changes. However, this has not been the case, and for this and other reasons, research workers have begun to question the efficacy of medication in general.

CONCERNS ABOUT ACADEMIC ACHIEVEMENT   Numerous studies have shown that improvement in academic achievement is disappointing (Gadow, 1983). Weiss, Kruger, Danielson and Elman (1975) conducted a five-year study on attention deficit children, some of whom received methylphenidate or chlorpromazine and others who took no medication. The final outcome was that no significant differences between the groups were found in academic performance. Barkley and

Cunningham (1978) reviewed more than 100 studies on the effect of medication and academic performance and concluded that behaviour appears to improve but cognitive abilities do not. Two possible explanations of these results concern *state-dependent learning* (SDL) and *drug dosage levels.*

SDL refers to the possibility that information learned under the influence of a drug may be recalled with maximum strength only when the drug state is reintroduced (Overton, 1978). The underlying assumption here is that information learned while in the presence of a specific drug is lost or partially lost when its retrieval is required in a different state – i.e., in the absence of the drug, at a different dosage level, or in the presence of a placebo. If it were shown that SDL operated in attention deficit children under stimulant medication, then academic gains might be demonstrated only if the child was kept under medication. Fears about the side-effects of drugs, however, would make the medication alternative less appealing.

At present, it is not clear whether SDL is operative with attention deficit children under stimulant medication. Swanson and Kinsbourne (1976) and Swanson, Eich and Kinsbourne (1978) found evidence for SDL in these children, but several recent studies have not (Gan & Cantwell, 1982; Weingartner, Langa, Grice & Rapoport, 1982). This confusing state of affairs should be resolved by further research, but at the moment SDL remains a *possible* explanation for the lack of academic progress made by attention deficit children treated with stimulant drugs.

A second possible explanation for poor academic gains has to do with drug dosage levels. As you should be aware, while a certain amount of a drug may have a beneficial effect, much less of it may have no effect, and much more of it may have disastrous effects. Some researchers fear that too great a dose of medication may actually prevent school learning from taking place, even though the child's behaviour is quiet.

Sprague and Sleator (1977) investigated the effects of two dose levels of methylphenidate on the ability of attention deficit children to perform a simple learning task and on their classroom behaviour. The drug doses were .3 mg/kg and 1 mg/kg. Learning was measured using a simple short-term memory task in which children were presented repeatedly with a matrix of children's pictures. After a few seconds they had to decide whether a new picture had been in the matrix or not. Classroom behaviour (the Connors Teacher Rating Scale) and heart rate were also measured.

Sprague and Sleator's results, shown in Figure 11-9, clearly indicate that learning on the memory task peaks at the dose of .3 mg/kg and declines at the dosage of 1 mg/kg. On the other hand, teacher ratings peak at the 1 mg/kg level. Heart rate declines a little at the lower dose but increases dramatically at the 1 mg/kg level. These results suggest that the children at the higher dosage were able to sit still (and this appealed to teachers), but

FIGURE 11-9
The results of Sprague and Sleator's
(1977) study

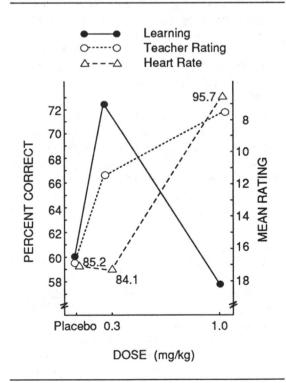

were unable to learn even simple information; surely the effect upon normal school learning would have been no less, and perhaps greater. Sprague and Sleator (1976) went on to propose theoretical dosage-response curves, which are examined in Figure 11-10. It must be emphasized that these curves are hypothetical; if they are confirmed by future research, they will suggest that far greater care be taken in the prescribing and monitoring of stimulant medication.

CONCERNS ABOUT SIDE EFFECTS It is agreed by most physicians that the most common short-term side-effects – loss of appetite, insomnia and stomach ache – are not serious and can be controlled by changes in dose levels and at the time of drug administration. However, two other side effects, changes in cardiovascular activity and the development of tics, cannot be as easily discounted.

The cardiovascular changes are increased heart

Interpreting Theoretical Dose-Response Curves

The interpretation of Sprague and Sleator's proposal is quite plain. There is an optimum level of drug dosage that facilitates learning. When the drug dosage is increased, learning is reduced but improvement in observable behaviour is accompanied with increased side effects (e.g., changes in heart rate). The point to be stressed here is that the physician relies on teacher and parent observations to monitor the effect of medication on behaviour. Positive reports might imply improved behaviour, even though learning is not increased. If Sprague and Sleator are correct, we have to re-evaluate our approach to the use of stimulant medication with children. Above all, the amount of medication must be carefully monitored with the smallest effective dose being the one that is administered. Moreover, medication should be used only with drug responders who have not responded to other forms of treatment.

FIGURE 11-10

Theoretical dose-response curves of Sprague and Sleator's proposal

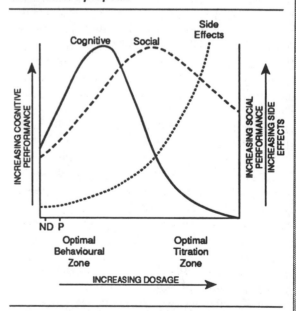

rate and systolic blood pressure (Ballard, Boibeau, Sleator, Massey and Sprague, 1976). (See also Figures 11-9 and 11-10.) While the increases are very small and the stimulants are unlikely to have any harmful effects on health in the short term, prolonged and sustained changes in cardiovascular activity might well have deleterious effects.

Barkley (1981) notes that one serious side effect of stimulant medication that should receive serious attention is the increase of nervous tics, especially the cases of irreversible Tourrette Syndrome (a neurological disorder consisting of continual motor tics accompanied by compulsive vocalizations). Barkley's concern is that some attention deficit children can develop tics or Tourrette Syndrome in response to methylphenidate. While only ten cases or so of such a response have been reported in the literature, he recommends that children with a history of tics or who are highly anxious should not be treated with any stimulant medication and calls for further investigation into this phenomenon.

Concerns have also been expressed about other long-term effects, especially drug addiction, suppressed growth, and declining benefits for treated children. The first of these, the fear that children will become addicted to the stimulant drugs, is now discounted by most researchers (e.g., Barkley, 1981), especially if treatment is carefully monitored.

A more serious side effect is physical growth suppression. Safer and his colleagues (Safer & Allen, 1973; Safer, Allen & Barr, 1972) reported that children who were on medication for three years or more were likely to suffer reduction in both height and weight. Subsequent studies have produced conflicting results (McNutt, Ballard, Boileau, Sprague & von Newmann, 1973; McNutt, Boileau & Cohen, 1977). In an extensive review on this matter, Roche, Limplan, Overall and Hung (1979) concluded that there is reasonable evidence that the taking of medication at high doses and over an extended period of time moderately suppresses weight gain, but that the evidence is less supportive for the suppression of growth in stature. Given the seriousness of this effect, further research must be undertaken.

The final concern about long-term effects is that initial behavioural changes for the good will not be maintained. For example, it is possible that children could build up a tolerance to stimulant medication (Weiss, 1981), and thus revert to their old behaviours. It is also possible that if nothing is done to improve the children's academic and social skills, then the attention deficit behaviour may return in time, particularly after the medication is removed. All of these concerns suggest extreme caution in the prescribing of stimulant medication, and the need for further research.

CONCERNS ABOUT CHILDREN'S ATTRIBUTIONS   It is also important to consider how the children themselves interpret their reactions to the medication. Whalen and Henker (1976, 1980) have shown that treated children tend to interpret their improved behaviour as due to the drugs and not to themselves. In other words, they still see themselves as having a problem, one which is only temporarily removed by medication; in the language of social psychology, they "attribute" their performance to an outside agent, not to themselves. This could further damage their already fragile self-concepts (see Chapter 10), and increases the chances that their attention deficit behaviours will return when medication is removed. Whalen and Henker suggest that, if drug therapy is to be undertaken, effort must be devoted *also* to teaching the now quiet child academic and social skills, and encouraging the child to believe that he or she is at least partly in control and responsible for improvements.

EVALUATION   Drug therapy is still a controversial topic, and there are firm opinions on both sides. Only future research can begin to resolve the issue. Fortunately or unfortunately, as educators it is never our decision to prescribe medication or not; we can, however, advise that educational and psychological issues should not be ignored in any drug program. Furthermore, we can also suggest other forms of treatment (behaviour modification and cognitive control) that have less potential for harm.

Behaviour Modification

The second traditional treatment for attention deficit has been behaviour modification (or behaviour therapy), in which the consequences of the attention deficit are manipulated to encourage the children to behave in some other manner. Behaviour modification works upon the symptoms of the problem, on the assumption that once those have been removed the problem no longer exists. Behaviour modification is a technique which originated in behaviourism (see Chapter 4), and thus is founded on the principle that behaviours or actions are controlled by their consequences. Undesirable behaviours can be eliminated, it is said, by removing their desirable consequences (this procedure is called *extinction,* because you want to extinguish the undesirable behaviour), and desired behaviours can be encouraged by providing rewards (called *reinforcers,* because they strengthen the response) when the correct behaviour or an approximation is produced.

For example, a behaviour modifier would start targeting an undesirable behaviour (e.g., shouting in the classroom) and a desired replacement (e.g., sitting quietly). The first step would be to identify any factors that were reinforcing the shouting, and remove them. These could include the teacher's giving of attention, or the laughing of the child's classmates. At the same time, it would be necessary to institute a reinforcement program to strengthen the desired behaviour. Initially, for example, the child could be given points towards extra free time (or anything else that was desired and suitable) in return for a minute's silence. Eventually the same points would cost more silent time. For a more detailed examination of behaviour modification, consult the recommended readings given at the end of this chapter.

HOW EFFECTIVE IS BEHAVIOUR MODIFICATION WITH ATTENTION DEFICIT CHILDREN? As usual, the answer is not clear. Many studies can be cited in which impressive gains have been claimed (e.g., Kent & O'Leary, 1976; Weissenburger & Loney, 1977). However, these gains are often in the classroom behaviour domain,

as opposed to the more cognitive academic skills domain. Furthermore, there is often evidence that even the behavioural improvements disappear after the study (and the reinforcers) terminate (e.g., Kent & O'Leary, 1976). In fact, Lahey *et al.* (1979) question whether there is solid research evidence for improvements in attention level, impulsivity, or perceptual or cognitive skills.

To make a long story short, there are now concerns that behaviour modification's benefits, if they exist, are confined to the behavioural area, do not generalize to academic areas, and may not last. These concerns led several researchers to pursue an amalgamation of cognitive and behavioural techniques, to attempt to strengthen the behavioural effects cognitively, and to exploit the behavioural improvements to allow for cognitive improvements. The secret, it seems, is that generalization to academic skills does not necessarily happen by itself; if you want cognitive improvements, you have to build in some cognitive training. We will refer to these newer methods as *cognitive control* approaches, though some term them *cognitive behaviour modification,* or *self-instructional training.*

Cognitive Control

Cognitive control is the blending of two schools of thought – cognitive therapy and behaviour therapy (Kauffmann & Hallahan, 1979). Ledwidge (1978) describes cognitive control as a cognitive therapy aimed at changing cognitions, which occurs through the modification of behaviour by means of self-statement (e.g., self-instruction, internalized speech). Furthermore, Ledwidge (1978) states that the main difference between cognitive therapy and behaviour therapy is that behaviour therapy attempts to change behaviour using essentially non-verbal means, whereas cognitive therapy relies heavily on speech as the instrument of change. Both therapies, however, evaluate treatment success in terms of overt behaviour. The essence of cognitive control training is to teach children a set of verbal techniques that they can use themselves to control their own behaviour. In other words, and in terms of our information integration model, the planning system is taught to control the processing and attention systems.

Most training procedures follow closely the instructional training program developed by Meichenbaum and Goodman (1971). Essentially, the program includes five steps which feature combinations of modeling, overt and covert rehearsal, prompts, feedback, and social reinforcement (Meichenbaum, 1977). The training sequence is as follows:

1. An adult model first performs the task while talking out loud to himself or herself (cognitive modeling).
2. The child then performs the same task under the direction of the model's instructions (overt external guidance).
3. The child next performs the task while instructing himself or herself out loud (overt self-guidance).
4. The child then whispers the instructions as he or she proceeds through the task (faded overt self-guidance).
5. Finally, the child performs the task while guiding his or her performance via private speech (covert self-instruction).

An example of the modelled instructions follows: the task is the copying of line patterns:

Okay, what is it I have to do? You want me to copy the picture with the different lines. I have to go slow and be careful. Okay, draw the line down, down, good; then go to the right, that's it; now down some more and to the left. Good, I'm doing fine so far. Remember, go slow. Now back up again. No, I was supposed to go down. That's okay. Just erase the line carefully.... Good. Even if I make an error I can go on slowly and carefully. Okay, I have to go down now. Finished I did it. (Meichenbaum and Goodman, 1971, p. 117)

While the model thinks aloud, certain types of self-statements are incorporated into the conversation:

1. The problem at hand is defined ("What is it that I have to do?")

2. Statements are used to focus attention and guidance statements are included ("Carefully … draw the line down").
3. Self-reinforcing comments are employed ("Good, I am doing fine …").
4. Self-evaluative coping statements and error-correcting options are contained within the guiding self-statements ("That's okay … even if I make an error I can go on slowly").

These statements, when internalized, will enable children to define and organize the task, guide themselves through the specific steps, and reward themselves for successful completion of the task or provide themselves with the confidence and means to correct possible errors.

Douglas (1980) has presented one of the best descriptions of a cognitive control program that can be adapted to suit the individual needs of children. Essentially the program is made up of three phases. In phase I, the emphasis is placed on trying to help children understand the nature of their problem and how it affects their behaviour. Phase 2 stresses the importance of the children's role in problem solving and motivates them to become more involved in this role. Phase 3 concentrates on the teaching of strategies to improve self control and problem solving behaviour. Details of this program are highlighted in the box that follows.

HOW EFFECTIVE IS COGNITIVE CONTROL?   Numerous studies have been undertaken using cognitive control with children, some with children who were not experiencing learning problems, including impulsiveness, aggression, emotional disturbance and attention problems (e.g., Meichenbaum & Goodman, 1971; Douglas, Parry, Marton & Garson, 1976). Furthermore, other studies have included the key element of cognitive control – conscious control of strategies – without making explicit references to it or employing it in its entirety (e.g., Egeland, 1974). In general, the findings have been very positive, showing decreased hyperactive behaviour, increased attentional skills (for instance, on the Matching Familiar Figures Test), and gains in academic achievement.

Douglas's Cognitive Control Program

Level I: Helping Children Understand the Nature of their Deficits and How Training Can Help

1. Providing an explanation of the nature of the child's attentional, inhibitory, and arousal modulating deficits.

2. Helping the child recognize how these deficits affect his daily functioning and create problems for him.

3. Convincing him that the deficits can be modified and motivating him to share actively in the process.

4. Introducing the child to the basic elements of the cognitive training approach.

Level II: Strengthening the Child's Motivation and Capacity to Deal with the Problem-solving Role

1. Providing success experiences within the training sessions by:

– breaking tasks into component parts,

– presenting tasks in gradually increasing order of difficulty,

– tailoring teaching material to individual child's capacities,

– providing systematic reviews of material covered.

2. Arranging success experiences at home and at school by:

– helping parents and teachers organize demands made on child to coincide with his ability to meet them successfully,

– encouraging parents and teachers to reward genuine attempts at mastery, as well as successes.

3. Teaching child general rules for approaching tasks, including:

– defining task demands accurately,

– assessing one's own relevant knowledge and / or the available cues in a situation or problem,

– considering all possible solutions,

– evaluating relative effectiveness of solutions considered,

– checking work carefully.

4. Discouraging passivity and encouraging independent effort by:

– addressing child with a title like "Mr. Problem Solver",

– discouraging undue dependence on trainer,

– discouraging mimicking of trainer's strategies or parroting of instructions; encouraging child to produce his own strategies and to restate instructions in his own words,

– shifting responsibility for correcting work and administering rewards to child,

– helping child learn to differentiate between his careless errors and errors that reflect genuine problems with understanding.

5. Making child aware of behaviours and attitudes on his part which interfere with problem solving by:

– drawing his attention to flagging attention or "hyped up" behaviour,
– discouraging excessive talking,
– reminding him to "work beyond" superficial aspects of a situation or problem,
– discouraging unreasonably low criteria for success.

Level III: Teaching Specific Problem-Solving Strategies

1. Modeling and teaching strategies directed toward improving attention and concentration. These strategies might include:

– organized and exhaustive scanning techniques,
– focusing strategies; checking for critical features,
– careful listening for essential information.

2. Teaching strategies and offering management suggestions directed toward increasing inhibitory control and developing organizational skills. This might be accomplished by:

– teaching child to sit on hands until he has thought through possible solutions,
– encouraging parents and teachers to provide special places for keeping important materials and helping the child remember to use them,
– encouraging the use of a special notebook for classroom assignments; keeping notebook in special place,
– modeling the use of lists of events or assignments to be remembered, assembling necessary materials for projects, laying out clothes and books for following day.

3. Teaching strategies and offering management suggestions directed toward improved control of child's level of alertness and arousal. This might include:

– labeling of arousal states,
– teaching the child to exhort self or calm self using verbal self-commands,
– suggesting interesting "breaks" between periods of concentrated work,
– being sensitive to the fact that child may need stimulation to combat boredom.

4. Teaching other specific strategies child has failed to learn, for example,

– rehearsal strategies and mnemonic devices,
– strategies required for particular academic activities (e.g., steps involved in adding fractions or in writing an essay).

(Further references to studies using cognitive control are given at the end of this chapter.)

Of course no training technique is perfect, and few escape the critics. O'Leary (1980) has suggested several weaknesses in the cognitive control research to date, and some possible future directions. In spite of such constructive criticisms, however, the evidence seems clear that cognitive control is a technique that should be considered in trying to improve attention deficits. (See the box above for an example of the use of cognitive control.) Even if stimulant medication has been prescribed, it would be useful to implement a cognitive control program at the same time, to ensure that any temporary behavioural gains are not wasted.

Attention Deficit Hyperactive Disorder: Cognitive Control Techniques

This example of a remedial intervention using cognitive control relates to children such as Peter, the attention deficit child described in the case study on p. 137.

Problem

The child does not stay on task, is unattentive, and appears to be easily distracted. He or she is always on the go – a classic hyperactive child.

Solution

We suggest that a good starting point is to try and improve on task behaviour by training the child to complete a variety of tasks.

The Tasks

We believe that the tasks should be non-academic in nature and appealing to the student. Puzzles and mazes are two examples. We further recommend that you start with tasks that are not too challenging. The reason for this is that your initial concern should be in developing a cognitive strategy and only with success should you provide more challenging tasks. You could use commercially prepared puzzles or the type of puzzle used in Camp and Bash's (1981) *Think Aloud* program (e.g., Ralph the Bear, a 7- or 9-piece puzzle) along with mazes similar to the Subtest of the WISC-R (Wechsler Intelligence Scale for Children, Revised). We have found that it can be very effective to take a photograph of a sporting figure and make a puzzle out of it. Using a character or object of interest to the student is often very motivating.

Training Program

Anticipate spending about eight to ten sessions with the child over several weeks.

You might want to use the successful completion of a task as a criterion to re-evaluate the student. The task or tasks should be done over a time period of ten minutes with assistance from you.

The first five or six sessions would incorporate the basic training technique developed by Meichenbaum. Each session, therefore, will provide training in self-verbalization. Thus, you perform the task first, talking out loud. Then have the child perform the task instructing himself or herself out loud under your guidance.

Next, you perform a similar task but this time you whisper to yourself. Then the child completes a task also whispering the way in which he or she is solving the problem. Finally, the student performs a task but internalizes his or her speech. Self-verbalizations should include (1) problem identification, (2) the identification of a strategy, (3) self-coping statements, and (4) self-evaluation. Depending on how successful you are, the last session should have the student complete the tasks using internalized speech only.

What follows is an example of how you might solve a problem talking out loud, during the initial sessions of the training program of self-verbalization. In this case, the puzzle is a cut-up picture of a hockey player.

What is it that I have to do? I have to put all the pieces together to make a picture of a hockey player. (Identification of problem)

Well, I could look at all the pieces and try to form the picture in my head, but that may be too hard. Or I could look for the different colours of the uniform and match them, or look for the hockey helmet and start from there. Yes, that's what I'll do, look for the helmet. (Identification of strategy)

Here goes. All the pieces are in front of me, let's see. This is part of a leg. I don't need that yet. Ah! This looks like part of the helmet – it is, good! Let me place it at the top. Now where is the other part? No, this isn't it. Here it is. Good, the head and shoulders are now in place. Okay, part of the number on his sleeve is missing. Let's see if I can find that. Here it is. Part of his other arm is missing, mmm ... ah! Glove and arm – this fits. Things seem to be going well. (Self coping statements)

Let me continue. Here is a part of a leg and skate; this doesn't fit. That's okay, I'll put it aside and look at the other pieces. Part of his upper leg is here and the piece fits, and here is the part of the other leg. Only two pieces left. Both pieces with

skates – here is the left skate – now the right. Great! Finished it.

It was a good idea to start from the head and work down to the skates on the ice. Thinking in steps really helped me put this picture together. (Self- evaluation)

During the training sessions it might be helpful to have cue cards to aid the student in solving the problem. A cue card would include four questions: What Is My Problem? How Can I Do It? Am I Using My Plan? How Did I Do? Or these statements could be on separate cards accompanied by the corresponding pictures of Ralph the Bear from the *Think Aloud* program (Camp and Bash, 1981).

Treatment of Test Anxiety

There appear to be two broadly different approaches to reducing test anxiety that can be used together. The first approach is to employ such traditional techniques as systematic desensitization or relaxation training to reduce the amount of anxiety felt in the testing situation. Burchfield *et al.* (1985) have referred to these as *physiological* approaches because they focus on eliminating the physiological response of anxiety. In a sense, these are equivalent to the behaviour modification approach to attention deficit, because they concentrate on the response (anxiety) as the problem.

The second approach is more cognitive in nature, and seeks to give the student both cognitive control techniques to monitor and regulate anxiety and study skills to eliminate the cause of the anxious response. While Burchfield *et al.* (1985) term these *psychological* approaches, it should be clear that both approaches are very psychological in nature. (We do not know of any attempts to employ drugs to control test anxiety, but undoubtedly they have been made; presumably depressants rather

than stimulants were employed. Given the lack of a clear physiological / arousal cause for test anxiety, at best medication might be expected to produce a calm student who still does poorly on the test.)

In a review of test anxiety treatments, Denney (1980) noted that cognitive techniques have been more successful. He and Meichenbaum (1977; Meichenbaum & Butler, 1980) would agree that a combination of relaxation and cognitive techniques would be best. Meichenbaum has termed this approach a "stress innoculation" program, with three components:

1. Teach the students to understand stress in general and their own stress problem in particular.
2. Practise the use of each of the newly learned skills, including relaxation, cognitive strategies, and verbal self-instruction.
3. Practise the same skills first with imagined and then with real stressful situations.

This program should remind you of the cognitive control techniques discussed above for use with attention deficit children. The five steps of verbal self-instruction (Meichenbaum, 1977) and

Douglas's outline of a cognitive control program can both be applied, with obvious modifications, to the treatment of test anxiety in older students.

The recommended readings at the end of this chapter include a number of other applications of cognitive control techniques which illustrate the great generality of this approach. Most applications share these two features: (a) neutralizing lower-level responses (e.g., arousal), while (b) teaching the student higher-level (cognitive) strategies for overcoming the source of the original problem.

Treatment of Hypoactivity

This is a short section, because we know of no cognitive approaches to the treatment of hypoactivity, and we must even admit that we don't have any firm ideas about what might work. The major difficulty is that practically no cognitive research has specifically addressed hypoactivity. When hypoactive behaviour has been addressed, it has more often been considered an emotional disturbance (e.g., Conger & Keane, 1981).

If hypoactivity is seen as a mild form of autism (see p. 140), then some research with autistic children may be relevant. For example, Fish (1976) has pointed out that stimulant drugs make autistic children worse, whereas they are sometimes helped by drugs that could loosely be termed sedatives or tranquilizers; this supports the argument that their attention problems are opposite in nature to those of attention deficit children. Behaviour modification has been attempted with virtually every type of psychological problem, but the unresponsiveness of hypoactive children may make it a difficult approach to use with them. This problem is even more likely with regard to cognitive control techniques, which require the active participation of the child.

In short, we must hope for far more research to be done with hypoactive children, designed to explore the nature of their problem and ways to overcome it.

Summary

This chapter has provided an overview of attention-based learning problems. We have seen that attention deficit and hypoactivity seem to represent opposite ends of the arousal continuum, though much more remains to be learned about hypoactivity. We have also seen that some problems not normally included under the label of learning problems, such as test anxiety, have an attention/arousal component. We think that much more research is needed, and that more educators need to become aware of the effect of attention and arousal upon academic learning.

We have also reviewed diagnostic and remedial techniques, concentrating upon attention deficit. Because arousal is (to some degree) a lower-level function, and because it can be medically altered, physiological techniques have been and will be popular. We have attempted to show the positive and negative effects of medication, but have, in the end, recommended caution. In particular, it must be emphasized that even if medication works for some, it will not work for all. By far the greatest enthusiasm today is for cognitive control techniques: these treat children as intelligent human beings, aim to make them independent, and – best of all – have been shown to be effective. If you learn nothing else from this chapter, learn about cognitive control.

RECOMMENDED READING

There are many sources now available regarding attention deficits. In addition to the ones cited in this chapter, you may wish to consult:

Routh, D.K.
    1986. Attention deficit disorder. In R.T. Brown and C.R. Reynolds (eds.). *Psychological perspectives on childhood exceptionality*. New York: Wiley.

Physiology of Arousal
Ornstein, R. & Thompson, R.F.
1984. *The amazing brain.* Boston: Houghton Mifflin.
A gentle introduction to the brain and arousal.
Hassett, J.
1978. *A primer of psychophysiology.* San Francisco: W.H. Freeman.
A far less gentle book, though one deeply devoted to the measurement of arousal.

Test Anxiety
Sarason, I.G. (ed.)
1980. *Test anxiety: Theory, research, and applications.* Hillsdale: Lawrence Erlbaum Associates.

Drug Therapy
Pelham, W.E.
1986. The effects of psychostimulant drugs on learning and academic achievement in children with attention deficit disorders and learning disabilities. In J.K. Torgesen and B.Y.L. Wong (eds.). *Psychological and educational perspectives on learning disabilities.* Orlando, Florida: Academic Press.
A comprehensive treatment of the effects of stimulant medication on academic achievement.

Cognitive Control
Kendall, P.C. & Hollon, S.D. (eds.)
1979. *Cognitive-behavioural interventions: Theory, research, and procedures.* New York: Academic Press.
In addition to the references given in the text, this book provides an idea of how widely cognitive control techniques have been applied.
Abikoff, H.
1987. An evaluation of cognitive behaviour therapy for hyperactive children. In B.B. Lahey and A.E. Kazdin (eds.). *Advances in clinical child psychology, Vol. 10.* New York: Plenum Press.
A recent review of the effectiveness of cognitive control with attention deficit children.

CHAPTER 12

Successive Processing

AS WE ARGUED in Chapter 5, successive processing problems can be of two types. The more general type of problem spreads across all or most instances of successive processing, appearing in most academic areas. This is almost certainly a problem with successive processing itself. The second kind of problem is confined to instances of successive processing within a given academic area, and is clearly more accurately described as a problem with successive processing in reading, or successive processing in arithmetic, etc. Both of these types of successive processing problems will be dealt with in this chapter.

We begin by reviewing the importance of successive processing in cognition, and the way in which it has been described by other theorists and practitioners. Then we summarize the aspects of the achievement areas that may be affected by successive processing problems, and illustrate those problems with examples of classroom performance. In the third section we will present methods which a classroom teacher or psychologist can use to assess successive processing informally, both generally and within specific achievement areas. Finally we will discuss approaches to improving poor successive processing; this discussion will be dominated by the question: Is poor successive processing due to low *ability* (thus unlikely to be

improved), or to a *difficulty* (requiring considerable skill development), or to an *inclination* on the child's part not to use it (thus encouraging optimism about remedial prospects)?

Successive Processing in Cognition

Luria (1966) and Das *et al.* (1975, 1979) have described successive processing as a major subgrouping or category of cognitive processes. Not surprisingly, many other authors have described a similar category, though they have used many different names. Within the psychology of intelligence, successive processing has been studied either as a rote memory ability or as a part of analytic reasoning. Most psychometric batteries of mental tests include measures of rote memory, in which subjects are presented (visually or auditorially) with a series of items (letters, numbers, pictures, objects, words, etc.), and later have to recall them (verbally, in writing, etc.) in correct serial order (e.g., Cattell, 1971; Ekstrom, French, Harman & Derman, 1976; and Guilford, 1967). Jensen (1969, 1974) has referred to this group of skills as Level I ability, in which stimulus input is not transformed prior to response output. Clearly, these skills tap the essence of successive processing, keeping processed information in correct temporal order; however, by employing only rote memory tasks, they stress only the use of successive processing in lower-level tasks. Luria and Das *et al.* have stressed that successive processing is also required in many higher level tasks (such as the determination of syntax to aid reading or language comprehension). Because it is difficult to devise tasks at this higher level that measure *only* successive processing, it does not seem to have emerged as a separate factor (at this level) in tests of mental abilities.

Many mental tests require adequate levels of successive processing for their successful completion. Examples of these would be tests of analytic reasoning (in which a set of procedures must be followed, in order) and, of course, language-based tests of comprehension. In these cases the tests do not measure successive processing by itself, but rather measure a combination of skills, one of which is successive processing.

Successive processing has also featured prominently in information processing theories, though again under other names. Most theories contain a short-term or working memory (refer back to our discussion in Chapter 4), which is responsible for holding input information in serial order, to allow for further processing. In turn, further processing can result in higher-level sequences of information which are also held in this working memory. As we saw in Chapter 7, sequences of letters can be processed into words, then sequences of words can be processed into phrases, then phrases into ideas, and so on. This is presumably the same rote memory that the psychometricians test, but used in such instances for far more complex tests. The term "successive processing" is intended to capture this range of cognitive activity.

Learning problem children have been described as deficient in many skills which are related to successive processing, including serial memory, sequencing ability, analytic thinking, and selective attention. Torgesen (1978) has reviewed a great deal of research which indicates that many learning problem children perform worse than normal chil-

dren on serial memory tasks such as remembering a series of numbers or words. He concluded that there were two major factors underlying this poor performance, inefficient serial memory *strategies* and inefficient (or slow) *encoding of information* in working memory. In the strategy area, learning problem children were less likely than normal children to use memory techniques such as naming and rehearsal of items to be remembered (see Chapter 14). The result of either or both of these difficulties is to make inefficient use of working memory space. To fail to encode items quickly or completely increases the likelihood that required information will not be in working memory at the same time, decreasing the chances of appropriate temporal links between items. To fail to repeat or rehearse the given information also decreases the chances of temporal (successive) links being formed.

Learning problem children have also been described as poor in sequencing – that is, in perceiving, following, or retaining temporal order (e.g., Bakker, 1972). A common reading error, for instance, is to misread "saw" as "was". While there is general agreement that learning problem children have serial order or sequencing problems, there is not much agreement about how this weakness should be interpreted (e.g., Vellutino, 1979, especially pp. 212-231 and 338-342).

Inefficient use of working memory can also give the appearance of not paying attention. You should recall our discussion in Chapters 5 and 6 of this point: poor attention can arise from attention / arousal system difficulties, giving rise to the syndrome known as attention deficit, or it can be a by-product of other processing problems. Some working memory / successive processing tests have been used to measure selective attention or "freedom from distractibility". The latter term has been applied to a group of the subtests that form the Wechsler Intelligence Scale for Children (usually abbreviated as the WISC, or the WISC-R since its 1974 revision). Rugel (1974), among others, suggested that the Digit Span, Coding and Arithmetic subtests measure the degree of attention which subjects can devote to a task, and subsequent authors have shown that learning problem children perform poorly on these subtests (Smith, Coleman, Dokecki & Davis, 1977). Each of these subtests requires the child to pay careful attention to sequences of information, retain his or her place in the problem, and perform a series of operations or responses. (Some authors refer to these tests as "sequential" measures.) We wish only to emphasize that poor working memory / successive processing skills could give rise to poor performance on these tests and thus to an appearance of poor selective attention or distractibility. Torgesen and Houck (1980) have shown, for instance, that learning problem children who perform poorly on the Digit Span Test (and not all do) do so largely because of inefficient stimulus encoding. Vellutino (1979) has concluded that many so-called selective attention problems are in reality due to inefficient verbal coding. Again, inefficient or incomplete encoding decreases the chances that rehearsal can take place and that temporal links between elements can be formed.

It has also been suggested that learning problem children have a different *cognitive style* – that is, a different habitual and general approach to thinking – than do their normally achieving peers. Learning problem children have been said to be less *analytic,* in the sense that they tend to be more *impulsive* (e.g., Kagan, 1965) and more *field dependent* (Keogh & Donlon, 1972). Impulsivity has been dealt with in Chapters 6 and 11, and we need only add here that, like distractibility, it can be a by-product of inefficient processing skills. Field dependence (as opposed to field independence) describes a cognitive style in which the person accepts the given information as it is, without restructuring it. Field dependence produces *passive* learning instead of active, *analytic* learning. To a large extent, field dependence is due to lack of use of simultaneous processing skills (see Chapter 13), which are required to detect the relationships or patterns upon which the restructuring is based. Again, however, poor successive processing skills can give rise to field dependent performance, in that problem restructuring and analysis requires the sequencing of a number of steps and / or the systematic exploration of a set of possible actions; inefficient successive processing will result in the loss of one's place in the sequence and subsequent failure in the task.

As we have emphasized throughout this book, our point is that the concept of successive processing provides a convenient and useful integrating framework for interpreting these diverse research findings. Other authors would prefer other frameworks, but we would argue that the major competing frameworks, described in the preceding paragraphs, do not offer the breadth of the successive processing concept, and thus are able to emphasize only one aspect of learning problems.

Successive Processing Learning Problems

In Chapters 7, 8, and 9 we examined the achievement areas of reading, spelling, arithmetic and mathematics, and indicated how learning problems could arise. Potential learning problems were described in information processing terms, and classified as largely due to problems in successive processing, simultaneous processing, or planning. In order to emphasize the concept of successive processing, we will cut across those achievement areas in this chapter. The reader should not lose sight of the fact that various learning problems can co-exist and that successive processing problems can give rise to others, and vice versa.

Table 12-1 lists the learning problems that were ascribed to successive processing. Any of these problems can occur in isolation, but they are more likely to accompany each other, particularly within achievement areas. For example, in spelling, if the word to be spelled is initially mispronounced, the child could be expected to then poorly analyze the (mispronounced) word into units, and then to make sequence errors in spelling. Lower level or initial errors are likely to produce errors at higher levels or at further stages in an achievement task. It is also likely that problems will occur across achievement areas, particularly if the problems are due to a more general difficulty (e.g., inability to hold sound

TABLE 12-1
Learning problems ascribed to successive processing

Achievement Area	Learning Problem Symptoms	Causal Descriptions
Reading	Lack of word analysis skills; inability to "sound-out" unknown words; guessing of words from context and/or first letters	Lack of phonetic knowledge Lack of ability to hold sound sequences Inclination toward global meaning
	Lack of comprehension of syntactic structure; failure to realize importance of word order; failure to read with "expression", failure to form syntactic chunks	Unfamiliarity with particular syntax Inability to hold word sequences Inclination toward global meaning
	Lack of comprehension of story sequence	Unfamiliar context Inability to retain main idea sequences Inclination toward global meaning
Spelling	Failure to pronounce (repeat) word correctly	Unfamiliarity with words or sounds Inability to retain sound sequence
	Failure to analyze word into sound segments	Lack of specific phonetic / syllabic knowledge Inability to retain sound sequence
	Failure to retain place in word being spelled; loss of sound segment; repetition of sound segment	Unfamiliarity with word Inability to retain sound sequence (while spelling)
Arithmetic	Loss of place in sequence of calculations; omission of step in mental arithmetic	Unfamiliarity with number fact knowledge Inability to retain operation sequences
Mathematics	Lack of word analysis, syntactic or story sequence comprehension skills in word problems Loss of place in problem solution sequence; omission of a step	See Reading section Unfamiliarity with problem content Inability to retain solution step sequences

sequences) or inclination (e.g., toward global meaning rather than analysis).

The third column of Table 12-1 contains causal descriptions of the learning problems. These descriptions fall into three categories: those due to lack of specific knowledge (of sounds, syntaxes, words, etc.), those due to low ability to hold sequences (of sounds, words, etc.), and those due to an inclination away from sequential / analytic (successive) thinking. Again let us stress that these can occur in isolation or in combination, and that one category can cause another (e.g., disinclination to use successive processing will result in less practice of it, and thus in a lower level of ability to use it).

Examples of Successive Processing Problems

In this section we present examples of the problems listed in Table 12-1. We have had to be selective in choosing these examples, so the full range of possible problems, combinations and causes is not included here. Keep in mind that these are *potential* problems; few children are likely to have all of them, and no single problem is necessarily present in a learning problem child. Our purpose here is to illustrate the range of successive processing problems, to give you a feeling for what other examples could exist.

Word Analysis Problems

Successive processing is required in phonic word analysis in order to break the word into its sound-parts, so that each can be pronounced, and then smoothly blended. For example, consider a child trying to pronounce the word "development". Although the word is likely to be unfamiliar, it is phonically regular, and can be broken into pronounceable parts. A child with poor successive processing skills (of either the general or specific type) may try to avoid this approach, guessing from the first letter and the length of the word that it is "downstairs". This represents a disinclination to

use the analytic, successive approach. If asked to sound the word out, he or she may produce "dee-lop-ent", clearly the result of omitting several letters or syllables. Finally, children with successive processing problems can get to the point where they can pronounce each of the syllables, but can't blend them to produce a word (e.g., "de-vel-op-ment"). Especially if the word is unfamiliar to the child, this is not surprising. However, some children experience this problem with familiar words too; in these cases, "Say the word faster" doesn't seem to help. (This problem will be dealt with in the first case study later in this chapter. Refer also to the description of phonological dyslexia in Chapter 7.)

Syntax Comprehension Problems

Successive processing is required to hold a sentence's words so that their syntax can be processed to permit deeper analysis of the sentence's meaning. For example, in reading the sentence "The cat on top of the table was purring", the first seven words need to be held so that it can be seen that "on top of the table" describes where the cat was, and then "the cat" needs to be retained to connect with "was purring". If "on top of the table" pushed "the cat" out of working memory, the child may pronounce "was purring" correctly, but is unlikely to be able to read it with expression or explain the sentence's meaning. This problem is accentuated in learning problem children who are likely to be reading slowly, and whose working memories are thus unlikely to contain relevant prior information.

Story Sequence Comprehension

More advanced texts, such as many encountered in high school or beyond, often present a segment of information (e.g., an incident) in the middle of the text, without specifying how it is related to what immediately precedes or follows it. Because this segment may be crucial for later comprehension, it may need to be retained. Children with successive processing problems are less likely to be able to or to want to retain many such unintegrated segments, and so are likely to lack the necessary data for later comprehension. For example, much of the mystery in mystery stories comes from realizing that many characters *could* have committed the murder. If you can't remember the earlier parts of the story, there is no enjoyable surprise when the solution is revealed, at least no more than in observing some random event. (This type of problem is described in the second case study presented later in this chapter.)

Successive Processing in Spelling

Several aspects of spelling problems can be caused by poor use of successive processing. As in reading, poor pronunciation can result, which renders successful spelling unlikely (e.g., spell government: "govamint – g-o-v-a-m-i-n-t"). Similar problems result from breaking the word incorrectly into parts. Even more successive processing errors result from loss of place in the word being spelled (e.g., omission of the second syllable "e" in elephant; repetition of a syllable, as in "statististics" for statistics). These problems should be addressed by further processing (simultaneous processing, performance monitoring), but they stem initially from successive processing.

Sequence in Arithmetic

Consider an arithmetic problem such as $2 \times (7 + 2 + 4 + 8) - 7 = ?$ Sequence is involved in remembering the rules of arithmetic (such as performing the operations in the brackets first) and in remembering to perform all of the indicated operations. A successive error of the first type would be "Well, 2×7 is 14, plus 2 is 16, plus 4 is 20, plus 8 is 28, minus 7 is 21". An example of the second type of error would be "Okay, first I've got to add the numbers; 7 plus 2 plus 4 plus 8 is 21, and 21 minus 7 is 14". As in the spelling example, further processing may catch these errors; in the case of arithmetic any monitoring usually requires a repetition of the solution process, because there is nothing obviously wrong about 14 as an answer to that problem!

Observation and Assessment of Successive Processing Problems

In this section we discuss informal measures of children's successive processing skills. Formal, standardized tests will be mentioned when they exist, but this discussion is aimed more at the classroom teacher who does not have access to restricted psychological tests. Where standardized tests or norms do not exist, of course, an appreciation of whether or not the child is performing worse than normal can only be gained by testing a variety of children, most of whom are "normal". This is a valuable experience which is well worth the effort required, even for the users of standardized tests.

We begin by describing tests that have been used to measure successive processing in general, rather than with any particular achievement area. You should be aware, however, that *all* tests assess learned knowledge to some degree, so there is no such thing as a content-free test of successive processing. Instead, these tests employ content which almost all children have learned well, thereby decreasing the effect of the prior knowledge factor.

General Measures

Commonly used measures of successive processing require the child to reproduce a sequence of stimuli, which can be numbers, letters, words, pictures, or nonverbal sounds. In order to minimize the effort of prior knowledge, the actual items (the numbers, letters, etc.) should be very familiar to the child. The most common formal test in this area is the Digit Span Test, which appears in the WISC-R and the Illinois Test of Psycholinguistic Abilities (ITPA), and has been used by Das and his colleagues to measure successive processing (Das *et al.*, 1979). The procedure is quite simple: the teacher or tester reads a series of numbers to the child, at a rate of approximately one per second (this is the procedure followed in the WISC-R). The series start at lengths of two numbers for demonstration purposes, and become longer until the child makes two consecutive errors at the same length. Two lists are available at each length, so if the child makes an error on the first, the second is given. If that list is remembered correctly, then the first list of the next higher length is given, and so on. A variety of scoring procedures can be followed, the simplest being to record the greatest series length that the child can recall correctly; this is called the digit *span*. More complex scores can be obtained by counting the total number of items (i.e., numbers) that the child remembers correctly, including those in series which were not recalled totally correctly. For informal testing, the span score is more appropriate. (Typical scores are given in Table 12-2; as you can see, average scores increase with age.)

The teacher should be able to construct similar tests, using letters, common words or pictures. (Keep in mind that the letters and words should not rhyme, or this will penalize the children employing phonetic coding; see Chapter 7, pp. 86-87.) You should find that, as the items become less familiar or predictable (there are ten digits, twenty-six letters, and a large number of possible words), the span scores decrease; comparable scores are also presented in Table 12-2.

Nonverbal successive tests could be constructed from series of simple pictures (see the Visual Sequential Memory subtest of the ITPA), or from series of sounds (e.g., teacher taps a pattern "tap-tap, tap-tap", which the child has to reproduce, or the teacher has several blocks and taps them in a particular order which the child has to repeat).

In the tests described so far, the child has only to remember a series of stimuli; these are relatively "pure" measures of successive processing. Other examples of similar tests are given by Kaufman and Kaufman (1983) and Das and Naglieri (1990). One can also test successive processing in more complicated situations, in which the child has something else to do in addition to remembering the series. The advantage to these techniques is that they prevent the child from using a variety of strategies (such as rehearsal or chunking) which can artificially inflate span scores. Because the child is occupied processing other information while attempting to remember, these are referred to as *working memory span tests;* not surprisingly they yield smaller spans than the simpler tests. We'll describe four working memory span tests.

The simplest is called Backward Digit Span, and is similar to Digit Span except that the child has to repeat each series in reverse order. Typical results are shown in Table 12-2.

TABLE 12-2

Average scores on different span measures for different age groups

| Age (years) | Span Measure | | | | |
	Digit	Letter	Word	Backward Digit*	Counting*
2	2	–	3	–	–
4	4	–	3.5	–	–
6	4.5	4	4	1.5	1.5
8	5.5	4.5	4.5	2.5	2.5
10	6	5	4.5	2.5	3
12	6.5	5	5	3	3.5
Adult	7	6	5	3.5	–

Note: Averages have been rounded to the nearest 0.5, and are estimates based upon Dempster (1981), Wechsler (1974), and Case, Kurland, Goldberg (1982). Spans marked with an asterisk (*) are *working memory spans*, and therefore are predictably lower.

A more complicated test is called Visual Short-Term Memory. In its simpler form, cross-shaped grids of numbers are shown to the subjects (see the left-hand side of Figure 12-1), who then have to reproduce the numbers in an empty grid (see Das *et al.,* 1979). This test is more complicated than Digit Span because the child has to span the grid in a particular order (e.g., left-to-right, top-to-bottom), and then write the numbers in the same temporal order according to the same spatial scanning order. By late elementary school, most children have little difficulty with this simple version of the task. In the more complicated versions, a series of irregular grids is used, which increase in size from the five-digit grids of the simple version to nine digits (see the right-hand side of Figure 12-1). Because the grid shape changes from series to series, the child can not simply use the same spatial scanning order throughout. The more complicated version of this test has been described by Kirby and Biggs (1981).

The third working memory span test was devised by Case, Kurland and Goldberg (1982) and is called the Counting Span Test. The child is shown a series of one, two or more cards, face down. On each card is a number of shapes, some of which are coloured and some of which aren't. The child is supposed to count the coloured shapes, out loud and one by one. The first card is turned up, the child counts, then that card is turned down; the second card is turned up, the child counts again; and so on until all of the cards have been counted. At the end of the set of cards, the child is asked to recall how many shapes were counted on each of the cards. Typical results are shown in Table 12-2; as you will see if you try the test yourself, this test is more difficult than it first appears.

The fourth working memory span test is called a Reading Span test (Daneman & Carpenter, 1980). Subjects are required to read a series of statements, judging after each whether it is true or false. At the end of the series (usually two to five statements), the subject is asked to recall the last words of each of the sentences. Again this task is more difficult than it seems. Daneman and Carpenter found that university students could rarely remember more than four words. Try the example given in the box below for yourself.

To our knowledge, Daneman and Carpenter's test has not been given to young children, nor to learning problem children, perhaps because of the reading required. However, Daneman and Carpenter also presented an auditory version of the test (the Listening Span Test) which could be used, and other authors have presented alternative approaches which may be simpler to use with children (e.g., Masson & Miller, 1983). Development of such tests and their uses with learning problem children should soon be addressed by further research.

Successive Processing in Reading

Table 12-1 can act as a blueprint for designing successive processing tests in the various academic skill areas. In reading, these tests would be aimed at the subskills of word analysis, syntactic analysis, and story sequence comprehension. (Kirby and Robinson, 1987, have examined the successive processing skills of children with reading problems.)

FIGURE   12-1

Examples of the simple (left) and complex (right) visual short-term memory items

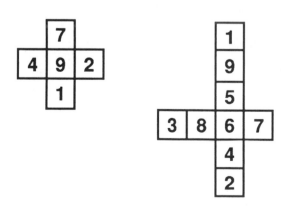

Reading Span

The important point to remember in measuring a working memory span (like Reading Span) is that you want the person to be actively processing the information (thinking about it) was well as passively storing it. Daneman and Carpenter (1980) did this by requiring their subjects to judge whether each of a set of sentences was correct; at the end of the set, they were asked to remember the last word of each of the sentences.

Try the examples below. Use two cards or sheets of paper to expose only one sentence at a time. After each, decide whether it is true or false, and then go on to the next. When you come to the line "Last words", write down as many of the preceding sentences' last words as you can remember in the spaces provided. (The correct answers are given on the next line.)

Set A
Jaguars and lions are two types of cat that live in South American jungles. True or false?

The United States originally consisted of thirteen colonies that had broken away from England. True or false?

Last words? _____ _____

Correct answers: jungles England

Set B
Each Canadian province has a one-house Parliamentary system. True or false?

Ludwig Beethoven became profoundly deaf in his later life. True or false?

In 1936, King George V was forced to choose between his throne and marriage. True or false?

Last words? _____ _____

Correct answers: system life marriage

Set C
The theory of relativity explains why light can move in curved paths. True or false?

Brass is an alloy composed of a mixture of copper and lead. True or false?

In the eighteenth century, the Black Death devastated many countries. True or false?

"Sons and Lovers" is T.S. Eliot's most famous novel. True or false?

Last words? _____ _____ _____ _____

Correct answers: paths lead countries novel

How'd you do? Remember you have to get them in the right order to be scored correct. Also, we hope you didn't forget to answer seriously whether each statement was true or false.

Some suggestions have already been made in Chapter 7 about possible word analysis tasks, for example the syllable and phoneme segmentation tests devised by Mann, Liberman and Shankweiler (1981). These assess oral language skills that should exist prior to reading. In both the basic technique is to say a word to the child, asking him or her to tap once for each sound unit (syllable or phoneme). Typical results are presented in Chapter 7 (see p. 87). Of course, examples would have to be given, and it is normally very difficult to explain the phoneme task to younger children.

The basic word analysis task is to present an unknown word and ask the child to pronounce it. If word *analysis* skills (as opposed to recognition skills) are being tested, phonologically regular words should be used and not "sight" words. In fact, nonwords can be very useful, as long as they are phonologically regular (e.g., "fandalazo", "kalanogra", etc.). Many such activities can be turned into games: for example, present phonologically regular nonwords as well as "illegal" nonwords ("trzl", "fnalgmr"), and ask the children to separate them into two sets, those that could be words and those that couldn't. Another example would be to present nonwords which, when correctly pronounced, are actually real words (e.g., "payshunts", "eenuf"), and ask the children to supply the real words. Examples of this latter test can be found in some measures of language aptitude (e.g., Carroll & Sapon, 1959), though easier examples would have to be found for younger children. (See Case Study I for a description of a child with problems in this area.)

At the syntactic level, a number of tests already exist. For example, one can observe which syntactic constructions a child uses correctly in oral language (for example, the Developmental Sentence Scoring technique of Lee, 1974); this does not provide an exhaustive list of the ones that *could* be understood, either orally or in reading, but it does tell the teacher which ones the child is most comfortable with, and major omissions would suggest some specific teaching activities. Other tests present the children orally with a syntactic construction, asking them to select a picture which rep-

resents the meaning of the construction. For example, if the presented sentence was "The boy was going to write a letter", one picture would show a boy with a completed letter, another with a pen and a blank sheet of paper. For more examples, see the Northwestern Syntax Screening Test (Lee, 1974), or Carrow's (1973) Test of Auditory Comprehension of Language. Other syntactic tests require the child to repeat sentences one at a time as the sentences increase in syntactic complexity. For example, to be able to repeat the sentence "While the hay at the back of the barn is dry, it is still necessary for more to be bought", the child will have to chunk it into a small number of units before it will fit into working memory. That chunking almost certainly has to be done on the basis of the sentence's syntax; the chunking requires simultaneous processing, but the basis for it is successive processing of the word order. Successive processing is then required to retain the sequence of chunks. Sentence repetition is one of the subtests in the Carrow Elicited Language Inventory (Carrow, 1974).

More informal measures of syntax are also possible. Many teachers use a procedure known as miscue analysis (Goodman & Burke, 1972), in which they record the errors that a child makes in oral reading, and rate these errors for their syntactic acceptability (among other things). Presumably, a child who is syntactically competent will tend to make errors which are syntactically acceptable in the passage, whereas a less syntactically competent child will tend to make errors which are constrained in other ways (for instance, graphically or semantically). This same approach could be used in a cloze task, in which the child supplies the missing word, or in the "inserted cloze" task, in which the child judges the correctness of inserted words, some of which have been designed to be syntactically wrong (see Kirby & Teasdale, 1987).

We know of no tests that have been designed to assess story sequence comprehension; however, it is possible to suggest some informal measures. Formal tests have probably been avoided because it is difficult to separate story *sequence* comprehension from other aspects of comprehension. Just as the other levels of successive processing involve the

Successive Processing:
Case Study I

Angela is a student in the third grade. She has been described by all of her teachers as a poor reader, and each year she has been seen, increasingly, as a disruptive influence in class. After several months in grade three, she was referred to the school psychologist, who was to investigate her reading and behaviour problems.

The psychologist decided that it was unlikely that Angela had a primary attention system problem even though she was rather impulsive and overactive in class, because those symptoms had begun to develop only recently. The psychologist decided to proceed on the hypothesis that Angela had a basic reading problem, a problem which made her frustrated and irritable in class. The test results that are relevant to us here come from the WISC-R, and from some informal reading tasks that the psychologist used. Angela's scores from the WISC-R (standard scores ranging from 1 to 19, with an average of 10) are given below:

Subtest	Score
Information	11
Similarities	10
Arithmetic	4
Vocabulary	11
Comprehension	9
Digit Span	2
Picture Completion	12
Picture Arrangement	10
Block Design	12
Object Assembly	11
Coding	4

These test results yield a Verbal IQ of 94, a Performance IQ of 98, and a Full Scale IQ of 95. They are consistent with the teacher's intuition that Angela is of normal ability. However, the breakdown into verbal and performance scales doesn't help us diagnose Angela's problem. If we look instead at the subtests which measure Rugel's (1974) Freedom from Distractibility (see page 160), the picture becomes clearer. The three subtests Arithmetic, Digit Span and Coding have, by far, the lowest scores of all the subtests. Angela clearly has a problem with distractibility. This doesn't solve her impulsivity problem, but it does provide support for that description of her behaviour. If her impulsivity had been apparent since she began school (which it hasn't), attention / arousal problems might have to be considered. In this case, the WISC-R results tell us that she is impulsive for her age, but that she is of average ability and, therefore, should be doing better in reading.

The reading tests told the psychologist and the teacher a lot more. From twenty minutes of reading, Angela was seen to have at least three problems: she tended to guess words from their first few letters, she tended to follow phonic "rules" even when they didn't apply, and she would often pronounce a "word" which she knew wasn't a real word.

Angela was first asked to read a number of words in isolation (that is, not in sentences), and then to read several stories. Here are some examples of Angela's word reading:

For "dream"	she said "drawn".
For "something"	she said "summer".
For "island"	she said "is-land".
For "saucer"	she said "sanker".
For "imagine"	she said "im-a-gine" (to rhyme with sine).

From these few examples it can be seen that she was guessing words from their first one or two letters, and that she was incorrectly pronouncing the letters in some words, thus producing non-words (as in "island"). When Angela said "is-land", she was asked if she had ever heard that word before: she said she hadn't, but she *did* think that the word on the page was a real word. She responded similarly when questioned about several other mispronunciations. She did not seem surprised that many of the words she read didn't make sense.

Here is an example of her story reading, taken from a longer passage.

Actual text: "The lions' final act was in progress. Jack stood waiting to clear the ring."

Angela's version: "The lions' funny … accent was in … pro-grest. Jack still … waiting … the clean ring."

Here again we can see that Angela was guessing at words: during the test she gave the strong impression that she thought speed was more important than accuracy, but even when she laboured over a word (for instance, "progress"), she often pronounced non-words. The result, whether she took her time or not, was incomprehensible to her and the listener.

Analysis

Angela was caught in a vicious circle. She clearly did not use her knowledge of phonic rules and exceptions to pronounce words correctly. Combined with her impulsivity (which may have resulted in part from her frustration in reading), this made her read quickly: it seemed that she thought it was better to get the wrong answers quickly rather than slowly!

Remediation

The psychologist and the teacher decided that this vicious circle had to be broken before Angela could make any progress. The key elements in the program they designed for Angela were:

1. to bring her back to basic phonics rules, to reinforce their importance in her mind;

2. to keep the phonics practice interesting and brief; and

3. to encourage her to use her knowledge of real words to guide her reading.

The first of these elements involved considerable training in successive processing, as Angela did not like to go through a word sound by sound. In order to get the idea of sequential processing across to Angela without using the reading content that she found so frustrating, it was decided to begin with some of the successive processing exercises designed by Krywaniuk and Das (1976). As Angela succeeded in these tasks, word-based tasks were slowly introduced. Where possible, these were presented as games in which other children could participate. It was not considered necessary to teach Angela many phonics rules, as her problem was not that she didn't know them, but that she didn't use them. A variety of tasks was designed in which she had to pay attention to the completed word, and to the sequence of sounds or syllables. One of these had her look up words in a dictionary.

During all of these tasks Angela received as much attention as possible, made as few mistakes as possible, and was shown how to correct her mistakes as quickly as possible. Most importantly, no single task or lesson lasted more than ten minutes, so that her interest remained high.

The third element of the program provides an example of how simultaneous processing can be used to overcome a successive processing problem. One of Angela's problems had been that she blindly read words without paying much attention to their meaning or, as it often turned out, to their lack of meaning. The first goal here was to convince Angela that the meaning of what she read was more important than the actual words. This came as a surprise to her, as all her previous teachers (in her opinion!) had always stressed how important it was for the words to be correct. Again, games were used as often as possible, especially those that involved other children. For example, one game required the children to pick out non-words from groups of words and, later, non-words or wrong words from sentences. In more traditional reading tasks, Angela was encouraged to write or tell her own stories, which she later had to read aloud: it was easy to convince her then that she hadn't used any non-words or words she didn't know in her stories! Other tasks involved having her read, and then stopping her, closing the book, and having her retell the story to that point. All of these techniques emphasized the importance of meaning, and balanced the emphasis upon word-attack skills in other parts of the program.

Progress

Angela had acquired her reading and behaviour problems over several years, so it was not surprising that it took many weeks for much progress to be seen. Even after six months she was not reading as well as many of her classmates, but most of her behaviour problems had disappeared, and her reading had improved dramatically. Perhaps most importantly, she no longer found reading to be unpleasant. Her teacher continued to monitor her progress carefully, but had been able to give up designing special exercises for her after the first six weeks. Angela's family had agreed to try some of the games and reading tasks at home, which allowed her much more practice and some variability, all in a non-threatening environment.

Angela should be able to become and remain at least an average reader. Her progress beyond that point will depend upon her other skills, her interests, and her future teachers. The remedial program succeeded in eliminating a barrier to her success, but it cannot guarantee how far she will proceed.

holding of a series of words or chunks, successive processing at the story level involves the holding of a series of story segments, such as events or episodes. Again, segment *order* is often important for later interpretations. For example, a story could contain two episodes, one in which an impoverished family is described, and one in which the father commits a bank robbery. If the family episode is remembered as preceding the latter, the interpretation would be that the man was forced into crime by poverty. If the sequence is remembered in the reverse order, the moral is quite different: crime leads to ruin.

To assess this process one could either present children with story segments and then ask them to place them in correct order, or present them with a complete story and later ask them to recall it,

recording the order of events they produce. An example of the former approach is the Picture Arrangement subtest of the WISC-R, in which children are given a number of pictures and asked to rearrange them so that they make a story. This is a complex skill, requiring considerable simultaneous processing skill to relate components between pictures and to construct a unitary story. (In fact, A. Kaufman and N. Kaufman (1983) found that a similar test called Photo Series was more related to simultaneous processing than successive.) Informal versions of the picture arrangement test can be constructed by cutting up comic strips and asking the children to rearrange them. To emphasize the importance of sequence, rather than overall (simultaneous) concept, pictures should be chosen that have no obvious underlying story (e.g., cat, house, pencil); children could then be asked to supply different stories, based upon different sequences of the same pictures.

When asking children to recall a narrative, a story could be presented either orally or in writing though, of course, only the latter would require reading. In either case it would be preferable if the story were constructed of a series of episodes which could stand more or less alone; in this way, more than one plausible sequence is possible, placing more stress upon successive processing of order. If the story is more integrated than that, such that the order of events could be deduced by someone who hadn't read the story, then simultaneous processing (of one story theme or plot structure) will dominate; this is probably the explanation of Kaufman and Kaufman's (1983) finding for the Photo Series test. (See Case Study II for a description of an adolescent with problems remembering story sequence.)

Successive Processing: Case Study II

Our second case study of successive processing problems is very different from the first. In fact, Danny, a fourteen-year-old high school student, would not be traditionally regarded as learning disabled at all. However, as you will see, he did have a learning problem. His problem was a difficulty in remembering the sequence of episodes within a story.

In elementary school Danny had been seen by his teachers as slightly above average in ability. This view was backed up by his achievement performance and by an IQ test (which showed an IQ of 110, though the records did not indicate which test was given). Even at the age of fourteen, in his second year of high school, Danny was still doing reasonably well in most of his subjects.

The first teacher to notice a problem was Danny's English teacher. The class had been asked to read a ten-page story and then, several days later, to retell that story in writing without referring to the actual text. Students then had to go on to say what should have happened next. Danny did much worse than expected; he could remember only the beginning and the end of the story. While that would have been sufficient information to reconstruct most stories, it wasn't in this case because the narrative was complex. In fact, the beginning of the story was quite misleading, suggesting that the main character was a nasty person. It went on to describe a series of events which didn't overtly have much to do with each other. It was necessary, however, to follow these parts of the story in order to understand their impact upon the main character. In the end, the main character faced a dilemma: he could do the "right" thing or, instead, he could attempt to make a lot of money. A reader who had followed the story could see that all the episodes tied in together, and that they implied that the character would opt for the "right" choice.

When the teacher thought about the story later, she realized that Danny had probably never before encountered a story that wasn't straightforward. At the time, however, she was surprised at Danny's poor performance, and gave him a second chance to read the story. When that didn't help him to respond, she sat down with Danny to watch him read the story in question and a variety of other texts, and to ask him questions as he went. The teacher realized that Danny was reading in a relatively superficial and passive manner. As he read, he'd get an idea of what the text was about, changing that basic idea (really a main idea – see Chapter 7) as the story unfolded. However, all that he held on to at any one point was that single main idea. When an episode wasn't related to the main idea, Danny either ignored it, or discarded the old main idea for a new one derived from the most recent episode. This meant that Danny could easily retell a simple story (the kind whose plot would easily fit into a thirty-minute television show), but got lost as soon as anything complicated happened.

If Danny had been of low-average ability, perhaps this wouldn't be all that surprising. The teacher recognized, however, that someone of Danny's overall ability should be able to do better, and that this type of learning problem would be a major handicap in the future.

Analysis

Danny's approach to reading was not a bad one, at least not for simple texts. It is possible that Danny's general ability had given him the opportunity to become lazy; perhaps less able students would have to worry about the details, but Danny could generally figure them out from the higher level (main idea) information that he could remember. This is certainly a very efficient use of working memory resources. Unfortunately, Danny had no detail-storing strategy to fall back upon when things became complicated.

Danny's problem was with the use of successive processing to remember large units of information. A quick series of word and number memory tests showed that he had no difficulty with successive processing of simple elements; the problem began to appear only as the units to be recalled increased in size. This is certainly not the type of learning problem that would prevent one from learning to read, and it may even be one that Danny would have corrected himself in time. yet such learning problems shouldn't be underrated: while they persist, they can prevent a lot of learning and, perhaps, leave the student discouraged with school in general. The fact that the learning problem looks solvable doesn't mean it's not a problem.

Remediation

The teacher decided to discuss the problem with Danny and design some remedial activities together. (This is a sensible approach that should be used more often, especially with adolescent students.) The teacher was able to make Danny begin to understand the problem, though he was far from convinced that it was very serious. Mostly on the teacher's suggestions, they arranged activities around three goals for Danny:

1. Concentrating on each idea as it was encountered (not giving up on any as being unimportant too soon);

2. Taking notes as he read, and then diagramming or mapping the connections between the ideas. These diagrams would then led to the main ideas of the text; and

3. Learning something about the structure of texts, so that he would be better equipped to analyze them.

The first of these goals focuses on content and is specifically designed to improve successive processing; it ensures that the sequence of ideas is processed and retained in the right order. The same is true for note-taking and generating lists of ideas in the second goal. Diagramming ideas, however, shows the relationships among them, and thus involves simultaneous processing. The third goal focuses on content to improve simultaneous processing. The student learns that texts are of different types, and that those different types have predictable structures (e.g., introduction, setting, characters, problems, resolution, end). These predictable general structures are called story grammars, though they don't apply only to stories.

For each of these goals, Danny was to have lots of practice – analyzing texts, reorganizing texts that had had their sentences scrambled, and filling in missing paragraphs.

Sounds like a lot of work, doesn't it? The teacher soon realized that all of his students could benefit from this type of program, and not only in English class. Discussions with other teachers, from English, History, Science and Social Science, resulted in joint efforts to select texts and to provide idea lists and diagrams for students' use. The teachers soon realized that what they were doing was trying to show their students how to comprehend – something that, perhaps, should be more heavily emphasized in school.

Progress

And what about Danny? As you might expect, the program worked. Danny soon saw what he had been doing wrong, and after a few weeks of practice he was able to drop some of the "supports" that he had been given (the listing of ideas, diagrams, etc.). Those supports became strategies that he could use when texts became difficult, or if he knew they were very important (e.g., when studying for an exam). His achievement returned to its previously high level, and he became even more interested in reading. One point that he kept emphasizing was that he now felt he had more control over his learning. A success story!

Successive Processing in Spelling

The task of spelling fortunately has fewer levels than reading, so there is much less need for an elaborate series of measures when testing successive processing. The basic requirement for assessing the different spelling problems listed in Table 12-1 is to observe the child's spelling performance at various stages in the spelling process (cf. Figure 8-1). The first problem mentioned in Table 12-1 is the correct pronunciation of the word to spell; this can be easily assessed by asking the child to repeat orally presented words of increasing difficulty, noting the particular sounds that cause problems and the number of sounds that the child can repeat.

The second problem concerns the segmenting of the word to be spelled into sound segments. This skill could be assessed by the syllable and phoneme segmentation tasks that were described in Chapter 7 (see p. 87). Other tests could involve the presentation of segmented words, which the child has to judge for correctness.

The third problem is maintaining one's place in the word being spelled. The most straightforward way to assess this is to inspect words the child has misspelled, once you have assured yourself that the word was pronounced and segmented correctly. More indirect measures could involve asking the child to judge whether given spellings are correct, after you have placed errors of a successive kind among the spellings. To ensure that holistic word recognition is not taking place, this technique could make use of phonologically regular nonwords. The types of errors inserted would include syllable (or phoneme) omission and repetition.

Successive Processing in Arithmetic and Mathematics

Two types of successive problems are apparent in arithmetic and mathematics tasks, those which are really reading or oral language problems (inability to interpret the words or sentences of a problem), and those which involve the loss of one's place during the execution of a number of problem steps. The first type has already been dealt with in the reading section above; all that needs be said beyond that is that mathematics problems contain some of the strangest syntax that children encounter in school, which they seldom encounter anywhere else.

The second type of problem is similar to the last of the successive spelling problems, loss of place during execution of a series of steps. In order to observe such a difficulty, it is first necessary to ensure that the child knows the correct series of steps; if the steps are not known, as is more common, then the problem is more correctly described as a simultaneous problem (see Chapter 13) or as a planning or strategic problem (see Chapter 14). To detect whether a step has been omitted, the child's work can be inspected (written work would be available for mathematics problems but not, of course, for mental arithmetic). If written work or partial answers are not available, then one can only judge by the incorrect answers given: is there any plausible way that they can be obtained by omitting a step in the correct solution procedure? Again, children could be provided with solved problems, and asked to judge their correctness. The inclusion of solutions which clearly omit or repeat steps should identify children with successive processing problems in this area.

Improving Successive Processing Skills

If a child is performing poorly in the successive aspects of achievement or general cognitive tasks, three explanations are possible:

1. The child has a low level of successive processing potential. By this we mean that the child's ability to employ successive processing is not good, and that remedial efforts to improve it are not likely to be successful. This explanation depends upon *potential,* an upper limit to future performance. It is never certain in testing that a child's potential, as opposed to the current level of performance, has been measured. However, if competent and extensive efforts have been made to teach a child a particular skill, such as phonic decoding, without success, a reasonable (though still not certain) conclusion is that that child lacks the requisite ability to learn that skill. Such a child may qualify for the label "phonological dyslexic" (see Chapter 7). In these cases, it may be more effective to attempt to design an alternative form of instruction (e.g., emphasizing a visual, whole-word approach) than to continue to stress the very skills that the child lacks.

2. The child has not developed to his or her potential in successive processing ability. Abilities develop in response to experience, practice and instruction; if some children have missed out on some of this, they may well have a difficulty in using successive processing, but the difficulty can be overcome. In these cases, it is preferable to improve the successive processing skill (and thus, for instance, phonic decoding) than to attempt an alternative and less certain form of instruction.

3. The child is not inclined to use successive processing when it is the optimal approach. A child may avoid successive processing in general, or merely in an achievement area (e.g., reading), or even within an aspect of an area (e.g., decoding). This inclination is not originally due to a lack of ability, though it may result in a lower level of skill. In these cases, the child requires strategy instruction, combined with some skill training.

These three explanations are difficult to distinguish in practice. Because we have no infallible measures of potential, the first explanation should be invoked only after extensive effort has been expended trying to implement explanations two or three. How long one should attempt to improve skills before opting for an alternative method of instruction is impossible to state as a rule. This decision must be based upon two factors: one's confidence that skill training has been tried as completely as possible, and the likelihood that the alternative method of instruction will be effective. If, as some have argued, whole-word based reading instruction can work only if the children teach *themselves* phonic skills, this option will not be effective for children with low successive processing ability.

It is also difficult to distinguish between explanations two and three, in that a lower skill level will tend to produce an inclination not to use that skill, and vice versa. Fortunately, the remedial activities suggested by these explanations are not very different, both recommending structured practice and strategy instruction in different proportions. In the remedial suggestions which follow we indicate both types of activities; it is the individual teacher's task to decide upon relative emphases. If a particular child improves quickly in a task, or "gets the hang of it" after brief instructions about how to approach the task, clearly the problem was largely strategic. In other cases, considerable structured practice will be required.

A word of caution: what follows are *guidelines* for designing remedial instruction, not a complete curriculum syllabus. We emphasize prototypical activities and tasks, leaving it to the teacher to design the individual child's instructional program and to integrate these activities into classroom routines.

If you look back at Table 12-1, you will see that the "causal descriptions" fall into three groups: content familiarity, sequence memory, and strategies. These are likely to interact in any particular child's poor achievement.

Content Familiarity

If children are unfamiliar with the task content, they are likely to take longer to encode that information; thus, it will absorb more of their working memory resources. If the unfamiliarity is with the whole item (unfamiliar digit, character, or sight word), this is more a problem of simultaneous processing (see Chapter 13). However, unfamiliarity is also likely to reflect a problem with the sequencing of items, as in sequences of letters that make a word (decoding) or sequences of numbers in an arithmetic problem (counting, adding). Unfamiliarity does not prevent recognition (encoding), but it slows it down. The problem is fundamentally the same, whether the units are sounds, letters, words, numbers or groups of words or numbers.

The solution to the unfamiliarity problem is practice, and the secret to the use of practice is to keep it interesting. As a rule, practice will be most effective if it is used individually, if it is not used for long periods continuously (depending upon the age and patience of the children), and if it can be employed in novel contexts (e.g., games, microcomputers). As just one such example, the teacher could construct a card-matching game, which children could play in groups of four to eight. The cards could have words, for instance, printed on them, care being taken that these words are phonetically regular. Two children at a time would turn cards over, and points would go to the child who first correctly recognizes that two cards are identical. Clearly, this game could also make use of sight words, thus helping simultaneous processing (see Chapter 13). It would not be difficult to adapt such a game for individual use on a microcomputer: in this way the student could practise "in private", and keep a record of the amount of time needed to make a correct decision.

Sequence Memory and Strategies

The essence of successive processing is to maintain a set of items in order in working memory; failing to do so is the source of most successive processing problems. Therefore, the basic remedial approach should be to teach children to remember sequences of items, and the strategies to use in doing so.

Sequence memory training could employ academic content and academic skills (such as in reading and remembering words), or could, instead, begin with content that was less academic (and, therefore, less intimidating). It could be done initially with numbers, letters, words or pictures that were presented in an obvious order (as in Digit Span types of tests), and later with the same stimuli presented so that order was not apparent (such as the Visual Short-term Memory test described earlier in this chapter; see Figure 12-1). In these tasks, the teacher might give the children a chance to approach the problem in their own way, and then allow them to check their own performance, pick out their errors, and try to suggest ways in which they went wrong. By careful probing and suggesting, the teacher should elicit from the children ideas about how to improve performance. If even that fails, the teacher should suggest a strategy: in the span tasks, this would be to name each of the items in turn, and then rehearse them. Thus if the numbers to be remembered were 6, 4, 7, 2, 9, 3, the child could be encouraged to say "6, 4, 6-4, 7, 2, 7-2, 9, 3, 9-3" several times, or "6, 4, 7, 6-4-7, 2, 9, 3, 2-9-3", and then "6-4-7-2-9-3" several times more. If the teacher begins with a series of a length that is just at or below the children's level of skill, some improvement should be quickly apparent. It is important that improvement happens as quickly as possible, that the children are aware of it, and that they understand how their new strategy has produced success, for their active cooperation is necessary for the practice to be successful. Sequence memory training could be applied to reading (words, etc. that the child has read), spelling (sounds, letters, groups of letters) or arithmetic and mathematics (numbers, formulas, etc.).

In the case of the more complex tasks, the further component of sequential scanning would have to be added. It would be best if this were added to the span-type tasks initially in a simple form, before gradually increasing in complexity (see Figure 12-2). The teacher should emphasize that a consistent scanning sequence is important, such as top-to-bottom, left-to-right. If the child has difficulty with that sequence, then the teacher should cover the entire matrix, uncovering the boxes one by one in the correct order. By this means, the correct strategy will be encouraged, a strategy that

FIGURE 12-2

A possible sequence of item types for number-memory training. Multiple examples would be provided of each form, and the set could be repeated for other stimulti (e.g., letters, words, pictures, objects).

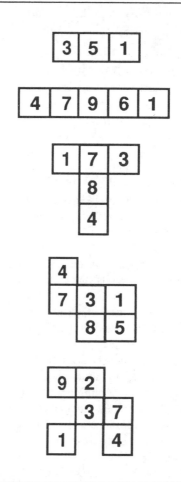

makes use of successive processing. Again, it is worth emphasizing that the teacher should wherever possible construct these activities into enjoyable games, and should not persist with them after the children begin to lose interest. One way of maintaining interest is to shift the content or context of the task, while keeping the process the same. Table 12-3 contains a list of possible successive

TABLE 12-3
Possible successive processing training tasks

Say and write alphabet letters or numbers in order.

Repeat random letter, number or word sequences (and then do it backwards!).

Memorize poems, songs, or lines in a play (the more fun the better).

After hearing a story, repeat the events in order.

Follow the instructions for a complex task, e.g., cooking from a recipe.

Copy a rhythmic pattern by clapping.

Repeat sentences of increasing length.

Give a visitor directions for travelling to a particular place.

Arrange cut-up comic strips in order.

Write the steps involved in performing an everyday activity (e.g., cutting the grass, washing the car, vacuuming).

Plan a sight-seeing trip.

Activities involving counting or time-telling.

Repetition of tongue-twisters (e.g., She sells sea shells by the sea shore).

Games involving the identification of missing letters or syllables in words (e.g., bo-le, s-ool).

processing training tasks that employ a variety of contents and contexts.

In reading, sequence memory would be taught with respect first to words the child has read, then phrases, sentences (ideas), and main ideas or story segments. At the sentence level, children could be taught a variety of methods for improving their memory. One such technique relies upon syntactic analysis; without necessarily teaching grammar, you could ask children to practise dividing sentences into "the bits that go together" such as in "The little boy / likes to feed / the cows / that live in the barn". Subtle syntactic distinctions, such as between tenses, could also be practised.

More complex sequencing tasks would involve more complex items, such as story elements or instructions. D. Kaufman and P. Kaufman (1979) used cards which on one side had a series of pictures connected by arrows, so that a coherent story sequence was indicated. Children were asked to verbalize the story on that side, after which the cards were turned over. On the reverse side were the same pictures, but in a different order. The children's task was to draw arrows between the

pictures, to reconstruct the sequence of the first side. This procedure could begin with simple series of two or three pictures, and build up to larger sets. Effort should be made to keep the pictures as independent as possible, so that the child's memory is largely formed by the sequence of pictures seen and not by any predominant semantic theme. (To reiterate the point made about the Photo Series test on pp. 171-172, if the overall theme or plot is apparent, simultaneous processing will become more important.)

A development of this technique involves the reading of a multi-element story by the children, who subsequently recall the sequence of events. As in the picture tasks, it is important not to use this task merely as a test, but as an opportunity to teach. The children should be encouraged to see where they went wrong, to go back to the story to correct their recall, and to try again. This process should be begun with simple stories, proceeding to the complex only when the basic skills and the simple stories have been mastered. Teaching in this case would also include some story analysis – asking the children to divide the story into segments and say how one segment leads to the next. Successive processing would be encouraged by the sequential aspects, but there would be no reason to avoid helping simultaneous skills, by looking at relationships and integration, as long as this focus did not detract from the development of the successive skills.

Further complex successive training tasks could be designed around the following of instructions: games could be devised in which the children must perform a series of actions in a particular order. This could be done with groups of children, each having to check the actions of the others. This approach could be adapted to mathematical problem solving, the point being to remember a sequence of planned operations.

For further examples of successive processing training activities consult the list of recommended readings at the end of this chapter. Two case study examples of successive processing problems are presented in this chapter. As we have emphasized elsewhere, these are intended as examples, not as the definitive statement of the only two types of successive processing problems that exist; they aren't!

Summary

In this chapter we have looked at successive processing, both as a general category of mental ability and as specifically applied in a variety of achievement areas. We began by explaining that other theories have used similar concepts, and that successive processing problems have been frequently seen as the source of learning problems. Table 12-1 contains a list of the commonly described successive learning problems.

A variety of measures of successive processing were presented, most available to the classroom teacher. A number of achievement area examples of successive processing were also described; these, in particular, emphasize that successive processing normally operates in conjunction with other skills. These various measures are best understood both as potential areas of difficulty for students and as areas in which remediation may need to take place.

The final section of this chapter outlined how to approach the remediation of successive processing problems. If you have followed us to this point, you should be able to see that the theory, the measurement, and the remediation form an integrated unit; ideally, they all support each other, and combine to help you understand learning problems caused by weaknesses in successive processing.

RECOMMENDED READING

Successive Processing Problems
We've avoided giving you the detail of the studies showing learning problem children to have successive processing problems. The following two references can be consulted if you would like to pursue that point:

Leong, C.K.
   1980. Cognitive patterns of "retarded" and below average readers. *Contemporary Educational Psychology, 5,* 101-117.

Kirby, J.R. & Robinson, G.L.W.
   1987. Simultaneous and successive processing in reading disabled children. *Journal of Learning Disabilities, 20,* 243-252.

Successive Processing Training
Das, J.P., Naglieri, J.A. & Kirby, J.R.
   In press. *The assessment of cognitive processes.* New York: Allyn & Bacon.

Kaufman, A.S. & Kaufman, N.L.
   1983. *Kaufman Assessment Battery for Children. Interpretive Manual.* Circle Pines, Minnesota: American Guidance Service.

Kaufman, D. & Kaufman, P.
   1979. Strategy training and remedial techniques. *Journal of Learning Disabilities, 12,* 416-419.

Krywaniuk, L.W. & Das, J.P.
   1976. Cognitive strategies in native children: Analysis and intervention. *Alberta Journal of Educational Research, 22,* 271-280.

Trifiletti, D.T., Trifiletti, R.M. & Trifiletti, R.J.
   1982. *WISCR-80. An Educational Program for the Weschler Intelligence Scale for Children, Revised.* Jacksonville, Florida: Precision People.

CHAPTER 13

Simultaneous Processing

THE SECOND MAJOR CATEGORY of information processing skills is simultaneous processing. In this chapter we examine simultaneous processing both as a general information processing skill, and as it is manifested in a variety of more specific contexts, including reading, spelling, and mathematics.

We begin by elaborating upon the definition of simultaneous processing given in Chapter 5. We review how other approaches to cognition have dealt with what we term simultaneous processing. As you will see, simultaneous processing appears in far more different and complex ways than does successive processing. In the second section of the chapter we describe how simultaneous processing is manifested in various achievement areas. In the third section, we present methods that classroom teachers or psychologists could use to observe simultaneous processing, both generally and within specific achievement areas. Finally, we present approaches to improving poor simultaneous processing. This discussion is largely dominated by the question of whether poor simultaneous processing is due to low *ability* to use simultaneous processing, to a more changeable *difficulty* in using it, or even to an *inclination* on the child's part not to use it. As we suggested in the preceding chapter, if poor processing is due to low ability, then remedial

approaches may have to concentrate on teaching the children alternatives, which could be extremely difficult. On the other hand, if skill development or strategy instruction seem possible, they are the preferred paths to take.

We repeat here our usual caution: the attention, processing and planning systems normally work in a coordinated fashion, as do simultaneous and successive processing. We focus in this chapter upon simultaneous processing, but you should not lose sight of its interdependent relationship with the other functions.

Simultaneous Processing in Cognition

You should remember from Chapter 12 that successive processing has a number of rough equivalents in other cognitive theories (e.g., rote memory, sequencing ability, and so on). Simultaneous processing, on the other hand, represents a level of generality which is not common in other cognitive theories; however, virtually all of those theories have one or more narrower elements which would be included under the general umbrella of simultaneous processing. In employing the broader term, we do not deny the usefulness of the narrower terms in many contexts; we do suggest that there is some value in acknowledging the relationships, through simultaneous processing, between these narrower constructs.

The essence of simultaneous processing is that a number of independent elements are present at the same time in working memory, such that the *relationships* are observed between them. These relationships are used to produce or construct a new entity which is in some sense an *integration* of the previously existing separate elements. Defined in this way, simultaneous processing can be seen in all theories of cognition and in all theories of achievement task performance. We do not have space in this section to consider all of these manifestations; therefore, we have had to be selective. As a result, we have chosen three areas to review: spatial skills and imagery, semantic processing, and reasoning.

While simultaneous processing and its variants have been common in theories of cognition, they have not been as prominent in explanations of learning disabilities. To a large extent, this has been due to the fact that simultaneous processing skills have been regarded as too related to intelligence; since learning disabled children have, by definition, to be normal in intelligence, children with low simultaneous skills have not been considered. One exception to this rule, which has been discounted, was the theory that learning disabled children have visual perception or visual-motor difficulties. (Refer back to Chapter 2 to see the evidence which supported this theory and the evidence which subsequently cast doubt upon it.) Of course, it is possible that simultaneous processing problems do not occur in the absence of a general processing problem. However, we suggest that there is evidence of learning problems due to simultaneous processing problems, learning problems that have not been typically considered by learning disability theorists. It is possible that some of these problems are rare (e.g., regarding sight-word skills), while others (e.g., in mathematical problem-solving) have been ignored in the concentration upon reading, and others (e.g., in reading comprehension) ignored in the concentration upon early skills.

Spatial Skills and Imagery

The spatial ability referred to by psychologists usually involves the mental holding of a non-verbal figure, and performance of some transformation upon the mental representation. The figures themselves differ in complexity or difficulty, as do the transformations to be performed. Figure 13-1 contains several examples of figures and transformations. In the first example, the subject must take a relatively simple figure, mentally rotate it, and then compare the result with another figure. The second example is a more complex figure which also must be rotated and compared. The third example is often referred to as a paper folding test. The figure itself is quite simple, only a piece of paper. However, the transformations, successive foldings of the paper, punching a hole through the folded paper and then unfolding the paper, are relatively complex. The fourth example involves a relatively complex figure (a cube) and a relatively complex transformation (three dimensional rotation).

These tests assess simultaneous processing because the subject takes the stimulus input (a series of lines and dots on a page), forms it into a holistic figure, and then manipulates that figure as a single unit. Similar skills are required in many other tasks, including recognizing a friend's face, following directions on map, deciding if the sofa would fit on the other side of the living room, and deciding whether it would look better there. Spatial skills are crucial in everyday life, and in much academic learning (e.g., understanding diagrams), but have not been as widely studied as have verbal skills.

An exception to this rule is the study of mental imagery, which has been shown to be a powerful memory technique. The work of Paivio (e.g., 1971), among others, has shown that visualizing the object represented by a word is a good technique for remembering the word. This, of course, is more true for words representing concrete objects than those representing more abstract concepts. The well known maxim "A picture is worth a thousand words" derives from the same phenomenon: a picture can represent in a single entity many pieces of

FIGURE 13-1
Spatial ability tasks

Here are four examples of spatial ability tests. (The correct answers are given at the end of the box.)

Example 1

Examine this figure:

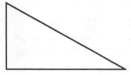

Which of the figures below can be produced by simply rotating the above figure (that is, without picking it up and turning it over)?

    (a)   (b)   (c)   (d)

Example 2

Examine this figure:

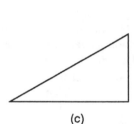

Which of the figures below can be produced by simply rotating the above figure (that is, without picking it up and turning it over)?

   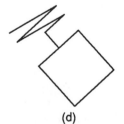

    (a)   (b)   (c)   (d)

F I G U R E   1 3 - 1 Continued
Spatial ability tasks

Example 3

The next line of figures describes a piece of paper being folded, and a hole being punched in it.

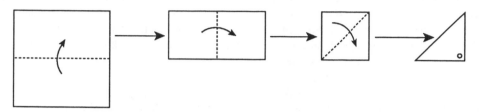

Which of the following figures show what the paper will look like when unfolded?

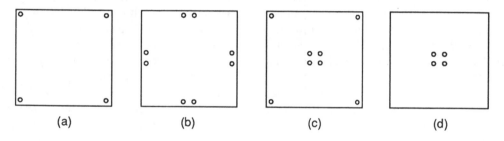

| (a) | (b) | (c) | (d) |

Example 4

Examine the following cube
(each of its six faces is different):

Which of following could be the same cube rotated?

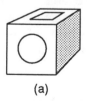 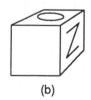

| (a) | (b) | (c) | (d) |

Correct answers

Example 1: a, d   Example 3: b
Example 2: b, c   Example 4: b, c

information and even more efficiently the relationships among those pieces of information. Furthermore, imagery provides a second code for verbal information, which increases the chances of recall and can prevent overloading of the verbal system (e.g., Brooks, 1968).

Spatial and imagery skills of the type described above play important roles in a number of achievement areas. Mathematics and scientific problem solving are the clearest examples: students need mentally or physically to construct a representation of the problem situation (e.g., a diagram). Geometry is an obvious example in which spatial skills are crucial. However, examples on other areas are also important. Even in a humanities subject such as history, maps are frequently employed to represent physical movements of armies or peoples, and diagrams to represent balances of historical forces. In language learning, imagery has been shown to assist in learning new vocabulary (this is called the "keyword" method; see McDaniel & Pressley, 1984). Students benefit in many academic subjects if they can visually represent some information while also verbally representing other information.

In reading, the ability to visualize the events described provides not only a second means of remembering the information, but also a valuable comprehension check. If the events are successfully visualized then comprehension is taking place, and if the visualization produced is assessed against other criteria, such as information occurring in the text, then errors in comprehension can be detected relatively quickly.

The role of these spatial skills in learning problems has not been researched to any great degree. Some evidence does exist, however, to indicate that difficulties in the spatial area are related to difficulties in mathematics and that training can improve spatial skills and transfer to mathematics achievement as well (Kirby, 1984).

As we have observed throughout this book, learning disabilities research has been constrained in many ways. The relative lack of attention given to mathematics and problem solving may have resulted in underestimating the importance of simultaneous processing skills, such as those represented by spatial skills, in producing learning problems. Similarly, the assumption that learning disabled children had to be normal in intelligence, combined with the fact that many intelligence tests include simultaneous processing items of a spatial nature, may have prematurely eliminated these skills from consideration as involved in learning problems. Much more research is needed in these areas; in the meantime, we suggest that teachers and psychologists keep an open mind about the possible roles of spatial skills in learning problems.

Semantic Processing

While simultaneous processing is most easily seen in spatial tasks, it is also clearly demonstrated in verbal tasks which require the relating or integrating of discrete pieces of information. Many examples of simultaneous processing in the verbal domain can be given. When a student inspects a list of words and mentally categorizes them as examples of furniture, animals and food, that student is employing simultaneous processing. In order to produce that categorization, separate words such as "chair" and "table" must be semantically analyzed, lists of potential features assembled, and the appropriate common features selected as the basis of the correct categorization. Another example of simultaneous processing would be to answer the question, "How is a lead pencil like a glass of beer?" Again it is necessary to assemble a list of characteristics of each of the items mentioned, to look for a commonality. (The answer, in case you're curious, is that both a lead pencil and beer contain carbon.) Both of these tasks require the semantic encoding of discrete items at the same time, so that common features can be identified.

Simultaneous processing is also involved when the semantic coding of words is used to construct a new meaning. For example, in comprehending the simple statement "The cat is black", the semantic element "cat" must be combined with the element blackness. More spatial or relational statements such as "The book is on the table" or "Peter is taller than Fred" illustrate the point as well, indicating an interaction between verbal and spatial domains. However, the same relating or integrating operation (simultaneous processing) is required when the content is abstract, not visual. For example, in comprehending "The soldiers were brave", there is no visual equivalent to "brave", but the two entities "The soldiers" and "bravery" still have to be linked or related in memory for comprehension to occur.

The comprehension of verbal material, in listening or in reading, requires that a considerable number of such semantic connections or relationships be formed. This is true within phrases (e.g., linking nouns with adjectives), at the sentence level (relating noun with noun, noun with verb), and at the paragraph level (identifying the referent of a pronoun), and beyond (recognizing the allegorical significance of an otherwise irrelevant intrusion upon the plot). The same is true in producing a response. For example, in answering the question "Is it ever right to steal", a variety of simple responses are possible: "No, because it's wrong to steal"; "Yes, if you have to"; "Yes, if you're not caught." Each of these simple answers is relevant in that it is related to, or addresses, the question. However, an even better answer can be constructed by relating these separate responses: "In general it's wrong to steal, but other principles are more important, such as the sanctity of life. It would be okay to steal to save a life." Answers of this type demonstrate what Biggs and Collis (1982) term "relational thinking".

Relatively little research has assessed the role of the semantic simultaneous processing factors in learning problems. Several reasons for this can be identified, again relating to the definition that learning disabled children are of normal intelligence. Comprehension skills, particularly in the listening domain, have been seen traditionally as too related to intelligence for a child to be normal in one and disabled in the other. The work of Wiig and Semel is an exception (e.g., Wiig, 1976; Semel & Wiig, 1982). By analyzing language functions into their component parts, Wiig and Semel have isolated aspects of comprehension which are associated with learning problems, some of which they ascribe to simultaneous processing. These comprehension components are less awesome than general

comprehension, and therefore seem more amenable to training. The analytic approach of Wiig and Semel to language corresponds to our analytic approach to intelligence. The simultaneous language functions that they find associated with learning problems involve the comprehension or production of comparative, passive, possessive, familial, spatial and temporal relationships, all of whch can be seen to have a simultaneous processing basis (see Wiig, 1976, p. 8). A second type of simultaneous processing problem, the inability to retrieve word meanings accurately, is related to the severe disability termed *deep dyslexia,* which was described in Chapter 7 (p. 90).

Reasoning

In the preceding sections we have seen examples of simultaneous processing in the spatial and verbal domains. This third section concerns reasoning tasks, which can be in either domain. Psychologists divide reasoning into two types, inductive and deductive. In inductive reasoning, a set of stimuli are inspected to determine a rule of similarity or difference; for example, which of the following words doesn't go with the others: saw, wood, hammer? This is another example of a situation in which lists of features or characteristics of elements must be compared and analyzed for similarity or dissimilarity. The lists of features must exist at the same time in working memory in order for the comparison process to be successful (see Pellegrino, 1985, for a readable review of inductive reasoning).

The second type of reasoning, deductive reasoning, involves the drawing of legitimate conclusions from given premises. For example, if Mary is taller than John (premise 1) and John is taller than Fred (premise 2), who is the tallest? Simultaneous processing is involved because the relationships expressed within and between premises must be constructed. This task is more like the "The soldiers were brave" task mentioned in the last section, in that elements with no inherent relationship (Mary, John; soldiers, bravery) are arbitrarily related. (See

Johnson-Laird, 1985, for a review of deductive reasoning.)

Once we begin to consider the area of reasoning, we are clearly stepping over the bounds of what is normally considered intelligence. A traditional approach to learning disabilities which requires that its subjects be of normal intelligence could not, therefore, consider reasoning skills as a source of learning disabilities. Our learning problem approach is not so constrained. Intelligence, or reasoning for that matter, is the result of the coordinated action of a number of cognitive skills, processes, and strategies, any one of which can be malfunctioning. There is no necessity to exclude reasoning skills, or more generally simultaneous processing, from consideration.

There are two separate issues here, whether problems in simultaneous processing are associated with learning problems, and whether simultaneous processing problems can be overcome. The answer to the first question is not yet clear. While we have shown (in Chapters 7, 8 and 9) the involvement of simultaneous processing in achievement tasks, there have not yet been appropriate studies done to link simultaneous processing with learning problems. Far more evidence exists to implicate arousal, successive processing and planning problems as causing learning problems. Our conclusion would be that simultaneous processing *is* so involved, though perhaps primarily in areas not commonly studied in learning disability research (e.g., mathematics, reading comprehension). There is certainly good reason for concluding that it *might* be involved.

The answer to the remediation question is also not clear; given the concentration upon simultaneous processing skills in most individual and group measures of intelligence, and the relative stability of such measures, simultaneous processing may be more difficult to improve than the other processes we have considered. This problem is most apparent when the tasks considered are reasoning tasks. However, even for reasoning tasks there are examples of successful remedial instruction. The best examples are provided by the work of Feuerstein and his colleagues (e.g., Feuerstein,

Rand, Hoffman & Miller, 1980; Feuerstein, Miller, Hoffman, Rand, Mintzker & Jensen, 1981). Their Instrumental Enrichment Program concentrates upon training a set of cognitive processes or functions, most of which are clearly related to simultaneous processing skills.

The Instrumental Enrichment Program has been used to improve the cognitive functioning and achievement of low functioning children and adolescents (many of whom would be labelled retarded or mildly retarded). The box below illustrates the approach and some of the materials used by Feuerstein and his colleagues. Instead of accepting test performance as a measure of immutable intelligence, they analyze test items for the processes required, and then explicitly train these processes extensively over a two or three year period. In this way, it could be argued, they are not training simultaneous processing at a general level, but rather are giving their subjects extensive training in a large array of independent simultaneous processing operations. The results they have obtained are still controversial. It is not yet clear that they have taught transferable skills – that is, skills that can be used in tasks other than those specifically used for training. However, their research is exciting and extremely encouraging. It also underlines the point that children with severe learning problems may require very extensive practice and training, far more extensive than would be obtained in a normal school environment.

Examples of Simultaneous Processing Problems

In this section we present examples of the achievement problems which may be due to problems with simultaneous processing. Once again, we emphasize that we have been extremely selective in describing these examples. Our purpose here is to illustrate the types of problems produced, not to provide complete descriptions of individual children. We would not expect all affected children to

Instrumental Enrichment

Feuerstein's approach to remediation is to train the cognitive processes that are required before achievement area skills can be mastered. He deliberately *excludes* curriculum content to concentrate upon these cognitive process skills. Once the basic processes have been trained, "bridging" activities are begun, to connect the processes to curriculum content.

Instrumental enrichment is based upon the concept of "dynamic assessment", in which the children's competence is judged not on the basis of the current (static) level of performance (as in most ability tests), but rather in terms of the amount of improvement shown as a result of instruction. The approach indicates explicitly that enhancement of cognitive processes often takes place under the guidance of an adult or teacher (the adult "mediates" the child's learning).

Instrumental enrichment usually employs an extensive series of paper-and-pencil exercises which can take 200 to 300 hours to complete. The emphasis is upon several hours of intensive practice per week, the program lasting many months. The skills are taught by means of a number of *instruments,* each of which is a cognitive task requiring several skills. Some of the instruments used are:

– organization of dots, in which the child learns to recognize dot patterns in an amorphous field;

– orientation in space, which deals with spatial relationships;

– numerical progressions, which concern recognizing number patterns;

– categorization, which focuses on classifying information; and

– syllogisms, which deal with formal logic.

The essence of Feuerstein's approach is extensive practice on numerous variants of each of these tasks, together with explicit instruction about how to perform them, and instruction in "meta-learning habits" (i.e., rules for "learning how to learn").

For example, the organization of dots exercises require the student to recognize dot patterns, forming shapes such as squares and triangles. In early exercises, the three dots forming a triangle are separate from those forming a square, and a few of the lines connecting the dots are drawn in. As the exercises proceed, the problems become more difficult; few or no lines are provided, the two patterns begin to overlap, the orientations of the patterns change, and the sizes of the patterns change. Through extensive practice of items that increase in difficulty, pattern recognition skill is established and strengthened. Other patterns are then introduced, and the usefulness of pattern recognition in other areas demonstrated.

For further details and examples, and for evidence regarding the effectiveness of Instrumental Enrichment, consult the following references: Feuerstein *et al.,* 1980; Feuerstein *et al.,* 1981; Feuerstein & Hoffman, 1980; Savell, Twohig & Rachford, 1986; and Rand, Tannenbaum & Feuerstein, 1979.

TABLE 13-1
Learning problems ascribed to simultaneous processing

Achievement Area	Learning Problem Symptoms	Causal Descriptions
Reading	Failure to recognize sight words, or read familiar words, quickly	Unfamiliarity of word
		Inability to integrate visual stimuli
	Failure to use word shape cues	Inclination to phonic analysis
	Failure to interpret word meaning	Unfamiliarity of word
		Inclination toward word identification (naming) only
	Failure to interpret sentence meaning	Unfamiliarity of words, concepts or context
		Inability to perceive or understand relationships
		Inclination away from meaning or abstract meaning
	Failure to interpret passage meaning (e.g., to select or construct main ideas, to construct themes)	Unfamiliarity of concepts or context
		Inability to perceive or understand relationships (especially inferences)
		Inclination toward surface level of text, away from interpretation, inferencing or elaboration

show all of these achievement problems, nor would only these simultaneous processing problems be observed in a given child; they could well co-exist with arousal, successive processing or planning problems.

Table 13-1 describes the achievement problems that have been ascribed in preceding chapters to simultaneous processing problems, in the areas of reading, spelling and mathematics. The learning problem symptoms are given as they would be observed by a classroom teacher. The third column contains our descriptions of the processes underlying those problems. In general these problems stem from two types of difficulty: either absence or inefficiency of a particular simultaneous code, or an inclination away from using such codes.

Word Identification Problems

Skilled reading requires that some words be identified "visually" – that is, without phonic (successive) analysis of letter sequences. Such words include sight words (see Chapter 7 and Table 8-1), but can also include many others encountered frequently. For the case of these latter words, it would be too inefficient to have to sound them out each time they were to be read. (An example would be the word "simultaneous" in the present chapter.) The main characteristic of a word identification problem involving simultaneous processing would be difficulty or inability to recognize words visually, without phonic analysis. This would not have to be a consistent problem; it may occur only

TABLE 13-1 *continued*

Achievement Area	Learning Problem Symptoms	Causal Descriptions
Spelling	Failure to use visual code for word or syllable (producing "Phoenician"-like errors)	Unfamiliarity of visual code unit or word
	Use of inappropriate visual code (producing "Chinese"-like errors)	Inability to retain visual code
	Failure to perform visual check after word spelled (failure to correct)	Inclination toward phonetic spelling
Arithmetic	Failure to recognize numbers or symbols	Unfamiliarity of code units, including lack of automaticity
	Slow computing of basic operations	Inability to perceive or understand relationships, operations, transformations
	Errors in place value	Inclination towards computation rather than pattern recognition
Mathematics	Failure to comprehend words, sentences, passages	See Reading section
	Failure to use required knowledge schemas (e.g., dollars and cents)	Unfamiliarity of concepts, operations, patterns, spatial aids, or problem types
	Failure to recognize problem types	Inability to perceive or understand relationships (especially transformations)
	Failure to use / construct spatial aids	Inclination to verbal, not visual material

for some words, especially hard or new words, and it may only result in an increase in the time that a child needs to "learn" a new word.

A secondary problem might be difficulty in using "word shape" information. For example, the shape ⌐_⌐ could fit many three-letter words. In skilled reading, this word shape should provide some clues as to what the word is, before you look at it directly, that is, while you are still looking at a word to the left of it. (See Haber & Haber, 1981, for more on this, as well as the section below on observing simultaneous processing in reading.)

Word Meaning Problems

In this case the difficulty is not in word identification but rather in word interpretation. Word interpretation is a function of the connections which exist in long-term memory between the auditory or visual stimulus of the word and other concepts. Students with an impoverished conceptual network are unlikely to be able to interpret words quickly or flexibly enough to proceed far in reading. This problem may be manifested in the treatment of words as objects rather than symbols and, of course, will interfere with reading comprehension.

Sentence Meaning Problems

After words are correctly identified and interpreted, their meanings must be integrated to produce propositional representations of sentences. This involves relating word meanings and grammatical structures. For example, in the sentence "The boy chasing the cow was fat", it is important to relate "fat" to the boy, not to the cow. Reading which is too oriented to phonic analysis or even just to word identification will produce meaning problems at the sentence level and beyond. Except in unusual situations, this problem is most likely a function of what the readers are *trying* to do – that is, a function of their strategies.

Passage Interpretation Problems

Problems may also occur at the level integrating meaning across sentences. These, in turn, can vary from relatively simple problems at the paragraph level – that is, integrating the meaning of three or four sentences – to those at a higher level selecting, integrating and abstracting important ideas contained or implied within a larger text. With longer texts, the bounds of working memory are exceeded if more complex strategies are not employed. Two types of problems can appear here, one being the inability to *select* the main idea of a passage, the other the inability to *construct* a main idea (or a theme) from a passage. The second problem becomes more and more important as the texts become more abstract or literary in nature. Selecting main ideas may be as easy as summarizing the plot, whereas constructing the themes may require interpreting why the author wrote the text.

Spelling Problems

Two sorts of spelling problem can be ascribed to simultaneous processing. The first of these is the lack or non-use of a visual code for the word or syllable being spelt, which would be related to word identification problems described above. The second simultaneous problem is the failure to perform a visual check after spelling to ensure that the word

does correspond to a familiar pattern. Both of these would produce errors of the Phoenician kind (see Chapter 8) if phonics were relied upon, or of the Chinese kind if the poor visual codes were used anyway.

Arithmetic Operations Problems

As we saw in Chapter 9, one simultaneous processing problem in arithmetic is the lack of automaticity of the basic operations. Poor performance is characterized by very slow computing of even very simple number facts (see the description of Kirby and Becker's, 1988, research, pp. 111-113). More basic problems could also concern number identification and understanding of place-value (for instance, failure to recognize that the 7 in 170 stands for 7×10).

Mathematics Problems

Examples of ineffective simultaneous processing in the mathematics domain relate to the absence or inefficiency of particular knowledge schemas, or to a disinclination to use them. Word problems follow several patterns, and inability to recognize these will usually produce failure. It is important to emphasize here the spatial domain, as many problems require the use of spatial information or the construction of spatial representations such as graphs or diagrams. It seems likely that many children simply do not understand such spatial "aids", and therefore avoid them (see Kirby, Moore & Schofield, 1988).

Observation and Assessment of Simultaneous Processing Problems

In this section we present a variety of techniques for assessing simultaneous processing. We mention formal standardized tests when these exist, but our emphasis is more upon informal testing in the classroom context. We begin by considering measures of a general nature, followed by those specifically taken from the reading, spelling and mathematics areas. Remember that, while these tests measure simultaneous processing, they also require other skills for successful performance. A single test score is never enough to diagnose the nature of a child's problem.

General Measures

In describing general measures, we can refer most easily to the work of Das *et al.* (1975, 1979), Das and Naglieri (1990), and of A. Kaufman and N. Kaufman (1983). We will not describe all of the general simultaneous processing measures that these authors have described, but rather a representative sample. The interested reader, and in particular the psychologist aiming to assess simultaneous processing in a formal way, is advised to consult those sources.

Figure Drawing Tests

Many of the tests which have been employed by Das and his colleagues and by Kaufman and Kaufman to measure simultaneous processing involve the drawing or copying of non-verbal figures, or the construction of non-verbal representations with concrete materials (e.g., blocks). In this area several standardized tests exist, some of which are relatively easily administered by teachers, others of which can only be administered by trained psychologists. We consider in depth a test called the Figure Copying Test, but also describe more briefly some of the other measures.

The Figure Copying Test is illustrated in Figure 13-2. The original test was devised by Ilg and Ames (1964), but has since been adapted for use with different kinds of children. Figure 13-2 contains two representative figures which children are required to copy; Figure 13-3 shows examples of how some children do copy the cube. An important feature to keep in mind in assessing such figure copying is that, as far as simultaneous processing is concerned, the important aspects to assess are whether the overall *proportions* of the figure and the geometric *relationships* among the figure's elements are maintained. For example, the copy of the circle should have the general appearance of a circle. If it is too egg-shaped, irregular or not complete, then the overall proportions have not been maintained. Similarly, the copy of the cube shape should have the general appearance of a cube, and should also maintain geometric relations; for example, the angles of the front face of the cube should be roughly right angles, and the length of the bottom front line should be slightly longer than the length of the back top line. To score a test like this it is necessary to make up a set of scoring criteria which fit the description of simultaneous processing. Sample criteria are given in Figure 13-2. Not surprisingly, as children become more cognitively mature, they become more able to perform these tasks. Average scores for the two items shown in Figure 13-2 are presented in Table 13-2, for various age groups.

To perform tests such as figure copying successfully, it is necessary to see the figure as a single unit – for example, to see a set of lines as a cube. This is clearly an example of simultaneous processing, by which a set of discrete stimuli, the lines, are processed into a unitary representation, the cube. The drawing is then performed to duplicate that encoding. This usually results in a face-by-face drawing, in the order shown in item (a) of Figure 13-3, and in competent drawings such as item (c). If the "cubeness" is lost at this stage, the three-face copies that appear can resemble a more flattened cube, as in item (d). If, instead of coding the lines as a cube, the student merely copies them as a series of lines, he or she might attempt to draw it in the order indicated in item (b) of Figure 13-3. This order usually results in quite bizarre copies that do not resemble a cube at all, as that in item (e). (Try this yourself. See how difficult it is to draw the cube well when this approach is employed.)

Many other figure drawing tests exist. The Developmental Test of Visual-Motor Integration (Beery & Buktenica, 1967) is a group administered standardized test which is similar to figure copying. An individually administered psychological test which is often used to detect brain damage is the Bender Visual-Motor Gestalt Test (Bender, 1938).

The tests described so far require the copying of a figure which is still visible. It is also possible to test figure copying from memory, by presenting a figure and removing it before copying begins. This places demands upon memory, and if an incorrect (i.e., non-simultaneous) approach is employed, the memory demands will often be too great. It is also possible to ask children whether two drawings are identical, thereby avoiding the difficult of scoring children's drawings. A. Kaufman and N. Kaufman (1983) have employed such a task, called Face Recognition, in which subjects are shown the faces of one or more persons and then are asked to select those faces from a larger set. Simultaneous processing can also be tested by presenting incomplete figures and asking children to judge what figure is "really" there (e.g., A. Kaufman & N. Kaufman's, 1983, Gestalt Closure test).

FIGURE 13-2
Figure copying test

Circle

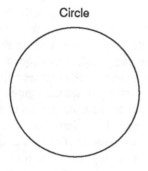

Cube

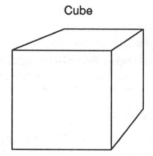

Scoring Criteria

Circle

1. Continuous line, with no extensions and no gap greater than 3 mm

2. Round, circular shape

3. Ratio of maximum width to maximum height in range 0.8 to 1.2

Cube

1. Cube shape (three-dimensional)

2. Square front (ratio of minimum side to maximum no less than 0.9) and bottom and top are within 5° of horizontal

3. Ratio of backmost top line to bottom front line in range 0.7 to 1.1

Note: These scoring criteria are based upon those developed by Leong (1974) and Kirby and Biggs (1981).

TABLE 13-2
Average scores for different age groups
for two figure copying items
shown in Figure 13-2

Age (years)	Circle	Cube
6	1.9	0.2
8	2.3	0.3
10	2.7	2.1
12	2.8	2.6

Note: For each item, the maximum score is 3. These averages
are based upon unpublished data held by Kirby.

FIGURE 13-3
Two ways to draw a cube, from figure copying test (The numbers on the edges of the cubes
in (a) and (b) indicate the order in which they are drawn in (c), (d) and (e) below.)

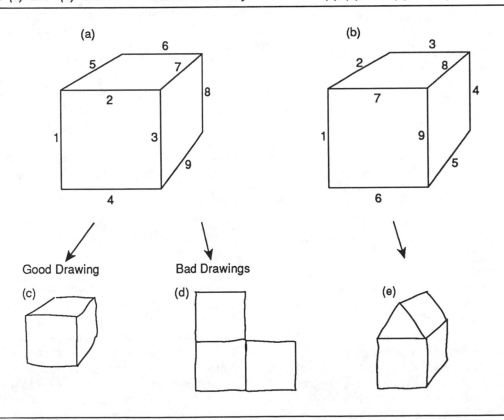

(a)

(b)

Good Drawing

Bad Drawings

(c)

(d)

(e)

Verbal Relations Tests

Many formal and informal tests exist to assess children's abilities to produce or comprehend verbal relationships. The most straightforward example would be a synonym test, in which the children have to select a word which means the same as another word. Such measures often appear on intelligence tests as vocabulary items. These measures assess simultaneous processing in that the children must search for long-term memory associates or relationships for the presented words. Other forms of verbal relationships would include antonyms, in which the task would be to pick out a word opposite in meaning; and categorization, in which children would be provided with a list of words and asked to form them into different groups. (To recognize category membership is to perceive common features among words, another clear example of simultaneous processing.) More complex examples of verbal relationships would include understanding family relationships (Who is your mother's brother's son?), spatial descriptions (The bus is behind the car; which is in front?), or metaphors (What does it mean to say "The sun was a red ball"?). (See Semel-Mintz and Wiig's, 1982, Clinical Evaluation of Language Functions test.)

Spatial Skills Measures

It is possible to construct many different measures with which to observe children's spatial skills. (The figure copying tests described above would be among these.) Standardized tests of spatial ability are quite common in intelligence tests and some measures may be available for general use (e.g., some of the Frostig, 1964, tests). However, many less formal measures are also available to the classroom teacher. One source of such observations would be the child's use of nonverbal aids such as maps, figures or diagrams. For example, one could show the child a map of the town in which the school was, or even a map of the school itself, and ask the child to locate certain features, buildings or classrooms. At a more basic level, it would be possible to assess children's understanding of rela-tional terms such as left and right, above and below, before and after, and so on. These terms are both spatial and relational in nature and underline the important of simultaneous processing in much verbal comprehension.

Reasoning Tasks

There are many standardized reasoning measures, some verbal and some nonverbal in content. Examples of these include the Raven Progressive Matrices (Raven, 1956) and the verbal analogy items contained in most group IQ tests. These tests require simultaneous processing in that different stimuli must be compared for common features or relationships, and these relationships then mapped onto other stimuli to produce the answer. This mapping process is also a relating operation.

We should not lose sight of the fact that reasoning tests are very complex in nature, and require many other skills beyond simultaneous processing. For example, in a verbal analogy task it is necessary for the subject to know the meanings of the words before relationships between those meanings can be identified. It is also necessary for the subjects to know the relationships themselves. If, for example, the relationship is one in mathematics of raising to the third power (e.g., 2, 8 [2^3], 512 [8^3]), and this third power relationship has to be applied to another set of numbers (e.g., 3, 27, ?), it is necessary for the subjects to know something about exponentials or, at least, about multiplication.

Simultaneous Processing in Reading

We describe three areas in which simultaneous processing can be observed in reading, but again we caution you to remember that a poor score in any of these areas could be for various reasons. Virtually any complex task in any achievement domain will require more than just simultaneous processing; therefore, students can fail at it for more than just the reason of poor simultaneous processing. If simultaneous processing is suspected, or simultaneous processing in reading, or even simultaneous processing in one aspect of reading such as word recognition, then this suspicion should be validated by the observation of related performances.

You should remember from Chapter 7 that simultaneous processing is involved in holistic word recognition that is not mediated by phonic analysis. There are a number of ways to observe this process in reading. One technique would be to show children a word for a brief length of time and ask them to identify it. The removal of the word should discourage phonic analysis, though the children may still be able to retain an image of the word and phonically analyze it. Holistic word recognition should produce a relatively rapid response, phonological analysis a more slow response, perhaps sound by sound. If you were to show children phonologically regular unfamiliar words or nonsense words, you would see clearly how they employ phonic analysis. They should perform very differently on visually recognized words. Furthermore, you could show them some words which were phonologically irregular and could only be correctly recognized holistically – e.g., enough, their, the, and one. Another approach would be to investigate children's knowledge of word shapes or outlines. A word shape (see the example earlier on p. 189) could be shown to the children and they asked to supply words which would fit that overall shape.

A second level of simultaneous processing in reading concerns the extraction of ideas or relationships from sentences. Sentences contain information which must be put together or integrated in order to be comprehended; thus, the latter part of a sentence may tell something more about a person or an object mentioned early in the sentence. For example, the sentence "The boy who chased the cow was fat" requires that the final adjective be associated with the first noun in spite of its proximity to the second noun. If a child were shown a picture of a fat boy chasing a skinny cow, he should indicate that this, rather than a picture of a skinny boy chasing a fat cow, correctly represents the sentence. Many similar examples could be constructed for use with children of different ages. In particular,

such examples could contain some of the relational terms described in the section above on verbal relations tests (p. 194): for example, "The book is on the chair", "The boy came before the car", "The girl is taller than the man". Children's comprehension of such terms could be assessed verbally, through picture recognition, or even through multiple choice written tests.

The final level of simultaneous processing in reading is at the paragraph or passage level, which requires children to relate information across sentences, paragraphs or even further. While reading at this level is not fundamentally different from the sentence level, in practice it is quite different because it places much more strain upon working memory in that pieces of information which are quite remote have to be integrated. Furthermore, it seems that children are far more likely to be thinking at the sentence level than at the passage level, perhaps because of working memory limitations. Finally, some processes such as inferencing are far more obviously involved at the passage level than at the sentence level, though they can be argued to be involved there as well. Many examples of semantic integration tasks could be constructed; two are shown in the box that follows. The first example is appropriate to early readers. The first sentence contains one piece of information, that some birds flew over a dog. The second sentence provides more information, that the dog was beside a tree. The third sentence then informs the reader more about the birds, that they were robins. A very basic example of semantic integration (simultaneous processing) would be for the reader to make the inference, which is highly constrained by the text, that the robins flew over the dog. This could be tested by asking the children to judge the accuracy, given the story, of various sentences.

The second example requires more advanced reading skills. In this case a much longer text is involved, and two pieces of information given early in the story must be related to a question occurring much later. The early pieces of information (in the context of a religious pilgrimage) are that any pilgrim who fails to bring a gift will result in the tribe's being punished, and that one pilgrim has

Semantic Integration

Example 1
Read the following three sentences:

1. The birds flew over the dog.
2. The dog sat beside a tree.
3. The birds were robins.

Now cover these three sentences up before reading on.

Which of the sentences presented below (A, B, C, D) did you read, in exactly the same words, above?

A. The birds flew over the dog.
B. The robins flew beside the dog.
C. The robins flew over the dog.
D. The birds flew beside the dog.

Solution: Students should recognize (A) as the same, as a "true statement". They might also pick (C), which is a true inference (showing use of simultaneous processing). They shouldn't pick (B) or (D), which are respectively a false inference and a false statement.

A second way to measure inferencing would be to use a slightly different question, such as "Given the story above, which of the following are almost certain to be true?"

Example 2
The following is a description of a text; there isn't enough room here to present the text in its entirety.

This three-page passage is a fictional account, developed by Moore (1986), con-cerning the pilgrimage of a tribe to a holy city. In the middle of the text, the following sentence occurs:

It was believed that when gifts were not received from each person on the pilgrimage, the gods frowned upon the tribe and the crops would be poor the next year.

Later, the following sentence occurs:

One tribesman, intent on material gain, had sold all his gifts.

There is no further development of this issue, and no explicit integration with the former sentence.

After another page or so, the story ends with the pilgrims at the holy city. Then several comprehension questions are asked, among them this one:

As a result of the pilgrimage described in this passage,

A. next year's crops would be very successful.
B. the tribe had no more goats.
C. next year's crops would not be very successful.
D. the tribe would not need to return for two years.

This is a much more difficult example of semantic integration, requiring the relating of two sentences which were far back in the text, and which did not seem particularly important (because they were not emphasized or developed) when read.

sold his gifts. If the readers are then or even much later asked what the gods were likely to do, only those who can link these two bits of information and make the appropriate inference will answer the question correctly. Tests such as these can be made more difficult by inserting increased amounts of information between the two bits which need to be integrated, or by making the bits of information less salient in the story. For example, if the general tone of the story is that the pilgrimage was very successful and that most of the pilgrims were very happy, it runs counter to the correct answer, which is that the gods will be unhappy.

Simultaneous Processing in Spelling

Measures similar to those used for the word recognition level in reading can be suggested for simultaneous processing in spelling. For example, children could be asked to spell sight words, words which cannot be produced through phonological analysis. Examples could include there, enough, though, and so on.

A less traditional measure would explore the number of ways a child had for representing spoken syllables in writing. A measure of the availability of such holistic representations could be provided, for instance, by asking the child to write down the sound "ti" as many different ways as possible. A child with a rich network of representations might produce a list such as tea, ti, te, tee, T, whereas a child with a less rich collection of representations may get no further than tea.

Another innovative measure might be to show children unfamiliar words or even nonsense words very briefly and then ask them to spell them in writing. If the presentation of the word is too brief for the child to name each letter or pronounce the word syllable by syllable, successful performance will require the formation of a holistic visual image during the brief presentation, followed by a slow decoding of that image into letters in writing. The formation of the holistic image, of course, is a measure of simultaneous processing. Phonological processing could be interfered with, at least in older

children, by making them repeat something else (e.g., "one, two, three, four") while they were looking at and writing the word.

Yet another example of simultaneous processing in spelling is the visual checking of a word following the spelling. This could be observed in children's own spelling by seeing whether they spontaneously go back to check words which have been incorrectly spelt. Alternatively and more simply, children could be asked to check lists of words to pick out those that have been incorrectly spelt. This task could be made more difficult by including in the list words which are pseudo-homophones – that is, words which, if pronounced, sound like real words though they are, in fact, not correct. Examples would include telefone, enuf, and sylee. A child with a good visual representation (simultaneous code) of words should perform more successfully on this task.

Simultaneous Processing in Mathematics

At a very basic level in mathematics one could concentrate on the simultaneous processing required for number identification. As in word identification, flash cards could be used to present numerals very quickly for the children to recognize. Similarly, dot patterns could be presented quickly, the child's task being to indicate how many dots have appeared.

A basic concept in arithmetic which requires simultaneous processing is the notion of *place value*. In the base 10 system, with which you should be familiar, this means that the number 206 means $(2 \times 100) + (6 \times 1)$, and so on. Children's competence with place value can be assessed in many ways. For example, in adding a column of numbers, the child has to carry correctly in order to obtain the desired result. If the numbers 10, 17, 22 and 104 are to be added (see Figure 13-4), the calculation requires that the 7, 2 and 4 be added first, giving 13; that 3 be written down and 1 carried; that 1 be added to the two 1s in the next column, plus the 2, giving 5; that the 5 be written down, and then the 1 brought down from the 104. Children beginning to learn

FIGURE 13-4
Place value in addition

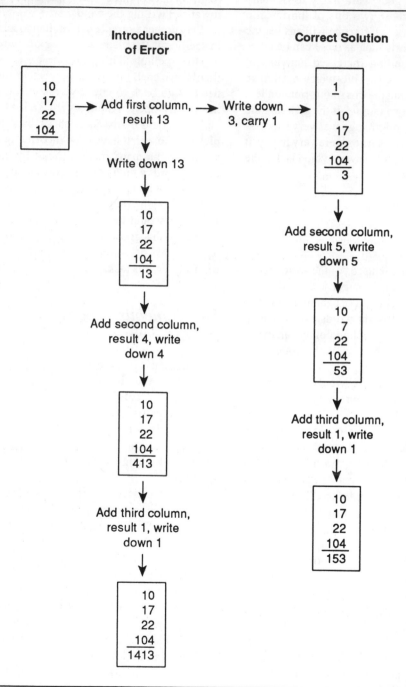

addition and place value often make errors such as writing down the 13 instead of just 3. So instead of the correct answer of 153, they may obtain an answer of 1413 (see this error in Figure 13-4). Other children, of course, may forget about the 1 they are carrying, and get an answer of 143. Similar examples can be found in subtraction, multiplication and division.

A related skill is that of estimation. If the addition problem above were shown to a child, along with four rough answers such as 150, 300, 1000, 100000, the child should be able to indicate which is roughly the answer without performing any computations. The response involves simultaneous processing because the child must produce a global or holistic representation of the numerals.

Another example of simultaneous processing, simplifying equations, is illustrated in the box below. You can see that the simpler items don't really require any computation at all, in that most of the terms on the left hand side also appear on the right hand side. The most efficient way to solve such problems is to compare the two sides and mentally cancel the common elements, leaving the result (in the first example, for instance) that X is

equal to 17. The Australian Council for Educational Research has produced a test called the Operations Test (A.C.E.R., 1977) which contains many such items, with simple or complex numbers and variables, and with simple or complex equation structures, which could be used to observe children's skills in this area. Of course, children can obtain the right answer through computation; to assess whether simultaneous processing is being efficiently used, it would be necessary to inspect the children's work, or even better, to watch them doing it. If computations are performed, the child is not performing the task in the most efficient manner. Similarly, if inappropriate cancellations are made, such as cancelling a positive 110 on one side with a negative 110 on the other side, simultaneous processing is being used, but incorrectly.

A more general indicator of simultaneous processing in mathematics would be the automaticity of basic operations. As discussed in Chapter 9, if basic operations have to be laboriously performed, more complex processing will be made less efficient. Children's simultaneous processing of basic operations could be tested by flashcards containing simple arithmetic problems such as $2 + 2$, $8 - 4$, and

Simplifying Equations

Solve the following equations for X:

A. $12 \times X = 17 + 12$

B. $7 \times (9 - X) = (9 - 4) \times 7$

C. $1042 \times X = 997 \times 1042$

D. $(137 \times X) \times 97 = (97 \times 103) \times 137$

E. $a + X = b + a$

F. $a + (2b + X) = (c^3 + a + b) + b$

Note that no computations are required.

Examples A and B involve simple numbers, C and D more complex numbers, and E and F variables. Examples A, C and E have simple structures, the remainder more complex structures.

so on. Slow responses probably indicate that the computation is being performed, whereas fast responses indicate that a fact is being recalled in a more holistic manner. Even if the computation has to be performed, as some of the research reviewed in Chapter 9 indicates, faster computation is advantageous and still represents more efficient simultaneous processing.

At the level of mathematical word problems, many examples of simultaneous processing are possible. Most word problems contain complex verbal information which must be comprehended for completion of the problem to be successful. In many cases inferences, or at least relationships between sentences, must be made. Therefore, virtually all of the examples of simultaneous processing in reading are also relevant to the solution of word problems in mathematics or science. More specific to mathematics and science are diagrams that often need to be constructed or employed, thus calling on simultaneous processing skills from the spatial domain at a higher level than reading comprehension would require.

Improving Simultaneous Processing Skills

As we indicated earlier in this chapter, there are three general types of explanation for poor performance in the simultaneous processing area. The first explanation is that the child has a low level of simultaneous processing ability or potential. As we have argued repeatedly in this book, this hypothesis is difficult to prove with any certainty. All tests measure performance rather than potential, and all require some sort of learned skills for successful performance. Therefore, just because a child performs poorly on a simultaneous processing test or even upon a range of simultaneous processing tests, he or she is not necessarily incapable of improving simultaneous processing skills. However, resources are limited in education, and it seems reasonable to assume that there will be some children whose

skills in this area are unlikely to improve greatly through instruction. (In fact, many researchers would argue that it would be far more difficult to improve simultaneous processing skills than other skills such as successive processing, on the grounds that simultaneous processing either *is* intelligence or is a very large component of it, and that intelligence is unlikely to be improved through training.) The second explanation of simultaneous processing problems would be that the child has not developed his or her abilities to the level to which they could be developed. In this case, extensive instruction and practice may be successful in improving performance. The third explanation is that the processing abilities are adequate, but for some reason the child chooses not to employ simultaneous processing to the extent that he or she should. This third explanation suggests that strategic instruction combined with some skill development should be employed. More than one explanation may be appropriate for some children.

The first explanation should be invoked only after remediation has been attempted for some time without success. If either or both of the second and third explanations are appropriate, then remediation should emphasize both skill development and strategy awareness, the relative proportions of each depending upon the individual case. It is highly unlikely that either skills or strategies would exist in good condition in the absence of the other. Therefore, it is likely that most children will need help in both areas. Furthermore, a difficulty in either area would be likely to produce a difficulty in the other.

In the suggestions that follow we have necessarily had to be brief. Our suggestions are not intended as an explicit curriculum, but rather as guidelines for the construction of curriculum materials and curriculum activities. We have divided simultaneous processing into three aspects: unit familiarity, construction of representations, and relating of units. Within each we will consider general skills unrelated to achievement areas and specific skills related to the achievement areas of reading, spelling and mathematics.

Unit Familiarity

Many of the problems identified in this chapter could be ascribed to a lack of familiarity with, or knowledge of, appropriate holistic units or codes. For example, if a drawing is to be coded not as a series of lines but as a cube, it is necessary for children to be familiar with cubes and with how they can be represented in two dimensional line drawings. Similarly, the coding of the meaning of a word, sentence, number, or collection of numbers requires that the holistic code be available to the child and that the child be sufficiently familiar with it to use it in a relatively automatic fashion. Knowledge and familarity can be increased through exposure, explanation, and practice, though this instruction may have to be very detailed and slow for some children. Case Study I below presents a case study of a child with problems in this area.

Simultaneous Processing: Case Study 1

This is a case study of a severe simultaneous processing problem, one which was apparent in much of the child's behaviour and allowed less optimism than most about remediation. We believe that it is important for you to examine some of the difficult cases, as well as those that have happy endings.

Allan was first brought to the attention of the school psychologist at the end of first grade, when he was almost seven years old. He had done poorly in kindergarten, but his parents had insisted that he proceed to first grade. His performance in first grade had been even worse; his parents were now willing to see him repeat a grade, but they wanted to know more about his problems, his chances for improvement, and steps they could take to help.

After interviewing the parents and the teachers, the psychologist came to the conclusion that Allan came from a good home in which there were no unusual pressures or crises. There hadn't been any unusual illnesses or absences from school, though Allan's mother remembered his birth as having been "rather difficult". Allan's two older sisters were doing well in school. Allan's hearing and eyesight had been tested; he had worn glasses since kindergarten.

Allan's first grade teacher described him as being of low general ability, except in oral language and music. He had particular problems with visual material, both words and pictures: even his artwork (painting and drawing) was poor for his age. The teacher had noticed that Allan was clumsy in the playground, and thought that his clumsiness had led to his lack of interest in sport. This teacher thought that Allan should repeat the grade, but was not optimistic about his future.

Assessment

The psychologist proceeded to give Allan a number of tests; we show here the results of only a few of them. In general, the results were consistent with the hypothesis that

Allan was poor in most of the areas of simultaneous processing. For example, his WISC-R scores were as follows:

Subtest	Score
Information	10
Similarities	4
Arithmetic	9
Vocabulary	11
Comprehension	9
Digit Span	10
Picture Completion	7
Picture Arrangement	10
Block Design	2
Object Assembly	3
Coding	9

These scores yielded a Verbal IQ of 91, a Performance IQ of 74, and a Full Scale IQ of 81. Without looking at the pattern of scores, it would be easy to decide that Allan was of low general mental ability (as had his teacher), and that his poor performance was hardly surprising. However, the subtest scores are uniformly low only for those requiring relating and integrating skills (similarities, block design and object assembly); scores are generally better for the rest. In fact, Allan's school performance wasn't really consistent with his being of low general ability either. The psychologist reported that he knew his alphabet, could count and perform oral arithmetic normally for his age, and generally gave the impression in his oral language of being of average ability.

As the teacher had observed, however, visual materials and spatial concepts gave Allan terrible problems. His reading was plagued by visual confusion (he said d for b, and vice versa), his spelling was classically "Phoenician", and he became confused by terms like "before", "after", "above", "below", "beside", "left" and "right".

Analysis

Allan had a severe problem in the simultaneous processing area. This problem was not confined to the visual modality, since he had difficulties also with oral language tests like the WISC-R Similarities test. His successive processing skills (other oral language skills, memory, etc.) were relatively unaffected. (The appearance of an overall low level of intelligence was primarily due to his low simultaneous performance.)

Remediation

It was clear that Allan's problem was a broad one, not to be solved by any brief intervention. This analysis was checked by trying, unsuccessfully, to change his strategies in relatively simple tasks. What Allan needed was an intensive and extensive program of simultaneous processing instruction to improve his relating and integrating abilities, perhaps along the lines of Feuerstein's Instrumental Enrichment approach. And there was no guarantee that even this would be successful.

Unfortunately, no such resources were available in Allan's school district. The psychologist, the first grade teacher, and Allan's parents decided that Allan should repeat first grade, that the teacher should attempt to help Allan in the classroom with a series of class-related simultaneous processing activities, and that his parents should try to do the same at home. The teacher and parents also agreed that they should try to be more understanding of some of Allan's weaknesses: for instance, they would try not to be too easily upset by his bizarre spelling.

The activities they selected were appropriate. At the general level, they included drawing, completing jigsaw puzzles, drawing and following maps, and even doing carpentry to develop Allan's skills. In the oral language area, Allan's entire family played verbal games which brought out relationships between words' meanings. At school, Allan was given extra practice in visualizing words, in tracing them correctly spelled, and so on.

Unfortunately, it seems there was not enough time or support to carry out these activities often enough. Perhaps because of this, perhaps because of Allan's low ability, or perhaps because of both factors, Allan did not improve significantly. While he did make some progress, his classmates always made more; as a result, he never improved his position in the class. Furthermore, as he went on in school, his subjects called for more simultaneous processing (e.g., in comprehension and problem solving) so, in reality, he was falling further and further behind.

When we last had contact with him, he was in early high school and not doing very well. None of his subsequent teachers had kept up his extra work in school, and his parents had stopped doing anything special at home. Everyone, Allan included, had resigned themselves to his dropping out of school in a few years to look for an unskilled job.

Allan's case is evidence that some children's problems will survive the best-intentioned intervention program if it is not sufficiently intensive and extensive. This may be particularly true of more severe simultaneous processing problems. Feuerstein's success with very intensive and extensive programs leads us to some optimism, but the resources must be available to allow for success.

Construction of Representations

Once the child is familiar with the correct form of coding, instruction should be designed to ensure that the appropriate codes will be used when necessary – that is, that the child will be able to construct holistic representations. For example, in figure copying tasks a child could spontaneously inspect the drawing and code it as a collection of lines. This is most likely to occur if the child feels required to respond quickly, to begin drawing as soon as possible. Such children might be encouraged to take their time, and to produce a verbal description of the figure to be drawn before beginning to draw; thus, the teacher might require the child to begin by describing it as a collection of lines, and describing how the lines are related, but might also require the child to produce an *overall* description of it – e.g., as a cube – before beginning to draw it. Instruction could begin with figure copying and proceed to copying from memory, and so on. More advanced drawing instructions could teach children to copy or recall figures in a rotated form, rotated by 90 or 180°, or in a mirror image form.

Other forms of representation could be used; for instance, children could be taught to draw a figure from someone else's perspective. Children could also be taught to visualize the features represented on a geographical map. Many other activities could be designed using materials such as blocks, jigsaw puzzles, and so on. Case Study I deals with a child who needed help in these areas.

In the reading area, representation could be taught both for the meanings of sentences (learning to pick out the picture which best represents a sentence) or for longer segments of text (picking out the main idea in a paragraph). In the latter case, instruction could proceed from picking out main ideas, to the construction of main ideas, to the construction of summaries for longer segments of text.

Eventually children could be taught to produce thematic organizers to aid their own learning, and to construct summaries or organizers for different purposes or from different points of view. See Case Study II for an example of a simultaneous processing problem in summarization.

Representation skills in spelling involve visual codes for syllables and words. Children could be taught to close their eyes and "see" a word, or even to touch words made from letter-shaped blocks. For example, a game could be played in which children have to imagine a word, and then mentally go through it to count the letters made only of straight lines, etc.

In mathematics, representation could be taught at the number, equation or word problem levels. At the number level, children could be asked to represent statements such as $3+4$ by a single number, or single numbers by a series of more complicated statements (e.g., $7 = 3 + 4 = 6 + 1 = 8 - 1$, etc.). At the word problem level, a child could be asked to draw an appropriate diagram to represent the problem. Many more examples could be designed, specific to various problem formats.

Relating

The final and most complex level of simultaneous processing is the relating of items of information. At this level, different pieces of information are represented in memory, and these codes are compared for either common features or underlying relationships. If the question were "How is a cat like a dog?", a variety of common features might be listed: they're both animals, they both have fur, they both have four legs, and so on. On the other hand, if the question were "How is a cat like a lead pencil?", the list of common features would be much shorter, consisting perhaps only of the item they both contain some of the same chemicals.

Relating is more complex when the relationship to be found is not a concrete one, such as being an animal or being blue, but is rather more abstract in nature. An example of such an abstract relationship would be that one element is a member of the class

of the other, such as a dog is an animal. In mathematics, such a relationship would exist where one number is seen as the result of performing a certain operation, such as raising it to the third power, on another number. These types of relationships are the basis of many of the measures which we have described in this chapter as tests of inductive or analogical reasoning. Feuerstein and his colleagues have presented many examples of how to train such relating operations (see the box on Instrumental Enrichment). Other examples are presented in Table 13-3.

In reading, relating can be taught at the word, sentence and passage levels. If children are experiencing difficulty in relating at either of the higher levels, training should begin at a lower level. For instance, children could be encouraged to list common features of different words, those features becoming more abstract or less salient as training progressed. Sentences would be similarly compared: do they say the same thing? How is what one says related to what the other says?

The work of Biggs and Collis (1982) could be used as the basis for many remedial activities in the reading or problem solving domains. Biggs and Collis identify much poor or immature performance as being "multi-structural" in nature. By this they mean that children produce an answer which may contain many appropriate features, but the features are not integrated into a coherent response. Thus, contradictory pieces of information may be given and integrating principles ignored. The multi-structural response is one which contains much of the correct information, yet that information is not integrated into a *relational* answer (Biggs and Collis' term).

How would one go about training relational thinking in this type of task? The first step would be to ensure that the children possess all of the relevant information. Rather than presenting the task and then asking for a single response, it is more useful to leave the task in front of them, and ask them, in a group, to suggest points that might be relevant to an answer. In other words, the children are encouraged to *withhold closure* until as much problem and solution information as possible can be

TABLE 13-3
Sample tasks for training simultaneous processing (especially relating)

– Recognize patterns (pictures, faces, words, numbers, anything).
– Match similar or opposite items (pictures, words, etc.).
– Categorize items (types of food, people, etc.).
– Draw conclusions from presented facts (e.g., detective game).
– Construct designs from pictures by drawing (or with blocks, etc.); then reproduce them in rotation or mirror image.
– Do jigsaw puzzles.
– Learn place value with blocks.
– Use imagery to learn new words or lists of old words.
– Supply crucial missing details in stories.
– Find hidden pictures in larger pictures.
– Look for hidden words.
– Find words that rhyme.
– Learn to use maps, to find objects or describe where they are.
– Draw maps of the school; of how to go home; etc.
– Add different prefixes and suffixes to words.
– Play games like "Concentration" which require visual memory.
– Make up summaries of newspaper stories.
– Think of and draw different ways to rearrange a room's furniture.
– Practise three-dimensional craft work (carpentry, pottery).

considered. Consider, for example, the question "Why are some children unhappy?" The teacher or group leader might write down the suggested aspects to the answer on pieces of paper which could then be reorganized or shuffled, and grouped according to common aspects (e.g., reasons relating to home problems, school problems, etc.). Ideally, the children should be asked to form these groupings themselves, and then express the integrated idea represented by a group of answer features. The result of this task should be two or more ideas relating to the same question, but not perhaps to each other. The final task then is to have the children integrate these disparate ideas (e.g., to relate home problems to school problems). In some cases this may be possible within the problem context itself, but in other cases it may be necessary to invoke outside knowledge (e.g., information about personality types). A crucial aspect of this type of training is

that it is not didactic; rather, it involves the teacher *interacting* with one or more children, probing their knowledge and guiding their thinking. Case Study II presents a related example concerned with summarizing text.

In spelling, relational thinking might involve the recognition of common spelling patterns in different words. This would not necessarily be a primary focus of intervention, but could be a component in spelling training.

In mathematics and problem solving, relating would be found in the recognition that a given problem was of a certain type – i.e., that certain generalized solution steps were appropriate. Training could involve the recognition of common problem features, or the interaction between parts of the solution (see Biggs and Collis, 1982; their book contains many examples from the mathematics and science areas).

Simultaneous Processing:
Case Study II

Nicolle, a 14-year-old high school student, was having difficulties with relational thinking, particularly in extracting the main ideas from the texts she was reading. The first teacher to notice her problem was her grade nine science teacher, Mr. Smith. He observed that Nicolle was often unable to give a summary of anything that she had read, unless the text itself contained an explicit summary. When asked what a text had been about, her tendency was either to concentrate upon a relatively unimportant detail, or to generalize to too vague a level.

Assessment
The first step Smith took was to discuss Nicolle with her other teachers. Their reaction disappointed him: basically they thought she was not very clever, and was "working to her ability". While agreeing that Nicolle was no genius, Smith thought that she should be doing better than she was.

The next step was to see the school psychologist, who agreed to interview Nicolle and give her the WISC-R. The psychologist's report confirmed the teachers' consensus that Nicolle was of low-average ability (Verbal IQ: 94, Performance IQ: 86, Full Scale IQ: 89). It showed the following subtest scores:

Subtest	Score
Information	10
Similarities	6
Arithmetic	11
Vocabulary	10
Comprehension	8
Digit Span	9

Picture Completion	9
Picture Arrangement	9
Block Design	7
Object Assembly	5
Coding	10

When Mr. Smith described Nicolle's problem again, the psychologist pointed out that Nicolle's WISC-R results were lowest for the subtests most requiring relating and integrating: Similarities, Block Design, and Object Assembly. Smith asked whether this could mean that Nicolle had a low level of "relating and integrating ability". The psychologist said it could, though he pointed out that it could also mean that Nicolle simply did not know how to relate and integrate things.

Smith decided to pursue the problem, convinced that he could explain relating and integrating to Nicolle enough to improve her performance in science. His first step was to observe how Nicolle went about making summaries. He began by asking her to read a number of texts that were well within her reading ability. One was an elementary school passage on dinosaurs; this passage was only one paragraph long, and said that although many dinosaurs were giants, some were as small as chickens. When Nicolle was asked to recall the main idea of this passage after several minutes, all she could say was "It was about dinosaurs". Only specific questions like "How big was the smallest dinosaur?" drew out the important information in the text. The teacher then gave her back the text, and asked her to write a two-sentence summary of it, one that would pick out the main ideas and be useful for studying. Her first attempt was:

> The largest dinosaur was Brachiosaurus, who weighed over 51 tons. Brachlosaurus is the largest animal ever to have lived on this earth.

Lest you think that this is not too bad a piece of writing for a 14-year-old, you should know that both of these sentences appear in the text; in fact, they are the last two sentences of the paragraph.

By working with her more closely, Smith was able to make her realize that it was important that the passage said that one dinosaur had been as small as a chicken. Even then, however, her summary was:

> The largest dinosaur was Brachiosaurus, who weighed over 51 tons. The smallest dinosaur was Compsognathus, who only grew to about the size of a chicken.

Not surprisingly, the second sentence was also taken word-for-word from the text. Nicolle resisted attempts to have her rewrite those two sentences in her own words, or to write them at a higher level of abstraction (e.g., "While many dinosaurs were large, some were as small as chickens").

Smith could see in this passage and others that:

1. Nicolle was missing the main points;
2. she was often concentrating upon details;
3. these details were often the wrong details;
4. the details she selected were often interesting in spite of being unimportant; and
5. even when Nicolle was given the "right" information, she was unable to rewrite it more concisely or more abstractly.

These problems all stemmed from being unable to relate ideas in seeking out the main ones, and then being unable (or unwilling) to reprocess those ideas into more abstract ones.

In consultation with the school psychologist, Smith decided on a two-part plan to help Nicolle. The first part was to work on relating and integrating as general simultaneous processing skills, the second to work more specifically on summarization skills. For the first part of the program, Smith selected activities from Feuerstein's Instrumental Enrichment Program, and made up other similar tasks and games. For example, a typical relating activity for Nicolle was to say how two words or pictures were alike or unlike; a typical integrating activity was to look for a pattern in a set of numbers, pictures, or words, and then use this pattern to make up more examples or sets.

For the second part of the program, which was followed more or less at the same time as the first, Smith relied upon the research of Brown, Day and Jones (1983) on "The development of plans for summarizing texts", and of Winograd (1984) on "Strategic difficulties in summarizing texts". He taught Nicolle the following sequence of steps in summarizing:

1. Figure out what the passage is mainly about.
2. With the text covered up, write down this main idea.
3. With the main idea in mind, go through the text, underlining the most important parts and crossing out the unimportant details.
4. Write down the important ideas that have been picked out, in any order, on separate slips of paper.
5. Look for patterns in the ideas, e.g., ideas that go together.
6. Reorder the ideas, getting rid of the ones that say the same thing as others, and putting together the ones that are about the same things.

7. Make a plan for putting all of the remaining ideas into a few sentences, making sure that the main idea is still clear.

8. Write the summary.

9. Check to see that nothing important has been left out, nor anything unimportant included.

10. Rewrite if necessary.

Progress

As you might expect, success was not obtained overnight. Smith found that Nicolle needed a lot of practice in following the plan, particularly when it came to seeing how ideas were related (steps 5 and 6), to making a plan (step 7), and actually writing the summary (step 8) when the main idea wasn't literally expressed in the text (that is to say, when it was only implied).

After three months of an hour or two of instruction per week (at which point the teacher could not longer find the time to spend with her), Nicolle had made great progress in the general simultaneous processing areas. She seemed, not surprisingly, to enjoy most the tasks that least resembled school tasks. As long as she was familiar with the relationship involved, she became quite adept at identifying patterns and rules.

However, she continued to have difficulty in "creating" new rules: this weakness may have reflected her low-average level of intelligence, and may be an enduring limitation for her, although this is by no means certain.

More importantly, Nicolle also made progress in the more school-related area of summarization. She became quite good at picking out main ideas, especially if they were clearly expressed in the text. She learned to discriminate between what was interesting and what was important, and became skilled at selecting the most important information to include in her summary. From the reports of other teachers, she was able to apply these skills to other subject areas as well. The major problems that remained after three months were constructing a main idea if it were not explicitly expressed, and rewriting the main idea to a higher level of generality. Again, it is possible that these are limitations imposed by Nicolle's level of general intelligence; it is also possible that she will take much longer to acquire these skills.

Both Smith and Nicolle had reason to be proud, because she had made more progress than many had thought possible. However, they also encountered limitations that Nicolle might never be able to overcome.

For further examples of simultaneous processing training the reader is advised to consult Das, Naglieri and Kirby (1990), A.S. Kaufman and N.L. Kaufman (1983), or the extensive work of Feuerstein and his associates (see recommended readings).

Summary

This chapter has examined simultaneous processing, as it is described in our theory and as it has appeared in a variety of other theories. The essence of simultaneous processing is the recognition of relationships between discrete items in working memory, and the use of these relationships between discrete items in working memory, and the use of these relationships to form new integrations in memory. Without denying the importance of successive processing, it seems clear that simultaneous is more complex, more related to what we normally term "higher mental abilities"; therefore, it is understandable that it has appeared in so many forms in so many theories. It is important to keep in mind that simultaneous processing can be examined at a number of different levels: at a very high level, as a general process; at a middle level, as a group of distinct skills (for instance, spatial ability); or at a much lower level of generality involved in a variety of specific achievement tasks.

The major learning problems ascribed to simultaneous processing are listed in Table 13-1. These are seen as being caused by either the lack of a particular code or ability, or by the inclination not to use simultaneous processing.

We provided descriptions of ways to measure simultaneous processing, both at the general process level and in the context of specific achievement tasks. As we have done throughout this book, we emphasized the importance of your understanding the basic concepts so that you can generate your own measures.

The final section of this chapter provided guidelines for and examples of remediating simultaneous processing problems. For remediation purposes, we divided simultaneous processing into three types: unit familiarity, construction of representations, and relating of units. Again, we hope that you can see the important links among the basic theory, the methods for observing simultaneous processing, and the approaches to remediation. Simultaneous processing, at least in some of its forms, may prove more difficult to improve than successive processing, but its importance in cognition and school achievement justifies considerable effort in trying to do so.

RECOMMENDED READING

Simultaneous Processing Training
Further suggestions for training activities can be found in the following sources:

Das, J.P., Naglieri, J.A. & Kirby, J.R.
In press. *The assessment of cognitive processes.* New York: Allyn & Bacon.

Feuerstein, R., Rand, Y., Hoffman, M.B. & Miller, R. 1980. *Instrumental enrichment.* Baltimore: University Park Press.

Kaufman, A.S. & Kaufman, N.L. 1983. *Kaufman Assessment Battery for Children. Interpretive Manual.* Circles Pines, Minnesota: American Guidance Service.

Trifiletti, D.T., Trifiletti, R.M. & Trifiletti, R.J. 1982. *WISCR-80. An Educational Program for the Wechsler Intelligence Scale for Children, Revised.* Jacksonville, Florida: Precision People.

Relational Thinking
Biggs, J.B. & Collis, K.F.
1982. *Evaluating the quality of learning: The SOLO Taxonomy.* New York: Academic Press.

This book describes how to evaluate the Structure of Observed Learning Outcomes (SOLO). Of particular interest is the distinction between *relational* and less developed forms of thinking or performing. Many examples are considered, in most achievement areas.

Comprehension
Comprehension and simultaneous processing are intimately linked. The following book, which we also suggested in Chapter 7, provides excellent suggestions:

Pearson, P.D. & Johnston, D.D.
1978. *Teaching reading comprehension.* New York: Holt, Rinehart & Winston.

CHAPTER 14

Planning and Strategies

MUCH COGNITIVE THEORY and research is based upon the idea that mental abilities have two major aspects, processing and planning. The former is concerned with the actual performance of a task, the latter with the *control* of the processing involved in that performance. In this book, we have divided the processing domain into two parts, successive and simultaneous processing (see Chapters 12 and 13). As we have shown in previous chapters, the processing domain includes temporary knowledge stored in working memory, more permanent and schematic knowledge stored in long-term memory, and a large set of operations (some successive, some simultaneous, many both) for transforming stored or input information. We have also described, in Chapter 11, the attention/arousal system which is responsible for energizing the processing and planning systems.

Up to that point, the system described is quite passive, waiting for some input to trigger its processes. It is that passivity which exposes the description so far as incomplete, and which has stimulated a great deal of recent research. While much of this research has been in cognitive psychology and designed to discover more about cognition in general, it is worth noting that a good deal of it has been specifically concerned with learning problem children. As we will see, many learning problem children approach academic tasks in a passive, nonstrategic way. This has led to attempts to design diagnostic and remedial procedures that address the planning domain.

The emphasis upon planning highlights the idea that children's performance is limited not only by their abilities or skills, but also by how well they deploy or use those skills. A good analogy may be to a football team: even talented players need a coach, or at least good play selection. Furthermore, good coaching or play selection may compensate for lesser ability, allowing a team of average players to defeat a less well-organized team of stars. We suggest that more teachers should be aware of this strategic aspect of teaching, beyond that of skill development, the ultimate goal being to teach children to do their own planning.

We begin this chapter by reviewing other approaches to learning problems to see how planning and similar constructs have been treated by others. We then go on to give examples of successful and unsuccessful planning, suggestions for the testing or observation of planning, and finally guidelines for designing remediation to overcome planning problems. However, before we begin, it is necessary for us to state as clearly as we can what we mean by planning. As you will see, it goes far beyond what the word most simply implies.

What We Mean by Planning

Planning is all that which allows cognition and behaviour to be more than passive and nonstrategic. It is also what is required in approaching a problem or task for which we do not have a ready solution. Active, strategic problem solving usually requires dealing with an overload situation: it is precisely because too much information is presented, or too many options for processing it exist, that there is a problem. As will become clearer as this chapter unfolds, problem solving of this type requires:

1. the selection of relevant presented information;
2. the selection of relevant prior knowledge;
3. the selection of relevant prior operations to act upon (1) and (2);
4. the creation of relevant new operations, usually by redefining combinations of old ones;
5. the combination of (3) and (4), to act upon (1) and (2), to produce a resultant set of information; and
6. monitoring and evaluating operations, to keep track of how far we've progressed in (5), to test whether the results of (5) satisfy the original problem, or to test whether it's worth proceeding further.

That, however, is still an over-simplification. For instance, how is the "relevance" of information or operations in (1) to (4) determined? Do you simply select at random, gradually discarding the bits that don't work? Well *you* may, but if you do the odds are you're not very good at problem solving.

Of course, this is not the place to present a complete theory of problem solving. Current conceptions of problem solving are changing rapidly (Glaser, 1984), and the field is growing far too quickly for a one-chapter summary (see the recommended readings at the end of this chapter). In fact, the term "problem solving" is too broad for, like "intelligence", it describes the end result of the integrated functioning of the attention, processing and planning systems. For example, skilled problem solving requires extensive prior knowledge from which relevant information can be selected. The aspects of problem solving in which we are interested in this chapter are those described in (1) to (6) above, which are responsible for selecting information or operations, for selecting or constructing a strategy or sequence of operations for transforming information, and for monitoring performance. Planning, therefore, is the controlling of processing.

Conceptions of Planning and Learning Problems

Planning can be divided into three broad areas: those concerned with selective attention, strategies, and metacognition (Kirby, 1984; Kirby & Ashman, 1984). While other approaches are possible, or even preferable for some purposes, we find the three-part division relatively simple to grasp and reasonably useful to apply in studying learning problems. (See recommended readings for other approaches.)

Selective Attention

One of the basic characteristics of the information processing system which we have been describing is the limited capacity of working memory, which restricts the amount of information to which we can pay attention at any point in time. Selective attention is the process by which information is chosen for attention; it may involve scanning the environment for a stimulus, or searching long-term memory for a known bit of information. Here we refer to the conscious or effortful aspects of selective attention, not the more automatic aspects controlled by the attention/arousal system. Complex academic tasks such as reading require a tremendous amount of searching, selecting, and processing of information. For such tasks to be performed smoothly, the right information from the environment has to

FIGURE 14-1

Bottom-up and top-down forces acting upon selective attention

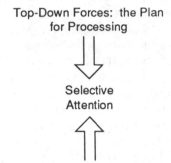

FIGURE 14-2

Interaction of bottom-up and top-down forces affecting selective attention

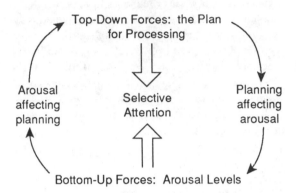

be combined (processed) with the appropriate schemas which have just been formed (from information presented earlier in the task) and with appropriate schemas from long-term memory. The organizing of this process is called selective attention, and normally takes place according to a plan.

Attention is not a simple process, and is still far from being completely understood. We have seen in Chapter 11 that attention is affected by arousal: arousal that is either too high or too low decreases the effectiveness of the selection process, preventing required information from being available for processing. If that is seen as a "bottom-up" effect (from the lower-level arousal to the higher-level selective attention process), it is also true that attention can be affected in a "top-down" fashion. Figure 14-1 shows these two forces acting upon selective attention. The top-down force is the plan under which processing is proceeding: a good plan will effectively guide the selection of information from environmental and memory sources, while a poor one will create a wretched mess. Arousal levels and the plan also interact, in that inappropriate arousal will hinder good planning, and poor planning may make the child more bored (arousal level too low) or more anxious (arousal level too high).

These effects are shown in Figure 14-2.

The result is that arousal and planning effects are difficult to separate. As we have already dealt with arousal problems in Chapter 11, we will concentrate in this chapter more upon the planning problems. However, you shouldn't lose sight of the interaction portrayed in Figure 14-2.

One of the tasks requiring selective attention in which learning problem children perform poorly is the Matching Familiar Figures Test, which was discussed in Chapter 11. It requires children to find the match of a particular picture from a group of very similar pictures. For adults this is a simple task, depending upon how similar the variations are to the standard picture. However, for young children, selective attention factors are even more important. When an adult or a skilled child performs this task, he or she inspects the standard picture for a key element, and then scans carefully through the options in a standard order (for instance, left-to-right, top-to-bottom), to see which possess or do not possess that key element. Ones not possessing the element are mentally cancelled from the set, and then another search takes place for a second key element. This systematic and *reflective* element-by-element and picture-by-picture strategy continues until only one remains. When learning problem children perform this type of task, their behaviour is much more *impulsive* in nature. Instead of selecting a single element for comparison, they respond quickly, without necessarily considering all of the options. For example, impulsive children are often observed to select answers which they have not yet visually inspected (see Messer's, 1976, review of research on this task).

Poor performance in this task can be due to inappropriate arousal (see Chapter 11) or to use of an inappropriate plan or strategy, as Figures 14-1 and 14-2 emphasize. In a simple task such as this, adults or skilled children may have an automatic plan to apply. Younger children, however, may need to construct such a plan for the first time while they are performing the task, and learning problem children may not be able to construct such a plan without explicit instruction. Remediation may consist of instruction in a specific scanning strategy (the element-by-element one described above), or in the more general technique of cognitive control or self-instruction (as described in Chapter 11, p. 152). Thus, even if the problem is originally in the attention/arousal system, remediation may make

use of the planning area; in this way a systematic plan may be used to control inappropriate levels of arousal. Some success in tasks such as this may serve to make the child less anxious, to lower arousal levels and, therefore, to allow for more appropriate planning.

A second selective attention task is presented in the box below. It distinguishes between central and incidental task information. Hagen (1967) showed that children recall increasingly more central information as they mature cognitively, whereas incidental recall stays constant. Thus, for young children, memory is deployed more indiscriminately to central and incidental information, whereas for older children, central information forms a much larger proportion of what is remembered.

Learning problem children perform poorly in tasks such as the one shown, remembering as much incidental information but less central information than other children (see Hallahan & Reeve, 1980, for a review). Though there is still debate about the implications of this finding, recent research emphasizes that it is at least partly due to differences between learning problem and normal children in their use of strategies (Worden, 1983).

Central vs. Incidental Information

In Hagen's (1967) experiment, children were presented with series of cards similar to the ones overleaf.

The cards were then covered and the children were shown a picture of an animal. The children were asked to indicate which card had the animal on it. From a number of trials like this, Hagen gave each child a score for *central* memory.

Next, Hagen showed the children a set of cards which had only animals on them, and asked the children to say which furniture picture went with each animal picture. (The animals and items of furniture had always appeared in the same pairs.) From the responses Hagen derived an incidental memory score for each child.

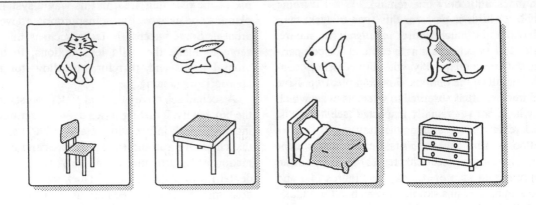

Hagen's results for children in grades 1, 3, 5 and 7 are shown in Figure 14-3 below. Central memory performance increases sharply with age, whereas incidental memory remains roughly constant. This means that irrelevant (incidental) information takes up proportionately more space in the memories of the younger children.

F I G U R E   1 4 - 3
Development of memory performance (based on information given by Hagen, 1967)

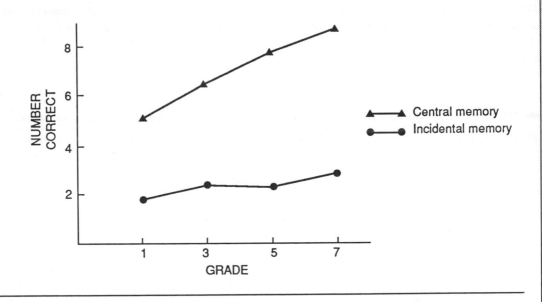

While we know of no studies which have been designed to improve the performance of learning problem children in such tasks, it seems reasonable that a variety of instructional devices could be used to highlight the central task information, or a graduated series of tasks could be presented in which the non-central information was introduced very slowly. If this approach were combined with instructions emphasizing the importance of the central information and showing how to verbalize and rehearse that information, performance should improve.

How do problems of selective attention intrude in the academic domain? Reading, for example, requires a very systematic scanning of visual information. If the scanning takes place in anything but a left-to-right, top-to-bottom manner, problems can result. However, a certain number of regressions – that is, looking back in the text – are required to interpret the meaning of the text correctly. If a child looks back to the wrong place in the text, confusion will result, just as it will if the same child then fails to find the place at which he or she stopped reading. Most academic tasks are complex, in that too much information is present and too many options exist for processing it. Successful performance requires a systematic plan of action which can function automatically.

Strategies

Plans consist of a set of strategies for handling a task, and strategies themselves consist of a series of processes for transforming task information. Consider the following problem: you are presented with a series of cards, each of which has a word printed on it (see Table 14-1). You are told that you have two minutes to study those cards and that later you will be asked to recall them. You are allowed to move the cards around while you study them. What do you do?

If you are like most adults, you'd read through them quickly and realize that the words fall into four different categories: animals, furniture, clothing and transportation. A good strategy to employ in this task is to move the cards into their four

TABLE 14-1

Words used for memory task by Moely, Olson, Halwes and Flavell (1969)

dog	bed	train	bicycle
table	truck	mitten	dress
car	hat	lion	camel
shoe	elephant	lamp	television
cow	chain	bus	boat
tie	horse	couch	sweater

categories, read through each category several times, and then try to repeat each group to yourself without looking. If this strategy is followed, recall should be practically perfect.

Children, especially younger children, perform poorly in this task (Moely, Olsen, Halwes & Flavell, 1969), partly because of the strategies they employ (or fail to employ). Some children roam from card to card in a random fashion, making no attempt to group the cards, to rehearse the words on the cards, or to test their memory. More successful children may employ a systematic, though less than ideal, strategy, such as rehearsing the entire list of twenty-four words without any grouping. Some children invent quite complicated strategies, such as moving the cards into alphabetic order and then rehearsing the words in groups according to their initial letter. These strategies may work partially, and might have been quite successful in other tasks, but are not particularly successful in the task described.

Learning problem children have been shown to perform poorly on tasks requiring spontaneous use of strategies (e.g., Torgesen, 1978; Worden, 1983), especially memory tasks. However, when the task is designed to force the subjects to use an appropriate strategy, learning problem children improve greatly (see Worden's, 1983, review). This shows clearly that these children are capable of employing appropriate strategies, but that they don't spontaneously choose to in given tasks. Since use of strategies is not their only problem, however, differences continue to exist between normal and learning problem children after strategy instruction (Torgesen & Houck, 1980). Poor spontaneous strategy selection is perhaps only part of the problem, and may even be a consequence of some other problem.

The disposition toward poor strategy use is compounded when the task is an academic one in which the children have already experienced considerable failure, or in which they are unfamiliar with the task content. For example, it is less likely that an appropriate strategy will be used in reading when basic word identification skills cannot proceed in an automatic fashion. Strategies interact with selective attention such that a poor strategy results in inappropriate information in working memory, which further prevents selection of an appropriate strategy. Repeated failure can lead to learned helplessness (see Chapter 10), and to poor strategies such as guessing, or waiting for someone to supply the answer.

Strategies which already exist in a child's cognitive repertoire may be automatic – that is, able to operate smoothly without absorbing much in the way of working memory resources. But many learned strategies are not yet at that automatic level, and others even have to be specially constructed for the task at hand. What is an automated strategy for the normal child may require more cognitive effort for one with a learning problem, and the partially automated strategy of the normal child may not be possessed by the learning problem child at all. For example, the skilled reader may have a variety of strategies at hand for determining the meaning of an unknown word encountered while reading a paragraph, whereas the learning problem child has few or none. Although any generalization about teaching methods is unsafe, it is fair to add that most normal reading instruction does not emphasize strategies to be employed during reading; instead, reading is presented as a skill of correct word identification, with comprehension following as a "natural" process (cf. Durkin, 1978-1979).

Metacognition

The third aspect of planning is metacognition, the awareness or knowledge we have about our own cognitive processes (Brown, 1980; Flavell, 1970). It includes knowledge about our cognitive skills (for instance, how many numbers can I remember?), about the nature of tasks (for example, in reading am I supposed to understand what the sentences mean?), and about the value of alternative strategies (for example, it's a good idea to underline the most important ideas in a passage). The regulation of selective attention and the selection or construction of appropriate task strategies are dependent upon the child's metacognitive awareness of what the task requires and how best to approach it (Lupart & Mulcahy, 1984). If the child does not understand the value of a given strategy in a particular task, he or she is less likely to use that strategy, or to use it well.

Are learning problem children less metacognitively aware than normal children? The answer seems certain to be yes, particularly with respect to megacognitive knowledge about academic tasks. However, it is not yet possible to decide whether this difference in metacognitive awareness is primarily responsible for their academic difficulties, or whether it is the academic difficulties themselves which have produced the lack of metacognitive knowledge. The second position is almost certainly true to some extent, though it is possible that the first is true as well.

For example, several studies have shown that children increase in metacognitive knowledge about reading as they become more skilled in reading (Myers & Paris, 1978; Moore & Kirby, 1981; Kirby & Moore, 1988). (The box below contains several of the questions asked in these metacognitive awareness studies and some of the answers given by children in the various grade groups.) Presumably, similar findings would be obtained in other achievement areas, or in any skill area. However, this does not answer the question of whether the lack of metacognition has contributed to the poor achievement, or whether it is a byproduct of low skill levels.

Metacognition in Reading

How aware are children of the nature of reading and of reading strategies? This question has been addressed by Myers and Paris (1978) and Moore and Kirby (1981; Kirby & Moore, 1988). Here are some of the questions asked in the Kirby and Moore (1988) study:

(1) What do you do differently when you read fast from when you read slow?

(2) What does the first sentence usually do in a story?

These questions (and others) were asked of a number of children (both good readers and poor readers) in grades 2, 4 and 6.

Kirby and Moore gave each answer a score, according to the system shown opposite. Figure 14-4 shows the average scores for good and poor readers at the three grade levels.

Scoring Scale

Question 1:

0 – don't know, nothing, or irrelevant
1 – make mistakes, say the words faster
2 – skip the hard words
3 – skip the easy or unimportant words
4 – coherent strategy (e.g., look at beginnings or ends of paragraphs)

Question 2:

0 – don't know, nothing, or irrelevant
1 – mechanical answers (e.g., begins with a capital letter; "once upon a time")
2 – tells what happened first
3 – introduces who, what, where, etc.
4 – overview of story

FIGURE 14-4
Scores for metacognition in reading (Kirby & Moore, 1988)

Question 1

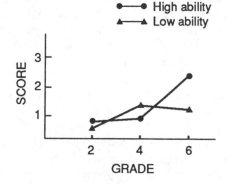

Question 2

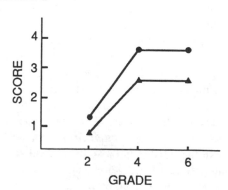

While much research still needs to be done with respect to metacognition in learning problem children, it does seem that this is an area of weakness for them. We would not suggest that metacognition instruction in the absence of academic skill training should be undertaken, but rather that some aspects of instruction regarding metacognition should be included in a comprehensive remediation program. We should remember that learning problem children, while not academically skilled, are reasonably intelligent and should be able to grasp what a task is about, even if they are not yet able to perform it. An initial metacognitive appreciation that the goal of reading is the extraction of meaning should facilitate the learning of comprehension strategies. As we will see later in this chapter, this proposal suggests that remedial efforts should be aimed not only at the bottom-up processes of word recognition and phonetic decoding, but also at the top-down processes of metacognitive awareness and strategy selection.

Learning Problems in Planning

In Chapters 6, 7, 8 and 9, we reviewed the areas of classroom behaviour, reading, spelling and mathematics and discussed the various types of learning problems which could arise in these areas. As we have seen in the preceding chapters, many of those achievement problems can be related to problems in the area of attention and of simultaneous and successive processing. We also saw that many problems are caused at a higher level, by the inefficient control of attention or processing. These control problems are problems of planning. Again, we emphasize that problems in the attention, processing and planning systems are interrelated. A problem in planning is just as unlikely to exist in isolation as are problems in the other areas. Proper planning in an academic context requires not only extensive knowledge but also the skillful and flexible integration of that knowledge with incoming information. Competent planning requires attention to be selectively deployed, both to incoming information and to known information, and the selection of an appropriate strategy based upon a

metacognitive appreciation of the task and of one's own skills.

Some children's learning problems seem to exist largely in the planning area, others have problems in the arousal or processing areas; yet other children have problems in several of these domains. It would not be unreasonable to expect children's problems to spread, so that an initial planning problem could produce a poor approach to successive tasks, with the result being less practice in successive processing and a lower level of that processing skill (see Figure 5-5). Because of this interdependence of the cognitive systems and their problems, remediation should be designed to take them all into account, regardless of which system is the primary focus. With that cautionary reminder, we turn now to the planning problems identified in Chapters 7, 8 and 9 in the specific achievement areas.

Table 14-2 lists the learning problems ascribed to the planning component of information processing in the various achievement areas. Learning problem symptoms are described and causal descriptions of the resulting factors in those learning problems are given. If you scan down the causal description column of Table 14-2, you can see that there are basically four sorts of planning problems. The first type of planning problem is essentially that there is no plan. (This is technically inaccurate, in the sense that processing is always taking place under the guidance of some sort of plan, even if that plan is extremely passive or misguided.) This type of problem can be seen both at the lower levels of cognition, as in identifying unknown words, and at the higher levels, as in comprehending a complicated passage if the child has no idea of how to proceed. To the extent that plans draw primarily upon either successive or simultaneous processing, the lack of an appropriate plan is also a processing problem.

The second type of problem observed in planning is that the wrong plan is employed. For example, it is not uncommon for beginning readers to believe that the purpose of reading is to correctly identify and pronounce the words on the page; therefore, they pay little attention to comprehending the message behind the words upon the page. This second category of planning problems is also related to processing problems.

TABLE 14-2
Learning problems ascribed to planning

Achievement Area	Learning Problem Symptom	Causal Description
Reading	Inability to switch word identification strategy according to task	Lack of alternative strategies (phonic, sight, contextual)
	Inability to employ second or third word identification strategy if first fails	Lack of flexibility in strategy-switching
	"Recognition" of incorrect word, not corrected after further reading	Lack of monitoring or evaluation
	Inability to comprehend clauses or sentences	Lack of general orientation to meaning extraction
		Lack of specific meaning extraction strategies
	Failure to correct misinterpretation of sentence	Lack of monitoring or evaluation
	Inability to extract main idea or theme, stated or implied, of a passage	Lack of orientation to meaning extraction
	Non-use or misuse of instructional aids (organizers, diagrams, etc.)	Lack of specific strategies
		Use of incorrect strategy
	Failure to correct misinterpretation	Lack of monitoring or evaluation
Spelling	Inability to switch spelling strategy, according to word	Lack of alternative strategies
		Lack of flexibility in strategy-switching
	Repetition or omission of a sound unit	Failure to follow spelling plan, or to retain place in word being spelled
	Inconsistent spelling, repetition of errors, etc.	Lack of monitoring and evaluation
Arithmetic and Mathematics	Random attempt at solution; use of incorrect strategy	Lack of appropriate strategy
	Failure to switch strategies	Lack of strategy-switching flexibility
	Failure to engage in "guided trial and error" to generate solution	Lack of appropriate strategy
		Disinclination to use active approach
	Failure to use or construct aids such as diagrams	Lack of appropriate strategies
		Lack of monitoring and evaluation
		Disinclination to use aids

A third type of problem concerns loss of place within the correct plan. As we have described in the preceding sections, a plan consists of a series of steps; often these steps are interrelated, in that the results of one stage determine what occurs at the next stage. It is necessary to keep one's place in the sequence of steps, otherwise one may omit or duplicate a crucial operation.

The fourth type of planning problem involves the failure to change a plan in response to what has happened, particularly in problem solving situations in which there is no obvious plan for solving the task at hand. In these cases, it is necessary to formulate a tentative plan, proceed with it for some time, and evaluate how well it works. If it is unsuccessful, or if parts of it are unsuccessful, one must go back, change the plan in the appropriate places, and begin the task anew. This aspect of planning requires that performance be constantly monitored and evaluated with respect to one's goal in the task. In academic tasks it not uncommon for children to lose sight of the goal for which they were aiming, to fail to monitor their own performance, and to fail to take appropriate remedial action.

Our approach here is similar to that of the preceding chapters: we will present examples of each of the planning problems identified in Table 14-2. We emphasize that we have been selective in choosing these examples, as the full range of problems, causes and possible combinations cannot be presented here. Instead, we have aimed at presenting a reasonable cross-section of difficulties, coming from the various achievement areas.

Flexible Use of Word Identification Strategies

In reading, competent word identification requires the flexible integration of phonological, visual and contextual strategies. The skilled reader not only requires all three strategies to read successfully, but must also know when to rely upon one source of information more than another. For example, it is often not necessary to identify a word very precisely; the rough meaning of the word as derived from context may suffice. In other cases, a more precise identification may be required, one relying upon both visual and phonological information. If any of these information sources is over-emphasized or under-emphasized, reading problems can result. Further problems can result from failing to monitor the success of a given strategy.

Purpose in Reading

A second example of a planning problem at a much higher level in reading concerns purpose in reading. Once basic reading skills have been established, after say two or three years of reading instruction, it is common for children to be given passages to read from which they are supposed to learn information. By high school it is very common for children to be given a chapter or even a book to take home and "study". Yet it is clear from the performance of many children that they have little conception of how study is to take place or even what the goals of study are. This type of problem can be observed more simply in the situation in which a child is asked to read a paragraph and understand what it is about. At the broadest level this problem can derive from whether the child is attempting to extract meaning at all, and more specifically, from which exact comprehension strategies he or she is employing.

Spelling Strategies

Like word identification, spelling of new words requires the flexible interchange of visual and phonological strategies and the monitoring of success. As we saw in Chapter 8, competent spelling of new words requires the following of a plan which has the various components of pronunciation, syllable selection and so forth. Not surprisingly, problems can result if this plan is not followed, or if the place in plan is lost while spelling a word. See Table 14-2 for examples of this type of problem.

Simplifying Equations

It is possible to find many examples of poor planning in the area of arithmetic and mathematics. A not uncommon one concerns how to solve algebraic equations such as $147 + 1927 = x + 147 + 1027 + 800$. A poor strategy is to start adding and subtracting, which may produce errors and will certainly be slow. A better approach is to recognize that 147 appears on both sides, so it can be ignored, and that 1027 and 800 are just 100 less than 1927, so the answer must be 100. Associated with this problem is the fear induced in some children (and perhaps even some readers of this book) by the sight of numbers or, more terrifyingly, groups of numbers. What should otherwise be seen as a relatively simple problem becomes an unmanageable one because of the fear or anxiety generated by the problem content. (Anxiety makes one less likely to be able to step back from the problem and see the overview, and also more likely to make arithmetical errors if the slow calculations are performed.)

Alternate Solutions to Word Problems

A second example from the mathematics area concerns the ubiquitous word problem. As we have discussed in Chapter 9, such problems tell some of the strangest stories found in all literature, and in the strangest syntax. Word problems are intended to present far more complexity than would be found in a simple set of equations and, therefore, to assess the degree to which the learner can deal with this overload and generate an appropriate problem solving strategy. They may be deliberately designed to confuse and mislead. In many cases alternative strategies must be attempted, evaluated and discarded, before the correct one is hit upon. This requires a massive effort in planning, keeping track of the solutions or approaches that have been attempted and of what should be tried next.

Observation and Assessment of Planning Problems

Because the concept of planning is a relatively new one and also a very complex one, it should not be surprising that there are no specific standardized

tests that measure "planning ability". In fact, as Kirby and Ashman (1984) have shown, the very concept of a unitary planning ability is unlikely to be accurate. Instead, planning seems certain to have many different faces and to depend heavily upon one's experience and task-specific knowledge. Furthermore, it must be remembered that what may be a measure of planning in a particular situation, with a particular group of children, may become a measure of something else in a different situation or with a different group of subjects. For example, if you have the required basic skills in mathematics, a particular word problem may assess your ability to engage in problem solving or planning to solve it. In this sense, it's your problem solving ability which determines your level of success. However, for another person whose basic skills in mathematics are weak, whether or not the problem is solved is more dependent upon basic skills. You may fail to solve the problem because of your planning skills, but the other person will fail because of the lack of knowledge skills.

Accordingly, it is necessary to exercise some caution in describing measures of planning ability. We have listed below several general measures, many of which can be used by classroom teachers, as well as some more specific planning measures from the achievement areas of reading, spelling and mathematics. We have divided the general measures into those relating to selective attention, strategies and metacognition to emphasize these different aspects, but the achievement area measures combine these three aspects to show how they are integrated in the real world.

General Measures

Selective Attention

There are a great number of tasks which assess selective attention to external input, and many of these currently exist as children's games. One popular one is called Connecting the Dots, illustrated in Figure 14-5. (Psychologists have called this task Trail-Making; see Ashman & Das, 1980.) The aim of the task is to draw a line beginning at the dot numbered one, connect it to the dot numbered 2,

FIGURE 14-5

Sample page of connecting the dots
(based upon a test by Kirby and Ashman, 1984)

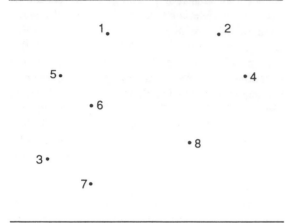

FIGURE 14-6

A sample from a maze test
(based upon examples used by Kirby and Ashman, 1984)

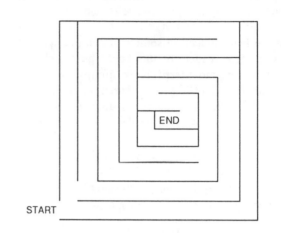

and so on until all the dots have been connected, as quickly as possible. In game applications of this task, the resultant drawing often forms a familiar figure. As a measure of planning, however, the overall figure is usually not relevant. This task appears to measure planning because the child must scan the visual environment – that is, the page – to find the next dot in correct sequence. If the child engages in a random scanning pattern, dot connecting is likely to be very slow or perhaps incorrect. Children can either be timed, to see how long they take to do a certain number of dots or pages, or they can be given a set amount of time to do as many as possible. Whereas many children show aversion to tests, they are greatly interested in tasks such as dot connection; in fact, they will work hard on other tests in order to be able to do this one.

A similar planning test is called Mazes. In this case, the child is presented with a visual maze, such as the one shown in Figure 14-6. The child's task is to draw a path through the maze, as quickly and as carefully as possible (see Kirby & Ashman, 1984). Again, children find this an interesting task. It appears to measure planning because at every choice point the maze must be scanned for the correct path. This task may also measure planning

because a variety of strategies are available to the children. For example, in a simple maze, it may be possible to plan the entire route through the maze before beginning to draw. This is likely to be quite successful in such situations. If, instead, segments of the maze are performed one-by-one, it is possible for the child to go down a major dead-end before realizing what has happened. On the other hand, segment-by-segment planning may be necessary in a more difficult maze. Skilled planners are familiar with their ability in this area, and select the appropriate amount of scanning ahead. Skilled planning should also result in careful, error-free performance; this can be assessed by assigning a penalty score to dead-ends entered, or lines illegally crossed. Performance can be timed, or the amount done in a set time counted.

A third planning task that relates to selective attention is the Matching Familiar Figures Test, which has been described previously in this chapter and in Chapter 11 (see p. 141). It requires children to match a particular picture with one of a group of six that are very similar. This test requires

FIGURE 14-7

Average performance levels of normal children on the matching familiar test (based upon Messer's, 1976, Table 1)

Response Time per Problem

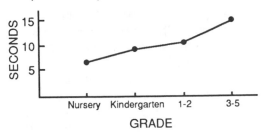

Number of Errors per 12 Problems
(more than one can be made per problem)

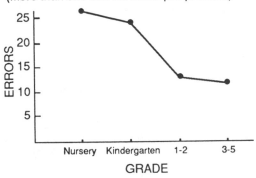

Scanning can be observed in tests which are not normally considered measures of selective attention, emphasizing the point that selective attention is required in most tasks. The Paper Folding Test is normally thought to be a measure of spatial ability (see Figure 13-1, Example 3). Richard Snow (1978) and his colleagues at Stanford University have observed the eye movements subjects make when solving these items (see the box below). Normally you would expect the subject to inspect the way the paper is folded, frame by frame, and then systematically examine the answer options to see which one is correct. Snow has found that this is, in fact, what subjects with good spatial abilities do, or more generally, what subjects do in problems that are well within their ability limits. When subjects attempt to solve difficult problems, it seems that their scanning strategies deteriorate and become more similar to those of subjects with low spatial skills. As the box below illustrates, this can result in a random scanning of the task, perhaps even beginning with the answer options before inspecting the problem, which is unlikely to be successful. The poor scanning may be both the *cause* and the *result* of poor performance in the task.

A final selective attention test is Verbal Fluency, in which the subject is required to scan long-term memory contents in order to, for instance, write down in three minutes as many words as possible beginning with the letter L. (Other authors have referred to tasks such as this as measures of creativity, divergent thinking, or verbal productive thinking; see Horn, 1976.) An unplanned approach to this task would be simply to wait until words beginning with L came to mind. With this approach, you would not be likely to come up with many L words in the time available. More planned approaches are possible. A common one adopted by school children is to scan around the classroom looking for objects which begin with L. This is a preferable strategy to just waiting, but you can see that it will likely result in nouns – particularly concrete nouns – being discovered, and virtually no adjectives, verbs or adverbs. A better strategy might be to decide that any word beginning with L is likely to have as its second letter a vowel;

children to search the visual display in a planned and systematic manner, to identify aspects or features of the standard item which may discriminate among the options available. Figure 14-7 shows some typical results: with increasing age, solution times increase and the number of errors made decreases. In tasks in which the discriminations to be made are very difficult, we see older or more able children taking longer to solve the problem than younger or less able children. A longer solution time in such tasks may be an index of a more planned performance.

Scanning Patterns in Paper Folding

The Paper Folding Test is usually thought of as a test of spatial ability (see Figure 13-1, Example 3, for a description of it). Snow (1978) has designed a version of this test so that subjects' *eye movements* could be observed; in other words, Snow was able to see what his test subjects were looking at, as they solved the problems. (See his paper for the details of how he did this.)

The results were quite striking. Figure 14-8 is an example of a competent high school student's performance. The student begins by following the problem through, from left to right, then goes back and forth between the first two stages of the problem before looking at four of the answer alternatives and responding correctly.

Figure 14-9 shows the performance of a less skilled high school student. As you can see, the person's approach is much more haphazard, never actually going through the problem in order; some answer options are scanned before the problem has been completed. Not surprisingly, an incorrect answer is given.

FIGURE 14-8
Scanning pattern of a competent student

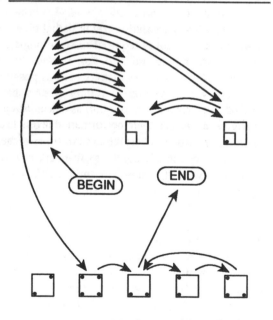

FIGURE 14-9
Scanning pattern of less skilled student

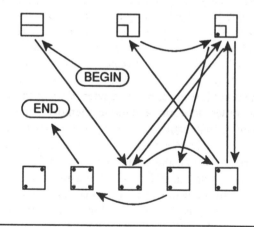

therefore, you begin with the sequence LA and try to think of LA words. So you could go, L-A-B, LAB, which would give you laboratory, then laborious, labour, labourer, and so on. After you had exhausted LAB words, you could try LAC words; e.g., lack, lace, and even lacrosse. Embedded within this strategy is another one, which says that when you hit upon a word such as labour, which you know has many different forms, generate those forms at that point. It can be difficult to determine which strategy a child is using, so usually only the number of words produced is counted. The more planful child should produce more words, though other factors (such as word knowledge) are also involved.

Strategies

Strategies can be observed at the perception, memory and problem solving levels. We have already described perceptual or scanning strategies in the selective attention section above. Typical memory tasks would be to memorize a list of words, or of word pairs. Practical examples would include going to the grocery store and trying to remember a shopping list, or attempting to learn the definitions of twenty new words in French. In memorizing a list of words, a basic strategy is to verbalize the words – that is, to name them. A better strategy includes systematic rehearsal; thus, the list is verbalized not just once, but a number of times in the same order, to form a durable memory for the sequence. Better still is to employ self-testing regularly, to see how well the list is being learned. Higher-level strategies capitalize on particular aspects of the words to be memorized. For example, if the words represent concrete objects, an imagery strategy (forming mental pictures of the objects) may be successful. If the words to be memorized fall into several conceptual categories, such as pieces of furniture, methods of transportation and so on, they could be mentally grouped into these categories, rehearsed within categories or even imaged within categories.

A planful subject will be likely to have a variety of such strategies available, and be able to select them as appropriate. The questions with respect to planning are first, whether any strategy is being employed; second, whether the strategy is appropriate; and third, whether there seems to be a flexible array of strategies which are brought to bear when performance fails or the task changes. In observing children's memory strategies, it is important to observe not only which strategies they spontaneously employ, but also which strategies they can employ when instructed to do so.

Strategies are also important in more conceptual areas, such as problem solving. Consider, for example, the following analogy problem: cat is to animal, as chair is to _____. Given that you do not know immediately how to solve this problem, what should you do? A useful strategy is to look first at the possible relationships between the first two words given. An obvious relationship may occur to you, that the first word is a member of the category represented by the second word; in this case, proceed to the next step. Otherwise, examine as many different relationships as possible. Then encode the third word, to see if a similar relationship could be mapped on to it to produce the missing fourth word. In doing this, of course, it is necessary to know how long to continue listing relationships between the first two words, and how long to continue attempting to map those relationships onto the third term. Verbal and nonverbal analogies are convenient ways of assessing children's problem solving strategies. In order to assess children's strategies as well as their performance levels (i.e., number correct), it is helpful to have them verbalize how they are solving the problem; this technique is also a component in improving their strategies.

Metacognition

Because metacognition refers to one's verbalizable conscious knowledge, the most obvious way to assess it is by interview, by asking children how they perceive a given task. In carefully designed situations it may also be possible to assess metacognition in more of a performance-oriented manner, for instance, in a task in which successful performance can only be attained if awareness of a particular feature of the task occurs. In the latter case, metacognition may be underestimated, due to the intrusion of other factors (for instance, if a person fails the task, it may be because of metacognitive knowledge or because of something else).

The purpose of assessing metacognitive awareness is to understand children's understanding of tasks, strategies, and their own abilities. For example, you may determine that a child knows a certain strategy (e.g., phonic decoding) and has the required knowledge skills (letter-sound correspondences); yet if that child does not appreciate that that strategy is useful in identifying new words (metacognitive awareness), there is a clear need for further instruction. Furthermore, the instruction required will have to be different from much standard instruction, in that it will have to *persuade* the child that the strategy is useful (cf. Paris, Lipson & Wixson, 1983).

Metacognitive questions can be asked of children regarding virtually any task or situation. For example, any of the memory tasks described above could be the subject of questions. Children could be asked how they would go about studying a list of twenty words. They could also be asked how they would teach a task to another child, perhaps a younger child. In this way, we may be able to get around the difficulty that many children have in verbalizing. This is a particular problem with young children, and may also be with learning problem children who approach tasks in a relatively passive manner. Accordingly, metacognitive interviewers may have to engage in substantial probing before children will verbalize what they, in fact, do know. As we will see in the remediation section below, one approach is to have the children do a task which you know they can do, and then ask them to verbalize how they did it. If you ask them to verbalize in isolation from performance, they may claim not to know how to do it or give an implausible answer. With the concrete task before them and success in that task already attained, it may be possible through skillful probing to elicit from them a description of what, in fact, they did do.

The danger in an interview is that children will not verbalize what they know. On the other hand, inferring metacognition from a performance is dangerous because children can sometimes do things of which they are not fully aware; similarly, the performance of the task may distract them from what they do know. The most typical of performance tasks have been termed comprehension monitoring tasks.

Measures in which performance requiring metacognitive awareness is observed are not pure measures of metacognition, but rather measures of metacognition in interaction with appropriate monitoring strategies and task-relevant knowledge. In these tasks, children are presented with information to understand (for instance, instructions for a game). Embedded in that information is either a critical gap or a critical error. Children can be observed first to see whether they notice the problem. If they don't, they can be specifically asked if anything is wrong, or even pointed towards the error and asked if that part is all right. Successful performance in these tasks requires recognition that *understanding* is required, and that understanding must be monitored and evaluated, perhaps beyond the sentence level.

Measures within Achievement Areas

Planning in Reading

We will discuss selective attention, strategy, and metacognition measures of planning at two levels in reading: at the word level and at the passage or comprehension level. The selective attention measures that were described above (see pp. 221-225) can mostly be translated into reading measures. For example, the Matching Familiar Figures Test can become a Matching Familiar Words Test, in which words have to be matched to a standard. Different items could contain regular or irregular words, or nonwords, to emphasize both phonic and sight skills. (As do all planning measures, this one clearly also requires other skills, e.g., phonic knowledge, successive processing). Word mazes could also be formed, the child's task being to discover hidden words in a matrix of letters. Search tasks could be devised as well: circle all the Es on a page; underline the word "cat" every time it appears; underline all the verbs; or underline all the examples of people. These selective attention measures can thus be designed to tap word-level or comprehension-level skills.

The word recognition strategies of phonic decoding, visual recognition, and use of context have already been discussed in Chapter 7. From the point of view of planning, one would want to know which of these strategies children possessed, which they could use spontaneously, and how easily they switch between them in appropriate situations. Goodman and Burke (1972) have described an approach to measuring these skills, based upon the errors children make in reading.

At the passage level, strategies can be described in general terms (meaning-oriented vs. pronunciation-oriented) or far more precisely (attempts to identify the referent of a pronoun, etc.), depending upon the child's level of skill. One would want to know here how many such strategies children possess, which they use, and how flexibly they can switch between them.

Metacognition about word identification has been assessed in a number of interview studies (Myers & Paris, 1978; Kirby & Moore, 1988). The box that follows highlights two metacognitive questions (at the word and sentence levels) and some typical results for grade 2, 4, and 6 children. In assessing metacognitive knowledge, of course, it is necessary to ensure that the child understands the answer given, and is not just repeating a response which has been rote learned. As we will discuss below in the remediation section, it is necessary to ensure in teaching metacognitive knowledge that *understanding* is communicated, not just specific knowledge of a rote nature.

Planning in Spelling

Many of the selective attention measures described above in the reading section would be appropriate for spelling: the Matching Familiar Words task is one example.

At the strategies level, informal observation could assess the degree to which children rely upon visual and phonological cues in spelling and the degree to which a non-preferred cue system can be employed if necessary. For example, a child given a non-word to spell could produce an acceptable version of that word employing the most common phonological sound-letter assignments. By itself, that task would assess largely phonological skills. However, the child could then be asked to supply some alternative spellings, perhaps making use of visual codes or less common phonological codes. For example, if the non-word to be spelt were "dite", the child might well come up with "dite" as a first spelling. Alternative strategies would be assessed by asking for other possible spellings, such as "dyte", "dight", "deight" and so forth. The number of alternative spellings produced would assess a child's flexibility in use of spelling strategies.

To our knowledge, metacognition in spelling has not been assessed, but possible questions could concern spelling a word that has not been heard before. At the performance level, children could be asked to inspect other children's dictation work and assess the correctness of spelling. If a word were included which was misspelt in the given context but could be a correctly spelled word in a different context, it would assess children's flexibility of monitoring spelling while also monitoring comprehension.

Planning in Mathematics

The selective attention tasks described previously could be easily applied to mathematics. For instance, there could be tests of digit matching or multi-digit number matching, or more complex measures (e.g., matching $4 \times 2 + 3$ with $2 \times 8 - 5$.

When we enter an area such as mathematics, the key factor of depth and breadth of content knowledge becomes even more apparent. When discussing planning, the danger is to talk as though plans or problem solving strategies exist in isolation from one's content knowledge. This is quite simply not the case. Not only are some content-specific problem solving strategies part of the knowledge in a

Metacognition about Words and Sentences

Here are two more questions from the Kirby and Moore (1988) study, which had previously been addressed by Myers and Paris (1978):

(1) When you're reading, what do you do if there's a word you don't understand?

(2) When you're reading a story, what do you do if there's a whole sentence you don't understand?

Children who responded with "Ask someone" were told, "Suppose no one else was around."

These questions were asked of good and poor readers in grades 2, 4, and 6, and their answers scored.

Scoring Scale

Question 1:

0 – don't know, nothing, or irrelevant
1 – skip it
2 – spell it
3 – sound out, syllabify, re-read
4 – look it up in a dictionary
5 – determine meaning from context

Question 2:

0 – don't know, nothing, irrelevant
1 – skip it
2 – implausible attempt (spell, sound out)
3 – external to text (dictionary, look at pictures)
4 – determine meaning from context

Figure 14-10 shows the results for the groups.

FIGURE 14-10
Scores for metacognition of words and sentences

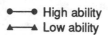

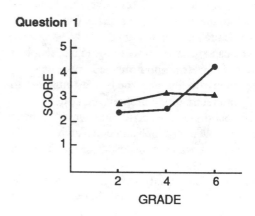

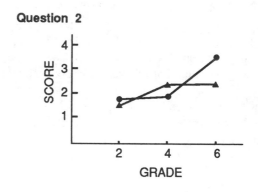

subject area (for example, how to solve particular algebra problems), but also some strategies cannot operate unless subject matter knowledge is highly automatized. We can see examples of this point in the box on simplifying equations. The first example is a simple algebra problem, in which no calculation has to be performed. The two numbers on the lefthand side of the equation have to be the same two numbers as on the righthand side of the equation; therefore, the question mark must represent the number 2. Children should be able to understand this type of problem long before they encounter formal algebra. However, consider the second example. The structure of this problem is formally the same as the first example; however, in this case there are more numbers, and the numbers themselves are much larger. It is not uncommon for children who can successfully solve the first example to take out their pencils and begin a laborious and often incorrect series of computations for the second. Such children clearly have the correct problem solving strategy, because they use it to solve the first problem. However, once the content of the problem gets beyond the child's level of automaticity, problem solving strategies break down and he or she is forced to revert to a lower level approach.

It is possible to devise a structured series of examples based upon the format contained in this box and observe how well children employ appropriate problem solving strategies. As we mentioned in Chapter 13, the Australian Council for Educational Research (1977) has produced a test called the Operations Test in which there are three types of problem content – simple numbers, complex numbers and variables – and two types of problem structure – simple equations such as those contained in this box and more complex equations (see the box on p. 199; also Collis, 1971). Such tests can be used to assess not only children's problem solving strategies, but also their familiarity with the subject matter content. Comparable tests could be devised in other areas of mathematics or problem solving. The key feature of such tests is that they identify different solution strategies and different degrees of content familiarity. This approach can even be taken with mathematical word problems. Mayer (1983) has shown that most word problems fit into one of a few different categories. Different

Simplifying Equations

In these tasks the goal is to determine what X is.

Example 1
$2 + 4 = 4 + ?$

Even young children who have never encountered algebra can solve problems like this, usually without doing any calculations. Their familiarity (automaticity) with these small numbers allows them to work with the *meaning* of the task, not just the details. Because of this they can explain that, if there is a 2 and a 4 on one side, then there has to be a 2 and a 4 on the other.

This is quite different from the second example.

Example 2
$1047 + 912 + 179 = 912 + ? + 179$

Because the numbers are less familiar, many children who successfully solved Example 1 without any calculations fail to do so in Example 2.

problem "types" in this case require different strategies, and within each type content could be varied from simple (or familiar) to complex.

With methods such as these, it is possible to assess the specific problem solving strategies which a child possesses and the facility with which that child can employ those strategies in different contexts of increasing complexity. Perhaps the most important aspect is for the teacher to accept that various strategies exist, and that it is important to assess them.

Improving Planning Skills

Our approach to remediation in the planning area is similar to that adopted in the preceding chapters: begin with the measures that have been used to observe planning skills, break those tasks down to determine the locus of the child's problem, and begin to teach at that point with simplified or familiar content. The goals are to improve the achievement areas, but it may be necessary to begin by teaching more general planning skills in a less complex and (for the child) less frightening context.

We will consider remedial approaches to planning problems in the selective attention, strategy, and metacognition domains, covering both general tasks and tasks within the areas of reading, spelling and mathematics. Before beginning, however, we hasten to remind the reader that planning problems seldom exist in isolation, that they usually exist in conjunction with deficient background knowledge and problems of simultaneous or successive processing or attention. In many cases, the beginning of remediation may be at the planning level. Nevertheless, as we have seen in the preceding chapters, by suggesting that remediation may begin at the planning level, we do not imply that this is the only source of learning problems.

Selective Attention

There have been many attempts to find ways to improve children's selective attention skills, par-

ticularly scanning skills such as those assessed by the Matching Familiar Figures Test. It is worth noting what doesn't work: several studies have attempted to improve students' scores by instructing them to take their time – that is, to slow down their processing (e.g., Kagan, Pearson & Welch, 1966). If, indeed, impulsivity were an isolated problem, perhaps delay training might work. However, delay training does not work. Before delay training, the children produce errors quickly; after it, they simply produce them more slowly! There is no evidence that merely instructing children to slow down is effective. The implications for the classroom are clear. Instructing children to slow down is unlikely to help. Shouting at children to slow down or take their time (as a frustrated and harassed teacher is likely to do) is more likely to be confusing or impulsivity-producing. If the children knew what to do when they slowed down, perhaps there wouldn't be a problem in the first place.

More successful attempts to improve scanning skills have involved modelling and strategy instruction (see Messer, 1976, pp. 1045-1046 for a review). In modelling the child may be shown a videotape of another child performing the task successfully. In some cases the child on the videotape may give explicit instructions or descriptions of how to perform the task. Either a child or an adult could go through the correct scanning strategy, slowly and systematically, giving the subject practice in each step in that strategy before tackling the entire task. Simple examples or content should be used first, before proceeding to the complex material included in the text. Yet another variant would be to adopt the self-instructional approach – that is, teaching children to monitor their own scanning so as to improve it (see pp. 151-152).

By far the most promising results have been achieved by combining strategy training with self-instructional training (e.g., Douglas *et al.*, 1976). We have already described these techniques in Chapter 11; an important point to note here is that this approach tackles attention, processing and planning, and that, within planning, the levels of selective attention, strategies and metacognition are addressed.

As we suggested in the assessment section above, the stimuli involved in a selective attention task can just as well be letters or numbers or nonverbal figures. In teaching scanning to a school-aged child, it may be worthwhile to begin with non-verbal stimuli, but proceed quickly to letters, letter combinations, numbers, and number combinations. With each of these different types of stimuli, the same scanning strategies could be emphasized: analyzing the display into elements, labelling the elements, if necessary labelling a sequence of elements, naming a sequence of elements, checking for identity in an analytic step-by-step fashion, and so on. As these strategies are unlikely to feel natural to the child, it is necessary to make certain that the child has some degree of success early in trying them out and begins to believe that they are useful. Particularly with young children, extrinsic reinforcement in the form of rewards or praise may be helpful.

Strategies

In improving strategies in a particular task, the first step is to assess the strategy that the children employ spontaneously. The next step, ideally, is to expose the children to a situation in which their spontaneous strategy fails, and fails obviously; this is a necessary step to motivate them to learn your strategy. In some situations this is easy to do; in others, extremely difficult. (See Case, 1980, for examples of this.) The third step is to teach your strategy, persuading the children that it is worth employing.

Instruction may take place through modelling, explicit verbal instruction, self-instruction, or some combination of these. If the strategy is complex – that is, has many steps or involves alternative strategies – it will be more effective to break it down, providing instruction, practice and feedback on each component before beginning to tie them together.

An important component of all strategies is the evaluation or monitoring of performance, which clearly involves metacognitive skills. Competent performance requires that performance be assessed in an on-going fashion, so that if it begins to fail, remedial action can be taken. This requires that the children share your goals of successful performance, and your perception of their lack of success. Like everything else, monitoring is more easily taught, and children more easily convinced, with easy or familiar material. Extremely obvious errors should establish the idea of monitoring, and it can then be gradually transferred to more difficult content.

As in teaching selective attention skills, it may be necessary to begin strategy instruction with an area other than an achievement area, for example, with memory strategies without any achievement content (e.g., Worden, 1983). The cognitive training program in the box below presents such an example. Strategies can also be taught in the context of a game. These situations should be enjoyable for the children, and because they do not involve an area of persistent failure, they should not spontaneously provoke the usual learned helplessness and failure-expectation responses (cf. Chapter 10). In the achievement area, many highly specific strategies need to be taught. For example, in word identification there should be general strategies of visual and phonic analysis, and use of context. Each of these would include more specific strategies dealing with particular rules or concepts. Other strategies should be used at the sentence comprehension level, for instance, analyzing syntax and semantics; yet further strategies at the paragraph or text level to extract main ideas, construct summaries, answer questions and so forth. An example of a student with study strategy problems is presented in the case study in this chapter. An overview of reading strategies can be found in Chapter 7, though a complete list is beyond the scope of this book. Similarly, Chapters 8 and 9 describe spelling and mathematics strategies. See the readings at the end of this chapter.

Planning: A Cognitive Training Program

Here is an example of a cognitive training program used in a short study undertaken by a graduate student. The study was designed to include three parts: a pre-test measure, a period of intervention, and a post-test measure.

Problem
The child lacks the strategies needed to enhance short-term memory.

Solution
Cognitive training to develop the meta-memory skills necessary for dealing with short-term memory tasks.

The Task
The central task of the program was devised to gain the interest of the child from the beginning, and characterized by its simplicity and lack of academic content. The student is required to remember twenty pairs of pictures. First, the pairs are all presented individually. Then the child is shown only one picture from each pair and is required to recall the picture not shown.

Training Program
Training procedures usually involve several sessions. In this particular example, four sessions are recommended.

Session 1
1. Tell the student that he or she could remember more by taking advantage of certain strategies or tricks.

2. Emphasize that these strategies would work with many kinds of memory problems in many situations.

3. Stress the fact that our memory is limited, that the memory test was difficult, and that using tricks can help.

4. Give the child twenty pairs of picture cards. Ask the child to present these to you while you verbalize the picture association process out loud. Overt verbalizations should include the following types of statements:

a) Definition of the problem: stating the nature and demands of the task. "I'm going to have to remember which picture goes with which picture. Later I'll see only one picture and I'll have to remember its partner."

b) Awareness of the need for attention: "I'm going to have to stop everything else and think about these pictures. I won't pay attention to anything else going on around me."

c) Awareness of strategy: "What plan am I going to use? I'm going to make a picture in my mind about the two pictures together. I'll make them go together somehow in my head."

d) Use of strategy throughout the task: "Let's see — bubble gum and cat. Gee, this one is difficult. I know, I'm thinking of that black cat with pink gum stuck in his hair. What a mess!"

e) Coping self-statements throughout the task: "My goodness, there are a lot of picture-pairs to remember. I guess that

I'll just have to try my best. I'll keep playing the game and see how it goes."

f) Positively reinforcing self-statements throughout the task: "I'm doing very well at using the memory plan." "I've really been paying attention well!"

g) Use of strategy in recall task: "Let's see – bubble gum. I can remember the bubble gum making a mess. Oh yes, bubble gum stuck in the cat's hair. The answer is bubble gum with cat."

h) Coping self-statements in recall task: "Let's see – bubble gum. I can remember something about a mess but I can't remember where. Think! (pause) Oh well, 'pass', I'll keep trying my best on the others. Nobody is perfect."

i) Positively reinforcing self-statements in recall task: "Gee, I'm doing quite well."

j) Stating merits of self-verbalization rehearsal: "Boy, I'm glad I used the memory plan. Thinking aloud, paying attention, and telling myself about pictures in my mind really helped me to remember."

5. The child is now required to do what you did, using the same pictures. Guide the child to use all of the above components of self-instruction throughout the memorization and recall task. Everything should be done out loud. At the conclusion of the task, congratulate the child and comment on how much self-verbalization helped him or her to remember.

Session Two

Provide the child with a flashcard listing the main components of self-instruction training. Read the list first, then have the child repeat each sentence. Tell the child that the card will be placed on the desk as a reminder of the rules of the memory game. The flashcard should include the statements:

– Talking to myself helps me to remember.
– I must tell myself to pay attention.
– I must use my memory plan all during the game. I must tell myself how the pictures can go together in a picture or a sentence in my mind.
– If I have trouble or make a mistake, I must tell myself it is okay and keep trying my best.
– When I do well, I must remember to congratulate myself.
– Talking to myself really helps me to remember!

Remind the child how to use these guidelines by modeling the use of self-statements for about five memory pairs from Session One. Now show the child twenty new sets of pictures consecutively for approximately ten seconds each. The child should use the self-verbalization strategies throughout the memorization and recall tasks. If the child has difficulty or fails to use any of the components, coach him or her. Conduct the entire session using normal talking voices. Encourage the child to express all thoughts out loud.

Following the recall task, tell the child that talking to himself helped him to remember.

Session Three

Session Three follows the same format as Session Two except for a few details. Present the child with twenty completely new sets of pictures. Tell the child to whisper quietly. Give very little prompting, compared with Sessions One and Two. Coach only when the child expresses a need for help.

Session Four

This session follows the same format as Session Three, but tell the child to vocalize internally throughout the task.

Study Strategy Problems:
A Case Study

David was a sixteen year old high school student who was having academic problems for the first time in his life. David had been in the top half of his class until the previous year, when his work had begun to slide. Nothing drastic at first, just lower marks than he expected. He managed to pass the year, but most of his teachers warned that his marks would have to improve or he could give up the idea of going to a good university after high school. The following year things were worse. The academic problems continued, and for the first time in many years David seemed to hate school. He even said that he didn't care if he went to university. David's parents and teachers were concerned that something had gone wrong, something that needed to be fixed right away.

Analysis

After much family turmoil, and discussions with the family doctor, a clinical psychologist, the school principal, David's teachers and the school psychologist, there emerged some agreement as to what the problem might be. The suggestion was that David had been too easily successful in his earlier schooling! While other students had been learning good study skills and strategies, David had been "coasting", relying upon his above average level of intelligence to get along and even to excel. This was a speculative interpretation, but it was backed by further investigation.

David's study habits were, in fact, terrible. In the past he had always managed to do his homework from one class during another class, while the teacher wasn't looking. Written essays were dashed off during the lunchtime before they were due. David did a lot of reading at home, but most of it was of very light fiction; the type of book he read hadn't changed much in several years. What had been relatively advanced reading for an eleven year old was now immature reading for a bright sixteen year old.

Remediation

The first step in helping David was to make him see the nature of the problem, and to agree that something needed to be done about it. This was more difficult than hoped, as David's attitudes about school had had several years to deteriorate. Combined with a healthy adolescent rebelliousness, these attitudes took considerable work to overcome.

David agreed to participate in a remedial program, though he insisted that he'd give it up if he didn't feel it was helping. One factor that seemed to convince him (or perhaps because he could use it as a justification with his friends) was the argument that he would never get a well-paying job without a good university degree. As in most cases involving adolescents, having David's agreement was crucial. Without it, the program would certainly have failed, particularly since part of the program was to get David to take more control of his learning. Deciding to try to improve was his first step in taking control.

David's teachers and the school psychologist designed a program with the following goals for David:

1. To understand better the goals of particular learning episodes;

2. To select the relevant material to learn;

3. To choose strategies for understanding and remembering the most important material;

4. To develop the habit of checking how well he was learning.

The aim was for David to practise these skills as often as possible, in as many different contexts as possible. For example, every day he was supposed to determine what the goals of at least one of his teachers had been that day in class. After an initial unwillingness to do it, and even a denial that it was possible, David soon found this to be an interesting task, particularly when he discovered that some teachers' goals were extremely difficult to unearth. After he had asked of them, unsuccessfully, what their goals had been, David's parents had to suggest that perhaps some teachers didn't have clear goals, and that it was probably not a good idea for him to pursue those teachers on that topic! David also had to overcome an unwillingness to accept that his teachers could be at fault, but once he did so, he gained a new sense of power.

As the program took shape, it became clear that David was developing better study habits as well, habits such as setting time aside to do homework at night, making plans for his week's studying, and making schedules for getting assignments in on time. The adults had decided (wisely, we think) to allow these improvements to happen as David progressed through the program, rather than beginning with them as a primary goal. Improving study habits would have been a reasonable but relatively uninteresting starting place. As it happened, David was able to see the need for organization and structure himself, once he saw the value of the activities going into that structure.

Many of the activities that David was asked to undertake were those of a good teacher: he was to make up objectives for lessons, plans for how the various lessons fitted together, and predictions of what tests and assignments were likely to be. The point is not that he became expert at these activities (the teachers themselves may not have been great at them), but rather that he was able to step back from his learning, to see how he could begin to take control of it. More specifically, he came to realize that he had to engage in active and planful learning if he was to get back on the track of achievement.

After several months of practice, with feedback from his parents and the school psychologist, David was able to continue more or less on his own. This is not a magical success story; after all, David began with a great deal of general ability. What the program accomplished was the establishment of a structure whereby that general ability could be manifested.

Other examples of study skill training programs are referred to by Biggs (1986) and Biggs and Rihn (1984).

Metacognition

For remediation to be successful, instruction should also include the metacognition level. An essential component to teaching children strategies and in particular a flexible combination of strategies, is to teach them an appreciation for the type of problem they are approaching and for the strategy or skill you are teaching. In many cases children do not understand what the actual goal of the problem is, or why the correct solution strategy works. Instruction at the metacognition level is aimed at developing these awarenesses in children, and has to take into account children's self-perceived goals and motives.

An excellent example of the importance of metacognition has been provided by Paris, Newman and McVey (1982). They taught first and second grade children a set of strategies for remembering twenty-four pictures, four from each of six categories (this task is similar to Moely *et al.*'s task, see p. 215). The strategies were to group the pictures during study, to label each picture, to rehearse the pictures in each group, to self-test, and to recall the pictures by group. Figure 14-11 shows the results of the Paris *et al.* study. On days 1 and 2, children were simply tested with no instruction. On day 3, all children were taught the strategies described above; half the children were merely taught the strategies, while the other half were also given an explanation of how the strategies should help memory. This second group should have been more aware of the strategies' value, and this heightened metacognition should have encouraged them to employ the strategies they were taught. As you can see, both groups improved in day 3, but the explanation group improved more. On days 4 and 5, all the children were tested again, without any further instruction. Whereas the strategies-only group sank back to its pre-instruction level, the explanation group maintained a high level of performance, due to their continued use of the strategies. Furthermore, Paris *et al.* interviewed the children to find out what they thought of the strategies; children in the explanation group were more likely to understand the value of the strategies, and children who

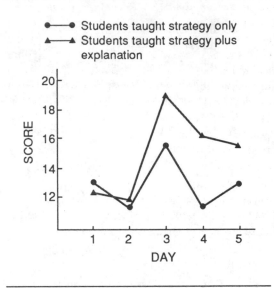

understood the strategies' value were more likely to use them.

The key to this example was that the metacognitive knowledge about the strategies was taught in the context of demonstrating those strategies, not in isolation. Explicit teaching of much metacognitive awareness by itself may have little impact. For example, if you examine many of the metacognition in reading questions studied by Myers and Paris (1978) or Kirby and Moore (1988), it is not clear that children would become better readers as a result of learning to answer these questions correctly. To know that some long stories take less time to read than some short stories is a *characteristic* of competent reading, but it is not necessarily a *cause* of competent reading. We are not advocating explicit instruction in this sense; instead, we would suggest that when a particular reading strategy is to be taught, the teacher should examine the knowledge implicit in that strategy and ensure that the children possess an adequate amount of it.

As emphasized in the preceding section, a crucial metacognitive skill is the evaluation of performance, the monitoring of success. It is our experience that children have very little familiarity with the detection or correction of errors, and then only with those produced by themselves. Explicit instruction in finding and correcting errors would seem to be quite useful, certainly as a first step in the development of monitoring and evaluating skills. If children are always presented with only "perfect" material, how can they learn to find errors? This problem is compounded when their own errors are always detected only by a teacher, and perhaps corrected only by a teacher. Such instruction encourages passive responding, with someone else taking responsibility for the monitoring of success. It is unlikely to produce successful metacognitive awareness and comprehension monitoring of performance.

An essential component in teaching metacognition is encouraging the child to be reflective, to step back from the problem and consider it in a broader context. One of our students described this process as "getting the bird's eye view". In school tests, this often involves trying to figure out what the teacher is trying to get at. A good exam writing strategy, for example, even if you don't know the answer to the question, is to put down as much as you know about things that might be related to the question or to the answer. This strategy is based upon the understanding that the teacher is trying to find out how much you know, not only whether you know the exact answer to the precise question tested. A second example would be the approach to an unfamiliar exam problem. A non-reflective solution would be to conclude, "I don't recognize this one, so I won't try it." A more metacognitive solution would be to go through the problem types which have been studied, based on the assumption that the exam is likely to contain only problems of these types. This, of course, assumes that the student is aware of the problem types which have been studied. How often is such "reflective" information taught? Each of the achievement areas could provide numerous examples of tasks in which metacognitive knowledge would be helpful but has probably not been taught.

For further examples of instruction in planning, see the suggested readings given below.

Summary

This chapter has described the element within the information processing system that makes it active, reflective, flexible, and strategic. In this sense, planning could be argued to be the most important part of the system, even though all parts are required. We described three levels of planning: selective attention, strategies, and metacognition. In recent years planning has been identified increasingly as a potential source of learning problems; we have listed a number of these problems in Table 14-2.

We described various methods for observing planning both at the general process level in selective attention, strategies, and metacognition, and in specific achievement tasks. These observation methods are linked to the types of learning problems that occur, and to the approaches to remediation suggested.

The last section of this chapter considered approaches to improving planning skills. Because some aspects of planning may be relatively easy to teach, it was suggested that planning instruction may be the first approach to any learning problem. The importance of metacognition in learning and learning problems can not be overemphasized: it is vital for teachers to lead their students toward undertanding what they are learning, why they should learn it, and how learning works.

RECOMMENDED READING

Theories of Problem Solving
If you're going to try to improve problem solving, it should be helpful to understand how it works. The following are three references which provide a broad overview:

Glaser, R.

1984. Education and thinking: The role of knowledge. *American Psychologist, 39,* 93-104.

Newell, A. & Simon, H.A.

1972. *Human problem solving.* Englewood Cliffs, New Jersey: Prentice-Hall.

Wicklegren, W.A.

1974. *How to solve problems: Elements of a theory of problems and problem solving.* San Francisco: Freeman.

Metacognition

This is still a relatively new concept in educational psychology, so it is difficult to assess whether it will retain the interest that it has at the time of this writing (1990).

Brown, A.L.

1978. Knowing when, where, and how to remember: A problem in metacognition. In R. Glaser (ed.). *Advances in instructional psychology,* Vol. 1, Hillsdale: Lawrence Erlbaum Associates.

Flavell, J.H.

1979. Metacognition and cognitive monitoring: A new area of cognitive-developmental enquiry. *American Psychologist, 34,* 906-911.

Lawson, M.J.

1984. Being executive about metacognition. In J.R. Kirby (ed.). *Cognitive strategies and educational performance.* Orlando, Florida: Academic Press.

Teaching Planning and Strategies

Case describes a general approach to strategy teaching which takes working memory space into account; Paris *et al.* demonstrate how metacognitive awareness and strategy instruction can be combined in teaching reading; and Tierney *et al.* present many ways of teaching comprehension strategies:

Case, R.

1980. Implications of neo-Piagetian theory for improving the design of instruction. In J.R. Kirby & J.B. Biggs (eds.). *Cognition, development, and instruction.* New York: Academic Press.

Case, R.

1985. *Intellectual development: Birth to adulthood.* Orlando, Florida: Academic Press.

Paris, S.G., Lipson, M.Y., & Wixson, K.K.

1983. Becoming a strategic reader. *Contemporary Educational Psychology, 8,* 293-316.

Tierney, R.J., Readence, J.E. & Dishner, E.K.

1980. *Reading strategies and practices: A guide for improving instruction.* Boston: Allyn and Bacon.

PART FOUR

Conclusion

CHAPTER 15

Retrospect and Prospect

IN A VERY DIFFERENT CONTEXT, Shakespeare once wrote "Stand not upon the order of your going, but go at once" (*Macbeth,* III, iv). In, other words, when the time has come to say goodbye, say it and go. The moral for writers of last chapters is that they should be brief and to the point. Accordingly, we seek to accomplish only two goals in this chapter:

1. to review our approach to learning problems, showing how it differs from other approaches, and showing how it addresses some of the issues we raised in Chapters 2 and 3; and

2. to discuss what the future may hold, for learning problem children who aren't helped, for those who are, and for the field in general.

Our Approach to Learning Problems

In this book we have attempted to put forward a coherent point of view, one that is relatively easy to learn and also manages to encompass current knowledge. This approach can be summarized in six points:

1. We adopt a theoretically uncommitted definition of what a learning problem is. In particular, brain damage (or dysfunction) is neither automatically included or excluded. We have tried to emphasize this approach by using the term "learning problem" rather than the more serious-sounding "learning disability".

2. We avoid the tendency of many writers to isolate a single or major cause or type of problem. Because of the complexity of school learning, it seems likely that more than one type of problem can arise. Our approach relies instead upon describing the cognitive machinery (processes, etc.) that is responsible for learning, and investigating which aspects of this machinery could and do break down to produce learning problems.

3. In order to describe the cognitive machinery, we need a theory of cognition. This theory can function at a broad level as a framework for guiding our thinking or at a far more precise level to provide an exact description of how specific tasks are performed. At the broadest level, we offer the consensus on cognition described in Chapter 4: information comes in and it is encoded, stored and used according to some sort of plan or stra-

tegy. (This description is so general as to be vague; thus, it is probably true. Nevertheless, it doesn't say much to guide us in helping children.) At a more precise level, we offer the PASS theory described in Chapter 5; this theory adds attention, defines and categorizes cognitive processes more precisely, and offers more detail on how cognition works. (This description is less vague, and therefore more likely to be wrong, or at least in need of amendment. At the same time, it retains enough generality to act as a useful framework.) At the most precise level, we offer the task analyses of reading, spelling and mathematics. (These descriptions are as detailed as possible, and thus most likely to be open to error. They are also, however, the clearest guide to diagnosis and remediation.) Even if you accept *none* of our levels of theory, we hope we have convinced you of the need for *some* theory.

4. Our approach to learning problems includes many problems not normally included as "learning disabilities". In addition to making specific reference to mathematics and spelling (which many would accept as learning problem areas), we emphasize that problems can occur in higher-level functions (such as comprehension or problem solving) as well as lower-level ones.

5. A consequence of this view of learning problems is that we see great relevance in studying normal learning for the understanding of learning problems. As we have said repeatedly, it is easier to know why something is not working if you know how it's supposed to work.

6. A second consequence of this view is that much of what we have said is as relevant to "normal learning" as it is to learning "problems". All children encounter problems in learning, and those problems are a function of the same cognitive system that produces "learning problems". By understanding cognition, we can help all children with their problems in learning, and prevent them from becoming "learning problem children". The study of learning problems need not be confined to "special" education.

The Future

If Children Aren't Helped

There is remarkably little evidence concerning what happens to learning problem children if their problems are not overcome. Many factors could account for this. For example, children identified as having a learning problem are the ones likely to receive help; thus they are the ones most likely to have their problems overcome. It is the ones who are *not* identified who are of interest but they are, by definition, not known to us. School systems can cover up the consequences of learning problems by continuing to promote children to the next grade or to graduate them in spite of poor academic achievement. Families with influence can do the same by finding a good (though perhaps simple) job for their poorly achieving relatives.

Many authors have commented on the likely future for learning problem children: poor achievement produces a dislike of school which can generalize to a dislike of society, early dropping out from school, juvenile delinquency, low level employment or unemployment (particularly for those coming from less-well-off families), and general unhappiness (e.g., Schonhout & Satz, 1983; Murray, 1976; Yule & Rutter, 1976). As the number of unskilled jobs available in society decreases, the lack of academic skills will become more and more significant, and thus more likely to contribute to unhappiness.

There is little evidence that learning problems simply go away if they are ignored. The original causes, such as poor attention skills, may disappear as the result of development, but they are very likely to leave behind a residue of poor academic skills and bad attitudes.

In short, the future for learning problem children is not very rosy, unless their problems can be overcome.

If Children Are Helped

By now we hope we've convinced you that learning problems are of different kinds and of different degrees of severity. Some are likely due to very specific brain damage, or at least some sort of neurological disorder; examples of these are the attention deficit hyperactives dealt with in Chapters 6 and 11, the phonological dyslexics mentioned in Chapters 7 and 12, and the deep dyslexics mentioned in Chapters 7 and 13. For some of these children, the future seems to depend upon a medical solution; if drugs can "correct" the arousal system problems that give rise to attention deficits, then they need be no more of a problem than diabetes or allergies. For higher-level problems such as deep dyslexia, however, medical solutions seem less likely to be effective, at least in the forseeable future. Children with such specific *disabilities* (in the sense that they are literally *unable* to do certain things) must hope for intensive or alternative forms of instruction to teach them another way of doing the same thing, just as physically disabled people must learn to write or drive cars in different ways. There is no reason to think that the future for these children is hopeless, but it seems unlikely that their problem will be overcome – circumvented, perhaps, but not cured.

We can be much more optimistic about the vast majority of learning problem children. There is general agreement among researchers and practitioners alike that learning problems need to be caught early, before a major academic skill deficit and learned helplessness have become established.

Early identification can be thought of in two ways. It is usually seen as picking out that "type" of child who is likely to develop a learning problem – for instance, those with poor attention or successive processing skills. This is certainly an important goal, designed to identify those children whose problems exist prior to their first encounter with academic learning – that is, those whose problems *originate* high in Figure 5-5. However, there are other learning problem children, whose problems are either specific to an academic area (e.g., phonics in reading), or specific to a cognitive process in an achievement area (e.g., successive processing required in maintaining word order in reading). For these children, learning problems begin to exist only as they begin to fail. Much more attention

needs to be devoted to identifying these early instances of learning problems to prevent poor learning, or the learning of incorrect skills, from taking place. Whereas the first type of identification will be made by a psychologist (on a teacher's recommendation), the second type is more likely to be made by the teacher alone and, we hope, overcome before a psychologist need be consulted.

How successful will we be in eliminating the vast majority of "garden variety" learning problems? To a large degree this depends upon the resources devoted to the problem. Just imagine the results of having one teacher per pupil: it is highly unlikely that very many "garden variety" learning problems would exist in such a system. Even children who were "prone" to develop learning problems would do far better in such a system, because their problems would be detected earlier and remedial steps would be instituted immediately. In case you doubt the value of individualizing instruction, Bloom (1984) has estimated that the *average* student in individualized instruction performs better than 98% of students in conventional instruction.

Individualized instruction sets an upper limit to optimism for learning problem children. It is easy to discount that as unrealistic, but it is worth keeping in mind as an educational (and societal) goal. Furthermore, the progress being made in intelligent computer-assisted instruction leads us to hope that great steps toward individualized instruction will soon become feasible. We would argue that individualized instruction will be most effective if the cognitive task-analysis-based methods of diagnosis and remediation described in this book are followed.

It is also necessary to describe the lower limit of optimism, particularly since individualized instruction will not happen completely or immediately. This is especially true for children who already have established learning problems. These children have spent several years or more acquiring those problems, and it is likely that several teachers and parents have done their best, admittedly in less-than-ideal circumstances, to overcome those problems. We would be unrealistic to expect that established learning problems will be overcome very quickly. Our best solutions lie in attacking established problems as well as we can (with, for example, the framework and techniques supported in this book), while also doing our best to minimize the number of new learning problems.

The Future of the Learning Problems Field

We hope that the future of this field is short; that learning problems will be eliminated. However, in the meantime, and in order to reduce the incidence of learning problems, researchers and practitioners must continue their efforts.

An important goal is for researchers and practitioners to work together. In the past, theories that were too esoteric (or just plain wrong) drove practitioners to anti-theoretical despair. Negative attitudes of practitioners acted to drive researchers away from practical problems, towards even more esoteric theories. In principle a theory should be extremely practical, helping teachers to understand the nature of learning problems and thus to employ efficient techniques to diagnose and remediate them.

The effective cooperation of teachers and researchers requires that each group learns from the other, and responds to the needs of the other. Teachers need to learn more theory than they may initially wish to in order to develop a deeper understanding of the nature of learning problems. They may also have to help researchers develop classroom materials and implement remedial programs. Researchers need to learn more about the practical conclusions from their work even if those conclusions aren't immediately apparent. Finally, they must help teachers by expressing their theories in a manner which can be understood by teachers.

We hope that this book contributes to bringing teachers and researchers closer together, and to helping them work together to overcome learning problems.

Summary

In this chapter we have reviewed our approach to learning problems, and indicated what we think the future holds, both for the children and for the field.

If this is your first time through the book, you're not finished yet. We'd recommend at least a second read of the book; you should find that much of it then makes more sense, or perhaps deeper sense.

Now is also the time to decide for yourself what learning problems are and what you can do about them. It's up to you to use whatever you've learned from this book.

References

Abikoff, H. 1987. An evaluation of cognitive behavior therapy for hyperactive children. In B.B. Lahey and A.E. Kazdin (eds.). *Advances in clinical child psychology, Vol. 10.* New York: Plenum Press.

Abramson, L.L., Seligman, M.E., & Teasdale, J.D. 1978. Learned helplessness in humans: Critique and reformulation. *Journal of Abnormal Psychology, 87,* 49-74.

Achenbach, T.M. 1978. The child behavior profile: 1. Boys aged 6-11. *Journal of Consulting and Clinical Psychology, 46,* 478-488.

Adelman, H.S. 1971. The not-so-specific learning disability population. *Exceptional Children, 37,* 528-533.

American Academy of Pediatrics. 1982. Policy statement. The Doman-Delcato treatment of neurologically handicapped children. *Journal of Pediatrics, 70,* 810-812.

American Psychiatric Association. 1987. Diagnostic and statistical manual of mental disorders. 3rd ed. revised. Washington, D.C.: American Psychiatric Association.

Ashcraft, M.H. 1982. The development of mental arithmetic: A chronometric approach. *Developmental Review, 2,* 213-236.

Ashcraft, M.H. & Battaglia, J. 1978. Cognitive arithmetic: Evidence for retrieval and decision processes in mental addition. *Journal of Experimental Psychology: Human Learning and Memory, 4,* 527-538.

Ashcraft, M.H. & Fierman, B.A. 1982. Mental addition in third, fourth, and sixth grades. *Journal of Experimental Child Psychology, 33,* 216-234.

Ashman, A.F. & Das, J.P. 1980. Relation between planning and simultaneous and successive processing. *Perceptual and Motor Skills, 51,* 371-382.

Australian Council for Educational Research. 1977. *Operations test: Mathematics Profile Series.* Hawthorn, Victoria, Australia: A.C.E.R.

Bakker, D.J. 1972. *Temporal order in disturbed reading-developmental and neuropsychological aspects in normal and reading-retarded children.* Rotterdam: Rotterdam University Press.

Ballard, J.E., Boileau, R.A., Sleator, E.K., Massey, B.H., & Sprague, R.L. 1976. Cardiovascular responses of hyperactive children to methylphenidate. *Journal of the American Medical Association, 236,* 2870-2874.

Bandura, A. 1969. *Principles in behavior modification.* New York: Holt, Rinehart & Winston.

Barkley, R.A. 1981. *Hyperactive children: A handbook for diagnosis and treatment.* New York: The Guildford Press.

Barkley, R.A. & Cunningham, C.E. 1978. Do stimulant drugs improve the academic performance of hyperactive children? A review of outcome studies. *Clinical pediatrics, 17,* 85-92.

Baron, J. 1979. Orthographic and word-specific mechanisms in children's reading of words. *Child Development, 50,* 60-72.

Baron, J. & Strawson, C. 1976. Use of orthographic and word-specific knowledge in reading words aloud. *Journal of Experimental Psychology: Human Perception and Performance, 2,* 386-393.

Baron, J., Treiman, R., Wilf, J. & Kellman, P. 1980. Reading and spelling by rules. In U. Frith (ed.). *Cognitive processes in spelling.* New York: Academic Press.

Barr, R.C. 1972. The influence of instructional conditions on word recognition errors. *Reading Research Quarterly, 7,* 509-529.

Barron, R.W. & Baron, J. 1977. How children get meaning from printed words. *Child Development, 48,* 587-594.

Barsch, R.H. 1965. *A movigenic curriculum.* State Department of Public Instruction. Madison, Wisconsin: 25.

Barsch, R.H. 1967. *Achieving perceptual motor efficiency.* Seattle: Special Child Publications.

Bateman, B. 1965. An educator's view of a diagnostic approach to learning disorders. In J. Hellmuth (ed.). *Learning disorders,* vol. 1. Seattle: Special Child Publications.

Bateman, B. 1974. Educational implications of minimal brain dysfunction. *The Reading Teacher, 27,* 662-688.

Beck, I.L., Pefetti, C.A. & McKeown, M.G. 1982. Effects of long-term vocabulary instruction on lexical access and reading comprehension. *Journal of Educational Psychology, 74,* 506-521.

Beery, K.E. & Boktenica, N.A. 1967. *The developmental test of visual-motor integration.* Chicago: Follett Publishing.

Bell, R.Q., Waldrop, M.F. & Weller, G.M. 1972. A rating system for the assessment of hyperactive and withdrawn children in pre-school samples. *American Journal of Orthopsychiatry, 42,* 23-33.

Bender, L. 1938. A visual motor Gestalt test and its clinical use. *American Orthopsychiatry Association Research Monograph,* No. 3.

Benton, A.L. 1975. Developmental dyslexia: Neurological aspects. In W.J. Friedlander (ed.). *Advances in neurology,* Vol. 7. New York: Raven Press.

Bibacc, R. & Hancock, K. 1970. Relationships between perceptual and conceptual cognitive processes. *Journal of Learning Disabilities, 2,* 17-22.

Biemiller, A. 1970. The development of the use of graphic and contextual information as children learn to read. *Reading Research Quarterly, 6,* 75-96.

Biggs, J.B. 1986. Enhancing learning skills: The role of metacognition. In J. Bowden (ed.). *Student learning and study skills.* Melbourne, Australia: Centre for the Study of Higher Education, Melbourne University.

Biggs, J.B. & Collis, K.F. 1982. *Evaluating the quality of learning: The SOLO taxonomy.* New York: Academic Press.

Biggs, J.B. & Rihn, B.A. 1984. The effects of intervention on deep and surface approaches to learning. In J.R. Kirby (ed.). *Cognitive strategies and educational performance.* Orlando, Florida: Academic Press.

Biggs, J.B. & Telfer, R.A. 1981. *The process of learning.* Sydney: Prentice-Hall.

Bloom, B.S. 1984. The 2 sigma problem: The search for methods of group instruction as effective as one-to-one tutoring. *Educational Researcher, 13,* 4-16.

Bond, G.L., & Tinker, M.A. 1967. *Reading difficulties. Their diagnosis and correction.* 2nd ed. New York: Appleton-Century-Crofts.

Bradley, C. 1937. The behavior of children receiving benzedrine. *American Journal of Psychiatry, 94,* 577-585.

Bradley, C. & Bowen, M. 1941. Amphetamine (benzedrine) therapy of children's behavior disorders. *American Journal of Orthopsychiatry, 11,* 92-103.

Broca, P. 1861. Remarks on the seat of the faculty of articulate language, followed by an observation of aphemia. In G. Von Bonim (ed.). *Some papers on the cerebral cortex.* Springfield, Ill.: Charles C. Thomas. 1960. (Originally Sur le siège de la faculté de langage articulé avec deux observations d'aphème (pert de parole), Paris, 1861.)

Brooks, L.R. 1968. Spatial and verbal components in the act of recall. *Canadian Journal of Psychology, 22,* 349-368.

Brown, A.L. 1978. Knowing when, where, and how to remember: A problem in metacognition. In R. Glaser (ed.). *Advances in instructional psychology,* Vol. 1. Hillsdale, New Jersey: Lawrence Erlbaum Associates.

Brown, A.L. 1980. Metacognitive development and reading. In R.J. Spiro, B.C. Bruce, & W.F. Brewer (eds.). *Theoretical issues in reading comprehension.* Hillsdale, New Jersey: Lawrence Erlbaum Associates.

Brown, A.L., Campione, J.C., & Day, J.D. 1981. Learning to learn: On training students to learn from texts. *Educational Researcher, 10,* 14-21.

Brown, A.L., Day, J.D., & Jones, R.S. 1983. The development of plans for summarizing texts. *Child Development, 54,* 968-979.

Brown, A.L. & DeLoache, J.S. 1978. Skills, plans, and self-regulation. In R. Siegler (ed.). *Children's thinking: What develops?* Hillsdale, New Jersey: Lawrence Erlbaum Associates.

Brown, J.S. & Burton, R.R. 1978. Diagnostic models for procedural bugs in basic mathematical skills. *Cognitive Science, 2,* 155-192.

Bruininks, R.H., Glaman, G.M., & Clark, C.R. 1973. Issues in determining prevalence of reading retardation. *The Reading Teacher, 27,* 177-185.

Bruner, E.C. 1971. Teaching disorders. In B. Bateman (ed.). *Learning disorders,* Vol. 4. Seattle: Special Child Publications.

Bryan, T. 1974a. An observational analysis of classroom behaviors of children with learning disabilities. *Journal of Learning Disabilities, 7,* 26-34.

Bryan, T. 1974b. Peer popularity of learning disabled children. *Journal of Learning Disabilities, 7,* 621-625.

Bryan, T. 1976. Peer popularity of learning disabled children. A replication. *Journal of Learning Disabilities, 9,* 307-311.

Bryan, T. 1981. Social behaviors of learning disabled children. In J. Gottlieb & S.S. Strichart (eds.). *Developmental theory and research in learning disabilities.* Baltimore: University Park Press.

Bryan, T. & McGrady, H.J. 1972. Use of a teacher rating scale. *Journal of Learning Disabilities, 5,* 199-206.

Burchfield, S.R., Stein, L.J. & Hamilton, K.L. 1985. Test anxiety: A model for studying psychological and physiological interrelationships. In S.R. Burchfield (ed.). *Stress: Psychological and physiological interactions.* Washington, D.C.: Hemisphere Publishing Corporation.

Burnette, E. 1962. *Influences of classroom environment on word learning of retarded with high and low anxiety levels.* Unpublished doctoral dissertation, Peabody College.

Butterfield, E.C., Wambold, C. & Belmont, J.M. 1973. On the theory and practice of improving short-term memory. *American Journal of Mental Deficiency, 77,* 654-669.

Canino, F.J. 1981. Learned helplessness theory: Implications for research in learning disabilities. *Journal of Special Education, 15,* 471-484.

Cannon, W.B. 1915. *Bodily changes in pain, hunger, fear and rage.* New York: Appleton-Century-Crofts.

Carpenter, T.P., Moser, J.M. & Romberg, T.A. (eds.) 1982. *Addition and subtraction: A cognitive perspective.* Hillsdale, New Jersey: Lawrence Erlbaum Associates.

Carroll, J.B. & Sapon, S.M. 1959. *Modern language aptitude test.* New York: The Psychological Corporation.

Carrow, E. 1973. *Test for auditory comprehension of language.* Boston: Teaching Resources Corporation.

Carrow, E. 1974. A test using elicited imitations in assessing grammatical structure in children. *Journal of Speech & Hearing Disorders, 39,* 437-444.

Case, R. 1980a. The underlying mechanisms of intellectual development. In J.R. Kirby & J.B. Biggs (eds.). *Cognition, development, and instruction.* New York: Academic Press.

Case, R. 1980b. Implications of neo-Piagetian theory for improving the design of instruction. In J.R. Kirby & J.B. Biggs (eds.). *Cognition, development, and instruction.* New York: Academic Press.

Case, R. 1985. *Intellectual development: Birth to adulthood.* Orlando, Florida: Academic Press.

Case, R., Kurland, D.M., & Goldberg, J. 1982. Operational efficiency and the growth of short-term memory span. *Journal of Experimental Child Psychology, 33,* 386-404.

Cattell, R.B. 1971. *Abilities: Their structure, growth and action.* Boston: Houghton Mifflin.

Cavanaugh, J.C. & Perlmutter, M. 1982. Metamemory: A critical examination. *Child Development, 53,* 11-28.

Chalfant, J.C. & King, F.S. 1976. An approach to operationalizing the definition of learning disabilities. *Journal of Learning Disabilities, 9,* 228-243.

Chapman, J.W. & Boersma, F.J. 1979. Learning disabilities, locus of control, and mother attitudes. *Journal of Educational Psychology, 71,* 250-258.

Clausen, J. 1973. Arousal theory in mental deficiency. In M. Hammer, K. Salzinger, & S. Sutton (eds.). *Psychopathology: Contributions from the social, behavioral and biological sciences.* New York: John Wiley.

Clements, S.D. 1966. Minimal Brain Dysfunction in Children, *NINDS Monograph No. 3,* Public Health Service Bulletin No. 1415. Washington, D.C.: U.S. Department of Health, Education & Welfare.

Cohen, S.A. 1971. Dyspedagogia as a cause of reading retardation: Definition and treatment. In B. Bateman (ed.). *Learning disorders,* Vol. 4, Seattle: Special Child Publications.

Colletti, L.F. 1979. Relationship between pregnancy and birth complications and the later development of learning disabilities. *Journal of Learning Disabilities, 12,* 659-663.

Collis, K.F. 1971. A study of concrete and formal reasoning in school mathematics. *Australian Journal of Psychology, 23,* 289-296.

Coltheart, M., Patterson, K., & Marshall, J.C. (eds.) 1987. *Deep dyslexia.* 2nd ed. London: Routledge & Kegan Paul.

Conger, J.C. & Keane, S.P. 1981. Social skills intervention in the treatment of isolated or withdrawn children. *Psychological Bulletin, 90,* 478-495.

Conners, C.K. 1969. A teacher rating scale for use in drug studies with children. *American Journal of Psychiatry, 126,* 885-888.

Conners, C.K. 1970. Symptom patterns in hyperkinetic, neurotic, and normal children. *Child Development, 41,* 667-682.

Conners, C.K. 1971. Cortical visual evoked response in children with learning disorders. *Psychophysiology, 7,* 418-428.

Conners, C.K. 1973. Rating scales for use in drug studies with children. *Psychopharmacology Bulletin. Special issue: Pharmacotherapy of Children,* 24-84.

Conrad, R. 1964. Acoustic confusions in immediate memory. *British Journal of Psychology, 55,* 75-84.

Cravioto, J. & De Licardie, E.R. 1975. Environmental and nutritional deprivation in children with learning disabilities. In W.M. Cruickshank & D.P. Hallahan (eds.). *Perceptual and learning disabilities in children, Vol. 2, Research and theory*. Syracuse: Syracuse University Press.

Cromer, W. 1970. The difference model: A new explanation for some reading difficulties. *Journal of Educational Psychology, 61,* 471-483.

Crowder, R.G. 1982. *The psychology of reading*. New York: Oxford University Press.

Cruikshank, W.M. 1972. Some issues facing the field of learning disability. *Journal of Learning Disabilities, 5,* 380-388.

Cruikshank, W.M., Bentzen, F.A., Ratzeburg, F.H., & Tannhausser, M.T. 1961. *A teaching method for brain-injured and hyperactive children*. Syracuse: Syracuse University Press.

Cruikshank, W.M., Bice, H.V., & Wallen, N.E. 1957. *Perception and cerebral palsy*. Syracuse: Syracuse University Press.

Daneman, M. & Carpenter, P.A. 1980. Individual differences in working memory and reading. *Journal of Verbal Learning and Verbal Behaviour, 19,* 450-466.

Das, J.P. 1973. The uses of attention. *Alberta Journal of Educational Research, 19,* 99-108.

Das, J.P., Kirby, J., & Jarman, R.F. 1975. Simultaneous and successive syntheses: An alternative model for cognitive abilities. *Psychological Bulletin, 82,* 87-103.

Das, J.P., Kirby, J.R., & Jarman, R.F. 1979. *Simultaneous and successive cognitive processes*. New York: Academic Press.

Das, J.P., Leong, C.K., & Williams, N.H. 1978. The relationship between learning disability and simultaneous-successive processing. *Journal of Learning Disabilities, 11,* 618-625.

Das, J.P. & Naglieri, J.A. 1990. *Cognitive assessment system*. Manuscript.

Das, J.P., Naglieri, J.A., & Kirby, J.R. In press. *Assessment of cognitive processes*. New York: Allyn & Bacon.

Davids, A. 1971. An objective instrument for assessing hyperkinesis in children. *Journal of Learning Disabilities, 4,* 499-501.

De Corte, E. & Verschaffel, L. 1981. Children's solution processes in elementary arithmetic problems: Analysis and improvement. *Journal of Educational Psychology, 73,* 765-779.

Delacato, C.H. 1966. *Neurological organization and reading*. Springfield, Illinois: Charles C. Thomas.

Denckla, M.B. 1973. Research needs in learning disabilities: A neurologist's point of view. *Journal of Learning Disabilities, 6,* 441-450.

Dempster, F.N. 1981. Memory span: Sources of individual and developmental differences. *Psychological Bulletin, 89,* 63-100.

Denney, D.R. 1980. Self-control approaches to the treatment of test anxiety. In I.G. Sarason (ed.). *Test anxiety: Theory, research, and applications*. Hillsdale, New Jersey: Lawrence Erlbaum Associates.

Douglas, V.I. 1980. Treatment and training approaches to hyperactivity: Establishing internal or external control. In C.K. Whalen & B. Hencker (eds.). *Hyperactive children: The social ecology of identification and treatment*. New York: Academic Press.

Douglas, V.I. 1983. Attentional and cognitive problems. In M. Rutter (ed.). *Developmental Neuropsychiatry*. New York: The Guildford Press.

Douglas, V.I., Parry, P., Marton, P., & Garson, C. 1976. Assessment of a cognitive training program for hyperactive children. *Journal of Abnormal Child Psychology, 4,* 389-410.

Downing, J. & Leong, C.K. 1982. *Psychology of reading*. New York: Macmillan.

Duffy, E. 1934. Emotion: an example of the need for reorientation in psychology. *Psychological Review, 41,* 184-198.

Duffy, F.H. 1981. Brain electrical activity mapping (BEAM): Computerized access to complex brain function. *International Journal of Neuroscience, 13,* 55-65.

Duffy, F.H., Denckla, M.D., Bartels, P.H. & Sandini, G. 1980. Dyslexia: Regional differences in brain electrical activity by topographic mapping. *Annals of neurology, 7,* 412-420.

Dunn, L. (ed.) 1973. *Exceptional children in the schools.* New York: Holt, Rinehart & Winston.

Dunlop, G., Koegel, R.L., & Burke, J.C. 1981. Educational implications of stimulus overselectivity in autistic children. *Exceptional Education Quarterly, 2,* 73-82.

Durkin, D. 1978-1979. What classroom observations reveal about reading comprehension instruction. *Reading Research Quarterly, 14,* 481-533.

Egeland, B. 1974. Training impulsive children in the use of more efficient scanning techniques. *Child Development, 45,* 165-171.

Ekstrom, R.B., French, J.W., Harman, H.H. & Dermen, D. 1976. *Manual for kit of factor-referenced cognitive tests.* Princeton, New Jersey: Educational Testing Service.

Elkind, D. 1983. Viewpoint: The curriculum disabled child. *Topics in learning and learning disabilities, 14,* 84-87.

Engelmann, S. & Bruner, E. 1974. *DISTAR reading: An instructional system.* Chicago: Science Research Associates.

Evans, J.R. 1977. Evoked potentials and learning disabilities. In L. Tarnopol & M. Tarnopol (eds.). *Brain function and reading disabilities.* Baltimore: University Park Press.

Eysenck, H.J. 1967. *The biological basis of personality.* Springfield, Illinois: Charles C. Thomas.

Farnham-Diggory, S. 1978. *Learning disabilities.* London: Open Books.

Federal Register. 1977. Washington, D.C. Dec. 29, 65082-65085.

Feingold, B.F. 1973. *Introduction to clinical allergy.* Springfield, Illinois: Charles C. Thomas.

Feingold, B.F. 1974. Hyperkinesis and learning disabilities limited to the ingestion of artificial food colors and flavors. *Presentation to legislative learnings,* Education Committee, Sacramento, July 31.

Feingold, B.F. 1975. *Why your child is hyperactive.* New York: Random House.

Feingold, B.F. 1976. Hyperkinesis and learning disabilities linked to the ingestion of artificial food colors and flavors. *Journal of Learning Disabilities, 9,* 551-559.

Ferguson, H.B. & Pappas, B.A. 1979. Evaluation of psychophysiological, neurochemical, and animal models of hyperactivity. In R.L. Trites (ed.). *Hyperactivity in children: Etiology, measurement and treatment implications.* Baltimore: University Park Press.

Feuerstein, R. & Hoffman, M.B. 1980. *The dynamic assessment of retarded performers.* Baltimore: University Park Press.

Feuerstein, R., Miller, R., Hoffman, M.B., Rand, Y., Mintzker, Y., & Jensen, M.R. 1981. Cognitive modifiability in adolescence: Cognitive structure and the effects of intervention. *Journal of Special Education, 15,* 269-287.

Feuerstein, R., Rand, Y., Hoffman, M.B. & Miller, R. 1980. *Instrumental enrichment.* Baltimore: University Park Press.

Fish, B. 1976. Pharmacotherapy for autistic and schizophrenic children. In E.R. Ritvo (ed.). *Autism: Diagnosis, current research and management.* New York: Spectrum Publications.

Fisher, D.F. & Frankfurter, A. 1977. Normal and disabled readers can locate and identify letters: Where's the perceptual deficit? *Journal of Reading Behaviour, 9,* 31-43.

Flavell, J.H. 1970. Developmental studies of mediated memory. In L. Lipsitt & H.W. Reese (eds.). *Advances in child development and behaviour,* Vol. 5. New York: Academic Press.

Flavell, J.H. 1976. *Cognitive development.* Englewood Cliffs, New Jersey: Prentice-Hall.

Flavell, J.H. 1979. Metacognition and cognitive monitoring: A new area of cognitive-developmental inquiry. *American Psychologist, 34,* 906-911.

Forness, S. & Estveldt, K. 1975. Classroom observation of children with learning behavior problems. *Journal of Learning Disabilities, 8,* 382-385.

Forster, G.G., Schmidt, M.S. & Sabatino, D. 1976. Teacher expectancies and the label "learning disabilities". *Journal of Learning Disabilities, 9,* 111-114.

Freeman, R.D. 1967. Controversy over "patterning" as a treatment for brain damage in children. *Journal of the American Medical Association, 202,* 385-388.

Freeman, R.D. 1976. Minimal brain dysfunction, hyperactivity, and learning disorders: Epidemic or episode? *School Review, 85,* 5-30.

French, J.D. 1960. The reticular formation. In J. Field, H.W. Magoun & V.E. Hall (eds.). *Handbook of physiology, Section 1, Neurophysiology,* Vol. 2. Washington, D.C.: American Physiological Society.

Frith, U. (ed.) 1980. *Cognitive processes in spelling.* New York: Academic Press.

Frostig, M. 1964. *The Marianne Frostig developmental test of visual perception.* Palo Alto, California: Consulting-Psychologists Press.

Frostig, M. & Horne, D. 1964. *The Frostig Program for the Development of Visual Perception.* Chicago: Follett.

Frostig, M., Lefever, D.W., & Whittlesey, J.R.B. 1961. A developmental test of visual perception for evaluating normal and neurologically handicapped children. *Perceptual and Motor Skills, 12,* 383-394.

Frostig, M., Maslow, P., Lefever, D.W., & Whittlesey, J.R.B. 1964. *The Marianne Frostig Development Test of Visual Perception* (1963 Standardization). Palo Alto, California: Consulting-Psychologists Press.

Furth, H.G. 1966. *Thinking without language.* New York: Free Press.

Geddes, W.H. 1983. Applied educational neuropsychology: Theories and problems. *Journal of Learning Disabilities, 16,* 511-514.

Gadow, K.D. 1983. Effects of stimulant drugs on academic performance in hyperactive and learning disabled children. *Journal of Learning Disabilities, 16,* 290-299.

Gagne, R.M., Major, J.R., Gerstens, H.L. & Paradise, N.E. 1962. Factors in acquiring knowledge of a mathematical task. *Psychological Monographs: General and Applied, 76* (7, Whole No. 526).

Gan, S. & Cantwell, D.P. 1982. Dosage effects of methylphenidate on paired-associate learning: Positive / negative placebo responders. *Journal of the American Academy of Child Psychiatry, 21,* 237-242.

Gardner, W.I., Cromwell, R.L., & Foshee, J.G. 1959. Studies in activity level. II. Visual. *American Journal of Mental Deficiency, 63,* 1028-1033.

Garner, R. & Alexander, P.A. 1989. Metacognition: Answered and unanswered questions. *Educational Psychologist, 24,* 143-158.

Geen, R.G. 1980. Test anxiety and cue utilization. In I.G. Sarason (ed.). *Test anxiety: Theory, research, and applications.* Hillsdale, New Jersey: Lawrence Erlbaum Associates.

Gelb, I.G. 1963. *A study of writing.* 2nd ed. Chicago: University of Chicago Press.

Getman, G. 1965. The visuomotor complex of the acquisition of motor skills. In J. Hellmuth (ed.). *Learning disorders,* Vol. 1. Seattle: Special Child Publications.

Gillingham, A. & Stillman, B. 1970. *Remedial training for children with specific disability in reading, spelling and penmanship.* Cambridge, Mass.: Educator's Publishing Service.

Ginsburg, H.P. (ed.) 1983. *The development of mathematical thinking.* New York: Academic Press.

Gittelman, R., Abikoff, H., Pollack, E., Klein, D.F., Katz, S., & Mattes, J. 1980. A controlled trial of behavior modification and methylphenidate in hyperactive children. In C.K. Whalen & B. Henker (eds.). *Hyperactive children: The social ecology of identification and treatment.* New York: Academic Press.

Gittelman-Klein, R. & Klein, D. 1976. Methylphenidate effects in learning disabilities: Psychometric changes. *Archives of General Psychiatry, 33,* 655-664.

Glaser, R. 1984. Education and thinking: The role of knowledge. *American Psychologist, 39,* 93-104.

Goldstein, K. 1936. The modifications of behaviour consequent to cerebral lesions. *Psychiatric Quarterly, 10,* 586-610.

Goldstein, K. 1939. *The Organism.* New York: American Book Co.

Golden, C.J. & Anderson, S. 1979. *Learning disabilities and brain dysfunction: An introduction for educators and parents.* Springfield, Illinois: Charles C. Thomas.

Goldstein, G.I. & Lancy, D.F. 1985. Cognitive development in autistic children. In L.S. Siegel & F.J. Morrison (eds.). *Cognitive development in atypical children: Progress in cognitive development research.* New York: Springer-Verlag.

Goodman, K.S. 1967. Reading: a psycholinguistic guessing game. *Journal of the Reading Specialist, 6,* 126-135.

Goodman, Y.M. & Burke, C.L. 1972. *Reading miscue inventory: Procedure for diagnosis and evaluation.* New York: Macmillan.

Goyette, C.H., Conners, C.K., & Ulrich, R.F. 1978. Normative data on revised Conners parent and teacher rating scales. *Journal of Abnormal Child Psychology, 6,* 221-236.

Gresham, F.M. 1988. Social competence and motivational characteristics of learning disabled students. In M. Wang, M. Reynolds & H. Walberg (eds.). *The handbook of special education. Research and practice.* Elmsford, New York: Pergamon Press.

Groen, G.J. & Parkman, J.M. 1972. A chronometric analysis of simple addition. *Psychological Review, 79,* 329-343.

Groen, G.J. & Resnick, L.B. 1977. Can preschool children invent addition algorithms? *Journal of Educational Psychology, 69,* 645-652.

Guilford, J.P. 1967. *The nature of human intelligence.* New York: McGraw-Hill.

Haber, R.N. & Haber, L.R. 1981. The shape of a word can specify its meaning. *Reading Research Quarterly, 16,* 334-345.

Hagen, J.W. 1967. The effect of distraction on selective attention. *Child Development, 38,* 685-694.

Hallahan, D.P. & Cruikshank, W.M. 1973. *Psychoeducational foundations of learning disabilities.* Englewood Cliffs, New Jersey: Prentice-Hall.

Hallahan, D.P. & Kaufman, J.M. 1975. Research on the education of distractible and hyperactive children. In W.M. Cruikshank & D.P. Hallahan (eds.). *Perceptual and learning disabilities in children, Vol. 2. Research and theory.* Syracuse: Syracuse University Press.

Hallahan, D.P. & Kauffman, J.M. 1976. *Introduction to learning disabilities: A psycho-behavioural approach.* Englewood Cliffs, New Jersey: Prentice-Hall.

Hallahan, D.P. & Reeve, R.E. 1980. Selective attention and distractibility. In B.K. Keogh (ed.). *Advances in special education,* Vol. 1. Greenwich, Connecticut: JAI Press.

Hallgren, B. 1950. Specific dyslexia (congenital word blindness): A clinical and genetic study. *Acta Psychiatrica Neurologica, Scandinavica, Suppl. 65,* 1-287.

Hammill, D.D. & Larsen, S.C. 1974. The effectiveness of psycholinguistic training. *Exceptional children, 41,* 5-14.

Hammill, D.D., Leigh, J.E., McNutt, G., & Larsen, S.C. 1981. A new definition of learning disabilities. *Learning Disability Quarterly, 4,* 336-342.

Hammill, D.D. & Wiederholt, J.L. 1973. Review of the Frostig visual perception test and the related training program. In L. Mann & D.A. Sabatino (eds.). *The first review of special education.* Philadelphia: JSE Press.

Haring, N.G. (ed.) 1974. *Behavior of exceptional children: An introduction to special education.* Columbus, Ohio: Merrill.

Harley, J.P., Ray, R.S., Tomasi, L., Eichman, P.L., Matthews, C.G., Chun, R., Cleeland, C.S., & Traisman, E. 1978. Hyperkinesis and food additives: Testing the Feingold hypothesis. *Pediatrics, 61,* 818-828.

Harris, A. 1961. *How to improve reading ability.* New York: David McKay.

Hassett, J. 1978. *A primer of psychophysiology.* San Francisco: W.H. Freeman.

Head, H.H.J. 1926. *Aphasia and kindred disorders of speech.* London: Cambridge United Press.

Hebb, D.O. 1955. Drives and the CNS (conceptual nervous system). *Psychological Review, 62,* 243-254.

Hermann, K. 1959. *Reading disability: A medical study of word blindness and related handicaps.* Springfield, Illinois: Charles, C. Thomas.

Hermelin, B.M. & O'Connor, N. 1970. Physiological responses and levels of arousal in the severely subnormal. In B.W. Richards (ed.). *Mental subnormality: Modern trends in research.* London: Pitman.

Hernandez-Peon, R. 1969. Neurophysiology of attention. In P.J. Vinken & G.W. Bruyn (eds.). *Handbook of clinical neurology,* Vol. 3. Amsterdam: North Holland Publishing Co.

Hessler, G. & Kitchen, D. 1980. Language characteristics of a purposive sample of early elementary learning disabled students. *Learning Disability Quarterly, 3,* 36-41.

Hinshelwood, J. 1917. *Congenital word-blindness.* London: H.K. Lewis.

Hinsley, D.A., Hayes, J.R. & Simon, H.A. 1977. From words to equations: Meaning and representation in algebra word problems. In M.A. Just & P.A. Carpenter (eds.). *Cognitive processes in comprehension.* Hillsdale, New Jersey: Lawrence Erlbaum Associates.

Hobbs, N. 1975. *Issues in classification of children.* San Francisco: Jossey-Bass.

Horn, J.L. 1976. Human abilities: A review of research and theory in the early 1970s. *Annual Review of Psychology, 27,* 437-485.

Hughes, J.R. 1978. Electroencephalographic and neurophysiological studies in dyslexia. In A.L. Benton & D. Pearl (eds.). *Dyslexia: An appraisal of current knowledge.* New York: Oxford University Press.

Hutchinson, N. 1989. Strategy instruction research in one knowledge domain: Algebra. *Canadian Journal of Special Education, 5,* 169-177.

Hynd, G. & Cohen, M. 1983. *Dyslexia: Neuropsychological theory, research and clinical differentiation.* New York: Grune & Stratton.

Ilg, F.L. & Ames, L.B. 1964. *School readiness: Behavior tests used at the Gesell Institute.* New York: Harper & Row.

Ingram, T.T.S. 1970. The nature of dyslexia. In F.A. Young & D.B. Lindsley (eds.). *Early experience and visual information processing in perceptual and reading disorders.* Washington, D.C.: National Academy of Sciences.

Jackson, H. 1931. *Selected Writings of John Hughlings Jackson.* 2 vols. London: Hodder & Stoughton.

James, W. 1890. *The principles of psychology.* New York: Holt.

John, E.R. 1977. *Functional neuroscience, Vol. 2. Neurometrics: Clinical applications of quantitative electrophysiology.* Hillsdale, New Jersey: Lawrence Erlbaum.

Johnson, D. & Myklebust, H. 1967. *Learning disabilities: Educational principles and practices.* New York: Grune & Stratton.

Johnson, S.M., Bolstad, O.D., & Lobitz, G.K. 1976. Generalization and contrast phenomena in behavior modification with children. In E.J. Mash, L.A. Hamerlynck, & L.C. Handy (eds.). *Behavior modification in families.* New York: Brunner-Mazel.

Jensen, A.R. 1969. How much can we boost I.Q. and scholastic achievement? *Harvard Educational Review, 39,* 1-123.

Jensen, A.R. 1974. Interaction of level I and level II abilities with race and socioeconomic status. *Journal of Educational Psychology, 66,* 99-111.

Johns, J.L. 1980. First graders' concepts about print. *Reading Research Quarterly, 15,* 529-549.

Johnson-Laird, P.N. 1985. Deductive reasoning ability. In R.J. Sternberg (ed.). *Human abilities: An information processing approach.* New York: Freeman.

Kagan, J. 1965. Reflection-impulsivity and reading ability in primary grade children. *Child Development, 36,* 609-628.

Kagan, J., Moss, H.A., & Sigel, I.E. 1963. Psychological significance of styles of conceptualization. In J.C. Wright & J. Kagan (eds.). *Basic cognitive processes in children. Monographs of the Society for Research in Child Development, 28,* (2, Serial No. 86).

Kagan, J., Pearson, L., & Welch, L. 1966. Modifiability of an impulsive tempo. *Journal of Educational Psychology, 57,* 359-365.

Kagan, J., Rosman, B.L., Day, D., Albert, J., & Phillips, W. 1964. Information processing in the child: Significance of analytic and reflective attitudes. *Psychological Monographs, 78* (1, Whole No. 578).

Kauffman, J.D. & Hallahan, D.P. 1979. Learning disabilities and hyperactivity (with comments on minimal brain dysfunction). In B.B. Lahey & A.E. Kazdin (eds.). *Advances in clinical child psychology,* Vol. 2. New York: Plenum Publishing.

Kaufman, A.S. & Kaufman, N.L. 1983. *Kaufman Assessment Battery for children. Interpretive Manual.* Circle Pines, Minnesota: American Guidance Service.

Kaufman, D. & Kaufman, P. 1979. Strategy training and remedial techniques. *Journal of Learning Disabilities, 12,* 416-419.

Kavale, K. 1981. Functions of the Illinois Test of Psycholinguistic Abilities (ITPA): Are they trainable? *Exceptional Children, 47,* 496-513.

Keeley, S., Shemberg, K., & Carbonell, J. 1976. Operant clinical intervention: Behavior management or beyond? Where are the data? *Behavior Therapy, 7,* 292-305.

Kendall, P.C., & Wilcox, L.E. 1979. Self-control in children: Development of a rating scale. *Journal of Consulting and Clinical Psychology, 47,* 1020-1029.

Kent, R.N. & O'Leary, K.D. 1976. A controlled evaluation of behavior modification with conduct problem children. *Journal of Consulting and Clinical Psychology, 44,* 586-596.

Keigh, B.K. & Donlon, G.M. 1972. Field dependence, impulsivity and learning disabilities. *Journal of Learning Disabilities, 5,* 331-336.

Keogh, B.K., Tehir, C., & Windeguth-Behn, A. 1974. Teachers' perceptions of educationally high risk children. *Journal of Learning Disabilities, 7,* 367-374.

Kephart, N.C. 1960. *The slow learner in the classroom.* Columbus, Ohio: Charles E. Merrill.

Kinsbourne, M. & Caplan, P. 1979. *Children's learning and attention problems.* Boston: Little Brown.

Kintsch, W. & van Dijk, T.A. 1978. Toward a model of text comprehension and production. *Psychological Review, 85,* 363-394.

Kirby, J.R. 1984. Educational roles of cognitive plans and strategies. In J.R. Kirby (ed.). *Cognitive strategies and educational performance.* Orlando, Florida: Academic Press.

Kirby, J.R. 1988. Style, strategy, and skill in reading. In R.R. Schmeck (ed.). *Learning strategies and learning styles.* New York: Plenum Press.

Kirby, J.R. & Ashman, A.F. 1982. *Strategic behaviour and metacognition.* Department of Education, University of Newcastle, N.S.W.: Final report, Australian Research Grants Committee.

Kirby, J.R. & Ashman, A.F. 1984. Planning skills and mathematics achievement: Implications regarding learning disability. *Journal of Psychoeducational Assessment, 2,* 9-22.

Kirby, J.R. & Becker, L.D. 1988. Cognitive components of learning problems in arithmetic. *Remedial and Special Education, 9*(5), 7-15, 27.

Kirby, J.R. & Biggs, J.B. 1981. *Learning styles, information processing abilities, and academic achievement.* Final report to the Australian Research Grants Committee. University of Newcastle, N.S.W.

Kirby, J.R. & Cantwell, R.H. 1985. Use of advance organizers to facilitate higher-level text comprehension. *Human Learning, 4,* 159-168.

Kirby, J.R. & Das, J.P. 1990. A cognitive approach to intelligence: Attention, coding and planning. *Canadian Psychology, 31,* 320-333.

Kirby, J.R. & Gordon, C.J. 1988. Text segmenting and comprehension: Effects of reading and information processing abilities. *British Journal of Educational Psychology, 58,* 287-300.

Kirby, J.R. & Moore, P.J. 1988. Metacognitive awareness about reading and its relation to reading ability. *Journal of Psychoeducational Assessment, 5,* 119-137.

Kirby, J.R., Moore, P.J., & Schofield, N.J. 1988. Verbal and visual learning styles. *Contemporary Educational Psychology, 13,* 169-184.

Kirby, J.R. & Robinson, G.L.W. 1987. Simultaneous and successive processing in reading disabled children. *Journal of Learning Disabilities, 20,* 243-252.

Kirby, J.R. & Teasdale, W.R. 1987. Children's monitoring of another's comprehension. *Australian Journal of Education, 31,* 73-85.

Kirk, S.A. 1962. *Educating Exceptional Children.* Boston: Houghton-Mifflin.

Kirk, S.A., McCarthy, J.J. & Kirk, W. 1968. *Illinois Test of Psycholinguistic Abilities.* Urbana, Illinois: University of Illinois Press. Revised Edition.

Kopitz, E. 1971. *Children with learning disabilities: A five-year follow-up study.* New York: Grune & Stratton.

Krupski, A. 1986. Attention problems in youngsters with learning handicaps. In J.K. Torgeson & B.Y.L. Wong (eds.). *Psychological and educational perspectives on learning disabilities.* Orlando, Florida: Academic Press.

Krywaniuk, L.W. & Das, J.P. 1976. Cognitive strategies in native children: Analysis and intervention. *Alberta Journal of Educational Research, 12,* 271-280.

Lahey, B.B., Hobbs, S.A., Kupfer, D.L., & Delamater, A. 1979. Current perspectives on hyperactivity and learning disabilities. In B.B. Lahey (ed.). *Behavior therapy with hyperactive and learning disabled children.* New York: Oxford University Press.

Lahey, B.B., Schaughency, E.A., Hynd, G.W., Carlson, C.L., & Nieves, N. 1987. Attention deficit disorder with and without hyperactivity: Comparison of behavioral characteristics and clinic-referred children. *Journal of the American Academy of Child and Adolescent Psychiatry, 26,* 718-723.

Lahey, B.B., Stempniak, M., Robinson, E.J., & Tyroler, M.J. 1978. Hyperactivity and learning disabilities as independent dimensions of child behavior problems. *Journal of Abnormal Psychology, 3,* 333-340.

Lambert, N.M. & Sandoval, J. 1980. The prevalence of learning disabilities in a sample of children considered hyperactive. *Journal of Abnormal Child Psychology, 8,* 33-50.

Lankford, F.G. 1972. *Some computational strategies of seventh-grade pupils* (Final report, Project No. 2-C-013). HEW / OE National Center for Educational Research and Development and The Center for Advanced Studies, University of Virginia. (Cited by Resnick & Ford, 1981.)

Larsen, S.C. 1976. The learning disabilities specialist: Role and responsibilities. *Journal of Learning Disabilities, 9*, 498-508.

Laufer, M.W., Denhoff, E., & Solomons, G. 1957. Hyperkinetic impulse disorder in children's behaviour problems. *Psychosomatic Medicine, 19*, 38-49.

Lawson, M.J. 1980. Metamemory: Making decisions about strategies. In J.R. Kirby & J.B. Biggs (eds.). *Cognition, development, and instruction.* New York: Academic Press.

Lawson, M.J. 1984. Being executive about metacognition. In J.R. Kirby (ed.). *Cognitive strategies and educational performance.* New York: Academic Press.

Learning Disability Quarterly, Vol. 5(4), 334-446.

Ledwidge, B. 1978. Cognitive behavior modification: A step in the wrong direction? *Psychological Bulletin, 85*, 353-375.

Lee, L.L. 1971. *Northwestern syntax screening test.* Evanston, Illinois: Northwestern University Press.

Lee, L.L. 1974. *Developmental sentence analysis: A grammatical assessment procedure for speech and language clinicians.* Evanston, Illinois: Northwestern University Press.

Leong, C.K. 1974. *Spatial-temporal information-processing in disabled readers.* Unpublished doctoral dissertation, University of Alberta.

Leong, C.K. 1980. Cognitive patterns of "retarded" and below-average readers. *Contemporary Educational Psychology, 5*, 101-117.

Lewis, M. (ed.). 1986. *Learning disabilities and prenatal risk.* Urbana: University of Illinois Press.

Liberman, I.Y., Shankweiler, D., Fischer, F.W., & Carta, B. 1974. Explicit syllable and phoneme segmentation in the young child. *Journal of Experimental Child Psychology, 18*, 201-222.

Liberman, I.Y. & Mann, V. 1981. *Should reading instruction and remediation vary with the sex of the child?* Haskins Laboratories, New Haven, Connecticut: Status Report on speech. (Research SR-65.)

Liberman, I.Y., Shankweiler, D., Blackman, B., Camp, L., & Werfelman, M. 1980. In P. Levinson & C.H. Sloan (eds.). *Auditory processing and language: Clinical and research perspectives.* New York: Grune & Stratton.

Licht, B.G. 1983. Cognitive-motivational factors that contribute to the achievement of learning disabled children. *Journal of Learning Disabilities, 16*, 483-490.

Lieberman, L.M. 1980. The implications of noncategorical special education. *Journal of Learning Disabilities, 13*, 65-68.

Lindsay, P. & Norman, D.A. 1977. *Human information processing.* New York: Academic Press.

Lindsley, D.B. 1960. The reticular activating system and perceptual integration. In D.E. Sheer (ed.). *Electrical stimulation of the brain.* Austin, Texas: University of Texas Press.

Logan, R.L. 1978. The effects of structured language programs on linguistic skills of culturally different children. *Dissertation Abstracts International, 38A*, 4096.

Lubar, J.F. & Deering, W.M. 1981. *Behavioral approaches to neurology.* New York: Academic Press.

Lund, K., Foster, G., & McCall-Perez, F. 1978. The effectiveness of psycholinguistic training: A re-evaluation. *Exceptional Children, 44*, 310-312.

Lupart, J. & Mulcahy, R. 1984. Some thoughts on research in learning disabilities and attention. In J.R. Kirby (ed.). *Cognitive strategies and educational performance.* Orlando, Florida: Academic Press.

Luria, A.R. 1961. *The role of speech in regulation of normal and abnormal behaviour.* Oxford: Pergamon Press.

Luria, A.R. 1966a. *Higher cortical functions in man.* New York: Basic.

Luria, A.R. 1966b. *Human brain and psychological processes.* New York: Harper & Row.

Luria, A.R. 1973. *The working brain.* Harmondsworth, England: Penguin.

MacDonald, T.H. 1980. How can I study science when I can't read the book? *Australian Journal of Reading, 3,* 137-142.

Macy, D.J., Baker, J.A., & Kosinski, S.C. 1979. An empirical study of the Myklebust Learning Quotient. *Journal of Learning Disabilities, 12,* 93-96.

Malmo, R.B. 1959. Activation: A neuropsychological dimension. *Psychological Review, 66,* 367-386.

Mandler, G. & Sarason, S.G. 1952. A study of anxiety and learning. *Journal of Abnormal and Social Psychology, 47,* 166-173.

Mann, L. 1971. Perceptual training revisited: The training of nothing at all. *Rehabilitation Literature, 32,* 322-335.

Mann, L. 1971. Psychometric phrenology and the new faculty psychology: the case against ability assessment and training. *Journal of Special Education, 5,* 3-14.

Mann, L. & Phillips, W.A. 1967. Fractional practices in special education: A critique. *Exceptional children, 33,* 311-319.

Mann, V.A., Liberman, I.Y., & Shankweiler, D. 1981. *A longitudinal study of some cognitive antecedents of reading proficiency.* Cited by Liberman and Mann, 1981.

Mash, E.J. & Dalby, J.T. 1979. Behavioral interventions for hyperactivity. In R.L. Trites (ed.). *Hyperactivity in children: Etiology, measurement and treatment implications.* Baltimore: University Park Press.

Masson, M.E.J. & Miller, J.A. 1983. Working memory and individual differences in comprehension and memory of text. *Journal of Educational Psychology, 75,* 314-318.

Mattes, J.A. 1983. The Feingold diet: A current reappraisal. *Journal of Learning Disabilities, 16,* 319-323.

Mattes, J.A. & Gittelman-Klein, R. 1981. Effects of artificial food coloring in children with hyperactive symptomology. *Archives of General Psychiatry, 38,* 714-718.

Mayer, R.E. 1985. Mathematical ability. In R.J. Sternberg (ed.). *Human abilities: An information processing approach.* New York: Freeman.

McDaniel, M.A. & Pressley, M. 1984. Putting the keyword method in context. *Journal of Educational Psychology, 76,* 598-608.

McLaughlin, J.A., Clark, F.L., Mauck, R.A., & Petrosko, J. 1987. A comparison of parent-child perceptions of student learning disabilities. *Journal of Learning Disabilities, 20,* 356-360.

McLeod, J. 1979. Educational underachievement: Toward a defensible psychometric definition. *Journal of Learning Disabilities, 12,* 322-330.

McNutt, B.A., Ballard, J.E., Boileau, R., Sprague, R.L. & von Newmann, A. 1976. The effects of long-term stimulant medication on growth and body composition of hyperactive children. *Psychopharmacology Bulletin 12,* 13-15.

McNutt, B.A., Boileau, R.A., & Cohen, M. 1977. The effects of long-term stimulant medication on the growth and body composition of hyperactive children. *Psychopharmacology Bulletin, 13,* 36-38.

Meichenbaum, D. 1976. Cognitive factors as determinants of learning disabilities: A cognitive-functional approach. In R.M. Knights & D.J. Bakker (eds.). *The neuropsychology of learning disorders: Theoretical approaches.* Baltimore: University Park Press.

Meichenbaum, D. 1977. *Cognitive-behavior modification: An integrative approach.* New York: Plenum Press.

Meichenbaum, D. & Butler, L. 1980. Toward a conceptual model for the treatment of test anxiety: Implications for research and treatment. In I.G. Sarason (ed.). *Test anxiety: Theory, research, and applications.* Hillsdale, New Jersey: Lawrence Erlbaum Associates.

Meichenbaum, D.H. & Goodman, J. 1971. Training impulsive children to talk to themselves: A means of developing self-control. *Journal of Abnormal Psychology, 77,* 115-126.

Meier, J.H. 1971. Prevalence and characteristics of learning disabilities found in second grade children. *Journal of Learning Disabilities, 4,* 115-126.

Messer, S.B. 1976. Reflection-impulsivity: A review. *Psychological Bulletin, 83,* 1026-1052.

Miller, L.C. 1972. School behavior checklist: An inventory of deviant behavior for elementary school children. *Journal of Consulting and Clinical Psychology, 38,* 134-144.

Mischel, W. 1974. Processes in delay of gratification. In L. Berkowitz (ed.). *Advances in experimental social psychology,* Vol. 7. New York: Academic Press.

Moely, B.M., Olson, F.A., Halwes, T.G. & Flavell, J.H. 1969. Production deficiency in young children's clustered recall. *Developmental Psychology, 1,* 26-34.

Moore, P.J. 1986. *Effects of geographical maps upon reading comprehension.* Unpublished Ph.D. thesis, University of Newcastle, N.S.W.

Moore, P.J. & Kirby, J.R. 1981. Metacognition and reading: A replication and extension of Myers and Paris in an Australian context. *Educational Enquiry, 4,* 18-29.

Morais, J., Carey, L., Algria, J., & Bertelson, P. 1979. Does awareness of speech as a sequence of phonemes arise spontaneously? *Cognition, 7,* 323-331.

Moruzzi, G. & Magoun, H.W. 1949. Brain stem reticular formation and activation of the EEG. *Electroencephalography and Clinical Neurophysiology, 1,* 455-473.

Murray, C.A. 1976. *The link between learning disabilities and juvenile delinquency: Current theory and knowledge.* Washington, D.C.: U.S. Government Printing Office.

Myers, M. & Paris, S.G. 1978. Children's metacognitive knowledge about reading. *Journal of Educational Psychology, 70,* 680-690.

Myklebust, H.R. 1954. *Auditory disorders in children.* New York: Grune and Stratton.

Myklebust, H. 1968. Learning disabilities: Definitions and overview. In H. Myklebust (ed.). *Progress in learning disabilities,* Vol. 1. New York: Grune and Stratton.

Myklebust, H.R., Boshes, B., Olson, D., & Cole, C. 1969. Minimal brain damage in children. (Final Report, U.S.P.H.S. Contract 108-65-142.) Evanston, Illinois: Northwestern University Publications.

Naglieri, J.A. 1989. A cognitive processing theory for the measurement of intelligence. *Educational Psychologist, 24,* 185-206.

Naglieri, J.A. & Das, J.P. 1988. Planning – Arousal – Simultaneous – Successive (PASS): A model for assessment. *Journal of School Psychology, 26,* 35-48.

National Advisory Committee on Hyperkinesis and Food Additives. 1980. *Final Report to the Nutrition Foundation.* New York: The Nutrition Foundation.

Neale, M.D. 1966. *Neale analysis of reading ability.* London: Macmillan.

Newcomer, P. & Magee, P. 1977. The performance of learning / reading disabled children on a test of spoken language. *The Reading Teacher, 30,* 896-900.

Newell, A. & Simon, H.A. 1972. *Human problem solving.* Englewood Cliffs, New Jersey: Prentice-Hall.

Office for Medical Applications of Research, National Institutes of Health. 1982. Defined diets and childhood hyperactivity. *Journal of the American Medical Association, 245,* 290-292.

O'Leary, S.G. 1980. A response to cognitive training. *Exceptional Children Quarterly, 1,* 89-94.

Orton, S.T. 1937. *Reading, writing, and speech problems in children.* New York: W.W. Norton.

Osgood, C.E. 1957. Motivational dynamics of language behavior. In M.R. Jones (ed.). *Nebraska symposium on motivation.* Lincoln: University of Nebraska Press.

Overmeier, J.B. & Seligman, M.E. 1967. Effects of inescapable shock upon subsequent escape and avoidance responding. *Journal of Comparative and Physiological Psychology, 63,* 28-33.

Overton, D.A. 1978. Major theories of state dependent learning. In B.T. Ho, D.W. Richards III, & D.L. Chute (eds.). *Drug discrimination and state dependent learning.* New York: Academic Press.

Owen, F.W., Adams, P.A., Forrest, T., Stoltz, L.M., & Fisher, S. 1971. Learning disorders in children: Sibling studies. *Monographs of the Society for Research in Child Development, 36,* (4, Serial No. 144).

Paivio, A. 1971. *Imagery and verbal processes.* New York: Holt, Rinehart & Winston.

Palmer, D.J., Drummond, F., Tollison, P., & Zingraff, S. 1982. An attributional investigation of performance outcomes for learning-disabled and normal-achieving pupils. *The Journal of Special Education, 16,* 207-219.

Paris, S.G., Lipson, M.Y., & Wixson, K.K. 1983. Becoming a strategic reader. *Contemporary Educational Psychology, 8,* 293-316.

Paris, S.G., Newman, R.S., & McVey, K.A. 1982. Learning the functional significance of mnemonic actions: A microgenetic study of strategy acquisition. *Journal of Experimental Child Psychology, 34,* 490-509.

Parke, R.D. & Collmer, C.W. 1975. Child abuse: An interdisciplinary analysis. In E. Hetherington (ed.). *Review of child development research,* Vol. 5. Chicago: University of Chicago Press.

Payne, C.A. 1984. *Children's phonological ability and memory for sentences.* Unpublished Master of Educational Studies Extended Essay, Department of Education, University of Newcastle, N.S.W.

Pasamanick, B. & Knobloch, M. 1973. The epidemiology of reproductive causality. In S.G. Sapir & A.C. Nitzburg (eds.). *Children with learning problems: Reading in a developmental-interaction approach.* New York: Brunner / Mazel.

Pearl, R. & Bryan, T. 1982. Mothers' attributions for their learning disabled child's successes and failures. *Learning Disability Quarterly, 5,* 53-57.

Pearl, R., Donahue, M., & Bryan, T. 1986. Social relationships of learning disabled children. In J.K. Torgeson & B.Y.L. Wong (eds.). *Psychological and educational perspectives on learning disabilities.* Orlando, Florida: Academic Press.

Pearson, P.D. & Johnson, D.D. 1978. *Teaching reading comprehension.* New York: Holt, Rinehart & Winston.

Pelham, W.E. 1986. The effects of psychostimulant drugs on learning and academic achievement in children with attention deficit disorders and learning disabilities. In J.K. Torgeson & B.Y.L. Wong (eds.). *Psychological and educational perspectives on learning disabilities.* Orlando, Florida: Academic Press.

Pelham, W.E. & Milich, R. 1984. Peer relations in children with hyperactivity / attention deficit disorder. *Journal of Learning Disabilities, 17,* 560-567.

Pelham, W.E. & Ross, A.O. 1977. Selective attention in children with reading problems: A developmental study of incidental learning. *Journal of Abnormal Child Psychology, 5,* 1-8.

Pellegrino, J.W. 1985. Inductive reasoning ability. In R.J. Sternberg (ed.). *Human abilities: An information processing approach.* New York: Freeman.

Phillips, B. 1978. *School stress and anxiety: Theory, research, and intervention.* New York: Human Sciences Press.

Pihl, R.O. & Parkes, M. 1977. Hair element content in learning disabled children. *Science, 1985,* 204-206.

Poggio, J. & Salking, N. 1979. A review and appraisal of instruments assessing hyperactivity in children. *Learning Disability Quarterly, 2,* 9-22.

Posner, M.I. & Boies, S.J. 1971. Components of attention. *Psychological Reports, 78,* 391-408.

Preston, J.P., Ray, R.S., Tomasi, L., Eichman, P.L., Matthews, C.G., Chun, R., Cleeland, C.S., & Traisman, E. 1978. Hyperkinesis and food additives: Testing the Feingold hypothesis. *Pediatrics, 61,* 818-828.

Pribram, K.H. 1971. *Languages of the brain: Experimental paradoxes and principles in neuropsychology.* Englewood Cliffs, New Jersey: Prentice Hall.

Prichep, L., John, E.R., Ahn, H., & Kaye, H. 1983. Neurometrics: Quantitative evaluation of brain dysfunction in children. In M. Rutter (ed.). *Developmental neuropsychiatry.* New York: The Guildford Press.

Rand, Y., Tannenbaum, A.J., & Feuerstein, R. 1979. Effects of instrumental enrichment on the psychoeducational development of low-functioning adolescents. *Journal of Educational Psychology, 71,* 751-763.

Rapp, D.J. 1978. Does diet affect hyperactivity? *Journal of Learning Disabilities, 11,* 56-62.

Raven, J.C. 1956. *Coloured progressive matrices.* London: H.K. Lewis.

Rayner, K. (ed.) 1983. *Eye movements in reading: Perceptual and language processes.* New York: Academic Press.

Resnick, L.B. & Ford, W.W. 1981. *The psychology of mathematics for instruction.* Hillsdale, New Jersey: Lawrence Erlbaum Associates.

Roach, E.F. & Kephart, N.C. 1966. *The Purdue Perceptual-Motor Survey.* Columbus, Ohio: Charles E. Merrill.

Robbins, M.P. 1966. A study of the validity of Delacato's theory of neurological organization. *Exceptional Children, 32,* 517-523.

Robbins, M.P. & Glass, G.V. 1968. The Doman-Delcato rationale: A critical analysis. In J. Hellmuth (ed.). *Educational therapy,* Vol. II. Seattle: Special Child Publications.

Roche, A.F., Lipman, R.S., Overall, J.E., & Hung, W. 1979. The effects of stimulant medication on the growth of hyperkinetic children. *Pediatrics, 63,* 847-850.

Rosenthall, R.H. & Allen, T.W. 1978. An examination of attention, arousal, and learning dysfunctions of hyperactive children. *Psychological Bulletin, 4,* 689-715.

Ross, A.E. 1976. *Psychological aspects of learning disabilities and reading disorders.* New York: McGraw-Hill.

Ross, D.M. & Ross, S.A. 1976. *Hyperactivity: Research, theory and action.* New York: John Wiley.

Rost, K.J. 1967. Academic achievement of brain injured and hyperactive children in isolation. *Exceptional Children, 34,* 125-126.

Rosvold, H.E., Mirsky, A.F., Sarason, I., Bransome, E.D., & Beck, L.H. 1956. A continuous performance test of brain damage. *Journal of Consulting Psychology, 20,* 343-350.

Rourke, B.P. 1983. Outstanding issues in research on learning disabilities. In M. Rutter (ed.). *Developmental neuropsychiatry.* New York: The Guildford Press.

Rourke, B.P., Bakker, D.J., Fisk, J.L., & Strang, J.D. 1983. *Child neuropsychology: An introduction to theory, research and clinical practice.* New York: The Guildford Press.

Routh, D.K. 1986. Attention deficit disorder. In R.T. Brown and C.R. Reynolds (eds.). *Psychological perspectives on childhood exceptionality.* New York: Wiley.

Rozin, P. & Gleitman, L.R. 1977. The structure and acquisition of reading II: The reading process and the acquisition of the alphabetic principle. In A.S. Reber & D.L. Scarborough (eds.). *Toward a psychology of reading. The proceedings of the CUNY conferences.* New York: John Wiley.

Rugel, R.P. 1974. WISC subtest scores of disabled readers: A review with respect to Bannatyne's recategorization. *Journal of Learning Disabilities, 7,* 48-55.

Rumelhardt, D.E. 1981. Schemata: The building blocks of cognition. In J.T. Guthrie (ed.). *Comprehension and teaching: Research reviews.* Newark, Delaware: International Reading Association.

Safer, D.J. & Allen, R.P. 1973. Factors influencing the suppressant effects of two stimulant drugs on the growth of hyperactive children. *Pediatrics, 51,* 660-667.

Safer, D.J., Allen, R.P. & Barr, E. 1972. Depression of growth in hyperactive children on stimulant drugs. *New England Journal of Medicine, 287,* 217-220.

Sandoval, J., Lambert, N.M., & Sassone, D. 1980. The identification and labeling of hyperactivity in children: An interactive model. In C.K. Whalen & B. Henker (eds.). *Hyperactive children: The social ecology of identification and treatment.* New York: Academic Press.

Santostefano, S. & Paley, E. 1964. Development of cognitive controls in children. *Journal of Clinical Psychology, 20,* 213-218.

Sarason, I.G. 1978. The test anxiety scale: Concept and research. In C.D. Spielberger & I.G. Sarason (eds.). *Stress and anxiety,* Vol. 5. Washington, D.C.: Hemisphere Publishing Corporation.

Sarason, S.B., Davidson, K.S., Lighthall, F.F., Waite, R.R., & Ruebush, B.K. 1960. *Anxiety in elementary school children.* New York: John Wiley.

Satterfield, S.H. 1973. Response to stimulant drug treatment in hyperactive children: Prediction from EEG and neurological findings. *Journal of Autism and Childhood schizophrenia, 1,* 36-48.

Satterfield, S.H. & Dawson, M.E. 1971. Electrodermal correlates of hyperactivity in children. *Psychophysiology, 8,* 191-197.

Schonhaut, S. & Satz, P. 1983. Prognosis for children with learning disabilities: A review of follow-up studies. In M. Rutter (ed.). *Developmental neuropsychiatry.* New York: The Guildford Press.

Schumaker, J.B. & Hazel, S.J. 1984. Social skills assessment and training for the learning disabled: Who's on first and what's on second? Part I. *Journal of Learning Disabilities, 17,* 422-431.

Schumaker, J.B. & Hazel, S.J. 1984. Social skills assessment and training for the learning disabled: Who's on first and what's on second? Part II. *Journal of Learning Disabilities, 17,* 492-499.

Schworm, R.W. 1982. Hyperkinesis: Myth, mystery and matter. *Journal of Special Education, 16,* 129-148.

Sedlak, R.A. & Wiener, P. 1973. Review of research on the Illinois Test of Psycholinguistic Abilities. In L. Mann & D.A. Sabatino (eds.). *First review of special education,* Vol. 1. Philadelphia: JSE Press.

Seligman, M.E. 1975. *Helplessness: On depression, development and death.* San Francisco: Freeman.

Seligman, M.E. & Maier, S.F. 1967. Failure to escape traumatic shock. *Journal of Experimental Psychology, 74,* 1-9.

Semel, E.M. & Wiig, E.H. 1975. Comprehension of syntactic structures and critical verbal elements by children with learning disabilities. *Journal of Learning Disabilities, 8,* 46-51.

Semel-Mintz, E. & Wiig, E. 1982. *Clinical evaluation of language functions.* Columbus, Ohio: Charles E. Merrill.

Shields, D. 1973. Brain responses to stimuli in disorders of information processing. *Journal of Learning Disabilities, 6,* 501-505.

Silver, A.A. & Hagen, R.A. 1966. Maturation of perceptual functions in children with specific reading disability. *The Reading Teacher, 19,* 253-259.

Silver, L. 1971. Familial patterns in children with neurologically-based learning disabilities. *Journal of Learning Disabilities, 4,* 349-358.

Silver, L.B. 1987. The "Magic" Cure: A review of the current controversial approaches for treating learning disabilities. *Journal of Learning Disabilities, 20,* 498-504.

Silver, L.B. 1979. The minimal brain dysfunction syndrome. In J.D. Nosphitz (ed.). *Basic handbook of child psychiatry, Vol. 2. Disturbances in development.* New York: Basic Books, Inc.

Siperstein, G., Bopp, M., & Bak, J. 1977. *Social status of learning disabled children.* Cambridge, Massachusetts: Research Institute for Educational Problems.

Siperstein, G.N. & Goding, M.J. 1985. Teachers' behavior toward L.D. and non-L.D. children: A strategy for change. *Journal of Learning Disabilities, 18,* 139-144.

Slingerland, B.H. 1974. *A multi-sensory approach to language arts for specific language disability children.* Cambridge, Massachusetts: Educator's Publishing Service.

Smith, F. 1978. *Understanding reading.* 2nd ed. New York: Holt, Rinehart & Winston.

Smith, M.D., Coleman, J.M., Dokecki, P.R., & Davis, E.E. 1977. Recategorized WISC-R scores of learning disabled children. *Journal of Learning Disabilities, 10,* 437-443.

Smith, S. (ed.) 1986. *Genetics and learning disabilities.* San Diego: College Hill Press.

Snow, R.E. 1978. Eye fixations and strategy analysis of individual differences in cognitive aptitudes. In A.M. Lesgold, J.W. Pellegrino, S.D. Fokkema & R. Glaser (eds.). *Cognitive psychology and instruction.* New York: Plenum Press.

Sowell, V., Parker, R., Poplin, M., & Larsen, S. 1979. Effects of psycholinguistic training on improving psycholinguistic skills. *Learning Disability Quarterly, 2,* 69-77.

Spielberger, C.D. 1972. Anxiety as an emotional state. In C.D. Spielberger (ed.). *Anxiety: Current trends in theory and research,* Vol. 1. New York: Academic Press.

Sprague, R.L. & Sleator, E.K. 1976. Drugs and dosages: Implications for learning disabilities. In R.M. Knights & D.J. Bakker (eds.). *The neuropsychology of learning disorders: Theoretical approaches.* Baltimore: University Park Press.

Sprague, R.L. & Sleator, E.K. 1977. Methylphenidate in hyperkinetic children: Differences in dose effects on learning and social behavior. *Science, 198,* 1274-1276.

Spring, C. & Sandoval, J. 1976. Food additives and hyperkinesis: A critical evaluation of the evidence. *Journal of Learning Disabilities, 9,* 560-569.

Stanley, G. & Hall, R. 1973. Short-term visual processing in dyslexics. *Child Development, 44,* 841-844.

Stanovich, K. 1982a. Individual differences in the cognitive processes of reading I. Word decoding. *Journal of Learning Disabilities, 15,* 485-493.

Stanovich, K. 1982b. Individual differences in the cognitive processes of reading II: Text-level processes. *Journal of Learning Disabilities, 15,* 549-554.

Stanovich, K.E. 1981. Relationships between word decoding speed, general name-retrieval ability, and reading progress in first grade children. *Journal of Educational Psychology, 6,* 809-815.

Sternberg, R.J. 1983. Criteria for intellectual skills training. *Educational Researcher, 12*(2), 6-12, 26.

Stevens, G.D. & Birch, J.W. 1957. A proposal for clarification of the terminology used to describe brain-injured children. *Exceptional Children, 23,* 346-349.

Strag, G. 1972. Comparative behavioral ratings of parents with severe mentally retarded children, special learning disabilities and normal children. *Journal of Learning Disabilities, 5,* 631-635.

Strauss, A.A. & Kephart, N.C. 1955. *Psychopathology and education of the brain injured child,* Vol. 2. New York: Grune and Stratton.

Strauss, A.A. & Lehtinen, L.E. 1947. *Psychopathology and education of the brain-injured child.* New York: Grune and Stratton.

Stroop, J.R. 1935. Studies of interference in serial verbal reactions. *Journal of Experimental Psychology, 18,* 643-661.

Suppes, P. & Groen, G.J. 1967. Some counting models for first-grade performance data on simple addition facts. In J.M. Scandura (ed.). *Research in mathematics education.* Washington, D.C.: National Council of Teachers of Mathematics.

Swanson, J.M., Eich, J., & Kinsbourne, M. 1978. State-dependent retrieval in hyperactive children. Paper presented at the annual meeting of the Psychonomic Society, San Antonio.

Swanson, J.M. & Kinsbourne, M. 1976. Simulant-related state-dependent learning in hyperactive children. *Science, 192,* 1354-1357.

Swanson, J.M. & Kinsbourne, M. 1980. Food dyes impair performance of hyperactive children on a laboratory learning test. *Science, 207,* 1485-1487.

Swanson, J.M., Kinsbourne, M., Roberts, W., & Zucker, K. 1978. Time-response analysis of the effect of stimulant medication on the learning ability of children referred for hyperactivity. *Pediatrics, 61,* 21-29.

Tarver, S.G., Hallahan, D.M., Cohen, S.B., & Kaufman, J.M. 1977. The development of visual selective attention and verbal rehearsal in learning disabled boys. *Journal of Learning Disabilities, 10,* 491-500.

Tatham, S. 1969-1970. Reading comprehension of materials written with select oral language patterns: A study at grades two and four. *Reading Research Quarterly, 5,* 402-426.

Taylor, I. 1981. Writing systems and reading. In G.E. MacKinnon & T.G. Waller (eds.). *Reading research: Advances in theory and practice,* Vol. 2. New York: Academic Press.

Teuber, H.L. 1960. Perception. In J. Fields, H.W. Magoun, & J.E. Hall (eds.). *Handbook of physiology,* Vol. 3. Washington, D.C.: American Physiological Society.

Thomas, C.J. 1905. Congenital "word-blindness" and its treatment. *Ophthalmoscope, 3,* 380-385.

Thomas, A. 1979. Learned helplessness and expectancy factors: Implications for research in learning disabilities. *Review of Educational Research, 49,* 208-221.

Tierney, R.J., Readance, J.E., & Dishner, E.K. 1980. *Reading strategies and practices: A guide for improving instruction.* Boston: Allyn and Bacon.

Torello, M.W. & Duffy, F.H. 1985. Using brain electrical mapping to diagnose learning disabilities. *Theory into Practice, 24*(2), 95-99.

Torgesen, J.K. 1977. Memorization processes in reading disabled children. *Journal of Educational Psychology, 69,* 571-578.

Torgesen, J.K. 1978-79. Performance of reading disabled children on serial memory tasks: A selective review of recent research. *Reading Research Quarterly, 14,* 57-87.

Torgesen, J.K. & Dice, C. 1980. Characteristics of research on learning disabilities. *Journal of Learning Disabilities, 13,* 531-535.

Torgesen, J.K. & Houck, D.G. 1980. Processing deficiencies of learning-disabled children who perform poorly on the digit span test. *Journal of Educational Psychology, 72,* 141-160.

Trifiletti, D.T., Trifiletti, R.M. & Trifiletti, R.J. 1982. *WISCR-80. An educational program for the Wechsler Intelligence Scale for Children.* Jacksonville, Florida: Precision People.

U.S. Office of Education. 1968. *First annual report of the National Advisory Committee on Handicapped Children.* Washington, D.C.: U.S. Department of Health, Education, and Welfare.

Vallins, G.H. 1965. *Spelling.* Great Britain: Tonbridge Printers.

Vellutino, F.R. 1979. *Dyslexia: Theory and research.* Cambridge, Massachusetts: MIT Press.

Wahler, R., Berland, R., & Coe, T. 1979. Generalization process in child behavior change. In B. Lahey and A. Kazdin (eds.). *Advances in child psychology,* Vol. 2. New York: Plenum Press.

Wardhaugh, R. 1969. *Reading: A linguistic perspective.* New York: Harcourt, Brace, and World.

Weiner, B. 1974. *Achievement motivation and attribution theory.* New Jersey: General Learning Press.

Weingartner, H., Langer, D., Grice, J., & Rapoport, J.L. 1982. Acquisition and retrieval of information in amphetamine-treated hyperactive children. *Psychiatry Research, 2,* 21-29.

Weiss, G. 1981. Controversial issues of the pharmacotherapy of the hyperactive child. *Canadian Journal of Psychiatry, 26,* 385-392.

Weiss, G., Kruger, E., Danielson, V., & Elman, M. 1978. Effect of long-term treatment of hyperactive children with methylphenidate. *Canadian Medical Association Journal, 112,* 159.

Weiss, B., Williams, J.H., Mangen, S., Abrams, B., Caan, B., Citron, L.J., Cox, C., McKibbern, J., Ogar, D., & Schultz, S. 1980. Behavioral responses to artificial food colors. *Science, 207,* 1487-1489.

Weissenburger, F.E. & Loney, J. 1977. Hyperkinesis in the classroom: If cerebral stimulants are the last resort, what is the first resort? *Journal of Learning Disabilities, 10,* 339-348.

Wender, P.H. 1971. *Minimal brain dysfunction in children.* New York: John Wiley.

Wender, P. 1973. Some speculations concerning a possible biochemical basis of minimal brain dysfunction. *Annals of the New York Academy of Sciences, 205,* 18-28.

Wender, P. 1976. Hypothesis for a possible biochemical basis of minimal brain dysfunction. In R. Knights & D. Bakker (eds.). *The neuropsychology of learning disorders: Theoretical approaches.* Baltimore: University Park Press.

Wepman, J.M., Cruikshank, W.M., Deutch, C.P., Morency, A., & Strother, C.R. 1975. Learning disabilities. In N. Hobbs (ed.). *Issues in the classification of children,* Vol. 1. San Francisco: Jossey-Bass.

Wernicke, C. 1906. Der aphasische symptoms-encomplex. In V. Leyden & U. Klemperer (eds.). *Deutsche Klinck am Eingange des 20. Jahrhunderts.* Berlin. Translated in E.G. Eggert (ed.). *Wernicke's works on aphasia: A source book and review.* The Hague: Mouton, 1977.

Werry, J. 1968. Studies on the hyperactive child IV. An empirical analysis of the minimal brain dysfunction syndrome. *Archives of General Psychiatry, 19,* 9-16.

Whalen, C.K. & Henker, B. 1976. Psychostimulants and children: A review and analysis. *Psychological Bulletin, 3,* 1113-1130.

Whalen, C.K. & Henker, B. (eds.) 1980. *Hyperactive children: The social ecology of identification and treatment.* New York: Academic Press.

Wicklegren, W.A. 1974. *How to solve problems: Elements of a theory of problems and problem solving.* San Francisco: Freeman.

Wiederholt, J. 1974. Historical perspectives on the education of the learning disabled. In L. Mann & D. Sabbatino (eds.). *The second review of special education.* Philadelphia: JSE Press.

Wiener, I. 1980. A theoretical model of the acquisition of peer relationships of learning disabled children. *Journal of Learning Disabilities, 13,* 506-511.

Wiig, E. 1976. Language and learning disabilities: Identification and evaluation. *Australian Journal of Remedial Education, 8,* 4-14.

Williams, N.H. 1976. *Arousal and information processing in learning disabled children.* Unpublished doctoral dissertation, University of Alberta.

Wine, J.D. 1982. Evaluation anxiety: A cognitive attentional construct. In H.W. Krohne & L.C. Laux (eds.). *Achievement, stress and anxiety.* Washington, D.C.: Hemisphere Publishing Corporation.

Winograd, P.N. 1984. Strategic difficulties in summarizing texts. *Reading Research Quarterly, 19,* 404-425.

Winzer, M., Rogow, S., & David, C. 1987. *Exceptional children in Canada.* Scarborough, Canada: Prentice-Hall.

Wong, B.Y.L. 1986. Metacognition and special education: A review of a view. *Journal of Special Education, 20,* 9-29.

Woods, S.S., Resnick, L.B., & Groen, G.J. 1975. An experimental test of five process models for subtraction. *Journal of Educational Psychology, 67,* 17-21.

Worden, P.E. 1983. Memory strategy instruction with the learning disabled. In M. Pressley & J.R. Levin (eds.). *Cognitive strategy research: Psychological foundations.* New York: Springer-Verlag.

Yerkes, R.M. & Dodson, J.D. 1908. The relation of stimulus to rapidity of habit-formation. *Journal of Comparative and Neurological Psychology, 18,* 459-482.

Yule, W. & Rutter, M. 1976. Epidemiology and social implications of specific reading retardation. In R.M. Knights & D.J. Bakker (eds.). *The neuropsychology of learning disorders: Theoretical perspectives.* Baltimore: University Park Press.

INDEX